Revised Fifth

Flea Market Trader

Edited by

Sharon & Bob Huxford

COLLECTOR BOOKS

A Division of Schroeder Publishing Co., Inc.

The current values in this book should be used only as a guide. They are not intended to set prices, which vary from one section of the country to another. Auction prices as well as dealer prices vary greatly and are affected by condition as well as demand. Neither the Author nor the Publisher assumes responsibility for any losses that might be incurred as a result of consulting this guide.

On the cover: basket $60.00-$75.00; tent $5.00-$10.00; Beton plastic soldiers $3.00-$4.00; Miss America comport $15.00, sugar $12.00, salt & pepper $20.00; Shirley Temple book, "The Littlest Rebel" $25.00-$30.00; Buttermold, wildflower $75.00-$150.00; baseball cards ca. 1950s 50¢-$3.50; teacher's bell $25.00-$35.00; blue & white cow pitcher $175.00-$200.00; 75th Anniversary commemorative Coke tray $5.00-$10.00; Star of Bethelem quilt $200.00-$300.00.

Additional copies of this book may be ordered from:

COLLECTOR BOOKS
P.O. Box 3009
Paducah, Kentucky 42001

@ $8.95 Add $1.00 for postage and handling.

Copyright: Bill Schroeder, 1985
ISBN: 0-89145-301-6

This book or any part thereof may not be reproduced without the written consent of the Author and Publisher.

INTRODUCTION

The Flea Market Trader is a unique price guide, geared specifically for the convenience of the flea market shopper. Several categories have been included that are not often found in general price guides, while others on antiques not usually seen at flea markets have been omitted. The new categories will serve to introduce you to collectibles that are currently coming on, the best and often the only source for which is the market place. As all of us who religiously pursue the circuits are aware, flea markets are the most exciting places in the world to shop, but unless you're well-informed on current values those 'really-great' buys remain on the table for the shopper that is. Like most pursuits in life, preparation has its own rewards, and it is our intention to provide you with the basic tool of education and awareness toward that end. But please bear in mind that the prices in this guide are meant to indicate only a general value. Many factors determine actual selling prices -- values vary from one region to another, dealers pay various wholesale prices for their wares, and your bargaining skill is important, too.

In our next edition, we hope to list the country's top flea markets for your convenience. If you have a favorite, write 'Flea Market Trader, 1202 Seventh Street, Covington, IN 47932'. Tell us what its schedule is (please be accurate), send us their mailing address and phone number, and we'll be happy to pass the information on to our readers. Also, if in your flea market jaunts you notice interest in new areas not covered in this issue, please make us aware of it so that if we possibly can, we will include it in the next edition.

We have organized our lisitings into general categories for easy use; if you have trouble locating an item, refer to the index. We assume that prices quoted by dealers are for mint items unless damage is noted. So our listings, when no condition code is present, reflect prices of items in mint condition. NM stands for minimal damage, VG indicates that the item will bring 40% to 60% of its mint price, and EX would be somewhere between the two. Nothing is listed in condition poorer than VG. Glassware is assumed clear unless a color is noted. Only generally accepted abbreviations have been used. Photos other than those we have taken are acknowledged on page 4, and we would like to take this opportunity to thank each author, dealer and auction house who allowed us to use their photographs.

The Editors

PHOTO CREDITS

American Beer Can Encyclopedia, Thomas Toepfer, pg 42-43

American Premium Guide to Baseball Cards, Ron Erbe, courtesy Books Americana pg 36

American Premium Guide to Coin Operated Machines, Jerry Ayliffe, courtesy Books Americana pg 295

American Premium Guide to Olde Cameras, David Sharbrough, pg 244-245

Antique Iron Identification and Values, Kathryn McNerney pg 33-36,145-152

Art Nouveau and Art Deco Jewelry, Lillian Baker, pg 116

Black Americana Newsletter, Linda Antonation, Editor and Publisher pg 48

Blue and White Stoneware, Kathryn McNerney pg 297

Blue Willow, An Identification and Value Guide, Mary Frank Gaston pg 328

Bottle Pricing Guide, 3rd Edition, Hugh Cleveland, pg 54

Butter Molds, An Identification and Value Guide, James E. Trice pg 58-59

C.E. Guarino, Box 49, Denmark, ME 04022, pg 257

Children's Glass Dishes and Furniture, Doris Anderson Lechler pg 17,83

Collectible Locks, An Identification and Value Guide, Richard Holiner pg 202

Collecting Toys, A Collector's Identification and Value Guide, Richard O'Brien, Books Americana pg, 33-34

Collector Prints, Old and New, Carl F. Lucky, courtesy Books Americana pg 258

Collector's Encyclopedia of Fiesta, Harlequin and Riviera, Sharon and Bob Huxford pg 146,174

Collector's Encyclopedia of Noritake, Joan Van Patten, pg 224

Collector's Encyclopedia of Occupied Japan Collectibles, Gene Florence pg 226

Collector's Encyclopedia of R.S. Prussia, Mary Frank Gaston, pg 175

Collector's Guide to Paper Dolls, Mary Young, pg 230-231

Doyle, Auctioneers and Appraisers, 98 Main St., Fishkill, NY, 12524 pg 164

Du Mouchelles, 409 Jefferson Ave., Detroit, MI 48226, pg 23,90-93, 99,107,114-115

Garth's Auctions, 2690 Stratford Rd., Box 369, Delaware, OH 43015 pg 108,111,197,261,273-274,283

Goofus Glass, Carolyn McKinley, pg 167

Guide to Pocket Knives, Value and Identification Guide, courtesy Books Americana pg 193-194

Identification and Value Guide to Scouting Collectibles, R.F. Sayers, Editor, Books Americana pg 288

Jack Sellner, Auctioneer, P.O. Box 113, Scottsdale, AZ 85252 pg 183-184

Maritime Auctions, R.R. 2, Box 45A, York ME 03090, pg 149

Metal Molds, Eleanore Bunn, pg 213-214

Modern Guns, Russell and Steve Quertermous pg 170-171

New England Auction Gallery, Box 682, Methuen, MA 01844, pg 27,75, 96-97,109,215,249,296

Oak Book, The; Jane Fryberger, pg 161

Nostalgia Company, The; 21 South Lake Dr., Hackensack, NJ 07601 pg 43,248

Old Fishing Lures, C. F. Luckey, courtesy Books Americana pg 151

Paper Collectibles, Robert D. Connolly, courtesy Books Americana pg 195,253

Pocket Guide to Depression Glass, Gene Florence, pg 62

Police Relics, G. E. Virgines, pg 31, 201

Primitives, Our American Heritage, Kathryn McNerney, pg 311

Railroad Collectibles, An Illustrated Value Guide, Stanley L. Baker pg 264-265

Red Wing Stoneware, Dan and Gail DePasquale, Larry Peterson pg 272

Rex Stark Auctions, 49 Wethersfield Rd., Bellingham, MA 02019 pg 60-61,88

Salt and Pepper Shakers, Helene Guaraccia pg 49,249,286

Shirley Temple Dolls and Collectibles, Patricia Smith, pg 74

Sotheby Parke Bernet, Inc., 980 Madison Ave., New York City, NY 10021 pg 159,162

Standard Encyclopedia of Carnival Glass, Bill Edwards, pg 65-66

Standard Modern Doll Identification and Value Guide, Patricia Smith pg 74

Willis Henry Auctions, 22 Main St., Marshfield, MA 02050, pg 290-291

World of Barbie Dolls, Paris and Susan Manos pg 135

World War II German Military Collectibles, Robert McCarthy, pg 220

300 Years of Kitchen Collectibles, Vols 1 and 2, Linda Campbell Franklin, Books Americana pg 58-59,106,150, 192,204,225

A B C Plates

Popular in the 1800s as well as the early years of this century, plates with the ABCs in their borders encouraged children toward learning their letters even during meal time. They were made from a variety of materials, but examples in earthenware with a colorfully printed central motif are most collectible, especially those dealing with sports, transportation, or a famous person, place or thing.

Bowl, Little Red Riding Hood center, alphabet rim, 7¾" 18.00
Bowl & plate, Humpty Dumpty, marked Arlow, Ireland 35.00
Cup, Ring Around Rosie, with children, German mark . 15.00
Cup, tin, early 48.00
Dish, Bo-Peep in center, ABCs & numbers, glass, 7½" .. 40.00
Dish, Dolly Dingle, signed Drayton, 7¼" diameter . 55.00
Mug, L For Lion Fierce In Eye..., green transfer, Adams, England 55.00
Mug, Red Riding Hood & Wolf, early 30.00

ABC plate with colorful kitten motif, manufactured by W. Adams and Co., Tunstall, England, 7½" diameter, $55.00.

Plate, A Party Of Four, Staffordshire, 6" 85.00
Plate, ABCs, stork, carnival glass 75.00
Plate, B Is For Bobby's Breakfast, red, two children & cow, 7" 72.00
Plate, Brighton Beach bathing pavilion, red transfer, 7½" 55.00
Plate, Catch It Carlo, multicolored, boy with girl & dog 46.00
Plate, cats teaching school, wearing dresses & suit, china, 7" 40.00
Plate, clock in center, irregular edge, amethyst glass, 7" . 75.00
Plate, clowns & ABCs 40.00
Plate, Hey Diddle Diddle, unmarked 48.00
Plate, Jumbo, tin, 6" 65.00
Plate, London Dog Seller, ironstone 48.00
Plate, man sliding downhill, multicolored, Staffordshire, 7½" 65.00
Plate, Old Mother Hubbard, color transfer, 7" 55.00
Plate, organ grinder & children, stippled ground, ABC border, 7½" 70.00
Plate, Sioux Indian Chief, brown, letter relief rim, 8¼" 60.00
Plate, Staffordshire, archery, 5¼" 85.00
Plate, Steeple Chase, Staffordshire, 7" 40.00
Plate, tin, bunny teacher .. 35.00
Plate, train transfer in center, 7½" 75.00
Plate, two children pulled in wagon by dog, brown center, 6¾" 32.00
Plate, Who Killed Cock Robin, tin, 1880s, 8" 75.00
Plate, 1893 Expo, with three buildings 75.00

Abingdon Pottery

Produced in Abingdon, Illinois, from 1934 to 1950, this company made vases, cookie jars, utility ware and lamps.

Ash tray, New Mode, #456 .	12.00
Basket, decorated, #582D . .	30.00
Bookends, seagull, #305, pair	40.00
Bowl, Chinese, oval, #345 . .	15.00
Bowl, console; star, #714 . .	12.00
Bowl, hibiscus, small, #527 .	25.00
Bowl, medium Shell, pink, #533	10.00
Bowl, oblong, pink with 2 pink geese: 1 upright & 1 feeding, #9701	30.00
Candle holder, Double Shell, pink, #505, pair	18.00
Candle holder, fern leaf, #434 .	12.00
Cigarette box, Trix, oblong, #348	16.00

Cookie jar, Bo Peep, #694 .	47.00
Cookie jar, Hippo, black, #549	50.00
Cookie jar, Jack-in-the-Box, #611	45.00
Cookie jar, Mother Goose, #695	35.00
Cookie jar, windmill, #678 .	40.00
Figurine, pouter pigeon, #388, 4¼"	25.00
Figurine, shepherdess & fawn, #3906, 11½"	225.00
Figurine, swordfish, #657 . .	30.00
Flower pot, Egg & Dart, medium, #366	10.00
Jam jar set, with tray, #666 .	25.00
Jar, Ming, with lid, #301 . .	28.00
Pitcher, Grecian, #613	12.00
Planter, fawn, #672	15.00
Plate, apple blossom, #415 .	14.00
Range set, daisy, yellow & brown, #690	38.00
String holder, mouse, #712 .	35.00
Teapot tile, Coolie, #401 . . .	35.00
Urn, Grecian, #553	25.00

Wall pocket, butterfly, pastels on white, 8½" x 8", $28.00.

Vase, anchor, #632	18.00
Vase, basketweave, small, #718	16.00
Vase, Fan, pink, #484	10.00
Vase, Hackney, #659	35.00
Vase, Tassel, #537	25.00

Advertising Collectibles

Competition among manufacturers of retail products since the late 1800s has produced multitudes of containers, signs, trays, and novelty items, each bearing a catchy slogan, colorful lithograph or some other type of ploy, flagrantly intent upon catching the eye of the potential customer. In their day, some were more successful than others, but today it is the advertising material itself rather than the product that rings up the big sales -- from avid collectors and flea market shoppers, not the product's consumers!

See also Coca-Cola; Labels; Planters Peanuts.

Ad Cards

America Baking Powder, Lady Liberty with shield & eagle	10.00
Arbuckle Bros Coffee, Egyptian map, Sphinx, 1889, 3x5"	2.25
Arm & Hammer, birds, lot of 49	20.00
Ayer's Cherry Pectoral, 7 pilgrims meet with Indians	8.00
Beverwyck Brewing Co, race horse & jockey, 1914 ...	3.00
Bluxome, die-cut lady with red hat & fan, VG	50.00
Boraxine, Makes Homes Healthy, boy in field with butterfly, VG	2.75
Brooklyn Bridge, between NY & Brooklyn, in color, 4x7" .	3.00

Trade card, Star Supply, birds and roses motif, $9.00.

Brown's Iron Bitters, lady's face looks through broken pane	10.50
Burdock Blood Bitters, child on toboggan, VG	7.50
Button's Raven Gloss Shoe Dressing, children, set of 6, G	15.00
Carolina Lily, multicolored circle, tipped-on albumen print of man	8.00
Celery Bitters, Steuben County Wine Co, cavalier with pipe	7.00
Church & Dwight Soda, set of 15, with original envelope .	8.00
Clark's Thread Co, girl sewing boy's coat, in color, 3x4½"	1.10
Currier & Ives, Bad Point on a Good Pointer, 1879 ...	50.00
Deering Twine Binder	2.50
Dental Mild Scotch Snuff, die-cut snuff box, yellow & black, VG	4.50
Domestic Sewing Machines, child blowing bubbles ..	5.00

Dr JC Ayer & Company, Sarsaparilla, Sunny Hours . 1.50
Dr Kilmer's Swamp Root Kidney, Liver & Bladder Cure, alligator 11.00
Dr Pardee's Celebrated Remedy, boy pulls dolly from creek, 5" 7.50
Easle, tipped-on albumen print of woman, VG 7.00
Eldorado Engine Oil, black & white, lady feeding horse, VG 3.25
Fleer, Three Stooges, black & white or color 2.50
GE Gray Artist-Photographer, floral litho, small . 5.00
Germania House Hotel, Cincinnati, Ohio, 1870 ..... 3.50
Gold Dust Twins, in tub, 1880s 12.00
Gowers & Stover Co, Oak Leaf Soap with muff, 3x5½" . 1.10
Heald & Co Portrait Photographers, multicolor litho, couple in boat 12.00
Heinz, die-cut pickles, with chef holding can & bowl . 8.00
Higgins Soap, days of the week, set of 7 .... 32.00
Ivory Soap, Maud Humphrey illustration, girl with washtub 35.00
J&P Coats, little girl with large umbrella, VG 3.00
Keer's Extra Six Cord Spool Cotton, Santa in green suit 5.00
Kendall's Spavin Cure, Black jockey on horse, groom at side, 4x6½" 12.50
Manhattan Biscuit Company, Indian on package 5.00
McCheany Bros Dentists, boys pulling Chinaman's braid 1.50
Moxie, roadster, man on horse 26.00

Old Judge Cigarettes, umbrella lifts, boy at store--at home 20.00

Quaker Bitters, girl 'Brighton Belle', Donaldson Bros, 6" 8.00
Quaker Oats, little girl stands on rocks with product, G . 2.50
Singer Sewing Machine Co, Columbian Exposition, set of 9 .... 4.00
St Jacob's Oil, New York Harbor, monk holding product, VG 4.00
Tobacco, steamship companies, lot of 7 .... 30.00

Banks

Atlantic Stove Co, stove, pot metal, 5¼" 40.00
Bokar Coffee, tin 10.00
Calumet Baking Powder, tin litho can, cardboard baby, 5" 50.00
Eight O'Clock, tin 10.00
F&M Bank, South Dakota, girl with balloon, tin, 4½x5½" 25.00
Ford Enrollment Plan, metal with leather cover 35.00
International Harvester Savings Bank, 4" 55.00
JP Seeburg, piano, nickled iron, 6¾" wide 210.00
Knox Hats, Santa with top hat, plastic, 6" 45.00
Magic Chef, stove, pot metal, 3½x3" 40.00
Pepsi-Cola bottle vendor ... 75.00
Pittsburgh Paints, house, glass 24.00
Red Top Cab, cab, cast iron, 4¼x8" 375.00
Rival Dog Food, can with picture of dog 15.00
Servel Electrolux, refrigerator, pot metal, 4" 10.00
Union Bank, safe, iron 25.00

Calendars

American Glass Co, ruler/blotter, black & white celluloid 8.50
Dr Pepper, 1944 .... 45.00

8

Ever-Ready, man shaving,
1933, 12x4" 25.00
Hood's Sarsaparilla, 1893 .. 24.00
John Deere Centennial,
1837-1937 .... 175.00
McCormick Reaper, Wyeth,
1931 .... 50.00
Orange Crush, 1953 ...... 40.00
Pepsi-Cola, 1941 .... 60.00
Sanford Ginger Ale, with
Black men, 1895 .... 40.00
Spanish American, mother &
child, 1944 .... 12.00

Clocks

A-C Spark Plugs, electric .. 30.00
Dr Pepper, 1944 .... 45.00
Kendall Motor Oil 65.00
Nash Coffee, tin 350.00
Pepsi-Cola, glass, 14" 75.00
Proctor and Gamble 145.00
Royal Crown Cola, reverse
painted sign & clock, 2 bot-
tles 110.00
Sauer's Flavoring Extracts,
Regulator, walnut 725.00
Vantage Cigarettes, battery
operated 20.00

Dolls

Alka Seltzer, Speedy, boy with
tablet in hand & on head,
bank, 5½" 7.50
American Beauty Macaroni
Co, Roni Mac, stuffed, 11",
1937 .... 25.00
Archie Comics, Archie, teen
doll wearing striped pants,
18", 1976 .... 8.00
Atlas Van Lines, Atlas Annie,
stuffed, message on tag,
15½", 1977 .... 5.00
Baby Magic, Snuggly Sammy,
multicolor, 24" tall, 1975 . 8.00
Baby Ruth, Baby Ruth,
painted face, stuffed cloth,
16", 1920s 12.00

Tony the Tiger, for Frosted Flakes,
molded plastic, 7¾" x 4½" , $5.00.

Baggies Food Storage Bags,
green inflatable alligator,
1975 .... 4.00
Beech-Nut Fruit Stripe Gum,
Gum Man, body is replica
of package, 7" 5.00
Betty Crocker, Betty Rose,
cloth, removable coat,
14½" 15.00
Big Boy Restaurant, Big Boy,
hands on suspenders, 10",
1974 .... 2.00
Blatz Beer, Blatz Beer Man,
can for body, no arms,
winking, 10" 15.00
Budweiser Beer, Bud Man,
Superman-like, rubber,
name on front, 18" 20.00
Burger Chef, chef's head with
chef hat, stuffed, 1970s . 5.00
Campbell Soup Co, Chef, boy
wears big white chef hat,
10", 1966 .... 10.00
Chee-tos, Chee-tos Mouse,
wears suit & tie, felt ears,
12", 1974 .... 5.00

Chrysler Corp, Mr Fleet, plastic, man with wrench, bank, 10″, 1973 .... 5.00

Clark Candy Bar, boy holds candy bar, soft vinyl, 7″ . 10.00

Exxon, tiger, 'Put a Tiger in Your Tank', plush, stuffed, 16″, 1973 .... 8.00

Fels-Naptha Soap, Anty Drudge, red dress with soap name, 11″, 1973 ... 55.00

Frostie Root Beer, Frostie Man, brown, long white beard, 16″, 1972 .... 8.00

Funny Face, Goofy Grape, purple, hat, 4 big teeth, pillow, 14″, 1975 .... 3.00

General Mills, Frankenberry, purple monster, twist waist, 7½″ 4.00

Gerber Products Co, Gerber Baby, flannel sleeper, rubber, 12″, 1954 .... 12.00

Junior Mints, Fonz, character from Happy Days TV show, 16″, 1976 .... 4.00

Big Boy, cloth pillow doll, 15½″ tall, $5.00.

Kellog Co, Rice Krispies, Snap, Crackle, Pop; stuffed, 12½″, 1948 .... 15.00

Kellog Co, Toucan Sam, stuffed, colorful toucan, long bill, 12″, 1964 .... 1.00

Ma Brown Pickles, Ma Brown, grandma wears wig & glasses, vinyl, 15″ 20.00

McDonald Corp, Ronald McDonald, clown, zipper front, red hair, 1971 .... 5.00

Michelin Tire , Michelin Tire Man, inflatable, white, 25″ 3.00

Mountain Dew, Hillbilly, with beard & ragged clothes . 20.00

Mr Bubble, bubble bath holder, pink plastic, 1 quart, 10″ 1.00

Mr Clean, bald white muscular man with arms folded, 8″, 1961 .... 20.00

Old Crow Whiskey, Old Crow, plastic, top hat & glasses, 4½″, 1950 .... 8.00

Pillsbury Co, Pillsbury Doughboy, white, cap & scarf detach, 16″, 1971.. 6.00

Planters Peanuts, Mr Peanut, peanut body, eyeglass, 21″, 1967 .... 5.00

Post Cereals, Sugar Bear, brown bear, name on shirt, 12½″, 1976 .... 5.00

Quaker Oats Co, Cap'n Crunch, sea captain, blue & yellow, 7½″ 4.00

Quaker Oats Co, Quisp, alien, propeller on head, Q on belt, 7″ 7.00

Shakey's Pizza Restaurant, Shakey Chef, chef with hat, white, 18″ 6.00

Fans

Baker's Chocolate, folding . 35.00

Coolerator girl, cardboard with wood handle 15.00

DeCoursey Ice Cream, with boy & girl twins 13.00

Edison Phonographs 15.00
Garrett Snuff, hunters pictured, 1937 .... 12.00
Generale Transat Lantique Steamship, signed, 1915 . 30.00
Moxie, Frances Pritchard holding glass 30.00
Moxie, Moxiemobile with boy on horse, 1922, NM 28.00
Pacific Tea Co, circa 1890s . 35.00
Putnam Dyes, British Dragoons, cardboard ... 8.00
Putnam Dyes, butterfly & Art Nouveau figures, cardboard 24.00
Singer Sewing Machines, paper, blue with roses .. 12.00
Vermont Insurance, President Coolidge, Keep Cool 22.00

Match Holders

Adriance Farm Machinery, wall hanging, colorful ... 70.00
Ceresota, EX 80.00
Coal & Lime, cast iron, wall hanging 45.00
DeLaval Separator Co, wall hanging 40.00
Fire King Gas Ranges, cast iron, duck figural, early . 50.00
Floyd & Co Clothiers & Hatters 25.00
Hanley Beer 24.00
JS Kemp Manufacturing, cast iron with crocodile paperweight, 8½" 50.00
Judson Whiskey, wall hanging, cast iron 40.00
Michigan Stove Co, iron ... 80.00
Old Judson, mom, dad & daughter, tin with scraper 75.00
Solarine Metal Polish 45.00

Match Safes

Anheuser Busch, German Silver, 'A' with eagle ... 50.00
Des Moines Insurance Co, 'Capital $100,000', old style 18.00
Dr Shoop's 95.00

Fontiues Gents Fine Footwear, Denver, pocket style 34.00
Gillette 22.00
Home Insurance, 2 fire fighters in relief 70.00
Juicy Fruit Gum 145.00
Look for Blue Union Label..., 1905 .... 50.00
Luden's Menthol Cough Drops, 5¢, under celluloid 55.00
Old Judson 135.00
Schlitz Milwaukee Beer, pocket size with cigar cutter 35.00
US Machine & Supply, 1880 . 10.00
Val Blatz Brewing Co 95.00

Pin-Backs

Buster Brown 18.00
Ceresota Boy 15.00
Cherry Mash 20.00
Davis Powder 10.00
Dutch Boy 12.00
Hood's Milk 5.00
Horlicks, with woman 15.00
Wool Soap 12.00
Yellow Kid 20.00

Pocket Mirrors

Adam Scheidt Brewery, with bottle, colorful 75.00

Pocket mirror, Hallock-Miner and Company, reversible happy and sad face, 2¼" diameter, $15.00.

American Line, large cruise
ship, colorful 35.00
Angelus Marshmallows, two
cherubs with product ... 75.00
AT Cook Seed Specialist, with
original envelope 38.50
Bingaman & Co Jewelers, Art
Nouveau lady, G 28.50
Coca-Cola, memo board, 50th
Anniversary, rectangular,
1936, NM 47.00
Dr Caldwell's Syrup Pepsin,
yellow box on blue 28.50
Duffy's Pure Malt Whiskey,
chemist at work 55.00
Dutch Java Coffee, celluloid
with kissing couple 24.50
Frisco Line, train running by
waterfall 65.00
Garrett's Baker Rye, with
nude 60.00
Mascot Cut Tobacco, with dog 55.00
Morton's Salt 30.00
Nature's Remedy 28.00

Queen Quality Shoes 40.00
RCA Victor, original 175.00
Red Seal Lye, with can 30.00
Sherwin Williams Paints, red
& white celluloid 17.50
Skeezix Shoes, Skeezix with
various birthstones 65.00
Starrett Tools, tools on red
celluloid 16.50
Stoddard Gilbert & Co, Old
Green 10¢ Cigar 38.50

Signs

Alt Heidelberg, tin, with boy,
19x9″ 22.00
Anheuser Busch, tin, Doctor
& stork, 7x12″ 50.00
Arm & Hammer Soda, with
emblem, black & gold,
16x12″ 24.50
Babbitt's Soap, paper, 2
babies, Our Twins, 24x15″,
EX 150.00

Salada, dimensional yellow teapot with black letters, 8½″ x 12″, $75.00.

Banquet Ice Cream, card-
board, 25x13" 55.00
Barbarossa Beer, canvas,
16x12" 45.00
Bartel's Beer, metal, round . 95.00
Braumeister, tin, multicolor
banner, 35x22" 68.00
Budweiser, neon, eagle
emblem with 'A', 26½x11" 65.00
Cataract Beer, tin lithograph,
1930s, 14" diameter 75.00
Coca-Cola, flanged, enamel,
Vendu Ice Glace, four col-
ors, NM 125.00
Coca-Cola, porcelain, Fountain
Service, 1935 .... 150.00
Coleman's Mustard, card-
board, dog & product,
framed, 24½x20" 275.00
Crosman Seeds, paper 195.00
Davis Carriage Mfg Co, tin,
carriage with horses, 1906,
7x20" 155.00
Doe-Wah-Jack, cardboard,
stoves, 14", M 300.00
Dr Pepper, porcelain, Good
For Life, colorful, 10x25",
VG 80.00
E&O Pilsner, beer, view of ci-
ty, tin, 11x9" 25.00
Feigenspon, tin, curled corner,
with girl 250.00
Fleischmann's Yeast, tin,
5½x8½", G 45.00
Garfield Tea, tin, with Presi-
dent Garfield, 28x20" ... 750.00
Hamilton Brown Shoe Co, tin,
oval, Shoes Wear Longer,
19" 20.00
Heidelberg Blatz, girl on bar-
rel, plaster, 1933, NM .. 300.00
IW Harper Whiskey, milk
glass, dog inside cabin,
1900, framed 750.00
Kayo Soda, embossed cartoon
character, 1930s, 14x29",
EX 58.00
McLaughlin Coffee, with box,
circa 1900 .... 65.00

Mennen Talcum Powder, 7
babies look over fence, cir-
ca 1900 .... 165.00
Moxie, tin, with buildings,
cars & buggies in street . 1,000.00
Musgo Gas, porcelain, with
Indian, 8" 550.00
New Scotch Snuff, tin, em-
bossed battleship, early,
VG 75.00
Pepsi-Cola, bottle, 28" 40.00
Pontiac Gas, porcelain, with
Indian, 36" 175.00
Post Toasties, paper die-cut . 225.00
Power Lube Motor Oil,
porcelain, with tiger 225.00

Tin Containers

Blanke's Mojav Coffee, red
with lady on horse 120.00
Bouquet Coffee 55.00
Brownie Peanuts, round ... 40.00
Buffalo Brand Peanuts, 10
pound 90.00
Camel Tube Patch 15.00
Dairy Made Baking Powder . 9.00

Seal of North Carolina Plug Cut
Smoking Tobacco tin, black with
yellow and red lettering, 6¼", $175.00.

Tiger Tobacco lunch pail, red basketweave with black tiger, large size, $35.00.

Davis Baking Powder, 3 ounce	10.00	Manchester Big Sioux Biscuits, Indian decor	50.00
Dove Brand Allspice	10.00	McNess Cocoa, sample	28.00
Feder's Eagle Brand Stogies, paper label, old, G	20.00	Mellrose Marshmallows	15.00
Flower Roses Talcum	15.00	Monarch Cinnamon, with lion, 3 pound, EX	17.50
Folger's Coffee, 5 pound, with ship	45.00	New Bachelor Cigars, round	100.00
Frishmuth's Whittle Cut Tobacco, round corners, EX	20.00	Old English Curve Cut Tobacco	20.00
Golden Dome Tea	45.00	Old Gold Smoking Tobacco, square corners, 1900s, G	20.00
Golden Rule Tea, 3 pound	40.00	Postum Cereal	15.00
Guasti Pure Grape Syrup, bear pulls cherub in chariot, 1 gallon	55.00	Raleigh's Talcum, with circus	15.00
Hercules Coffee	500.00	Rick's Canton Ginger	4.50
Java Mocha Coffee, pictures factory, 1900s, G	15.00	Sailor Boy Brand, 8¾x6½"	300.00
Kenny's Maid Coffee, 4	145.00	Sharp's Toffee	65.00
King Cole Coffee	125.00	Slippery Elm Lozenge	425.00
Krak-R-Jack Biscuits	40.00	Snap Shot Gun Powder, slain duck falling	75.00
Luzianne Coffee, Mammy pouring coffee, 1 pound	30.00		

Tip Trays

Bartel's Beer, shows 'Night Watchman,' pre-1920	135.00

Century Beer Schneider, old man, woman drinking .. 125.00

Christian Feigenspan Breweries, redhead in low-cut gown 90.00

Columbus Brewery, Christopher Columbus 135.00

El Ricardo Cigars, Spanish conquistador portrait ... 85.00

El Verso Cigars, man dreams of girl while smoking ... 55.00

Fairy Soap, EX 60.00

Globe-Wernicke, sectional bookcase ad 22.00

Harkert Cigar Co, Andrew White portrait 85.00

Hunt Shoe Co, close-up of stag 55.00

Iroquois, pre-prohibition ... 75.00

Korby's Whiskey, tramp steals whiskey from man . 65.00

Lewis 66 Whiskey, man eating lobster 60.00

Maltosia, pre-prohibition .. 40.00

Moehn Brewery 95.00

Monticello, EX 75.00

National Cigar, girl holds bouquet of yellow flowers .. 85.00

National San Iran, cowboy on horse, pre-1920 .... 275.00

Plymouth Gin, monk drinking 75.00

President Suspenders, with portrait, 4¼″ diameter .. 40.00

Red Raven Splits, World's Fair, 1904 .... 78.00

Ryan's Beer, Gypsy girl ... 80.00

West End Brewing Co, Victorian lady wrapped in flag 175.00

Trays

Arctic Ice Cream, polar bear . 165.00

Bartholomay, pre-prohibition 85.00

Budweiser, fox hunters, shadow of fox by fireplace . 75.00

Casey & Kelly Brewery, king holding mug, pre-prohibition 260.00

Cleveland Fruit Juice Co, tin lithograph, with dispenser, 1908 .... 195.00

Dobler Brewing Co, oval, with three beer wagons, 1906 . 175.00

Dr Pepper, girl with two bottles of product 150.00

Duesseldorfer Beer, baby holding bottle, pre-prohibition 350.00

Excelsior Beer, lady in sailor blouse, two bottles 325.00

Fredericksburg Brewery, San Jose, Dutch boy with tray, 1915 .... 45.00

Furnace Ice Cream, girl holding tray, 1920s 145.00

Green River Whiskey, old Black man with mule, 1890s 300.00

Hick's Capudine, several cherubs 150.00

Jacob Ruppert's, 19th century men served, pre-prohibition 225.00

Merrigan's Ice Cream, little girl & boy on beach, 1923 . 145.00

Monroe Brewery, king holding goblet, pre-prohibition .. 175.00

O'Keefe's Stock Ale, post-prohibition 37.00

Old Gold Leaf Rye, blonde lady, 1900 .... 150.00

Old Pepper Whiskey, Revolutionary War soldiers ... 180.00

Orange Julep, girl in swimsuit, EX 120.00

Pepsi-Cola, beach scene, round, EX 20.00

Pepsi-Cola, Coney Island, 1950s, M 25.00

Potosi Pure Malt Beer, red, white, gold & black 65.00

Red Raven, bird next to bottle, square, 1910 ...... 160.00

Red Raven, Papa has a headache, nude child with bottle 195.00

Roessle Lager, two old men at table drinking, pre-prohibition 150.00

Tam O'Shanter, beer tray, post-prohibition 40.00

Store box, Tanglefoot fly paper, wood with stenciled lettering, 6″ x 17″ x 10¼″, $25.00.

Akro Agate

This company operated in Clarksbury, West Virginia, from 1914 to 1951, manufacturing marbles, novelties, and children's dishes, for which they are best known. Though some were made in clear solid colors, their most popular and easy-to-identify lines were produced in a swirling opaque type of glass such as was used in the production of their marbles. Their trademark was a flying eagle clutching marbles in his claws.

Chiquita, creamer, opaque
green, 1½″ 4.00
Chiquita, cup, 1½″, with
saucer, 3⅛″ diameter,
transparent cobalt 8.00
Concentric Rib, cup, green,
1¼″, with white saucer,
2¾″ diameter 3.75
Concentric Rib, teapot, green
with white lid, 3⅜″ 6.50
Concentric Rib, 7 piece set in
box, various opaque colors 25.00
Concentric Ring, cup,
marbleized blue, 1¼″ . . . 28.00
Interior Panel, cereal bowl,
azure blue, 3⅜″ diameter 15.00

Interior Panel, creamer,
transparent green, 3⅜″ . . 10.00
Interior Panel, creamer,
transparent topaz, 1⅜″ . . 8.00
Interior Panel, cup, 1⅜″, with
saucer, 3⅛″ diameter, pink
lustre 13.00
Interior Panel, plate, azure
blue, 3¾″ 5.00
Interior Panel, plate,
lemonade & oxblood, 4¼″ 9.00
Interior Panel, sugar with lid,
green lustre, 1⅞″ 15.00
Interior Panel, sugar with lid,
red & white marbleized,
1⅞″ 30.00
Interior Panel, teapot with lid,
marbleized green & white,
3⅜″ 19.00
Miss America, creamer, forest
green 35.00
Miss America, cup & saucer,
white, no decal 31.00
Miss America, plate, white
with decal decoration . . . 20.00
Octagonal, cup, closed handle,
opaque pumpkin, 1½″ . . 20.00
Octagonal, pitcher, dark green 11.00
Octagonal, plate, opaque
yellow, 3⅜″ 5.50
Octagonal, plate, opaque
yellow, 4¼″ 3.00

Octagonal, sugar, open, white, 1¼" 10.50

Octagonal, teapot with lid, closed handle, green, white lid, 3⅝" 8.00

Pastry set, glass: 2 cake pans & covered bowl; + 4 utensils & booklet 40.00

Raised Daisy, creamer, opaque yellow, 1¾" 25.00

Raised Daisy, tumbler, opaque beige, 2" 16.00

Stacked Disc, cup, opaque yellow, 1¼" 4.00

Stacked Disc, tumbler, opaque white, 2" 3.00

Stacked Disc, 21 piece set in box, opaque green & white 35.00

Stacked Disc & Interior Panel, cereal bowl, opaque green, 3⅜" 14.00

Stacked Disc & Interior Panel, creamer, opaque green, 1¼" 5.00

Stacked Disc & Interior Panel, cup, transparent green, 1¼" 9.00

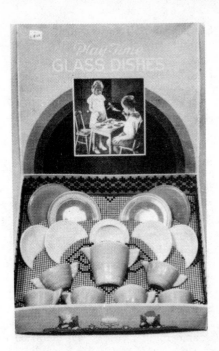

Concentric Ring, small size, in original box, $125.00.

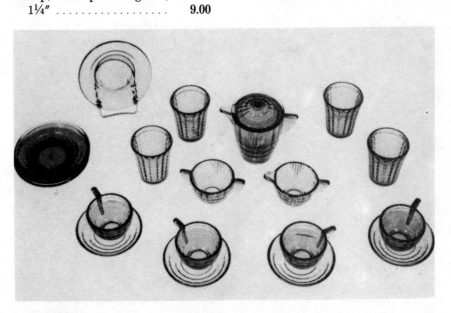

Stacked Disc and Interior Panel, transparent azure blue, twenty piece set in original box, $250.00.

Stacked Disc & Interior Panel, pitcher with lid, cobalt, 2⅞" 16.00

Stacked Disc & Interior Panel, plate, marbleized blue, 4¾" 10.50

Stacked Disc & Interior Panel, tumbler, transparent green, 2" 7.50

Stippled Band, creamer, transparent azure, 1½" . 20.00

Stippled Band, cup, transparent amber, 1¼" . 4.50

Stippled Band, plate, transparent amber, 4¼" . 6.00

Stippled Band, sugar, open, transparent green, 1¼" . 5.00

Stippled Band, teapot with lid, transparent azure, 3¾" . 36.50

Stippled Band, 8 piece set in box, small size, transparent amber 37.00

Aluminum

From the late 1930s until early in the 1950s, kitchenwares and household items were crafted from aluminum, usually with relief molded fruit or flowers on a hammered background. Today many find these diversified items make an interesting collection. Especially desirable are those examples marked with the manufacturer's backstamp or the designer's signature.

Bowl, grapes in relief, Hammerkraft, 11½" 7.00

Bowl, reticulated, crimped, poinsettias, Farber & Shlevin, 15" 7.00

Candy dish with cover, footed, blossom with bow, Rodney Kent 8.00

Casserole, Wild Rose Brilliantone, Continental Silver Co Inc 12.00

Coaster, set of 6, tulip design, Rodney Kent 6.00

Coffee pot, drip, with lid, 400 brand extra heavy, 6 cup, Unid 8.00

Two-tiered server, marked Buinlun in house-shaped backstamp, 10" x 9", $7.00.

Creamer and sugar bowl, #7007, marked Hand Forged Everlast, $7.50 for the pair.

Creamer & covered sugar, Continental, chrysanthemum design 10.00

Lazy susan, tulip decor, #413, Rodney Kent, 18″ 10.00

Perculator, 3 quart, complete, #843, Mirro 12.00

Plate, iris design, Chadwell, 13½″ 8.00

Server, 2 tier, bamboo design, Everlast 6.00

Teapot, coronation of Elizabeth, 1953 .... 9.00

Tray, grape cluster, loop handle, Buelinum, 17½″ 7.00

Tray, handles, crimped rim, Cromwell, 10x12″ 9.00

Tray, handles, pine trees, mountains, Arthur Amor, 11½x9″ 10.00

Animal Dishes with Covers

Popular novelties for parts of two centuries, figural animal dishes were made by many well known glass houses in milk glass, slag, colored opaque or clear glass. These are preferred by today's collectors, though the English earthenware versions are highly collectible in their own right.

British lion, milk glass 65.00

Camel, resting, head, neck & humps are cover, 5⅜ x6¼″ 110.00

Cat, black & white on white ribbed base 55.00

Chick & egg, milk glass, 1889 95.00

Cow on basket-type bottom, light amber 50.00

Crayfish, 4½x7½″ 125.00

Dog, Pekingese on rectangular basket, painted, 5″ 250.00

Dog, Scotty, rectangular, blue glass 50.00

Dove with hand, dated 125.00

Duck on basket, milk glass . 30.00

Eagle hovering over fallen bird, clear round ornate base, footed 95.00

Eagle sheltering eggs, milk glass, American Hen, 1898 65.00

Fish on boat, milk glass ... 22.00

Hen, lacy base, caramel slag, Atterbury 170.00

Lamb on lid, fluted box, 5½x3¾″ 22.00

Lovebirds, basket base 60.00

Quail, milk glass 45.00

Rabbit, Atterbury 155.00

Robin on nest, milk glass, Westmoreland 50.00

Rabbit, well detailed milk glass with glass eyes, 5″ x 10″, $125.00.

Rooster, blue with white head, blue ribbed base 25.00

Snail on strawberry, signed Vallerysthal 80.00

Squirrel, on fancy shaped dish, amber 75.00

Swan with closed neck, milk glass 110.00

Turkey, McKee 175.00

Turtle, feet & head on base, amber, large 100.00

Rabbit on sheaf of wheat, milk glass, black painted top, $135.00

Art Deco

The Art Deco movement began at the Paris International Exposition in 1925 and lasted into the 1950s. Styles of apparel, furniture, jewelry, cars, and architecture were influenced by its cubist forms and sweeping, aerodynamic curves. Sleek greyhounds and female nudes (less voluptuous than Art Nouveau nudes), shooting stars and lightning bolts, exotic woods and lush fabrics -- all were elements of the Art Deco era. Today's fashions, especially in home furnishings, reflect the movement; and collectors delight in aquiring authentic examples to re-create the posh Art Deco environment.

Ash tray, bronze terrier on green marble base, Germany 75.00
Bathroom set, yellow overlay glass, geometric, 6 piece . 250.00
Bookends, bronze over copper, girl kneeling, pair 125.00
Candlesticks, scrolled copper tubing & pewter, 8½x4" diameter 35.00

Centerpiece, apricot satin glass, 3 nudes support 10" bowl 325.00
Clock, giltwood triangle carved with overlapped square, French, 11" 385.00
Coffee pot, electric, chrome, inset handles, faucet knob . 25.00
Figurine, brass, Delilah at the Well 35.00
Flower frog, dancing girl, German porcelain, 8" 27.50
Gates, wrought iron, scalloped, in geometric frame, Subes, pair 440.00
Lamp, blue satin glass, nude playing harp, 12x6", pair . 300.00
Lamp, boudoir; panther figural with pink camphor shade 45.00
Light, hall; kneeling metal nude with beacon, marble, mahogany base 165.00
Perfume, frosted amethyst rose with butterfly stopper, 3½" 80.00
Pillow, lavender satin with lady walking greyhound . 20.00
Plaque, copper, stylized woman, Mitzi Otten, 5x9" 880.00

Dresser set, four pieces on 11" x 7¾" mirrored tray, $17.50.

Sculptural lamp, Au Cirque, bronze with glass shade, marble base with bird and clown hat, signed A. de Avier, 7″ x 10″, $300.00.

Radio, blue mirrored glass, Troy	650.00
Rug, geometric decor in blue & rose, Eric Bagge, 30x52″	450.00
Sculpture, bronze seated flapper, marble base, 4″	225.00
Vase, trumpet, frosted & clear glass, geometric base, Luce, 7″	375.00

Art Nouveau

'New Art' originated in the late 1890s in the L'Art Nouveau shop on the rue de Provence in Paris, and lasted until the 1920s. The style took themes from nature -- flowers, insects, fruits, animals and female nudes -- and used them in flowing, sensuous, asymetrical forms. It influenced every aspect of fashion -- jewelry, furniture, art, silver, glass, bronzes, and ceramics -- and many examples remain to delight today's collectors.

Birdcage, wire, ornate, revolving side wheel, dome top, 17″	55.00
Biscuit jar, wheel-cut intaglio florals, silver mounted, 12″	275.00
Bookends, Nouveau design, signed Clarence Crafters, pair	55.00
Box, blown-out pattern, gold with raised porcelain florals, hinged	180.00
Brush & mirror, silver, lady with flowing hair & lilies	225.00
Cigar holder, woman wearing flowing dress	80.00
Creamer & sugar, lustreware, artist signed, France, 1913	65.00
Desk plateau, lion & lioness at pool, bronze, after Radetzky, 15″	350.00
Desk set, dore bronze, marked JB, #1659, 8 piece	350.00
Dressing mirror, bronze, maiden, beveled mirror, 2 lights, 21″	1,500.00

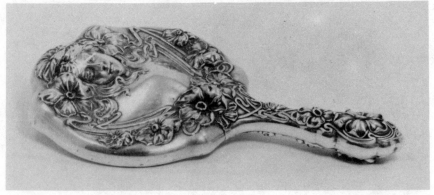

Hand mirror, sterling silver, lady's head and flowers in relief, 10″, $200.00.

Salt, glass, pedestaled with lid, cherub relief, 4½" .. 27.00

Tile, set of 3, relief cherubs with banner, JG Low, 6x18" 180.00

Bust of lady with flowers in her hair, uncolored porcelain face, hands and hair, pastel clothing, signed Made in Austria Ernst Wahl ss, Turn, Wien, $450.00.

Fire tender, double rod balustrade with floral filigree, glass squares... 525.00

Inkwell, figural dog & tree, hinged lid, 11" long 100.00

Pitcher, chalkware, lady with flowing hair molded in high relief 160.00

Candlesticks, silver plate by Wallace Bros., poppies and buds in relief, ca. 1908, 11", $250.00 for the pair.

Tray, shell shape, dish at each end with bird between, Herend 65.00

Vase, figural tree trunk, loop handle, 11½" 40.00

Figural light, silver plated female form, tripod base, ca. 1910, 10", $135.00.

Autographs

Autographs of famous people from every walk of life are of interest to students of Philography, as it is referred to by those who enjoy this hobby. Values hinge on many things -- rarity of the signature and content of the signed material are major considerations. Autographs of sports figures or entertainers often sell at $5.00 for small signed photos, and as little as $1.00 on 3" x 5" cards. Beware of forgeries. If you are unsure, ask established dealers to help you.

Abbott, George; signature on 3x5" card 15.00
Alberghetti, Anna Maria; inscribed signed photo, black & white, 8x10" 10.00
Ali, Muhammed; signed black & white photo, lengthy inscription, 8x10" 20.00
Andrews, Dana; inscribed signed black & white vintage photo, 8x10" 15.00
Arness, James; inscribed signed CBS publicity photo as Matt Dillon 20.00
Avalon, Frankie; inscribed signed black & white publicity photo, 8x10" ... 12.00
Basie, Count; jazz band leader, signed photo, 8x10" 38.00
Begin, Menachem; signed black & white matt finish photo, 3x4¼" 30.00

Bolger, Ray; inscribed signed black & white photo, 4x3" . 10.00
Borgnine, Ernest; 8 line note signed on bottom of letter to him 10.00
Boyer, Charles; signed black & white matt photo, close-up, circa 1930 .... 62.00
Buck, Pearl; signed 5x7" portion of cover of Today & Forever 20.00
Cary, Harry Jr; actor, in Western outfit, inscribed signed photo 17.00
Como, Perry; signed black & white photo, close-up, 5x7" 5.00
Crabbe, Buster; signed photo, Tarzan, holds knife, with Cheeta, 8x10" 29.00
Davies, Marion; signed matt finish portrait quality photo, circa 1935 ...... 30.00
Davis, Sammy, Jr; signed inscribed candid black & white glossy, 8x10" 10.00
Demarest, William; signed inscribed photo from My Three Sons, 8x10" 10.00
Dempsey, Jack; signed menu from Dempsey's Restaurant, dated 1971 .... 50.00
DiMaggio, Joe; signed 3½x5" snapshot, in action at Old Timer's Game......... 19.00

Cole Porter, composer, three bars of music plus small signed bust photo, fine condition, $225.00.

Dr. Martin Luther King, Jr., signature on consent statement to National Committee for a Sane Nuclear Policy, dated Dec. 20, 1960, $600.00.

Ferrer, Jose; inscribed signed photo as Toulouse-Lautrec, 8x10″ 17.00

Gable, Clark; signed bank check, 1949, dark 3½″ signature, M 150.00

Gar, Eddie; vintage inscribed signed matt black & white photo, 8x6″ 30.00

Gaynor, Mitzi; inscribed signed vintage black & white cheesecake pose 10.00

Gordon, Ruth; signed black & white vintage photo, 8x10″ 14.00

Grable, Betty; 2 lines & signature on postcard .. 22.00

Graham, Billy; signed photo on pamphlet What Is Conversion 13.00

Hayes, Helen; signed letter, 1 page, 1950s 16.00

Herman, Woody; orchestra leader, signed photo, with clarinet, 8x10″ 18.00

Howard, Moe; of the Three Stooges, signed bank check, 1971 .... 25.00

Jackson, Andrew; signed 1 page land grant, 1829, part of seal gone 275.00

Johnson, Celia; signed black & white photo, vintage, 8x10″ 14.00

Kennedy, John F; signed program for White House press dinner, 1963 ..... 700.00

King, Andrea; inscribed signed photo, glossy black & white, vintage 18.00

Lamour, Dorothy; inscribed signed black & white glossy, bust pose 15.00

Lee, Pinky; inscribed signed photo, color, in character, 8x6″ 12.00

Leigh, Vivien; signed 1 page letter, theatre stationary, 1955 .... 190.00

Lemon, Meadowlark; signature on 3x5″ card 9.00

Lincoln, Abraham; signed handwritten segment from larger document 900.00

Lombardo, Guy; signed photo of him conducting his orchestra, 10x8″ 19.00

Lovell, James A; astronaut, signed color photo, 8x10″ . 10.00

Loy, Myrna; signed black & white photo, Midnight Lace scene, 8x10″ 14.00

Lugosi, Bela; inscribed signed sepia photo as Count Dracula, 5x7″ 300.00

Mancini, Henry; American composer, signed photo, 8x10″ 14.00

Martin, Dean; vintage inscribed signed black & white photo, 8x10″ 10.00

Martin, Mary; inscribed signed photo, black & white, 8x6″ 10.00

Matthau, Walter; signed black & white photo from Casey's Shadow 10.00

McCarthy, Joseph R; signature on album page as Senator, 1948 .... 23.00

McIntire, Jim; actor, inscribed signed photo as Western character 17.00

Meredith, Burgess; inscribed signed color photo from Rocky, 8x10" 10.00

Merman, Ethyl; inscribed signed matt black & white photo, circa 1935 ...... 25.00

Moody, Dwight L; American evangelist, closely cut signature 10.00

Paige, Satchel; signature on white index card 16.00

Patterson, Floyd; signature on 3x5" card 9.00

Pulitzer, Joseph; signature in purple ink on card, New York, 1885 .... 75.00

Rand, Sally; hand written signed letter on personal stationery, 1 page...... 32.00

Remick, Lee; signed black & white photo, sexy pose, 8x10" 8.00

Reynolds, Debbie; inscribed signed photo, matt finish, circa 1955 .... 10.00

Rogers, Will; signature on card 125.00

Roosevelt, Eleanor; signed typed letter, Val-Kill Cottage stationery 22.00

Ruth, Babe; signature on card, 5x3" 225.00

Salk, Jonas; signed photo, head & chest view, 8x10" . 22.00

Scott, Randolph; signature on 3x5" card 10.00

Sills, Beverly; signed black & white photo, 3½x5¼" ... 10.00

Skelton, Red; inscribed signed photo, close-up, laughing, 8x10" 9.00

Sousa, John Philip; full signature on card 70.00

Stanwyck, Barbara; photo from Blowing Wild, with Cooper, Quinn & Roman. 18.00

Taylor, Elizabeth; signed photo in very short dress, ca 1955, 8x10" 18.00

Tierney, Gene; inscribed signed photo, circa 1935, close-up, 8x10" 25.00

Tucker, Sophie; signed announcement of appearance at Chez Paree 12.00

Vargas, Alberto; signed Vargas Girl print from Playboy, 8½x11" 39.00

Walcott, Jersey Joe; signed photo in boxing pose, 8x10" 19.00

Welch, Raquel; inscribed signed black & white photo, candid close-up 10.00

Wilson, Woodrow; signed 1 page letter, 1912 .... 130.00

Winters, Jonathan; typed signed letter, personal stationery, 1965 .... 15.00

Ziegfeld, Florenz; signed 1 page letter, Chicago, 1903 . 85.00

Automobilia

Many are fascinated with vintage automobiles, but to own one of those 'classy chassis' is a luxury not all can afford! So instead they enjoy collecting related memorabilia such as advertising, owners' manuals, horns, emblems and hood ornaments. The decade of the 1930s produced the items that are most in demand today, but the fifties models have their own band of devoted fans as well. Usually made of porcelain on cast iron, first year license plates in hard-to-find excellent condition may bring as much as $125.00 for the pair.

Left: Booklet, Inside Story of the New Dodge, ca. 1941, 16 pages, 5″ x 7″, $30.00; right: Folder with specs and cut-away pictures of New Hillman Husky, ca. 1959, 5″ x 7″, $20.00.

Booklet, Maxwell Motor Cars, 1912, 40 pgs 40.00

Booklet, Schedule of Repair Changes, 1926 Model T, 20 pg 17.00

Car clock, Pierce Arrow, electric, mid-'30s 100.00

Dash instrument panel, for Essex Super 6, 1926 .... 37.00

Gas tank straps, 1926-27 Ford, pair 20.00

Hood ornament, devil with tail wrapped around body, bronze 65.00

Hood ornament, Pontiac, 1950s 30.00

Hood ornament, woman with flowing hair, 1942 ...... 60.00

Horn, 1909 Buick, brass with original bulb 125.00

Horn, 1920s Steward Warner, hand operated 50.00

License plate, Hawaii, 1951, VG 25.00

Magazine, Auto Trade Journal, December, 1917 .... 20.00

Magazine, REO Review, October, 1921, many photos, 14 pgs 12.00

Magazine, The Horseless Age, October 6, 1912 .... 22.00

Manual, Cadillac, 1955 .... 10.00

Manual, Whippet Six Model 98 .... 25.00

Postcard, 1933 Ford, color . 25.00

Reward poster, stolen auto, 1928, 3x5″ 10.00

Token, 1934 Ford, NM 25.00

Wheel, wire, for 1933 Plymouth, 5 for 150.00

Autumn Leaf

Autumn Leaf dinnerware was a product of the Hall China Company, who produced this extensive line from 1933 until 1978 for exclusive distribution by the Jewell Tea Company. The Libbey Glass Company made coordinating pitchers, tumblers and stemware. Metal, cloth, plastic and paper items were also available. Today, though very rare pieces are expensive and a challenge to acquire, new collectors may easily reassemble an attractive, usable set at a reasonable price.

Baker, 2 pint 47.00

Bottle, Jewel-T Wagon, Jim Beam, empty 85.00

Bowl, cereal; mint gold 8.75

Bowl, fruit 4.00

Bowl, salad; 9″ 12.00

Bowl, vegetable; divided ... 50.00

Bud vase 165.00

Butter, 1 pound, with cover . 110.00

Teapot, Newport style, ca. 1933-35, 7½″, $100.00.

Cake plate	12.00	Mixer cover, Mary Dunbar,	
Cake safe, metal	25.00	plastic	22.00
Casserole, covered; 1½ quart,		Mug, Irish Coffee	55.00
tab handles	22.50	Mustard set, 3 piece	45.00
Cleanser can, metal	115.00	Pickle dish	14.00
Clock, original works	300.00	Picnic thermos	150.00
Coffee maker, drip, all china,		Pie baker	15.00
4 piece with insert	175.00	Platter, 11½″	14.00
Coffee pot, 8 cup	30.00	Salt & pepper shakers, Casper	12.00
Cookbook, Mary Dunbar		Salt & pepper shakers, range,	
Favorite Recipes	12.00	handled	15.00
Cookie jar, big ear	65.00	Saucer	2.00
Cookie jar, Tootsie	85.00	Saucer, St Denis	6.00
Creamer, New Style	8.00	Sifter, metal	85.00
Creamer, Old Style	15.00	Soup, coupe	10.50
Cup & saucer	8.00	Soup, cream	15.00
Custard cup	4.75	Spoon, stainless steel	6.00
Drip jar with cover	12.50	Sugar with lid, New Style	10.00
Fork, stainless steel	6.00	Sugar with lid, Old Style	15.00
Fruit cake tin	3.00	Teapot, Aladdin, 3 piece	30.00
Gravy boat	14.00	Tid bit tray, 3 tiered	45.00
Marmalade with cover &		Tray, glass, wooden handles	85.00
underplate	45.00	Tray, metal, oval	35.00

Warmer, oval 95.00
Warmer, round, with original
box 100.00

Aviation Collectibles

Collectors of aviation memorabilia search for items dealing with zeppelins, flying machines -- aircraft of any type, be it experimental, commercial, civilian or military. From airplane parts and pilot's gear to photos and magazines, there is a multitude of material relative to this area of interest.

Ad card, Runkel's Cocoa &
Chocolates, aviation heroes 30.00
Artificial horizon, standard,
luminous markings,
WWII, VG 30.00
Autograph, Wrong Way Corrigan, in flyleaf of That's
My Story 69.00
Book, Historic Airships, RS
Holland, 343 pages, 1928 . 15.00
Book, Lindbergh's Trophies &
Decorations, 64 pages,
1933 .... 35.00
Calendar, desk; Grumman
Aircraft, 18 color pages,
1943 .... 15.00
Card game, New Lindy Flying
Game, New York to Paris,
1927 .... 12.00
Fuel gauge, Luftwaffe markings, WWII 45.00
Goggles, Polaroid, black rubber & chamois, with box &
lenses, WWII 18.00
Helmet, type 1092, goatskin &
chamois, tagged, WWII
USN 40.00
Helmet, WWII aviator's, pilelined leather 45.00
Life vest, Mae West, gray,
WWII 20.00
Magazine, Aero Digest,
January 1941 .... 3.00

Match safe with compass,
WWII 6.00
Needle book, Trans-Atlantic
Aeroplane, Czechoslovakian 8.00
Photo album & scrapbook,
1920s 65.00
Pilot wings, pin-back sterling,
WWII, pair 35.00
Poster, aircraft in flight, black
& white, WWII, 1942 .. 8.00
Propeller, laminated wood,
metal edge & tip, 84" ... 225.00
Visor cap, khaki, leather bill &
strap, brass eagle 35.00

Avon

Originally founded under the title California Perfume Company, the firm became officially known as Avon Products, Inc., in 1939, after producing a line of cosmetics marketed under the Avon name since the mid-twenties. Among collectors they are best known not for their cosmetics and colognes, but for their imaginative packaging and figural bottles. Also collectible are product samples, awards, magazine ads, jewelry and catalogues.

1969 King Pin After Shave, white milk glass bottle, 4 oz., $5.00.

1967 Leather Spray Cologne Boot, brown plastic with gold ring below black cap, 3 oz., 6″, $4.00.

Alpine decanter, original, no box	35.00
Apple Blossom cologne, bubble sides, 6 ounces, 1941-1953	45.00
Bay Rum Keg	7.50
Bottle, 1926 Avon Lady, 1979	30.00
Bowl & pitcher, Victorian, marbeled, full, in box	25.00
Cake server, 1978	10.00
Candle holder, Martha Washington	10.00
Christmas Mouse, 5th Precious Moments	50.00
Daisy Bouquet set	28.00
Dueling Pistol Number 1	7.00
Gavel	4.50
Happy Father's Day set	15.00

1971 Liberty Bell Decanter, aftershave or cologne, glass with brown plastic top, 5 oz., 4½″, $6.00.

Kitten, milk glass	6.00
Lamp, cologne, base holds talc, full, carnival top	20.00
Li'l Tom Turtle soap	25.00
Parlor lamp, 1971	10.00
Pincushion doll, Bicentennial Betsy Ross	25.00
Scottie dog, milk glass, full, in box	10.00
Sheriff's Badge soap	25.00
Super Cycle, black glass, 1971	10.00
Teddy Bear Pen Award, 1979	17.00
Tiffany Sterling Acorn Necklace	80.00
Trading Post	42.00
Viking Horn	7.50
Whitey the Whale	10.00

Azalea China

Manufactured by the Noritake Company from 1916 until the mid-thirties, Azalea dinnerware was given away as premiums to club members and home agents of the Larkin Company, a door-to-door agency who sold soap and other household products. Over the years, seventy chinaware items were offered, as well as six pieces of matching hand painted crystal. Early pieces were signed with the blue 'rising sun' Nippon trademark, followed by the Noritake M-in-wreath mark. Later, the ware was marked Noritake, Azalea, Hand painted, Japan.

Basket, #193	115.00
Bouillon	12.00
Bowl, #55	88.00
Bowl, vegetable; oval, #172, 9½″	25.00
Butter tub	37.50
Candy dish, #313	450.00
Casserole, covered, #16	55.00
Celery dish, 12½″	30.00
Cheese, covered, #314	70.00
Coffee pot, #182	295.00
Compote, #170	80.00
Cream soup	70.00

Creamer, #122	50.00
Cruet, 6¼"	145.00
Cup & saucer, #2	13.50
Fruit bowl, large	210.00
Gravy boat, #40	25.00
Humidor	375.00
Jam jar with spoon	70.00
Mustard pot with spoon	47.50
Pitcher, milk; #100	120.00
Plate, breakfast; #98, 8½"	15.00
Plate, salad	7.50
Platter, 14"	38.00
Relish, 4 section, #119	99.00
Roll tray	35.00
Salt & pepper, #11, pair	10.00
Soup, flat, #19	15.00
Syrup pitcher	35.00
Teapot, gold finial, #400	300.00
Toothpick	90.00

Badges

'Wild West' badges and those once worn by officials whose positions no longer exist -- City Constable, for instance -- are tops on the lists of today's badge collectors. All law enforcement badges are considered collectible as well. Badges have been made in many materials and styles since the 1840s when they came into general use in this country. They were usually of brass or nickle silver, though even silver and gold were used on special order. Stars, shields, octagonals, ovals and discs are the most common shapes.

Badges such as this shield usually sell for around $100.00; the star-shaped railroad badge may bring as much as $150.00.

Chauffeur, brass, 1942	10.00
Constable, Kingston, Ohio seal, rounded shield, nickel, 1950s	35.00
Department of Public Safety, eagle & shield, men & sailboat, WWI	35.00
Deputy Marshall, star shape	45.00
Deputy Sheriff, ballpoint star, Texas Star in center	60.00
English Bobby, hat shield, crown on top of sunburst, 1880s, 4½"	35.00
Fire Department, ladder, pike & hydrant, early 1900s	24.00
Fireman, Cornwall, New York, cross type, 2"	10.00
Game Patrol, bear in relief on gold metal shield	28.00
Guard, Burns Detective, large ornate oval shape	12.00
Jewish Defense League, Protection of Girls & Women, star	25.00
Judge, Court of Indiana Offences, man in relief, gold & red	24.00

Police Captain, shield shape, gold finish, Indiana seal . 50.00

Police Reserve, Bedford, nickeled silver shield, enamel center 45.00

Police Reserve, Chicago, 6 point star, city seal, early 1900s 50.00

Post Office, old 23.00

Secret Service, Mexico, bronze & enamel, eagle with snake in beak 30.00

Sheriff, Arizona, gold, eagle top, raised star, blue letters 125.00

Sheriff, purse size, nickeled . 18.50

Telephone Company employee, California, blue with silver letter 20.00

Texas Rangers, cut-out star, marked 14 karat 175.00

Traffic Lieutenant, Watsonville School Police, California seal 25.00

Union Pacific Railroad, brass, logo shape, Spike Days 1929 .... 28.00

US Naval Station, Pearl Harbor, eagle with logo center, silver 20.00

Banks

The most popular (and expensive) type of bank with today's collectors are the mechanicals, so called because of the antics they perform when a coin is deposited. Over three hundred models were produced between the Civil War period up to the first World War. On some, arms wave, legs kick, mouths open to swallow up the coin, and other such amusing nonsense intended by the inventor to encourage and reward thriftiness. The registering bank may have one or more slots, and as the name implies, tallys the amount of money it contains as each coin is deposited. Many old banks have been reproduced -- beware! Condition is im-

portant; look for good original paint and parts.

Some of the banks listed here are identified by C for Cranmer, G for Griffeth, and W for Whiting, oft-used standard reference books.

Mechanical

Archie, bust of man, painted aluminum, EX 70.00

Artillery 325.00

Bad Accident 475.00

Bowling Alley 360.00

Bull Dog, standing, painted cast iron, 7″ long, EX .. 900.00

Cabin 365.00

Clown Bust, dots on hat, painted aluminum, EX .. 80.00

Clown on Globe, in original wood box 700.00

Creedmore, 1877, all original . 395.00

Darky in Cabin, G-39 ..... 225.00

Eagle & Eaglets, cast iron, G-78, 8″ 275.00

Elephant, man pops out of howdah 225.00

First National Duck Bank, Disney, tin, semi-mechanical 95.00

Frog & Old Man, old recast . 300.00

Greedy Nigger Boy, painted cast iron, EX 360.00

Halls Lilliput, type III, #113 . 225.00

Hunter, with pilgrim-type hat, painted cast iron & tin, 10″ long, G 200.00

Jolly Nigger, Starkey's patent 220.00

Key, figural large key, painted cast iron, 5¾″, VG 345.00

Lion & Two Monkeys 300.00

Marx Buddy, tin mechanical boy, glass candy container 295.00

Minstrel, German, relief face at top, tin litho, 7″, EX . 130.00

Monkey, sitting with arms raised, puts coins in mouth, early tin 225.00

Monkey, tips hat, tin litho, Chein 30.00

Artillery bank, red, white and blue, patented 1875-1897, $325.00.

Mule Entering Barn, cast iron,
   5¼″ 340.00
Mystery Bank, hand appears
   to grab coin, tin 45.00
Organ Bank, boy & girl ... 225.00
Organ Grinder 250.00
Paddy & the Pig 475.00
Scotsman, relief man on front,
   tin litho, 7″, EX 525.00
Smyth X-Ray Bank, cast iron,
   no finish, 5¼″ long 1,300.00
Speaking Dog, trap missing,
   original paint, 7x8″, G .. 450.00
Tank & Cannon, painted
   aluminum, tank 8¼″ long,
   EX 300.00

Registering Banks

Bee Hive, 1888 .... 165.00
Buddy L Savings & Record-
   ing, 6″ 80.00
Burdick Corbin Patent 1902,
   copper 48.00
Captain Marvel 75.00
Clown & Monkeys 25.00

Keep 'Em Sailing 100.00
Kingsbury Manufacturing
   Company clock, metal .. 40.00
Milk Pail, registers pennies,
   iron 85.00
Round Magic, dime register-
   ing 45.00
Snow White 45.00
Superman 75.00
Thrifty 30.00
Trunk, penny & dime register-
   ing, nickel plated 55.00
Uncle Sam's 3 Coin, Durable
   Toy & Novelty Company,
   metal, 6″ 50.00
Universal, tin, 3 coin, 1905 . 75.00

Still

Auto, painted cast iron,
   W-157, 6¼″ long, G 360.00
Bank Building, painted cast
   iron, W-423, 4″ 15.00
Battleship Oregon, painted
   cast iron, W-144, 5″ long,
   VG 220.00

Uncle Sam's 3 Coin Register Bank, $50.00.

Bear, brass, stealing pig,
W-246, 5½" 50.00

Bear, painted pot metal, head
opens, 5½" long, EX . . . 85.00

Ben Franklin, bust, pot metal,
W-313, 5¼", EX 30.00

Bird on Stump, painted cast
iron, W-209, 5", G 180.00

Buster Brown & Tige, painted
cast iron, W-2, 5", VG . . 100.00

Camel, painted cast iron,
W-201, 7¼", repainted . . 130.00

Cat, seated, painted cast iron,
W-248, 4", EX 100.00

Cat, with ball, painted cast
iron, W-247, 5¾" long,
restored 110.00

Cow, painted cast iron, W-188,
4½" long, VG 90.00

Crystal Bank, painted cast
iron & glass, W-243, 4¼",
VG 35.00

Dispenser, Bird Dog, painted
cast iron, W-107, 5½"
long, VG 45.00

Dispenser, cigarette machine,
Penny Smoke, 1¢ 240.00

Dispenser, on wheels, painted
cast iron, W-75, 4" long, G 140.00

Dispenser, painted cast iron,
W-216, 5" long, EX 300.00

Dog, on tub, painted cast iron,
W-54, 4", VG 90.00

Donkey, painted cast iron,
W-216, 5" long, EX 300.00

Ferry Boat, painted cast iron,
W-148, 7½" long, G 210.00

Gollywog, painted cast iron,
W-3, 6¼", EX 290.00

Home Bank, figural building,
painted cast iron, W-333,
4¼", EX 180.00

Horse, prancing, painted cast
iron, W-77, 4½" long, EX . 25.00

Indian, two-faced, painted
cast iron, W-291, 4¼", VG 800.00

Indian Family, cast iron,
W-289, 5" long, no paint . 445.00

Keg, stoneware with Albany
slip, 3¼" 20.00

Left: Lion, 5½″ x 4″, $75.00; right: Elephant on Tub, silver paint, $100.00.

Lamb, painted cast iron,
  W-192, long, G 65.00
Lucy Atwell Fairy House, tin 250.00
Mulligan the Cop, painted cast
  iron, W-8, 6″, EX 120.00
Mutt & Jeff, painted cast iron,
  W-13, 5¼″, repainted ... 130.00
Parrot, figural, pot metal,
  head opens, 4″, EX 180.00
Plymouth Rock, painted cast
  iron, W-292, 4″ long, G . 800.00
Possum, painted cast iron,
  W-205, 4¾″ long, EX ... 250.00
Professor Pug Frog, painted
  cast iron, W-230, 3¼″, EX 300.00
Rabbit, sitting upright,
  painted cast iron, W-98, 5″,
  VG 75.00
Rhino, painted cast iron,
  W-252, 5¼″ long, VG ... 275.00
Rooster, painted cast iron,
  W-187, 5″, EX 65.00
Safe, japanned & painted cast
  iron, W-347, 4½″, VG .. 50.00
Santa, at chimney, painted
  lead, W-238, 4¼″ long, G . 200.00
Shell Out, painted cast iron,
  W-293, 5″ long, repainted . 130.00
Singer Sewing Machine, tin
  lithograph, 5½″ 600.00

Statue of Liberty, painted cast
  iron, W-269, 6¼″, EX .. 55.00
Tank, WWI, painted cast iron,
  W-161, 6″ long, G 100.00
Trolley Car, painted cast iron,
  W-265, 4¼″ long, restored 140.00
Two-Faced Devil, painted cast
  iron, W-41, 4¼″, EX ... 550.00

Barber Shop

Though few fans of barber shop
memorabilia have any personal recall
of the old-time tonsorial estab-
lishments, the fancy blown glass
barber bottles, tufted velvet chairs,
and red, white and blue poles that once
hung at their doors kindle a spark of
nostalgia among them.

See also Shaving Mugs; Razors.

Bottle, clambroth, each with
  different label, set of 4 .. 100.00
Chair, Koch's, oak & brass
  with green tufted velvet
  upholstery 1,650.00
Chair, walnut with red velvet,
  carved swans, 1878 .... 850.00

Sign, neon, 1930s, 30x10" . **175.00**
Sterilizer jar, clambroth, with
    cover, star **37.00**

Baseball Cards

The first baseball cards were issued in the late 1800s by cigarette and tobacco companies who packed them with their products, primarily to promote sales. The practice was revived for a few years just before WWI, and again just in time to be curtailed by the Depression. From 1933 until the onset of WWII, and from early in the 1950s to the present, chewing gum companies produced sports cards, the most popular of which are put out by Bowman and Topps. The colored photo cards from the thirties are the most treasured, and any baseball great or Hall of Famer is the most valued in any particular issue.

Babe Ruth Story, 1948, #1,
    Story In The Making, NM **13.00**

Red Heart, 1954, Stan Musial, 2½" x 3¾", $50.00.

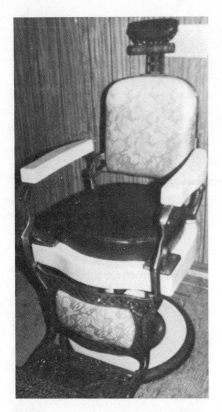

Barber chair, manufactured by E. Berninghaus Co., Cincinnati, Ohio, porcelain trim, cast iron frame, restored, $500.00.

Clipper, Improved Andis
    Master, Racine, Wisconsin,
    1924 .... **35.00**
Photo, tintype, barber in shop,
    late 1800s **35.00**
Pole, key wound, restored . **395.00**
Razor strap, leather, Double
    Duck **12.00**
Shaving lamp, soap container,
    burner, brush holder, or-
    nate, 7" **85.00**
Shoeshine stand, wood base,
    wrought iron chair &
    footrest **300.00**
Sign, embossed tin, pole &
    'Ask For Wildroot', 1940s,
    12x36" **35.00**

Babe Ruth Story, 1948, #8, Baseball's Famous Deal, VG 4.00

Batter-Up, 1934-1936, #117, Bill Dickey, NM 45.00

Batter-Up, 1934-1936, #15, Leroy Mahaffey, NM ... 9.00

Batter-Up, 1934-1936, #178, Don Brennan, VG 10.00

Batter-Up, 1934-1936, #6, Bill Terry, EX 12.00

Batter-Up, 1934-1936, #79, Tony Cuccinello, M 10.00

Bazooka, 1959, Bob Turley, M 26.00

Bazooka, 1959, Mickey Mantle, EX 100.00

Bazooka, 1960, #1, Ernie Banks, NM 10.00

Bazooka, 1960, #13, Willie Mays, NM 20.00

Bazooka, 1960, #23, Gil Hodges, NM 7.00

Bazooka, 1960, #4, Hank Aaron, M 25.00

Bazooka, 1961, #2, Mickey Mantle, EX 18.00

Bazooka, 1961, #36, Bill Tuttle, NM 2.50

Bazooka, 1961, #9, Frank Malzone, M 3.00

Bazooka, 1962, Ernie Banks, EX 25.00

Bazooka, 1962, Ken Boyer, NM 3.50

Bazooka, 1962, Norm Larker, M 3.00

Bazooka, 1963, #1, Mickey Mantle, M 28.00

Bazooka, 1963, #31, Frank Robinson, VG 6.00

Bazooka, 1963 All-Time Greats, #17, Babe Ruth, M 12.00

Bazooka, 1963 All-Time Greats, #6, Cy Young, M . 2.50

Bazooka, 1964, #12, Willie Mays, NM 15.00

Bazooka, 1964, #30, Brooks Robinson, M 10.00

Bazooka, 1965, #11, Boog Powell, M 2.25

Bazooka, 1965, #24, Jaun Marichal, M 8.00

Bazooka, 1965, #32, Sandy Koufax, M 12.00

Bazooka, 1966, #22, Carl Yastrzemski, EX 10.00

Bazooka, 1966, #38, Pete Rose, M 22.00

Bazooka, 1966, #48, Billy Williams, M 2.50

Bazooka, 1967, #11, Harmon Killebrew, EX 4.00

Bazooka, 1967, #22, Frank Robinson, M 7.50

Bazooka, 1967, #46, Al Kaline, NM 5.50

Bazooka, 1971, Brooks Robinson, NM 5.50

Bazooka, 1971, Roberto Clemente, M 9.00

Bell Brand, 1958, Johnny Podres, M 88.00

Bell Brand, 1960, #15, Roger Craig, M 5.50

Bell Brand, 1960, #9, Sandy Koufax, EX 13.00

Bell Brand, 1961, Gil Hodges, M 10.00

Bell Brand, 1962, Don Drysdale, M 10.00

Berk Ross, 1951, #1, Stan Musial, M 11.00

Berk Ross, 1951, #5, Whitey Ford, EX 5.00

Berk Ross, 1952, Billy Martin, M 14.00

Berk Ross, 1952, Mickey Mantle, EX 90.00

Berk Ross, 1952, Roy Campanella, EX 28.00

Berk Ross, 1952, Yogi Berra, EX 15.00

Bond Bread, 1958, Luke Easter, M 30.00

Bond Bread, 1958, Phil Cavaretta, EX 8.00

Bowman, 1948, #27, Sid Gordon, EX 1.80

Bowman, 1948, #4, Johnny Mize, EX 6.50

Bowman, 1949, #121, Mark Christman, M 2.00

Bowman, 1949, #224, Satchell Paige, NM 200.00

Bowman, 1949, #238, Bob Lemon, NM 40.00

Bowman, 1949, #50, Jackie Robinson, EX 30.00

Bowman, 1949 PCL, set of 36, NM, each 100.00

Bowman, 1950, #217, Casey Stengel, NM 13.00

Bowman, 1950, #98, Ted Williams, M 50.00

Bowman, 1951, #253, Mickey Mantle, NM 250.00

Bowman, 1951, #305, Willie Mays, NM 250.00

Bowman, 1951, #94, Clyde McCullough, M 2.00

Bowman, 1952, #196, Stan Musial, EX 30.00

Bowman, 1952, #217, Casey Stengel, EX 13.00

Bowman, 1952, #40, Bubba Church, M 2.00

Bowman, 1952, #8, Peewee Reese, NM 7.00

Bowman, 1953, #21, Joe Garagiola, EX 6.00

Bowman, 1953, #44, Bauer, Berra, Mantle, EX 25.00

Bowman, 1953, #93, Rizzuto & Martin, EX 16.00

Bowman, 1954, #66B, Ted Williams, NM 550.00

Bowman, 1955, #202, Mickey Mantle, EX 23.00

Bowman, 1955, #95, Sal Maglie, M 1.00

Briggs, 1953-1954, Willie Mays, NM 400.00

Butter Cream, 1933, Lefty Grove, NM 160.00

Cracker Jack, 1914, #111, Jim Callahan, NM 65.00

Cracker Jack, 1914, #18, Johnny Evers, NM 50.00

Cracker Jack, 1914, #60, Rollie Zeider, EX 19.00

Cracker Jack, 1914, #88, Christy Mathewson, pitching, EX 125.00

Cracker Jack, 1915, #103, Joe Jackson, EX 75.00

Cracker Jack, 1915, #366, Napoleon Lajoie, NM ... 100.00

Dan Dee, 1954, #14, Paul LaPalme, EX 17.00

Dan Dee, 1954, #3, Walker Cooper, EX 80.00

Darigold, 1959, Phil Ortega, NM 14.00

Delong, 1933, #3, Oscar Melillo, NM 48.00

Diamond Stars, 1934-1936, #1, Lefty Grove, EX 30.00

Diamond Stars, 1934-1936, #45, Jo-Jo White, M 8.00

Double Play, 1941, #101-102, D Dallesandro & Augie Galan, M 8.00

Double Play, 1941, #81-82, Ted Williams & Joe Cronin, 40.00

Drake's, 1950, #24, Yogi Berra, NM 60.00

Drake's, 1950, #5, Duke Snider, NM 60.00

Esskay, 1954, Robert D Kennedy, VG 40.00

Fro-joy Ice Cream, 1928, #1, VG 35.00

George C Miller Company, 1933, Dizzy Dean, VG .. 150.00

George C Miller Company, 1933, Lon Warneke, EX . 85.00

Glendale Meats, 1954, Matt Batts, EX 35.00

Goudey, 1933, #223, Dizzy Dean, EX 60.00

Goudey, 1933, #67, Guy Bush, NM 7.50

Hires, 1958, #44, Hank Aaron, NM 50.00

Hires, 1958, #61, Duke Snider, EX 13.00

Hunter's, 1953, Stan Musial, G 75.00

Hunter's, 1954, Tay Jablonski, VG 23.00

Hunter's, 1955, Jack Faszholz, G 14.00

Jello, 1962, #140, Jaun Marichal, NM 12.00

Jello, 1962, #188, Ernie Banks, NM 10.00

Jello, 1962, #27, Jim Gentile, M 3.00

Jello, 1962, #74, Steve Bilko, M 5.00

Jello, 1963, #139, Dick Groat, M 1.00

Jello, 1963, #187, Bob Aspromonte, M 17.00

Jello, 1963, #89, Ed Charles, NM 10.00

Johnston Cookies, 1953, #14, Walker Cooper, NM 3.00

Johnston Cookies, 1954, #34, Bob Thomson, NM 50.00

Johnston Cookies, 1955, Dave Jolly, M 7.50

Johnston Cookies, 1955, Lew Burdette, NM 9.00

Kahn's, 1955, Roy McMillan, NM 120.00

Kahn's, 1956, John Klippstein, EX 16.00

Kahn's, 1957, Frank Thomas, NM 15.00

Kahn's, 1957, Roberto Clemente, NM 75.00

Kahn's, 1958, Lawrence Brooks, EX 14.00

Leaf, 1948-1949, #111, Jerry Priddy, M 6.00

Leaf, 1948-1949, #50, Dick Wakefield, M 5.50

Lummis Peanut Butter, 1949, Puddinhead Jones, NM . 40.00

Mothers Cookies, 1952, #11, Bill MacCawley, EX 10.00

Mothers Cookies, 1952, #4, Chuck Connors, VG 30.00

Nabisco Team Flakes, 1969, Pete Rose, EX 18.00

Num Num, 1952, #16, Bob Kennedy, EX 95.00

Num Num, 1952, #6, Early Wynn, VG 14.00

Play Ball, 1939, #132, Jim Brown, M 12.00

Play Ball, 1939, #50, Charlie Gehringer, EX 11.00

Play Ball, 1940, #225, Shoeless Joe Jackson, EX 35.00

Play Ball, 1940, #82, Hank Gowdy, M 3.50

Red Heart, 1954, Sammy White, NM 6.00

Red Man, 1952, Cliff Chambers, M 2.00

Red Man, 1952, Yogi Berra, EX 8.00

Red Man, 1954, Roy Campanella, EX 10.00

Remar Bread, 1946, Johnny Price, EX 4.00

Remar Bread, 1949, Jack Jensen, EX 6.00

Rodeo Meats, 1955, Jim Finigan, EX 18.00

Rodeo Meats, 1956, Vic Power, VG 18.00

Smith's Clothing, 1947, #22, Max Marshall, VG 75.00

Smith's Clothing, 1948, #25, Bob Klinger, EX 6.00

Sommer & Kaufman, 1949, #1, Lefty O'Doul, EX 16.00

Sommer & Kaufman, 1949, #18, Floyd J Vaughn, VG . 13.00

Stahl Meyer, 1953, Roy Campanella, NM 160.00

Sunbeam Bread, 1946, Guy Fletcher, NM 7.00

Topps, 1952, #1, Andy Pafko, EX 10.00

Topps, 1952, #261, Willie
Mays, EX 150.00
Topps, 1952, #37, Duke
Snider, NM 13.00
Transogram, 1969, Harmon
Killebrew, NM 9.00
Union Oil, 1958, Marshall
Bridges, EX 14.00
Wilson Weiners, 1954, Ted
Williams, VG 2.50
Yuengling's Ice Cream, 1928,
#5, Gabby Hartnett, EX . 6.00

Baskets

Hand crafted baskets made from 1860 until around the turn of the century are commanding good prices on today's collectibles market, and early factory-made baskets are gaining in interest. Most valued are the Nantucket Lighthouse baskets and Shaker miniatures. Those designed for a specific use -- cheese baskets, herb baskets, and egg baskets, for example -- are preferred over the general purpose type.

See also Indian Artifacts.

Bushel, factory made, attached handles, late 1800s .. 75.00
Bushel, woven splint with bentwood rim handles, painted, 15x22" 60.00
Buttocks, splint, square mouth, brown & natural design, handle, 11x12".. 145.00
Buttocks, white oak, splint handle, 7x12" 75.00
Cheese, splint, miniature, 1½" diameter 65.00
Compote, stripped & unstripped willow, geometrics, 1850s, 9x7" 80.00
Egg, Maine Indian, splint, oval, rustic, gray patina, 5x10" 85.00

Market basket, double woven top, three colors, hand carved handle, 8½" x 19½" x 13", $140.00.

Picnic basket, hickory splint, 14½" x 12½", $38.00.

Egg, open weave splint, ash rim, splint wrapped handle, 1800s 270.00

Field, oak splint, carved bow handles, 14x18x9" 85.00

Garden, plaited, wide splint, oak handle 85.00

Gathering, double handle, rectangular, leather shoulder straps, 29" 150.00

Indian, pear shaped, splint with striped design, 2 colors, 13" 40.00

Long needle pine, thread constructed and decorated, 4x2½" 25.00

Market, splint, nailed rim, bentwood handle, 12x20" . 25.00

Melon rib, splint, good age, 3¾" (+ handle) x6x7", EX 135.00

Miniature, buttocks, old worn black finish, handle, 2¼" diameter 175.00

Miniature, melon, ribbed ash splint, hickory handle, 5" diameter 115.00

Miniature, splint, fine weave, 5" diameter, 3½" handle . 145.00

Oriental export, with lid, polychrome painted florals, 8x9½" 30.00

Picnic, willow, 2 wrapped handles, hinged cover, 12x8x9" deep 110.00

Potato, hickory, reinforced center base splints, whipped edge 90.00

Splint, bentwood rim handles, old patina, 13½x23x35", VG 85.00

Splint, oak, flat bottom, handle, early 1900s, 13x21" . 55.00

Storage, checkerwork, painted, hickory splint-wrapped rim 95.00

Bauer

The Bauer Company moved from Kentucky to California in 1909, producing crocks, gardenware, and vases until after the Depression when they introduced their first line of dinnerware. From 1932 until the early 1960s, they successfully marketed several lines of solid color wares that are today very collectible. Some of their most popular lines are Ring, Plain Ware, and Monterey Modern.

Batter, bowl 20.00

Candle holder, Monterey, turquoise, #417, each 12.00

Coffee server, Ring, metal handle with raffia, dark blue, 8 cup, #94 .... 35.00

Custard cup, Ring, dark blue, #34 .... 6.00

Gravy boat, Ring, oval with undertray, orange-red, #99 36.00

Mug, Ring, Barrel, orange-red 20.00

41

Planter, ivory, signed, oval,
13" long 29.00
Pudding dishes with metal
holders, Mission, 6
assorted colors, set 45.00
Sherbet, Ring, dark blue, #83 . 30.00
Sugar bowl, Ring, open,
orange-red, #40 . . . . 8.00

Beer Cans

The earliest beer cans, the flat
tops, were introduced in 1934 and
came with instructions on how to use
the punch opener. Cone tops, patented
in 1935, are rare today and usually
bring the highest prices. From 1960
on, these were replaced by the pull-tab
type which is still in use. Condition is
very important. Rust, dents, scratch-
es, or other such defects lessen the
value considerably.

A-1 Phoenix Suns, bank top,
1974-75 . . . . 5.00
Adler Brau, straight side steel 10.00
Big Cat Malt Liquor, Pabst
Brewery, Milwaukee, pull
top, 16 ounces 8.00
Black Label, silver can,
straight side steel 7.00

Blatz, Pabst Brewery, flat top,
12 ounces, 1952 . . . . 2.50
Canadian Ace Beer, Chicago,
Illinois, cone top, quart . 50.00
Canadian Ace Bock, straight
side steel 22.00
Drewry's Beer, character
series, pull top, 16 ounces . 40.00
Fisher B, Lucky, straight side
steel 7.00
German, Trains, 12 pack cans 36.00
Krueger Cream Ale, Newark,
New Jersey, cone top,
quart 145.00
Mickey's Malt Liquor, flat top 45.00
Old Dutch Ale, Aztec
Brewery, San Diego, cone
top, 12 ounces 400.00
Pfeiffer, black shoe soles . . 13.00
Pilser's Ale, Metropolis
Brewery, New York, cone
top, 12 ounces 350.00
Red Top Extra Pale, yellow
label with red letters, cone
top, 12 ounces 55.00
Schlitz Lager, Milwaukee,
Wisconsin, cone top, 12
ounces 135.00
Schlitz Vitamin D Beer, cone
top, 12 ounces 60.00
Waynesboro, Pennsylvania,
Fire Department, 4 cans,
set 3.00

Left to right: Skol, Atlas Company, Chicago, IL, flat top, $40.00; Snowcrest, Grace, Santa Rosa, CA, flat top, $125.00; Soul Stout Malt Liquor, Maier, Los Angeles, CA, pull top, $125.00; Spur Stout Malt Liquor, Sick's Rainier, Seattle, WA, pull top, $40.00; Stag, Carling Brewery, Belleville, IL, pull top, $5.00.

Left to right: Schmidt's First Premium, Schmidt, Logansport, IN, cone top, $75.00; Schmidt's City Club, Schmidt, St. Paul, MN, cone top, $30.00; Schmidt's City Club, Schmidt, St. Paul, MN, cone top, $40.00; '76 Ale, Terre Haute Brewery, Terre Haute, IN, cone top, $75.00.

Beer Collectibles

Beer can collectors and antique advertising buffs as well enjoy looking for beer related memorabilia such as tap knobs, beer trays, coasters, signs, and the like. While the smaller items of a more recent vintage are quite affordable, signs and trays from defunct breweries often bring three digit prices. Condition is important in evaluating early advertising items of any type.

Bottle, Coors, comic ghoulish face with logo	250.00
Bottle, Old Bohemian Beer, unopened, 1940s, M	10.00
Calendar, Blatz Brewery, 1904, Victorian girl, 18x27"	225.00
Corkscrew/opener, Anheuser Busch Malt Nutrine, bottle shaped	18.00
Framed paper, Mountain Whiskey, girl & waterfall, 24x20"	150.00
Glass, Gluek's, Enjoy Your Gluek's in Bottles	40.00
Glass, Miller High Life, reverse on glass, 24x10"	175.00
Hand mirror, Duffy's Pure Malt	30.00

Key ring, Hamm's, Theodore Hamm's 100th Anniversary	10.00
License holder, Hamm's, metal frame	25.00
Mug, Blatz Brewing, looks like barrel	12.00
Paper, Pabst Brewing, paper, Wright Brothers scene, original frame	60.00
Pin-back button, Miller High Life, celluloid girl extension	25.00
Pocket knife, Anheuser Busch, unusual design	95.00
Sign, Anheuser Busch, paper, Custer's Last Fight, frame & label	420.00
Sign, Eichler's Beer, wooden, green background with red letters	130.00

Tray, Trommer's Malt Beer, $25.00.

43

Sign, Heileman's Brewing, paper, Old Style Lager with old-time pub 90.00

Sign, Jac Schmidt Brewing, paper, farm scene, cardboard self frame 45.00

Sign, Lone Star Beer, tin, embossed 16.00

Sign, Michelob Beer, electric, logo, hung by chain, 20x5" 18.00

Sign, Miller Lite, lights up . 15.00

Sign, Olympia Beer, electric, It's The Water, G 20.00

Sign, Pabst, tin, hands hold bottle, factory, 1910, 36x48" 350.00

Statue, officer, Anheuser Busch, papier mache, 20" . 450.00

Statue, Pfieffer Brewing, Pfieffer's Fifer 30.00

Tap knob, Drewry's Beer .. 17.00

Tap knob, Michelob Beer .. 20.00

Tap knob, Old Reeding Beer, plastic 10.00

Tap knob, Old Style Beer, round 20.00

Tap knob, Peerless Beer, round 20.00

Thermometer, Fitger Brewing 18.00

Tray, Falls City Beer, girl sitting on horse, 13" diameter 275.00

Tray, International Brewing, Iroquois with full headdress 40.00

Tray, Jac Schmidt Brewing, City Club Beer 32.00

Tray, Miller High Life, Girl on Moon 43.00

Tray, Olympia Beer, preprohibition, horseshoe & waterfall 220.00

Tray, Oneida Brewing, Roderic, dog, fair scene . 45.00

Tray, Schlitz Brewing, hops on front, world on back . 26.00

Tray, Theodore Hamm's Brewing, bears & lake scene 28.00

Windmill, Heinekin, electric, 18x11" 18.00

Bells

Of the many types of bells available to the collector today, perhaps the most popular are the brass figurals. School bells, sleigh bells, and dinner bells are also of interest. Bells have been made from a variety of materials -- even glass and wood.

Art glass, blue cased with white, applied fruit, 6" .. 60.00

Church warden's, cast in bronze with turned wood handle, 1732, 14" 125.00

Cow, bronze, cast tassel clapper, 5" 12.50

Crystal, band of ferns & shells, acid etched decor, 4½" .. 25.00

Sleigh bells, four on original leather strap, 15½", $80.00.

Cast iron with bird figural top, 4″, $32.00

tury. The Norton Company made redware and salt glazed stoneware for more than one hundred years. The Fenton pottery (1847-1858) produced much the same type of ware, but in addition also made several lines of a more artistic nature. Their most famous product was Rockingham, a brown mottled glazed ware, and though it was manufactured by many other firms until well into the 20th century, it's not unusual to hear an especially good piece referred to as 'Bennington.' Fenton also made scroddled ware, graniteware, parian, and flint enameled ware. Possibly only one in five Fenton pieces were marked, either with a variation of the '1848' impressed mark, or the 'USP/United States Pottery Company' backstamp, as the firm was known for the last six years of its existence.

Dinner, Wallace, sterling silver, small, .95 ounces .	25.00
Elizabethan woman with clapper feet, figural, brass, 3½″	25.00
Gong, brass, within ornate framework, hammer on each side, 7x5½″	125.00
Lady, wearing full skirt with hat & fan, figural, brass, 6″	110.00
Lady wearing pleated bonnet, figural, French porcelain .	80.00
Railroad Crossing, 1909, 12″ diameter	95.00
Sleigh, head harness, nickel plated, large string	120.00
Storks in nests, two fish as handle, brass, 4¾x4″	75.00

Bennington

Bennington, Vermont, was the location of two important potteries that operated there from the late 1700s until the close of the next cen-

Book flask, brown & yellow mottled, 4½x6¼″	350.00
Candlestick, flint enamel, 9½″, M	525.00
Creamer, cow figural, flint enamel	450.00
Crock, J & E Norton, saltglaze with cobalt flowers, tendrils, 2 gallon	160.00
Croup kettle, cover, Rockingham, 6½″	350.00
Flowerpot, attached saucer, embossed cattails, dark brown glaze, 8″	60.00
Jar, J & E Norton, saltglaze, fancy cobalt floral, 1½ gallon, EX	175.00
Jar, J Norton & Co, saltglaze, cobalt bird on flower, 1½ gallon	245.00
Jug, E & LP Norton, saltglaze with cobalt flower, 2 gallon, M	175.00
Jug, J & E Norton, saltglaze with cobalt bird on stump, 1 gallon	265.00

Teapot, scroddled ware, $250.00.

Jug, J & E Norton, saltglaze
with cobalt flower, 2 gallon,
EX 175.00
Jug, J Norton, saltglaze with
cobalt butterfly, ovoid, 2
gallon, EX 275.00
Picture frame, oval, Rock-
ingham, 10¾", 2" wide . 475.00
Pie plate, Rockingham, 10", M 130.00
Spittoon, with cameo, 10½" . 145.00
Tulip vase, flint enamel, 10" . 450.00
Wash bowl, Rockingham,
1849 mark 375.00

Big Little Books

Probably everyone presently in
the forty to sixty age bracket owned
a few Big Little Books as a child. Today these thick hand-sized adventures
bring prices from $10.00 to $75.00 and
upwards. The first was published in
1933 by Whitman Publishing Com-

pany. Dick Tracy was the featured
character. Kids of the early fifties
preferred the format of the comic book,
and Big Little Books were gradually
phased out. Stories about super
heroes, and Disney characters bring
the highest prices, especially those
with an early copyright.

Air Fighters of America, 1941,
VG 12.00
Allen Pike of the Parachute
Squad, 1941, VG 15.00
Andy Panda and the Pirate
Ghosts, NM 9.00
Apple Mary and Dennie's
Lucky Apples, 1939, VG . 15.00
Arizona Kid on the Bandit
Trail, 1936, VG 10.00
Beasts of Tarzan, 1937, VG . 20.00
Blaze Brandon with the
Foreign Legion, 1938, EX . 15.00
Blondie, Count Cookie in Too,
1947, M 15.00

Blondie and the Bouncing
  Baby Dumpling, 1940, EX   18.00
Bob Stone, The Young Detec-
  tive, VG   15.00
Brad Turner in the Trans-
  atlantic Flight, 1939, VG   12.00
Bronco Peeler, The Lone
  Cowboy, 1937, VG   17.00
Buck Jones and the Killers of
  Crooked Butte, 1940, VG   20.00
Buck Rogers and the
  Planatoid Plot, 1936, VG   35.00
Buffalo Bill Plays a Lone
  Hand, 1936, VG   13.00
Buz Sawyer and Bomber 13,
  1946, VG   20.00
Captain Frank Hawks, Air
  Ace and the League of 12,
  1938, VG   12.00
Charlie Chan of the Honolulu
  Police, 1939, VG   20.00
Chester Gump at Silver Creek
  Ranch, 1933, VG   10.00
Chester Gump in the Pole to
  Pole Flight, 1937, EX   15.00
Convoy Patrol, 1942, VG   12.00
Dan Dunn and the Under-
  world Gorillas, 1941, VG   20.00
Desert Justice, 1938, EX   8.00
Detective Higgins of the Rac-
  quet Squad, 1938, M   12.00
Dick Tracy, Voodoo Island,
  1944, EX   25.00
Dick Tracy and the Spider
  Gang, 1937, VG   30.00
Don Winslow vs the Scorpion
  Gang, 1938, M   15.00
Donald Duck, Ghost of
  Morgan's Treasure, 1946,
  EX   22.00
Donald Duck Is Here Again,
  1944, EX   15.00
Fighting Hero's Battle for
  Freedom, 1943, VG   12.00
Flash Gordon and the Witch
  Queen of Mongo, 1936, VG   90.00
Flying the Sky Clipper with
  Winsie Atkins, 1936, EX   12.00

G Man and the Radio Bank
  Robbers, 1937, VG   25.00
Ghost Avengers, 1943, VG   18.00
Houdini's Big Little Book of
  Magic, 1927, VG   40.00
Huckleberry Finn (Mark
  Twain), 1939, NM   12.00
In the Name of the Law, 1937,
  EX   10.00
Jack Armstrong and the
  Ivory Treasure, 1937, VG   23.00
Jane Withers, In Keep
  Smilin', Movie Edition,
  1938, VG   20.00
Jimmie Allen in the Air Mail
  Robbery, 1936, VG   15.00
Kay Darcy and the Mystery
  Hideout, 1937, EX   12.00
King of the Royal Mounted
  and the Great Jewel
  Mystery, 1939, VG   15.00
Les Miserables, Movie Edi-
  tion, 1935, VG   20.00
Little Miss Muffet, 1936, VG   15.00
Little Orphan Annie in the
  Movies, 1937, VG   35.00
Lone Ranger and His Horse
  Silver, 1934, EX   30.00
Mandrake the Magician and
  the Flame Pearls, 1946, VG   45.00
Mary Lee and the Mystery of
  the Indian Beads, 1937, VG   13.00
Maximo the Amazing Super-
  man and the Crystals of
  Doom, 1940, VG   20.00
Men of the Mounted, 1933,
  VG   30.00
Mickey Mouse, The Detective,
  1934, EX   18.00
Mickey Mouse on Cave Man
  Island, 1944, EX   25.00
Mickey Mouse Sails for
  Treasure Island, 1933, EX   18.00
Moon Mullins and Kayo, 1933,
  VG   20.00
Mr District Attorney on the
  Job, 1941, VG   20.00
Og, Son of Fire, 1936, NM   18.00

Pat Nelson, Ace of the Test Pilots, 1937, EX 12.00

Phantom and the Sign of the Skull, 1939, EX 25.00

Pilot Pete, Dive Bomber, 1941, VG 8.00

Popeye and the Quest of the Rainbird, 1943, VG 25.00

Ray Land of the Tank Corps, USA, 1942, VG 15.00

Red Barry, Undercover Man, 1939, VG 20.00

Red Ryder and the Western Border Guns, 1942, EX . 22.00

Sequoia, movie with Jean Parker, 1935, VG 20.00

Shooting Sheriffs, Sheriffs of the Wild West, 1936, VG . 15.00

Skippy, The Story of; 1934, VG 20.00

Smitty in Golden Gloves Tournament, 1934, EX . 15.00

Speed Douglas and the Canal Sabotage Plot, 1941, EX . 12.00

Speed Douglas and the Mole Gang, 1941, VG 15.00

Sybil Jason in Little Big Shot, Movie Edition, 1935, VG . 18.00

Tailspin Tommy and the Hooded Flyer, 1937, EX . 22.00

Tailspin Tommy in the Famous Payroll Mystery, 1933, VG 20.00

Tailspin Tommy in Wings Over the Arctic, 1935, VG 20.00

Tarzan, Return of; 1936, EX . 25.00

Tarzan of the Apes, 1933, VG 58.00

Terry and the Pirates, 1935, EX 40.00

Tex Thorne Comes Out of the West, 1937, VG 14.00

The Texas Kid, 1937, EX .. 12.00

Three Musketeers, 1935, VG . 21.00

Tom Beatty, Ace of the Service, 1939, EX 12.00

Tom Beatty and the Big Brain Gang, 1939, EX 12.00

Tom Mix, Hoard of Montezuma, 1936, EX .. 20.00

Tom Mix in the Fighting Cowboy, 1925, EX 40.00

Tom Swift and His Giant Telescope, 1939, VG 40.00

Treasure Island, 1934, EX . 20.00

Uncle Don's Strange Adventure, 1936, EX 12.00

Will Rogers, 1935, VG 17.00

Black Americana

This is a wide and varied field of collector interest. Advertising, toys, banks, sheet music, kitchenware items, movie items, and even the fine arts are areas that offer the Black Americana buff many opportunities to add to his collection.

Ash tray, 'Sunshine Sam' around base, blue, red, brown & tan, 4x4″ 37.00

Bank, Mammy, red lips, hand on hip & stomach, slot in back, 6½″ 25.00

Sheet music, Turkey in the Straw, $24.00

Salt and pepper shakers, children's heads, $25.00 for the pair.

Bell, Mammy, brown & yellow underglazed, ceramic, 3″ . 18.00

Book, Liza Jane & The Kinkies, Mary Phipps, 1929, 45 pages, 8x11″ .. 35.00

Bottle opener, butler, cap comes out of bottom, opener inside, 5½″ 32.00

Cookie jar, Cooky chef & Mammy, Pearl china, pair . 250.00

Dart board, Sambo, metal holder, tin litho, Wyandotte Toys, 14x23″ 75.00

Doll, Aunt Jemima, in envelope with instructions, plastic, 1948 .... 42.00

Drawing, Water-Millions is Ripe, boy has melon, Sol Eytinge, 1879 .... 18.00

Figurine, cotton bale, boy eats melon, bisque, marked Japan, 3x3″ 50.00

Figurine, two boys with violin & mouth organ, Occupied Japan, pair, 5″......... 28.00

Grocery list, I'se Need Grocery List, Mammy grins, 12 items, 10x5½″. 15.00

Honey pot, Mammy, head lifts off, tongue spoon, Occupied Japan, 4½″............ 35.00

Match holder, painted Mammy on front, black, red & white, wood, 8″ 35.00

Perfume, Golliwog, head is stopper, big fur Afro, red lips, 3″ 65.00

Pie bird, Mammy, arms out, hole in chest, ceramic, 5″ . 25.00

Pincushion, Mammy, stuffed skirt holds pins, chalkware torso, 6½″ 30.00

Platter, Coon Chicken Inn, tan face in center, Syracuse, 1925, 9x11″ 160.00

Potholder, Mammy & chef, red, black & white, chalkware, 5½″ 36.00

Salt & pepper, Mammy & chef, light blue & yellow, pink lips, large 16.00

Sign, JP Alley's Hambone, man in airplane, cigar in mouth, 7″ 20.00

String holder, Mammy, plaid apron, brown underglazed face & hands, 6″ 38.00

Sugar, Mammy, holds flowers, 'Sugar' on her apron, flat back 18.00

Tea towel, Mammy washes dishes, two children, original label, 17x27″ ... 22.00

Teapot & sugar, brown face, strawberry spout, Japan, 3x6″ 55.00

Teaspoon, 'Coon Chicken Inn' on handle, silver plate, Victors, 6″ 16.00

Toothpick, Coon Chicken Inn, big grin & bow tie, heavy metal, 4″ 95.00

Black Cats

This line of fancy felines was produced mainly by the Shafford Company, although black cat lovers accept similarly modeled, shiny glazed kitties of other manufacturers into their litters -- er, collections. Some of the more plentiful items may be purchased for $6.00 to $10.00, while the Napco bank is worth around $75.00 and the nine-piece spice set in a wooden rack usually sells for $65.00.

Planter, 6¼" x 3" x 3", $10.00.

Ash tray, head, green eyes & open mouth, red bow ...	15.00
Canister with lid, green eyes, 6½"	25.00
Cigarette lighter	18.00
Cinnamon shaker	10.00
Condiment set, 3 piece	30.00
Cookie jar, head with lid, 5" .	45.00
Cruet, pair	20.00
Decanter, with 4 shot glasses, 8"	22.00
Envelope holder, yellow eyes, with sponge	25.00
Figurine, green eyes, 2" ...	4.00
Figurine, sitting, green eyes, pink nose, 14"	8.50
Mug, green eyes, 2"	6.00
Salt & pepper, green eyes, 4", pair	12.50

Salt & pepper, teapot shape, pair	12.00
Spice set, green eyes, wood triangular holder with 8 compartments	65.00
Sugar, green eyes, original label	12.00
Teapot, green eyes, 5½" ...	15.00
Utensil holder, green eyes .	25.00
Vase, green eyes, 6"	9.00
Wall pocket, green eyes ...	50.00

Blue and White Stoneware

Collectors who appreciate the 'country look' especially enjoy decorating their homes with this attractive utility ware that was made by many American potteries from around the turn of the century until the mid-thirties. Examples with good mold lines and strong color fetch the highest prices. Condition is important, but bear in mind that this ware was used daily in busy households, and signs of normal wear are to be expected.

Baked bean pot, Boston Baked Beans, 1 handle, 10" ...	200.00
Butter crock, cows, stencil decor, with bail	65.00
Canister, Coffee, Snowflake, original wood lid, china knobs, 6½"	110.00
Canister, Tea, Basketweave .	165.00
Cider cooler, Good to the Core, wood spigot, 15x13"	250.00
Creamer, Arc & Leaf Paneled, 4½x4" diameter	60.00
Crock, berry/cereal; Flying Bird, 2x4" diameter	95.00
Crock, milk; Daisy & Lattice, good color, 4x8"	110.00
Crock, pine cone, straight sides, 9½x5¾" diameter ...	175.00
Cup, Bow Tie with transfer of blue bird, 3"	75.00
Custard, Fishscale, 5"	75.00

Salt crock, butterfly pattern, no lid, $95.00.

Foot warmer, Henderson .. 150.00
Measuring cup, Flying Bird
   mug 159.00
Mixing bowl, Currants &
   Diamonds, 5x9½" 100.00
Mug, Rose & Basketweave,
   gold tracery 75.00

Pie plate, blue-walled brick-
   edged base, star mark,
   10½" 100.00
Pitcher, cluster of grapes on
   trellis, dark blue, 7x7",
   with lid 150.00
Pitcher, Indian wearing war
   bonnet, 8x6" 200.00
Refrigerator jar, with lid .. 125.00
Roaster, double, chain link,
   ear hand holds, 9x11"
   diameter 125.00
Rolling pin, with Butte,
   Nebraska advertising ... 185.00
Salt crock, butterfly, with lid . 125.00
Sand jar, polar bear & seals in
   relief, 13½" 250.00
Spittoon, lilies & plumes .. 125.00
Teapot, swirl, pulled ears, double bail handle, relief disks
   rim, 9" 450.00
Toothbrush holder, beaded
   panel with open rose ... 125.00
Water cooler, apple blossom,
   brass spigot with fishtail,
   17x15" 525.00

Pitcher, cows in relief, 8", $175.00.

Blue Ridge

One of the newest and most exciting collectibles on the scene today is American dinnerware. Some of the most attractive is Blue Ridge, produced by Southern Potteries of Erwin, Tennessee, from the late 1930s until 1956. More than four hundred patterns were hand painted on eight basic shapes. The Quimper-like peasant decorated line is one of the most treasured.

Betty, bowl, oval, 9″	5.00
Betty, cup & saucer	4.50
Betty, soup, coupe	3.50
Betty, vegetable bowl, 9″	7.00
Blue Heaven, bowl, 9½″	7.50
Blue Heaven, cup & saucer	5.00
Blue Heaven, fruit, 5¼″	1.75
Blue Heaven, platter, 11¾″	7.50
Boot vase, 9¼″	55.00
Fantasia, bowl, 5¼″	2.50
Fantasia, cereal, 6″	3.00
Fantasia, creamer & sugar with lid	10.00

Mardi Gras, coffee pot, square handle	30.00
Mardi Gras, creamer	7.00
Mardi Gras, sugar with lid	9.00
Roses, bowl, 5¼″	2.00
Roses, plate, 10″	4.00
Roses, relish, 3 part	16.00
Roses, soup with handles	3.00
Roundelay Green, creamer	2.50
Roundelay Green, oval bowl, 9¼″	6.50
Roundelay Green, vegetable bowl, 8¾″	4.50
Silhouette Blue, sugar with lid	4.50
Silhouette Blue, vegetable bowl, 9″	6.50
Silhouette Gray, creamer	3.50
Silhouette Gray, cup & saucer	3.50
Silhouette Gray, plate, 10½″	3.50
Water Lily, bowl, round	8.00
Water Lily, gravy	6.00
Water Lily, sauce dish	3.00
Water Lily, soup or cereal	6.00
Wild Strawberry, bowl, 5½″	2.00
Wild Strawberry, plate, 9½″	3.50
Wild Strawberry, platter, oval, 11″	5.00
Wild Strawberry, sugar with lid, large	5.00

Cigarette box with three ash trays, 3″ x 4″, $37.50.

Bottle Openers

Figural bottle openers are figures designed for the sole purpose of removing a bottle cap. To qualify as an example, the cap lifter must be part of the figure itself. Among the major producers of openers of this type were Wilton Products; John Wright, Inc.; L & L Favors; and Gadzik Sales. These and advertising openers are very collectible.

Alligator, #124	25.00
Auto jack	35.00
Canada goose, brass	50.00
Cliquot Club, Eskimo figural .	75.00
Cocker dog	15.00
Crab	15.00
Donkey, brass	25.00
Fish, #127	25.00
Flamingo	30.00
Four-eyed man	25.00
Goat, sitting, cast iron	45.00

Parrot, chrome on metal, with corkscrew, $25.00.

Green River Whiskey, with corkscrew	15.00
Handyhands on ash tray . .	50.00
Iroquois Indian, aluminum .	75.00
Lamppost drunk, brass . . .	20.00
Lobster, #134	15.00
Mademoiselle	45.00
Mallard	25.00
Nude, brass	50.00
Nude, copper color, reclining, unlisted	35.00
Palm tree drunk	25.00
Parrot, small	45.00
Pheasant, brass	35.00
Pixie, brass & steel, English registry mark, 1920s . . .	20.00
Sam Weller, figural	12.00
Setter dog	22.00
Silverman's Strand Theatre, leg with foot opener	7.00
Top hat man	25.00

Bottles

Bottles have been used as containers for commercial products since the late 1800s. Specimens from as early as 1845 may today be occasionally found; watch for a rough pontil to indicate this early production date. Some of the most collectible are bitters bottles, used for 'medicine' that was mostly alcohol, a ploy to avoid paying the stiff tax levied on liquor sales. Spirit flasks from the 1800s were blown in the mold and were often designed to convey a historic, political, or symbolic message. Even bottles from the 1900s are collectible, especially beer or pop bottles and commercial containers from defunct bottlers.

Bitters, African Stomach, round, amber, 9½"	35.00
Bitters, Augauer, Chicago .	28.00
Bitters, Cascara, square, amber, 9½"	23.00

Left to right: Poison, skull, in cobalt glass, 4¼″, $150.00; Triloids, triangular, blue glass, 3½″, $10.00; Tri-Seps, Milikins- Bernay's #2, amber glass, 3″, $10.00.

Bitters, Dr J Hostetter's Stomach, amber, square, 8¾″ 15.00

Bitters, Electric Band, square, amber, 9¾″ 18.00

Bitters, Hall's, barrel shape with 7 ribs on top & bottom, amber, 9″ 150.00

Bitters, Herb Wild Cherry, tall with 4 cherry trees, amber, 8¾″ 85.00

Bitters, Langley's Morning Star, 3 sided, amber, 12¾″ 90.00

Bitters, Poland Wine, labeled only, green, round, ¾ quart 20.00

Bitters, Prickley Ash Bitters Company, amber 20.00

Bitters, Prussian, square, amber, 8½″ 65.00

Bitters, Rex Kidney & Liver, Best Laxative & Blood Purifier 12.00

Bitters, Stoughton, labeled only, black, round 7.00

Bitters, unembossed, amber, 9″ 5.00

Dairy, bluish tinge, very old, bubbles in glass, pint ... 10.00

Dairy, cream top, Greenleaf, baby face, green pyre, square, quart 20.00

Dairy, cream top, Lake to Lake, Wisconsin, red pyre, square, quart 15.00

Dairy, cream top, red & orange pyre, double baby face, square, quart 35.00

Dairy, miniature milk, St Lawrence, bubble top ... 22.00

Berring Bitters, brown glass, 9½″, $10.00; bitters, aqua glass, 8½″, $20.00.

Dairy, Purdue University Creamer, square, embossed, quart 15.00

Figural, Aunt Jemima, ceramic, colorful, made in France, 10″ 40.00

Figural, Coachman, Van Dunks, puce or black ... 75.00

Figural, cornucopia, clear glass, Near Cut design, 9″ . 25.00

Figural, Honeymoon, emerald green 30.00

Figural, hound dog, amber glass, sheared lip for cork, 9½″ 17.00

Figural, Poland Water, amber, few light stains 250.00

Medicine, Agnew's Cure for the Heart, rectangular, clear, 8″ 20.00

Medicine, Bull Extract of Sarsaparilla, rectangular, aqua, 7″ 18.00

Medicine, Citrate of Magnesia, clear, embossed porcelain stopper 5.00

Medicine, Dexter's Indian Salve, round, aqua, 2¾″ . 10.00

Medicine, Dr Dieter's Zokoro, cork top, 10″ 20.00

Medicine, Dr McMunn's Opium, open pontil 18.00

Medicine, Dr SS Fitch, open pontil, flat lip 30.00

Medicine, Ebling's Herb Medicine, rectangular, aqua 15.00

Medicine, ER Durkee, open pontil, flat lip 16.00

Medicine, Gargling Oil, rectangular, cobalt, 5″ 30.00

Medicine, Graham's Dyspepsia Cure, rectangular, clear, 8¼″ 12.00

Medicine, LE Gibb's Bone Liniment, 6 sided, aqua, 4¼″ 15.00

Poison, ribbed, applied top, aqua, 10″ 38.00

Poison, Triloid's, cobalt, 100% labels 15.00

Whiskey, Avan Hoboken & Company, olive green, 11¼″ 22.00

Whiskey, Duffy Malt, amber, partial label, 10″ 10.00

Whiskey, John S Dunn, wood cased, 23″ 45.00

Whiskey, Little Brown Jug, brown pottery, 2¾″ 30.00

Boxes

Flea markets are a good source for various types of boxes -- wooden store boxes with stenciled advertising, ancient bentwood and bride's boxes, sewing and spice boxes, boxes of poplar and walnut, those with dome tops, and figurals. Old boxes are of interest to collectors of primitives, sewing notions, and advertising memorabilia. See Shaker category for other listings.

Bentwood, spring fastener, cut-out handles, burned florals, 10″ 65.00

Bible, book form, original paint, 13x12x4″ 300.00

Blanket style, rosewood graining with green band 350.00

Cat figural, porcelain, hand painted, 2½″ 395.00

Deed, flat top with mustard sponge decor, small 270.00

Parquetry inlay with lacquer interior, 7″ square 30.00

Persian brass, engraved, with hasp, 6″ long 30.00

Poplar, red with original brown graining, iron lock & hasp, 12″ long 50.00

Stamp, Gustav Stickley, copper 350.00

Tin, litho scenes on 4 sides, Mohawk Valley, Ft Johnson, 7x12″ wide ... 60.00

Dome-top box with straw applique, ca. 1830, 4″ x 8″ x 6½″, $85.00.

Bread Plates

Bread plates were very popular during the last part of the 1800s. They were produced by various companies, many of whom sold their wares at the 1876 Philadelphia Centennial Exposition. Though they were also made in earthenware and metal, the most popular with collectors are the glass plates with embossed designs that convey a historical, political or symbolic message.

Actress, Miss Neilson	65.00
Bates, Lieutenant Colonel John Coulter Bates, bust in center	95.00
Button & Daisy, amber, open handle	38.00
Continental, Give Us This Day	65.00
Crying Baby	38.50
Cupid & Venus	30.00
Cupid astride leaping lion, with handles	55.00
Deer & Pine Tree, amber ..	60.00
Diamond Grill, milk glass, Give Us This Day	30.00
Double Vine, 10½″ diameter	28.50
Faith, Hope & Charity	50.00
Fine Cut, lion head handles, amber	45.00
Frosted Lion, Give Us This Day Our Daily Bread, with handles, 12″	85.00
Gladstone	35.00
Golden Rule	47.50
Good Luck, Horseshoe, horseshoe handles	40.00
Liberty Bell, signer's, rectangular	85.00
Maltese Cross in Circles ...	17.00
Minerva Mars, round, with handles	60.00
Niagara Falls, late 1800s ..	60.00
Three Presidents	45.00
We Mourn Our Nation's Loss	55.00

Sheaf of Wheat, 12″, $30.00.

Brownies

The Brownie characters -- The London Bobby, The Bellhop, Uncle Sam and others -- were strange little creatures with pot bellies and long spindle legs who emerged in the night to do wondrous deeds for children to delight in discovering the next morning. They were the progeny of Palmer Cox, who in 1883 introduced them to the world in a poem called *The Brownies Ride*. Books, toys, napkin rings and advertising items are just a few of the items available to today's Brownie collectors.

Book, Adventures of a Brownie, Mulock, 1893	10.00
Book, Donohue, early, NM	30.00
Candlestick, Brownie with hands in pocket, majolica, 7½″	135.00

Child's table knife, silver plated brass, embossed ornate handle	17.00
Decalcomania Album #4, 9 pages of decals, NM	35.00
Doll, Soldier, paper on wood, with wood base, 1892, 12″	35.00

Book, *Queer People*, 1889, 8½″ x 10″, $50.00.

Game, Lotto, Brownies on cover of box	25.00
Label, orange, early 1920s, M	20.00
Magazines, Queer People, 1894, set of 8	75.00
Paint book, Whitman #669-10, circa 1949	25.00
Plate, Brownie decor, KTK & Co, 6"	20.00
Stamps, rubber, with various Brownies, set of 12	85.00
Stickpin, Brownie Policeman	15.00
Tray, with lithograph of Brownies	95.00
Watch fob, 3 Brownie faces, sterling	125.00

Butter Molds

Butter molds were once used to decorate and identify butter made by the farmer's wife who often sold her extra churnings at the market. Because the early molds were hand carved, none were exactly alike, and endless variation resulted. The ones most highly treasured today are those with animals or birds, or those with unusual shape or construction.

Box, fruit, 8 prints, 2 pound	75.00
Box, rectangular, two flowers, machine made, late 1800s	30.00
Elliptical, pear motif, hand carved	45.00
Plunger, 2-sided Canadian type, flower & leaves motif	50.00
Rose & bud, machine made, 3" diameter	30.00
Six-leaf flower, hand carved, 1830s	40.00
Sunflower with scored diamond center, turned case, 3½"	50.00

Butter mold, hinged construction, two leaves and three initials, 3" x 8½", $235.00.

Butter mold, five parts, simple star design, signed, 3½" x 2" x 2¾", $125.00.

Two acorns with leaf, good border, turned case, 4" .	65.00
Two acorns with rope edge, square, 2¾"	40.00
Two berries, two flowers, dovetailed with brass clasp	40.00
Wildflower & branches, beaded edge, 4½"	35.00

Butter Stamps

Butter stamps differ from molds in that the mold is dimensional while the stamp is flat, and was used not to shape the butter, but merely to decorate the top.

Acorn & leaf, two repeats, rectangular, 2½x5"	40.00
Eagle, round, turned handle, repaired, 4"	80.00
Floral & fern, round	40.00
Geometric wheel, age crack, 1880s, 4"	60.00
Leaf & flower, stylized, turned wood handle, 4¼" ...	40.00
Rose with leaves, machine made	35.00

Butter stamp, tulip and leaves design, large diameter, $100.00 to $125.00.

Rosebuds, 1880s, 2½"	80.00
Sheaf, early, deep cut, 4½" .	50.00
Thistle, hand carved	45.00
Tulip, simple, turned handle, 4½"	45.00

Campaign Collectibles

Pennants, buttons, posters -- in general, any thing related to presidential campaigns -- are being sought by collectors who have an interest in the political history of our country. Most valued are items from a particularly eventful period, or those things having to do with an especially colorful personality. Pin-back buttons, popular campaign tools since 1896, are particularly appealing.

Badge, silk, King's County Republican Committee, 1892	14.00

Plate, John F. Kennedy, 1917-1963, Royal Copenhagen, 3″, $50.00.

Bandanna, Teddy Roosevelt, battle flag, 1904	50.00	Button, William H Taft, celluloid with image, ¾″	18.00

Bandanna, Teddy Roosevelt,
battle flag, 1904 ...... 50.00
Book, Cleveland & Thurman
for President & Vice, 588
pages, 1888 .... 10.00
Bust, Grant, National
Favorite, signed/dated,
Dreyfuss, 1885, plaster . 400.00
Button, Carter, Re-Elect
Carter & Mondale, litho-
graphed metal 6.00
Button, Goldwater & Miller,
flashing 12.00
Button, McKinley &
Roosevelt, jugate 20.00
Button, Nixon for President,
picture on celluloid 12.00
Button, Rockefeller, celluloid
with image, 1½″ 10.00
Button, Stand by Wilson,
Man on the Job, celluloid,
1″ 22.00
Button, Thomas E Dewey for
President, celluloid with
image, 1¼″ 15.00

Button, William H Taft,
celluloid with image, ¾″ . 18.00
Button, 1952 Primary,
lithographed metal 30.00
Calendar, Wilkie & McNary
picture 20.00
Clock, Roosevelt, Spirit of
USA 75.00
Convention ticket, Democratic
National, 1892, Cleveland . 7.00
Doll, LB Johnson, in box .. 12.00

Bandanna, Parker-Davis, 24″, in mint
condition, $175.00.

Flag, Lincoln, 1860-1864 campaign 700.00
Guest ticket, Republican National Convention, 1900 . 15.00
Liberty Bell, Teddy Roosevelt, bronze bear on bell, 5″ base 37.50
License plate, 1960 Official Representative National Convention, M 12.00
Medal, pin-back, New Day, Franklin Roosevelt & John Garner 27.50
Mug, Franklin D Roosevelt, figural barrel, The New Deal shield, 4″ 32.50
Photo, Dewey, with back stand, entire face in color, 1944, 17x24″ 14.00
Photo, General MacArthur & Carl Bohnen, embossed sepia tones, 1942 ...... 20.00
Plate, Our Union for Ever, with George Washington, 1776-1876, 6″ 45.00
Poster, Nixon's the One, 28x20″ 45.00
Poster, Roosevelt & Truman, 11x15″ 20.00
Puzzle, Spiro Agnew wearing Superman suit, 16x20″ 5.00

Ribbon, Lincoln, 1860 ..... 120.00
Sheet Music, We Want Wilkie, 1940 .... 5.00
Tumbler, Roosevelt & McKinley pictured with eagle 58.00
Watch, Hero Spiro, 1970 .. 100.00

Candlesticks

Candles are among the earliest lighting devices known to man. Socket-type candlesticks were used in the 16th century; before that, candles were simply impaled upon a sharp pointed holder called a pricket. Gradually candlesticks became more refined, and during the 17th and 18th century, were often made of silver or other metals in elaborate designs that reflected the fashion of the day. Early American glass houses such as the Boston and Sandwich Glass Company produced exquisite candlesticks in lovely colors. Since then, they have been manufactured by all major glass companies, and are available in abundance today. Silver and brass figurals are also popular with collectors.

Brass, heavy with good detail, threaded, 1850s, 4″, pair . 90.00
Brass, pricket, sectional with joining rod, 16″ 85.00
Brass, push-up, beehive with diamond detail, 1880s, 9″, pair 90.00
Brass, push-up, square base with fluted standard, 6″, pair 55.00
Brass, rope twisted stem threads into round base, 5″, pair 195.00
Glass, amber, baluster with 6 panels & flared base, 6″, pair 35.00
Glass, clear flint, hexagonal, 7″, pair 35.00
Glass, electric blue, 6 panels, flared base, 6″, pair 50.00

Oilcloth banner, Franklin D. Roosevelt, 40″ x 54″, $250.00.

Champleve, multicolor enamels on brass, 8¼", $185.00, pair.

Hanging, long twisted wrought iron rod, 18" ..	85.00
Hog scraper, iron with push-up & lip hanger, 6¼" ...	95.00
Hog scraper, tin with push-up, marked Ryton & Walton, 7"	85.00
Iron spiral with wood base, top hook, 1750s	100.00
Pine, metal socket, wire spring clip, 7"	65.00
Tin, drip pan on stem, conical weighted base, 1700s ...	175.00
Turned wood stem in stone base, tin collar, 8½"	85.00

Candlewick

Candlewick was one of the all-time best-selling lines of The Imperial Glass Company of Bellaire, Ohio. It was produced from 1936 until the company closed in 1982. More than 741 items were made over the years and though

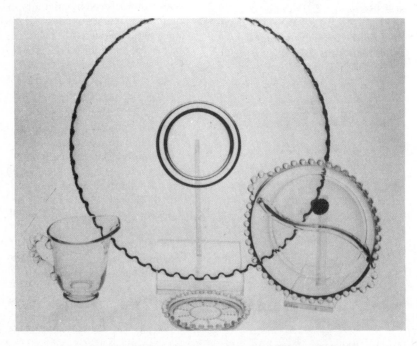

See the listings that follow for specific values.

many are still easy to find today, some (such as the desk calendar, the chip and dip set, and the dresser set) are a challenge to collect. Candlewick is easily identified by the beaded stems, handles, and rims characteristic of the tufted needlework of our pioneer women for which it was named.

Ash tray, cranberry color, round, #400/150, 6″	7.00
Ash tray, 4 piece bridge set, cigarette holder at side .	25.00
Bitters bottle, with tube, 4 ounces	32.00
Bowl, bouillon, 3 handles ..	12.50
Bowl, butter & jam, 3 part, 10½″	22.00
Bowl, heart shape with handle, 9″	19.00
Bowl, jelly with cover, 5½″ .	15.00
Bowl, round, 2 handles, 4¾″ .	12.00
Butter, covered, round, 5½″ .	17.50
Calendar, beaded edge, rectangular, #400/--	30.00
Candle holder, urn, holders on circular center bead, 6″ .	18.50
Cigarette set, box with 4 rectangular ash trays, 6 piece	32.50
Cocktail set, plate with indentation, cocktail, 2 piece .	14.50
Compote, bulbous beaded stem, 5″	12.00
Compote, footed fruit, crimped, 10″	22.50
Cordial, stem #3800, 1 ounce .	20.00
Cordial, 2-bead stem, #4000, rare series, 1¼ ounces ..	18.00
Deviled egg server, center heart handle, #400/154, 11½″	35.00
Hurricane lamp, #14994, 2 piece, 12″	20.00
Juice tumbler, beaded foot, #400, 5 ounces	10.00
Lazy Susan condiment set, #400/1510, 8 piece	88.00
Marmalade set, liner saucer, jar, lid & spoon	28.00

Oil & vinegar set, no handles, #400/2946, 3 piece	36.00
Pitcher, beaded handle, ice lip, 40 ounces	32.50
Plate, round, 2 open handles, #400/72D, 10″	24.00
Plate, serving, cupped edge, 13″	22.00
Plate, 2 handles, crimped, 6¾″	7.50
Plate, 2 handles, sides upturned, 9″	12.00
Puff jar, from boudoir set, #400/--	20.00
Punch cup	4.00
Salad set, 4 piece buffet: large round tray, divided bowl, 2 spoons	30.00
Salt & pepper shakers, bulbous, with beaded stem, chrome top, pair	6.00
Souvenir, Annual Glass Festival, Bellair, Ohio, #400/--	7.00
Toast, with cover, set	35.00
Tray, wafer, handle bent to center of dish, 6″	16.50
Vase, beaded foot, small neck ball, 4″	12.50
Vase, fluted rim, beaded handle, 8″	22.50

Candy Containers

From 1876 until the 1940s, figural glass candy containers of every shape and description have been manufactured for the use of candy companies who filled them with tiny colored candy beads. When the candy was gone, kids used the containers as banks or toys. While many are common, some, such as Charlie Chaplin by L.E. Smith, the Barney Google by Barrel bank, Felix on the Pedestal, or the Rabbit Family, are hard to find and command prices in the $450.00 to $600.00 range.

Wheelbarrow, with hard-to-find tin insert, 6″ long, $200.00.

Baby on log, papier mache, early 50.00

Battleship, Victory Glass Company 20.00

Boston Bean Pot, with closure . 40.00

Bulldog, round base 27.00

Cabin Cruiser, variation ... 12.00

Candelabra 30.00

Charlie Chaplin, Borgfeldt . 95.00

Chevrolet Station Wagon, 1938 .... 20.00

Chicken, nodding head, compo, German mark 30.00

Clown, pressed paper, 10½″ . 40.00

Colorado Boat, glass only . 40.00

Donkey Pulling Cart, original version 50.00

Duck, papier mache with wire legs, on stump, Germany, 3½″ 15.00

Dutch Windmill 45.00

Easter egg, papier mache, hand painted, large 22.00

Hen & chicks, papier mache, hand painted, Germany, 1917, 3x2″ 10.00

Hen on nest, papier mache, original label, 1924, 7x6″ . 45.00

House of Glass, cottage ... 100.00

Jack-O'-Lantern, straight eyes 75.00

Lantern, Victory Glass Company, brass cap 20.00

Liberty Bell, amber, aqua, or green; original screw closure 45.00

Lincoln Zephyr, glass wheels, 1936 .... 25.00

Locomotive, paper closing . 20.00

Mug, Necco Sweets 11.00

Orange, papier mache, early . 30.00

Pig, papier mache, green .. 55.00

Rabbit, papier mache, sitting on haunches, glass eyes, 5½″ 22.50

Rabbit Begging, screw bottom 45.00

Revolver, mercury glass, Pat
Pending, large 30.00
Rooster, papier mache with
wire legs, on stump, Ger-
many, 4″ 15.00
Safe, Penny Trust Company,
milk glass, gold decor,
original closure 45.00
Santa Claus Leaving Chimney 65.00
Santa's Boot, with wrap-
around label, paper cap . 22.50
Spirit of St Louis, glass only . 40.00
Suitcase, Variation A, clear
glass 20.00
Tank, Victory Glass Com-
pany, cardboard closure . 20.00
Ugly Duckling 75.00
Willy's Jeep, original paper . 18.00
World Globe, glass only ... 50.00

Carnival Glass

From about 1905 until the late
1920s, carnival glass was manufactured by several major American glass
houses in hundreds of designs and patterns. Its characteristic iridescent
lustre was the result of coating the
pressed glassware with a sodium solu-
tion before the final firing. Marigold,
blue, green, and purple are the most
common colors, though pastels were
also used. Because it was mass-
produced at reasonable prices, much of
it was given away at carnivals -- as a
result it came to be known as carnival
glass.

A Dozen Roses, bowl, footed,
amethyst, rare, Imperial,
8½″ 375.00
Acanthus, plate, marigold,
Imperial, 10″ 155.00
Acorn, bowl, green, Fenton,
8½″ 70.00
Acorn, plate, blue, scarce, Fenton, 9″ 480.00

Acorn Burrs, bowl, flat,
amethyst, Northwood, 10″ 120.00
Acorn Burrs, bowl, flat, green,
Northwood, 5″ 55.00
Acorn Burrs, butter with
cover, amethyst, North-
wood 225.00
Acorn Burrs, creamer,
marigold, Northwood ... 90.00
Acorn Burrs, punch bowl with
base, green, Northwood . 650.00
Acorn Burrs, punch cup,
green, Northwood 40.00
Age Herald, bowl, amethyst,
scarce, Fenton, 9¼″ 865.00
Amaryllis, compote, blue,
small, Northwood 140.00
American, tumbler, marigold,
rare, Fostoria 500.00
Apple Blossoms, bowl,
marigold, Dugan, 7½″ .. 30.00
Apple Panels, creamer,
marigold, English 30.00
Apple Tree, pitcher, marigold,
rare, Fenton 1,100.00
Arcs, bowl, amethyst, Im-
perial, 8½″ 42.00

Colonial Lady, Imperial, vase,
marigold, $300.00.

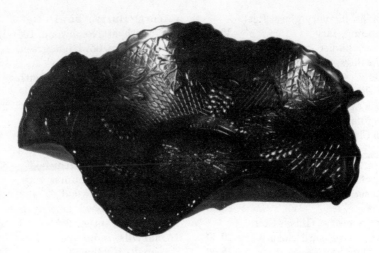

Concord, Fenton, 9″ bowl, blue, scarce, $95.00.

Art Deco, bowl, marigold, English, 4″ 25.00

August Flowers, shade, marigold 36.00

Australian Swan, bowl, marigold, Crystal Co, 5″ . 38.00

Autumn Acorns, bowl, green, Fenton, 8¾″ 50.00

Aztec, sugar, clambroth, McKee 150.00

Balloons, cake plate, marigold, Imperial 60.00

Banded Diamonds, tumbler, amethyst, rare, Crystal Co 350.00

Banded Panels, sugar, open, amethyst, Crystal Co ... 45.00

Basketweave & Cable, sugar, complete, white, Westmoreland 110.00

Beaded Acanthus, milk pitcher, green, Imperial ... 210.00

Beaded Cable, rose bowl, opalescent aqua, Northwood 365.00

Beaded Panels, compote, opalescent peach, Westmoreland 70.00

Beaded Shell, bowl, footed, amethyst, Dugan, 5″ ... 38.00

Beaded Shell, mug, amethyst, Dugan 85.00

Beaded Shell, water pitcher, marigold, Dugan 360.00

Bells & Beads, gravy boat with handles, amethyst, Dugan 60.00

Birds & Cherries, bon bon, green, Fenton 60.00

Blackberry, plate, marigold, rare, Fenton 275.00

Blackberry Block, pitcher, green, Fenton 600.00

Blackberry Wreath, bowl, marigold, Millersburg, 5″ . 50.00

Blossoms & Band, bowl, amethyst, Imperial, 5″ .. 28.00

Broken Arches, punch bowl with base, marigold, Imperial 290.00

Butterfly, bon bon, ribs on exterior, amethyst, Northwood 260.00

Butterfly & Berry, butter with cover, marigold, Fenton . 110.00

Butterfly & Berry, pitcher, marigold, Fenton 275.00

Butterfly & Berry, sugar with cover, blue, Fenton 150.00

Checkerboard, punch cup, amethyst, Westmoreland . 90.00

Cherry, bowl, footed, opalescent peach, Dugan, 8½″ . 190.00

Cherry, bowl, ice cream, green, Millersburg, 10″ 160.00

Cherry, sugar with cover, marigold, Millersburg ... 65.00

Cherry Circles, bon bon, blue, Fenton 55.00

Cherry Circles, compote, marigold, Fenton 50.00

Cobblestones, bon bon, amber, Imperial 75.00

Cobblestones, bowl, green, Imperial, 8½″ 75.00

Coin Dot, rose bowl, green, Fenton 75.00

Columbia, compote, green, Imperial 57.00

Coral, bowl, blue, Fenton, 9″ . 75.00

Coral, compote, marigold, rare, Fenton 65.00

Cornucopia, vase, white, Fenton, 5″ 100.00

Cosmos & Cane, bowl, marigold, 10″ 58.00

Cosmos & Cane, spooner, marigold 95.00

Country Kitchen, bowl, marigold, rare, Millersburg, 5″ 90.00

Crab Claw, fruit bowl with base, marigold, Imperial . 90.00

Crackle, bowl, amethyst, Imperial, 9″ 30.00

Crackle, tumbler, dome base, green, Imperial 26.00

Daisy, bon bon, blue, scarce, Fenton 75.00

Dandelion, tumbler, amethyst, Northwood 50.00

Diamond & Daisy, compote, blue, US Glass 60.00

Diamond Point Columns, powder jar with lid, marigold, Imperial 50.00

Diamonds, pitcher, marigold, Millersburg 135.00

Double Scroll, punch cup, marigold, Imperial 135.00

Dragon & Lotus, bowl, footed, green, Fenton, 9″ 85.00

Drapery, candy dish, ice blue, Northwood 95.00

Embroidered Mums, bowl, blue, Northwood, 9″ 59.00

Estate, perfume, aqua, Westmoreland 110.00

Feather & Heart, tumbler, marigold, scarce, Millersburg 82.00

Fentonia, creamer, blue ... 85.00

Fentonia, fruit bowl, marigold, 10″ 75.00

Fern, compote, marigold, Northwood 45.00

Field Flower, tumbler, green, scarce, Imperial 70.00

File, creamer, marigold, Imperial & English 100.00

Fishscale & Beads, bowl, amethyst, Dugan, 6″ ... 34.00

Flannel Flower, compote, marigold, large, Crystal Co 90.00

Floral & Grape, tumbler, white, Dugan 48.00

Floral & Optic, rose bowl, footed, aqua, Imperial .. 180.00

Flute, bowl, amethyst, Imperial, 5″ 65.00

Flute, salt dip, footed, vaseline, Northwood 75.00

Flute, tumbler, marigold, Imperial 45.00

Flute & Cane, wine, marigold, Imperial 40.00

Folding Fan, compote, blue, Dugan 75.00

Four Flowers, bowl, blue, 10″ 90.00

Frosted Block, creamer, marigold, Imperial 50.00

Golden Flowers, vase, marigold, 7½″ 48.00

Golden Harvest, decanter with stopper, marigold, US Glass 120.00

Graceful, vase, white, Northwood 85.00

Grape, bowl, footed, green, Fenton's Grape & Cable, 8¾″ 67.00

Grape, fruit bowl, marigold, Imperial, 8¾"	36.00
Grape, nappy, green, Northwood's Grape & Cable ..	65.00
Grape, plate, ruffled, marigold, Imperial, 8½" .	58.00
Grape, tumbler, green, Northwood's Grape & Cable .	70.00
Grape, tumbler, smoke, Imperial	50.00
Grape & Gothic Arches, bowl, marigold, Northwood, 10"	48.00
Grape & Gothic Arches, pitcher, blue, Northwood ..	115.00
Grape Delight, rose bowl, footed, blue, Dugan, 6" .	70.00
Grape Heavy, nappy, amethyst, Imperial	38.00
Grape Leaves, bowl, green, Northwood, 8¾"	75.00
Grapevine Lattice, plate, marigold, Dugan, 7"	70.00
Greek Key, bowl, green, Northwood, 7"	100.00
Hattie, bowl, amethyst, Imperial	58.00
Hawaiian Lei, creamer, marigold, Higbee	65.00
Heart & Vine, bowl, green, Fenton, 8½"	42.00
Hearts & Flowers, plate, marigold, rare, Northwood, 9"	170.00
Hobstar, cookie jar with lid, green, Imperial	95.00
Hobstar, fruit bowl with base, green, Imperial	75.00
Hobstar, sugar with lid, clambroth, Imperial	50.00
Hobstar & Feather, punch cup, blue, scarce, Millersburg	80.00
Hobstar Reversed, butter, blue, English	70.00
Holly, compote, amethyst, Fenton, 5"	36.00
Holly Panelled, bowl, amethyst, Northwood ..	70.00
Honeycomb & Clover, bon bon, amber, Fenton	70.00

Horses Heads, bowl, flat, green, Fenton, 7½"	80.00
Horses Heads, bowl, footed, marigold, Fenton, 7" ...	60.00
Illusion, bon bon, blue, Fenton	65.00
Inverted Coin Dot, rose bowl, green, Northwood or Fenton	60.00
Inverted Coin Dot, tumbler, amethyst, Northwood or Fenton	95.00
Inverted Feather, compote, marigold, Cambridge ...	45.00
Inverted Feather, cup, marigold, rare, Cambridge	50.00
Inverted Strawberry, bowl, marigold, 9"	68.00
Inverted Strawberry, celery with stem, amethyst, rare .	275.00
Jewelled Heart, bowl, amethyst, Dugan, 10" ..	95.00
Kittens, bowl, vaseline, scarce, Fenton, 4"	245.00
Kittens, spooner, marigold, rare, Fenton, 2½"	147.00
Knotted Beads, vase, blue, Fenton, 4"	37.00
Lattice & Daisy, bowl, marigold, Dugan, 9"	60.00

Imperial Basket, Imperial, marigold, rare, $48.00.

Lattice & Daisy, pitcher, blue, Dugan 185.00

Leaf & Beads, bowl, green, Northwood or Dugan, 9″ . 85.00

Leaf Chain, plate, amethyst, Fenton, 9¼″ 92.00

Leaf Tiers, sugar, footed, marigold, Fenton 88.00

Little Fishes, bowl, flat, green, Fenton, 5½″ 56.00

Long Hobstar, punch bowl with base, marigold 125.00

Louisa, candy dish, footed, amethyst, Westmoreland . 60.00

Lustre & Clear, shakers, marigold, Imperial, pair . 70.00

Lustre & Clear, tumbler, marigold, Imperial 40.00

Lustre Flute, bon bon, green, Northwood 55.00

Lustre Flute, punch bowl with base, amethyst, Northwood 160.00

Lustre Rose, pitcher, amethyst, Imperial 97.00

Many Fruits, cup, blue, Dugan 40.00

Maple Leaf, bowl with stem, marigold, Dugan, 9″ 70.00

Maple Leaf, butter, marigold, Dugan 100.00

Maple Leaf, sugar, marigold, Dugan 65.00

Mary Ann, vase, amethyst, two varieties, Dugan, 7″ . 80.00

Mirrored Lotus, bon bon, blue, Fenton 57.00

Mitered Diamond & Pleats, bowl, blue, English, 8½″ . 40.00

Moonprint, butter, marigold, English 100.00

Northwood's Nearcut, compote, amethyst 130.00

Octagon, butter, green, Imperial 126.00

Octet, bowl, white, Northwood, 8½″ 80.00

Open Rose, plate, amber, Imperial, 9″ 95.00

Hand vase, English, one shape, amethyst, $300.00.

Orange, hatpin holder, marigold, Fenton 126.00

Orange Tree, bowl, footed, green, Fenton, 9″ 110.00

Oval & Round, plate, green, Imperial, 10″ 74.00

Palm Beach, plate, amethyst, rare, US Glass, 9″ 250.00

Panelled Swirl, rose bowl, marigold 65.00

Panther, bowl, footed, marigold, Fenton, 10″ .. 95.00

Peach, bowl, white, Northwood, 5″ 60.00

Peacock & Urn, goblet, vaseline, rare, Fenton ... 90.00

Peacock At The Fountain, bowl, blue, Northwood, 9″ 98.00

Peacock At The Fountain, tumbler, ice blue, Northwood 165.00

Peacock Strutting, sugar with lid, green, Westmoreland . 60.00

Petals, compote, amethyst, Dugan 60.00

69

Pigeon, paperweight, marigold 80.00

Pinwheel, vase, amethyst, English, 6½" 85.00

Pony, compote, amethyst, scarce, Millersburg 70.00

Pretty Panels, pitcher, green, Northwood 160.00

Prism Band, tumbler, decorated, green, Fenton . 75.00

Quartered Block, butter, marigold 90.00

Rambler Rose, pitcher, marigold, Dugan 120.00

Raspberry, milk pitcher, marigold, Northwood ... 120.00

Robin, mug, smoke, old line only, Imperial 70.00

Rose Garden, bowl, amethyst, Norway, 8¾" 65.00

Royalty, fruit bowl with stand, smoke, Imperial . 135.00

Scale Band, pitcher, marigold, Fenton 110.00

Scales, bon bon, opalescent peach, Westmoreland ... 90.00

Shrine, champagne, clear, US Glass 90.00

Singing Birds, spooner, green, Northwood 120.00

Singing Birds, sugar, green, Northwood 155.00

Smooth Panels, pitcher, green, Imperial 170.00

Soda Gold, pitcher, marigold, Imperial 210.00

Souvenir Banded, mug, marigold 70.00

Split Diamond, butter, marigold, scarce, English . 70.00

Square Diamond, vase, blue, rare, English 125.00

Star of David & Bows, bowl, amethyst, Northwood, 8½" 60.00

Stippled Rambler Rose, nut bowl, footed, blue, Dugan . 75.00

Stippled Strawberry, butter, marigold, Jenkins 90.00

Style, bowl, amethyst, 8" .. 92.00

Sunken Daisy, sugar, blue, English 36.00

Swirl Hobnail, vase, green, rare, Millersburg, 7" 250.00

Swirl Variant, epergne, green, Imperial 170.00

Ten Mums, bowl, blue, Fenton, 8" 95.00

Thin Rib, candlestick, marigold, Fenton, pair .. 60.00

Thistle & Thorn, nut dish, blue, English 85.00

Three Flowers, tray, handle in center, smoke, Imperial, 12" 52.00

Thumbprint & Spears, creamer, green 56.00

Tiger Lily, pitcher, green, Imperial 195.00

Triands, celery vase, marigold, English 55.00

Tulip & Cane, goblet, smoke, very rare, Imperial, 8 ounces 70.00

Twins, bowl, green, Imperial, 9" 48.00

Valentine, bowl, amethyst, rare, Northwood, 5" 125.00

Victorian, bowl, amethyst, rare, 10" 175.00

Vineyard, pitcher, marigold, Dugan 85.00

Vintage, plate, blue, Fenton, 7" 120.00

Waffle Block, parfait glass with stem, marigold, Imperial 30.00

Waffle Weave, inkwell, marigold 85.00

Waterlily & Cattails, creamer, marigold, Fenton 80.00

Waterlily & Cattails, tumbler, amethyst, Northwood .. 165.00

Waterlily & Cattails, tumbler, marigold, Fenton 95.00

Weeping Cherry, bowl, flat base, amethyst, Dugan . 90.00

Whirling Star, compote, green, Imperial 62.00

Wild Fern, compote, amethyst, Australian ... 165.00
Wild Rose, bowl, flat, green, Northwood, 8″ 42.00
Wildflower, nappy with handles, pink, Dugan ... 70.00
Wildflower, plate, blue, Dugan, 9″ 96.00
Windsor, flower arranger, marigold, rare, Imperial . 85.00
Wine & Roses, wine, blue, Fenton 80.00
Winken, lamp, marigold ... 95.00
Wise Owl, bank, marigold . 46.00
Wishbone & Spades, plate, amethyst, rare, Dugan, 6″ 130.00
Woodpecker, wall vase, vaseline, Dugan 90.00
Wreath of Roses, compote, blue, Fenton 42.00
Zig Zag, tumbler, decorated, blue, Fenton 50.00
Zip Zip, flower frog holder, marigold, English 54.00
Zippered Heart, bowl, amethyst, Imperial, 5″ .. 48.00
Zippered Heart, bowl, marigold, Imperial, 9″ .. 70.00

Catalogs

Vintage catalogs are an excellent source of reference for collectors, as well as being quite collectible in their own right. While some collectors specialize in trying to accumulate a particular company's catalogs in sequence, others prefer to look for those specializing in only one area of interest -- knives, lighting fixtures, or farm machinery, for instance. Original catalogs are often hard to find, and several companies have reprinted some of their earlier editions.

AB Dick Company, Edison Mimeograph & Office Devices, 1891, 32 pages . 38.00

Montgomery Ward, 1922 Fall and Winter, $24.00.

AE Schmidt Company, billiard catalog, 1920, 26 pages 10.00
American Sawmill Machinery Company, #22, 1921, 208 pages 48.00
Art in Seed Bags, Stecher Litho Company, hard bound, 2 volumes 45.00
Arts & Gems, Schumann, cloth bound, 1891, 64 pages 15.00
Ball Brasses, drawer pulls & hardware, illustrated, 1940, 26 pages 7.00
Beckley Ralston Company, motorcar, boat & cycle accessories, 1914 .... 22.00
Blue Ribbon Foods, premium catalog, 1905 .... 6.00

Buckley Brothers, Kernel Of
Kentucky, milling, 1918, 8
pages 5.00
Case & Co, Hartford, Connec-
ticut, school desks, 1888,
24 pages, 9x6″ 25.00
Catalog of Seed Packets, San
Francisco, actual packets,
1920 .... 47.50
Colt, 1921, 40 pages, M ... 35.00
Edison Cylinder Records,
Gold Moulded, records to
February 1906 .... 15.00
Firebanks Company, tools,
cloth bound, 1918, 649
pages 45.00
Hamelt & Company Cowboy,
order blank & envelope,
1934, 128 pages 25.00
Hapgood Plow Company,
1892, 40 pages 10.00
Hudson Sporting Goods,
pre-1940 .... 15.00
Isaac Walker Hardware, 1925,
539 pages 55.00
Johnson, Smith & Company,
novelties & tricks, 1931,
700 pages 39.00
KC Card Company, Mason &
Company, gambling
devices, 1930 .... 45.00
Keen Kutter, cutlery,
mid-1920s 25.00
Majestic Company, circa
1931, building products, 28
pages 5.00
Marlin Firearms Company,
guns, illustrated, July
1915, 136 pages 85.00
McDonald Brothers, Special
Fall, heaters & lanterns,
1898, 17 pages 25.00
Northrup Seed Company, inserts, 1902, 80 pages ... 40.00
Pittsburgh Glass, Wallace &
MacAffe Company, 1880, 8
pages, 16x20″ 8.00
Sears Lighting Fixtures, 1922,
128 pages 25.00

Thayer & Chandler, Brass
Crafts, 1910, 16 pages .. 25.00
Victor Talking Machine Company, Victor Records, 1922 15.00
Western Auto Supply,
automobile accessories,
1928, 130 pages 9.00
Wisconsin Deluxe Company,
novelties, premiums, etc,
1945, 70 pages 25.00
Youth's Companion, prem-
iums, 1891 .... 15.00

Ceramic Art Studio

Whether you're a collector of
American pottery or not, chances are
you'll like the distinctive styling of the
figurines, salt and pepper shakers, and
other novelty items made by the
Ceramic Arts Studio of Madison,
Wisconsin, from about 1938 until
about 1952. They're among the most
recently recognized collectibles on the
market, and a trip to any good flea
market will usually produce one or
several good buys on their shelf sitters
or wall hanging pairs. They're easily
spotted, once you've seen a few examples, but if you're not sure, check
for the trademark: the name of the
company and its location.

Bell, Dance Hall Girl, long
decorated gown, 6½″ ... 45.00
Bud vase, Oriental figure playing mandolin, 6½″ 35.00
Ewer, jasperware, raised
white ballerina, Wedgwood
blue, 4″ 45.00
Figurine, lion & lioness,
bronze & brown, 5½″, pair 55.00
Figurine, Water Lady, waves
form dress, green finish,
12″ 55.00
Planter, Manchu, Oriental
man, 7″ 45.00

Figurine, antelope, avocado green glaze, 4″ x 4½″, $25.00.

Plate, Paul Bunyan, Wisconsin souvenir, lavender glaze, 5½″	45.00
Salt & pepper, pigs: girl in tutu & boy with sailor hat, pair	30.00
Vase, African Lady & African Man, brown & white matt, 8″, pair	60.00
Wall hangers, shadow dancers, 8″, pair	25.00

Character Collectibles

One of the most popular areas of collecting today, and one with the most available memorabilia, is the field of character collectibles. Flea markets usually yield some of the more common examples -- toys, books, lunch boxes, children's dishes, and sheet music are for the most part quite readily found. Trade papers are also an excellent source. Often you will find even the rare and hard-to-find listed for sale. Disney characters, movie stars, television personalities, comic book heroes, and sports greats are the most sought after.

Alice in Wonderland, billfold, 1950s	12.00
Alice in Wonderland, clock, with Mad Hatter	150.00
Alice in Wonderland, sewing cards	35.00
Amos & Andy, cardboard stand-up, Pepsodent	17.00
Amos & Andy, map of Weber City, in original envelope, M	22.00
Babe Ruth, digital clock	250.00
Bambi, figurine, standing, looks ahead, American Pottery, 7½″	80.00
Batman, ballpoint pen, clip is metal figure of Batman, 1966	10.00

Laurel and Hardy dolls, cloth and vinyl, 1973 on foot, Larry Harmon Picture Corp, Hong Kong, 14″, $8.00 each.

Batman, bicycle ornament, full figure, 1966 .... 10.00
Beatles, alarm clock, Yellow Submarine 325.00
Beatles, blow-up doll of Paul McCartney 35.00
Beatles, game, Flip Your Wig 30.00
Beatles, lunchbox, Yellow Submarine 25.00
Beatles, model of Yellow Submarine in box 145.00
Beatles, pin, pictures with names in filigree, large .. 40.00
Ben Casey, jigsaw puzzle .. 10.00
Betty Boop, tea set, 1930s, MIB 350.00
Betty Boop & Mr Boop, perfume, glass figural with paper heart, pair 50.00
Bing Crosby, recipe book, TV Special, Kraft 9.00
Blondie, coloring book, Whitman #680, 1944, 150 pages 10.00
Blondie & Dagwood, game, Westinghouse premium, 1940, MIB 45.00

Bonnie & Clyde, original handbill, photos post-death .. 15.00
Buck Rogers, Big Big Book, Planetoid Eros, 1934 ... 75.00
Buck Rogers, inlaid puzzle . 35.00
Buffalo Bill, story book, #164 12.00
Bugs Bunny, clock, other characters on dial, Warner Brothers 250.00
Bugs Bunny, Porky Pig, coloring book, Whitman #683 10.00
Buster Brown, dictionary, 1927, 324 pages 32.50
Buster Brown, knife, leg shaped 55.00
Buster Brown, pin-back button 20.00
Buster Brown, pitcher, with alphabet 95.00
Buster Brown, playing cards, no box 25.00
Buster Brown & Tige, cast iron bank 135.00
Buster Brown & Tige, china pin tray 30.00
Buster Brown & Tige, pocket mirror, 1946 .... 8.00
Buster Brown & Tige, wrist watch 55.00

Shirley Temple Christmas Doll Book, with doll, #1770, Saalfield, 1937, $30.00.

Captain Marvel, CM Club membership button, Fawcett Publishing, 1941 ... 10.00
Captain Midnight, decoder & manual with original mailer 70.00
Captain Midnight, mug, Ovaltine, radio premium, 1940s 20.00
Charlie Chaplin, mechanical plastic figure, Italy, 1950s 95.00
Charlie McCarthy, carnival figure, wearing monacle, 13″ 30.00
Charlie McCarthy, pencil sharpener, M 60.00
Charlie McCarthy, radio, 1930s 260.00
Cinderella, pastry set, Peerless Playthings Company, MIB 15.00
Cinderella, watch, with glass slipper, Disney, MIB ... 110.00
Cisco Kid & Pancho, Viewmaster reel #960 ... 10.00
Daddy Warbucks, nodder, bisque, Germany, 1930s, 3½″, M 95.00
Dan Patch, decanter 75.00
Davy Crockett, belt, leather . 12.00
Davy Crockett, cap pistol, pot metal & plastic 27.50
Davy Crockett, Indian Scout badge 5.00
Davy Crockett, ring, gold on plastic, firing rifle 12.00
Davy Crockett, tumblers, with name, dates & scenes, 4″, set of 4 .... 28.00
Dennis the Menace, wooden jumping jack figure, 6″ . 15.00
Dick Tracy, Aurora model kit 25.00
Dick Tracy, Bingo game ... 25.00
Dick Tracy, pop-up book, VG 65.00
Dick Tracy, red plastic wallet, Crime Stopper, 1960s ... 8.00
Dick Tracy, secret code maker in the original box 15.00
Dionne Quintuplets, ad for Quaker Oats chromium bowl, envelope 125.00

Hopalong Cassidy manual, 16 pages of ads, giveaway ideas, etc., to promote Hoppy on radio and in movies, movie matinees featured at 15¢, 10″ x 14″, $80.00.

Dionne Quintuplets, book, Here We Are--3 Years Old, 1937 .... 30.00
Dionne Quintuplets, cereal bowl, metal 28.00
Dionne Quintuplets, fan, School Days, with St Paul Milk advertising 17.00
Dionne Quintuplets, handkerchief showing various activities 37.50
Dionne Quintuplets, soap dolls, MIB 100.00
Disney, book, Ave Maria, Random House, 1940 ... 20.00
Disney, book, Robin Hood & His Merry Men, 1952, first edition 32.00
Disney, book, Schooldays in Disneyville, 1939, VG .. 15.00

Disney, Disneyland Pictorial
Souvenir, 1965, 34 pages . 15.00
Disney, Fantasia Unicorn,
carousel toy, 1940s, 25" . 220.00
Disney, matchbook cover,
WWII Disney Insignia,
Pepsi, set of 6 .... 12.00
Disney, sand pail, Gulliver's
Travels, 3" 25.00
Disney, sand pail, Treasure
Island, Mickey, Minnie &
friends, 4" 50.00
Disney, tablecloth, Mickey,
Minnie, Donald & Pluto,
52x80" 30.00
Disney, tumbler, All Star
Parade 10.00
Disney, War Insignia Stamp
Album, 1940s 25.00
Donald Duck, auto, Sun Rub-
ber, VG 40.00
Donald Duck, bank, as sailor
by lifesaver, composition,
1938 .... 125.00
Donald Duck, cast feet, felt
clothes, Schuco 750.00
Donald Duck, Coke bottle, 2
decals, 7 ounces, 1950s . 20.00
Donald Duck, convertible,
Line Mar, metal friction
toy, MIB 125.00
Donald Duck, Poster Paint
Set, Milton Bradley, com-
plete in box 35.00
Donald Duck, puppet made of
papier mache, 9" 60.00
Donald Duck, Sunshine
straws, box with straws,
1950s 15.00
Dopey, Castile Soap figural . 12.00
Dopey, doll, WD Enterprises,
compo, original clothes &
label, 1937 .... 195.00
Dr Kildare, nodder figure . . 20.00
Dr Seuss, Hanky Bird figure . 20.00
Dumbo, doll, gray & white
plush with celluloid eyes,
Character Novelty...... 20.00
Dumbo, hand puppet, Disney 12.50

Dumbo, salt & pepper, Leeds
China, 1940s, pair 15.00
Elvis Presley, billfold with col-
or saddle, M 100.00
Elvis Presley, dog tag
bracelet, 1956 .... 20.00
Elvis Presley, souvenir album,
1950s, 12 pages 20.00
Felix the Cat, animated clock 40.00
Felix the Cat, doll, composi-
tion, large 385.00
Felix the Cat, doll, stuffed
jointed, English, 1930s, 12" 135.00
Felix the Cat, rubber head,
wood body, Cameo 165.00
Ferdinand the Bull, bisque,
Japan, 1939 .... 27.50
Ferdinand the Bull, book,
1938, 16 pages 14.00
Ferdinand the Bull, hard rub-
ber figure, Seiberling ... 35.00
Fibber McGee, Bradley game
with instructions, 1936,
MIB 35.00
Flash Gordon, Jet Propelled
Kite in original box 20.00
Gene Autry, badge, Flying 'A'
Wings 15.00
Gene Autry, cowboy outfit,
MIB 125.00
Gene Autry, guitar, plastic, in
original case 55.00
Gene Autry, Sunbeam Bread
button, M 8.00
Gene Autry, wrist watch,
moving 6-gun, in original
box 225.00
Goldilocks, pop-up book, 1934 75.00
Goofy, blotter, Sunoco, 1939 . 15.00
Happy Hooligan, papier
mache nodder, 6½" 75.00
Hopalong Cassidy, alarm
clock, US Time Co, black
metal 80.00
Hopalong Cassidy, Chow Set,
3 pieces in original box . 65.00
Hopalong Cassidy, red plastic
pencil sharpener with Hoppy 12.00

Mickey Mouse, windup acrobat, plastic Mickey, 6″, $165.00.

Hopalong Cassidy, roller skates	45.00	Jackie Coogan, pencil box, tin	15.00
Hopalong Cassidy, silver metal ring with face	20.00	James Bond, Roger Moore doll, 11″	5.00
Hopalong Cassidy, stationery in folder	15.00	James Dean, necklace, 1955, rare	875.00
Hopalong Cassidy, View Master reel, Cattle Rustler, 1953	10.00	Jiggs, wood stand-up figure, 7″	15.00
Howdy Doody, bank, ceramic	65.00	Jiminy Cricket, wooden figure, jointed, 9″	75.00
Howdy Doody, handkerchief, red, white & blue cotton, 8″	15.00	Li'l Abner, picture puzzle on key chain, 1950s	8.00
Howdy Doody, Phonodoodle	13.00	Li'l Abner & Daisy Mae, rubber & cloth puppets, 1940s, pair	40.00
Howdy Doody, T-shirt, VG	12.50		
Humpty Dumpty, animated form, Baranger, 1939	775.00	Lindbergh, pencil box, with decals of plane & Lindy	40.00
Jack Armstrong, Explorer telescope, Wheaties premium, 1938	30.00	Little Lulu, bean-filled felt doll, red body & yellow cap, 10″	40.00
Jack Armstrong, Hike-O-Meter, for Wheaties	20.00	Little Orphan Annie, book, The Lucky Knife, Whitman, 1934	20.00
Jack Webb, police whistle	6.00		
Jackie Coogan, doll, papier mache	135.00	Little Orphan Annie, child's stove	35.00

Little Orphan Annie, doll, segmented wood, 5" 55.00

Little Orphan Annie, pop-up book 75.00

Little Orphan Annie, sheet music 10.00

Little Orphan Annie, wrist watch, New Haven, 1934 . 80.00

Little Orphan Annie & Sandy, painted lead figure, 1930s, 2" 12.00

Little Red Riding Hood, bisque figure, with wolf, 6", M 65.00

Little Red Riding Hood, child's sewing machine, made in Germany 65.00

Little Red Riding Hood, pop-up book, 1934 .... 18.00

Lone Ranger, book, Fran Striker, 218 pages, 1936 . 10.00

Lone Ranger, book bank, Zell, 1938 .... 40.00

Lone Ranger, ink blotter, Bond Bread 7.50

Lone Ranger, ring, Atom Bomb 35.00

Lone Ranger, Rodeo Set, Marx, MIB 65.00

Lone Ranger, uncolored coloring contest entry picture, 1950 .... 12.00

Lone Ranger & Silver, Hartland figures, MIB .. 75.00

Maggie & Jiggs, celluloid figures with movable arms, 6½" 225.00

Marilyn Monroe, calendar, salesman's sample 100.00

Marilyn Monroe, tin coaster . 25.00

Matt Dillon, Aladdin vaccuum bottle 6.00

Mickey, Donald, & Goofy, bisque, band concert, M ... 100.00

Mickey & Donald, Merry Christmas, 1948 Firestone giveaway, M 300.00

Mickey & Minnie, child's purse with pictures of both mice, 1930 .... 28.00

Mickey & Minnie, gold lustre tea set, Japan, 15 piece . 100.00

Mickey & Minnie, handkerchief 12.00

Mickey & Minnie, trapeze, windup, celluloid 375.00

Mickey Mouse, baseball player, hard plastic with rubber tail, 7" 12.50

Mickey Mouse, bicycle bell, chrome, 1930s 45.00

Mickey Mouse, bisque figure, plays saxophone, minor paint wear, 3¼" 30.00

Mickey Mouse, bisque figure holding cane, 4½" 85.00

Mickey Mouse, book, Brave Little Tailor, Whitman, 1939 .... 10.00

Mickey Mouse, book, Mickey Mouse Never Fails, 1939 . 55.00

Mickey Mouse, Bubble Buster in original box, EX 80.00

Mickey Mouse, carnival chalk figure, 1930s, 9¾" 95.00

Mickey Mouse, Choo-Choo #485, Fisher Price 40.00

Mickey Mouse, comic book, Cherrios premium, 'Secret Room' 5.00

Mickey Mouse, corn popper, 1930s, rare 185.00

Mickey Mouse, cup & egg cup combo, 3¾" 15.00

Mickey Mouse, hanky with paper label 28.00

Mickey Mouse, hard rubber figure, Seiberling Company, 6½" 125.00

Mickey Mouse, hard rubber fire truck 22.00

Mickey Mouse, Mickey Mousketooner 35.00

Mickey Mouse, milk pitcher, china, early 1930s, 2x3" . 125.00

Mickey Mouse, pen knife, Chicago World's Fair, 1933 35.00

Mickey Mouse, potty, graniteware, Germany .. 150.00

Mickey Mouse, pull toy drummer, Fisher Price, 11" . . 125.00
Mickey Mouse, race car, tin windup, in original box . 225.00
Mickey Mouse, sand pail, Mickey's Garden 15.00
Mickey Mouse, sand sifter with tools, metal 95.00
Mickey Mouse, spoon, Branford silver plate, 1930s . 15.00
Mickey Mouse, spoon, made for Post-O cereal 25.00
Mickey Mouse, target game in box 85.00
Mickey Mouse, Tool Chest, with Pluto & camping scenes, 1936 . . . . 80.00
Mickey Mouse, typewriter, Mouseketeer, with box . . 80.00
Mickey Mouse, Wilbur Chocolate Bar, M 90.00
Mickey Mouse, wrist watch, Bradley, 50th Birthday . 40.00
Mickey Mouse, wrist watch, Timex electric, 1970 . . . . 100.00
Minnie Mouse, bisque figure, wearing hat & holding umbrella, 4½" 75.00

Minnie Pearl, Chicken System promotional book, 1967, 100 pages 25.00
Monkees, playing cards, 1966 5.00
Moon Mullins, Crayon & Paint Book, 1932 . . . . 10.00
Moon Mullins, jointed wooden figure, 5½" 80.00
Moon Mullins & Kayo, bisque toothbrush holder 95.00
Mortimer Snerd, hair-growing figure 25.00
Mr Magoo, cloth & vinyl doll, 1962, 15" 25.00
Mr Spock, doll with vinyl head, Knickerbocker 10.00
Mutt & Jeff, tie tacks, pair . 65.00
Olive Oyl, jointed wooden figure, 5" 50.00
Peter Rabbit, bank 45.00
Pinocchio, bank, composition, Crown Company, 1940 . . 75.00
Pinocchio, cloth doll with hat, Knickerbocker, 18", EX . 85.00
Pinocchio, round tin lunch pail with characters, 1940 . . . 50.00
Pinocchio, soap figure in box, 1939 . . . . 25.00

Red Riding Hood cup, no mark, 3", $135.00.

Pluto, bisque figure, sitting with head forward, 2¾", EX 50.00

Pluto, pencil sharpener, celluloid 20.00

Pluto, planter, sitting with planter cart, Leeds China, 6½" 45.00

Pluto, Pop-up Kritter, Fisher Price, EX 25.00

Popeye, Big Big Book, Thimble Theatre, 1935 ...... 55.00

Popeye, book, Popeye Meets His Rival, Whitman 22.00

Popeye, handkerchief with allover picture 22.00

Popeye, Juggler game 55.00

Popeye, Magic Playground . 55.00

Popeye, Mattel music box . 49.00

Popeye, picture puzzles, 4 in original box, 1932 ...... 65.00

Popeye, ring toss, King Features, 1935, MIB ... 22.00

Popeye, sparkler, 1930s, good working condition 175.00

Popeye, tie clasp with enameled character 30.00

Porky Pig, bank, bisque, 4½" 135.00

Raggedy Ann, coloring book, Saalfield, 1945 .... 9.00

Roy Rogers, bandanna, silk . 15.00

Roy Rogers, boot, metal with copper finish & horseshoe base, 5¾" 26.00

Roy Rogers, box-type camera, EX 25.00

Roy Rogers, German binoculars, 1956, MIB .. 30.00

Roy Rogers, neckerchief slide 25.00

Roy Rogers, View Master reel, Holdup, 1953 .... 10.00

Roy Rogers & Trigger, figure & horse 50.00

Rusty & Rin Tin Tin, pen knife with Morse code on reverse, M 20.00

Schmoo, bank with card ... 20.00

Sergeant Preston, pedometer, M 36.00

Seven Dwarfs, books, Whitman, story of each dwarf, 24 pages, 7 books 350.00

Shirley Temple, book, Birthday Book, #1735, 1935 .. 60.00

Shirley Temple, book, Little Miss Broadway, M 25.00

Shirley Temple, books, Five Books About Me, in original box, EX 85.00

Shirley Temple, child's ring, sterling with picture of Shirley 150.00

Shirley Temple, doll buggy . 295.00

Shirley Temple, full page ad, Quaker Puffed Wheat .. 10.00

Shirley Temple, sheet music, On Good Ship Lollipop . 16.00

Skeezix, bank, 1926 .... 40.00

Smokey the Bear, figural cigarette snuffer & note holder 10.00

Sneezy, plastic figurine, 5¾" 10.00

Snow White, sheet music, Whistle While You Work, 1937, M 15.00

Snow White & 7 Dwarfs, cereal bowl, milk glass, 1938 .... 20.00

Snow White & 7 Dwarfs, picture plaque of Snow White 10.00

Soupy Sales, marionette, rubber face & compo body, 1966, 12" 25.00

Sparkle Plenty, soap figure, 1940s, MIB 17.50

Spiro Agnew, watch, original, runs 48.50

Superman, animated alarm clock, 1940 .... 550.00

Superman, Hidecraft billfold, 1947 .... 15.00

Superman, kiddie swim fins, official, MIB 25.00

Tarzan, button, Signal Club . 24.00

Tarzan, movie jigsaw puzzle, Pippins cigars premium, M 35.00

Three Little Wolves, book, linen, 1937, 10x15" 67.00

Thumper, Goebel, original tag, small 25.00
Tom & Jerry, figurines, Wade, England, MIB 25.00
Tom Mix, parachute, complete with launcher 60.00
Tom Mix, siren badge, Dobie County 25.00
Tom Mix, Straight Shooters ring 35.00
Uncle Willie & Emmie, bisque toothbrush holder, 1930s . 75.00
Wimpy, carnival chalk figure, 16" 75.00
Woody Woodpecker, animated alarm clock, Wood's Cafe 175.00
Wyatt Earp, Marshal's outfit, in box, 1950s 35.00
Yellow Kid, card, script ... 40.00
Zorro, wrist flashlight, 3 colors, 2½" diameter 12.00

Children's Books

Books were popular gifts for children in the latter 1800s; many were

Sunbonnet Babies, published by Rand McNally, 1902, $10.00.

beautifully illustrated, some by notable artists such as Frances Brundage and Maxfield Parrish. From this century, tales of Tarzan by Burroughs are fast becoming very collectible -- *Tarzan and the Leopard Men*, 1935, first edition, is worth about $185.00.

Alice's Adventures in Wonderland, Tenniel illustrated, Lothrop, 1898 . 40.00
Big Animal Picture Book, McLoughlin Brothers, 1900 .... 15.00
Book of Magic, puzzles, tricks & stunts, Houdini, 295 pages, 1927 .... 8.00
Brave & Bold, Alger 10.00
Chatterbox, 1917 .... 10.00
Daddy Jake & Runaway, Stories by Uncle Remus, Century, 1889 .... 125.00
Do & Dare, Horatio Alger, 1910 .... 8.00
Funny Jungleland, metamorphic, 1909 .... 45.00
Girl's & Boy's Book of Sports, 1 color, 11 woodcuts, 1840, NM 100.00
Grimm's Fairy Tales, Scharl, 212 illustrations, 1944 .. 7.00
Jack & the Bean Stalk, Chapbook, Turner & Fisher, 1840s, 4x6" 50.00
Little Friends Birthday Book, Tuck, Brundage illustrated, pre-1910 ..... 75.00
Little Lord Fauntleroy, C Scribner's Sons, 24 illustrations, 1914 .... 20.00
Mickey Mouse Silly Symphonies, pop-up, 1933 ... 95.00
Popeye Borrows a Baby Nurse 15.00
Robinson Crusoe, Riverside Press, EB Smith illustrated, 1909 .... 45.00
Rollo on the Thine, Abbott, illustrated, 218 pages, 1866 8.00

Sinbad the Sailor, Chapbook,
1 color, 9 woodcuts, 1840s,
4x6" 40.00
Songs of Summer, James
Whitcomb Riley, 190
pages, 1883-1908 .... 10.00
Summer Outing, WB Conk-
xey Co, 1901 .... 12.00
Sunshine for Little Children,
Maud Humphrey il-
lustrated 35.00
Tarzan & Foreign Legion,
Burroughs, ERB Inc, first
edition, 1947 .... 30.00
Who's Afraid of the Big Bad
Wolf, Disney Enterprises,
1933 .... 10.00

Children's Dishes

In the late 1900s, glass companies introduced sets of small scaled pressed glass dinnerware, many in the same pattern as their regular line, others designed specifically for the little folks. Many were of clear glass, but milk glass, opalescent glass, and colors were also used. Not to be outdone, English ceramic firms as well as American potteries made both tea sets and fully accessorized dinnerware sets decorated with decals of nursery rhymes, animals, or characters from children's stories. Though popularly collected for some time, your favorite flea market may still yield some very nice examples of both types.

China and Pottery

Basket, sugar, marked Basket
PP Salem China Co, 2¼" .   6.75
Bowl, Bunnykins, Royal
Doulton 19.00
Bowl, Davy Crockett Fron-
tiersman, 6" 7.50
Casserole, Bears, covered,
Made in Japan, 2¼" 13.50

Creamer, Mieto, marked Hand
Painted Made in Japan,
1⅞" 2.50
Creamer, Punch & Judy,
England, 3¼" 23.50
Creamer, stick spatter, Staf-
fordshire, England, 3⅛" . 32.50
Creamer, Sunset, Made in
Japan, 1⅞" 3.50
Creamer, tan & gray lustre,
Phoenix China Made in
Japan, 2¼" 7.50
Cup, Ballerina, marked
General Ind NY Japan,
1½" 2.50
Cup, Blue Portrait, Germany,
1⅝" 17.00
Cup, Bluebird Dinner Set,
Noritake, 1¼" 6.50
Cup, Circus Set, Edwin M
Knowles China Co, 2⅛" . 5.50
Cup, May, England, 2⅛" .. 13.00
Cup, Mickey Mouse, Occupied
Japan, 1¼" 7.50
Cup, Silhouette, Made in
Japan, 1½" 4.50
Cup, The House That Jack
Built, Germany, 1⅞" ... 11.00
Mug, Barnyard Scene, Royal
Windsor, England, 3¼" . 13.00
Mug, Brundage Girls, Ger-
many, 2¾" 29.00

Sugar bowl, Lamb pattern in milk
glass, 3¼", $195.00.

Plate, The Young Sailors, 3½", $45.00.

Plate, fish set, Austria, 6½" . 21.00

Plate, Merry Christmas, green
lustre, Leuchtenberg, Germany, 5" 6.00

Plate, Otter Cocoa Set,
Noritake, 4¼" 14.00

Plate, Saint Nicholas, Germany, 5⅛" 13.00

Plate, Sarreguemine, 6" ... 33.50

Platter, Pagodas, England,
6⅛" 26.00

Rolling pin, Mary Had a Little Lamb, 9" 57.50

Salt box, tan lustre floral,
Made in Japan, 2⅛" 16.50

Saucer, Cameoware, Harker,
4⅞" 2.25

Saucer, Girls with Pets,
Charles Allerton & Sons,
England, 4½" 2.50

Saucer, Joseph, Mary, &
Donkey, Germany, 4¾" . 4.50

Saucer, Silhouette, Noritake,
3¾" 2.50

Saucer, The Bridesmaid, Germany, 4⅞" 4.50

Set, Floral Medallion, Made in
Japan, 4 place service .. 26.00

Soup, Kite Set, England, 3½" 52.50

Spoon, Blue Onion Kitchenware, Germany, 5½" ... 55.00

Sugar with lid, Buster Brown,
Germany, 3¾" 60.00

Sugar with lid, Butterfly,
Made in Japan, 3⅛" 4.75

Sugar with lid, Floral Set, Nippon, 3" 8.00

Sugar with lid, gaudy
ironstone, England, 4" .. 37.50

Sugar with lid, Sunset, Made
in Japan, 3⅛" 4.50

Teapot, Roman Chariots,
Cauldon England, 3⅜" .. 53.00

Teapot with lid, Angel
Christmas set, Germany,
6½" 57.50

Teapot with lid, Geisha, 3¼" 23.50

Tray, clown, with duck & dog
on ball, Made in Japan,
4¼" 4.75

Tureen, Blue Marble,
England, 4¼" 42.50

Waste bowl, Water Hen,
England, 2½" 29.00

Waste bowl, waterfront scene,
unmarked 10.00

Pattern Glass

Acorn, creamer, crystal, 3⅜" 75.00

Acorn, spooner, crystal,
3⅛" 74.00

Arched Panel, tumbler, cobalt,
Westmoreland Glass Com-
pany 22.00

Austrian 200, creamer,
crystal, Greentown, 3¼" . 75.00

Baby Thumbprint, cake
stand, crystal, United
States Glass Company, 3" 68.50

Bead & Scroll, spooner,
crystal, 2¾" 57.50

Beaded Swirl, butter, crystal,
Westmoreland Glass Com-
pany, 2⅜" 49.50

Block, sugar with lid, blue,
4½" 97.50

Braided Belt, table set,
crystal, 4 piece 273.00

Bucket, butter, crystal, Bryce
Brothers, 2¼" 205.00

Button Panel 44, creamer, crystal, George Duncan's Sons, 2½" 42.50

Buzz Saw, spooner, crystal, Cambridge Glass Company, 2⅛" 21.00

Chimo, sugar with lid, crystal, 3" 58.00

Clear & Diamond Panels, spooner, green, 2¾" 32.50

Cloud Band, table set, white milk glass, Gillinder & Sons, Inc 325.00

Colonial, punch cup, crystal, 1⅞" 13.50

Colonial 2630, creamer, olive, Cambridge Glass Company, 2⅜" 33.00

Dewdrop Hobnail with Hobnail Base, spooner, Columbia Glass Co, 2¾" 65.00

Diamond Ridge, sugar with lid, crystal, 4⅝" 125.00

Doyle 500, tray, amber, Doyle & Company, 6⅝" 43.00

Drum, mug, crystal, 2" 34.00

Duncan & Miller 42, honey jug, crystal, 2⅜" 62.50

Dutch Kinder, chamber pot, blue milk glass, 2 1/8" .. 80.00

Fancy Cut, water set, crystal, Co-Operative Flint Glass Co 142.00

Fernland 2635, creamer, cobalt, Cambridge Glass Co, 2⅜" 38.50

Fine Cut, master berry bowl, crystal, 1¾" 62.50

Flute, small berry bowl, crystal with gold 23.00

Frances Ware, pitcher, blue, Hobbs, Brockunier & Company, 4¾" 93.00

Galloway, tumbler, crystal, 2" 6.00

Grapevine with Ovals, sugar with lid, crystal, McKee, 2⅞" 40.00

Hawaiian Lei, butter, crystal, 2¼" 36.00

Hobnail with Thumbprint Base No 150, tray, crystal, Doyle, 7⅜" 27.00

Horizontal Threads, table set, crystal, 4 piece 139.00

Inverted Strawberry, punch bowl, crystal, Cambridge Glass Co, 3⅜" 49.00

Kittens, cereal bowl, marigold, Fenton, 3½" 93.00

Lamb, creamer, crystal, 2⅞" 60.00

Liberty Bell, table set, crystal, Gillinder & Sons, 4 piece . 475.00

Lion, saucer, crystal, Gillinder & Sons, 3¼" 17.00

Long Diamond 15006, butter, crystal, US Glass Co, 2" . 125.00

Menagerie, spooner, blue, Bryce, Higbee Co, 2⅝" . 115.00

Michigan, butter, crystal with gold, US Glass Co, 3½" . 118.00

Nearcut, water tumbler, crystal, Cambridge Glass Co, 2" 6.00

Nursery Rhyme, master berry bowl, crystal, US Glass Co, 4¼" 55.00

Nursery Rhyme, punch cup, white milk glass, US Glass Co, 1⅜" 24.00

Oval Star 300, tray, crystal, Indiana Glass Co, 7¼" .. 73.00

Pattee Cross, punch set, crystal, US Glass Co, 7 piece 203.00

Pennsylvania, butter, green, US Glass Co, 3½" 145.00

Pennsylvania, creamer, green, US Glass Co, 2½" 73.00

Pert, sugar with lid, crystal, 5⅛" 138.00

Plain Pattern 13, butter, cobalt, King Glass Co, 1⅞" 145.00

Sandwich Ivy, creamer, amethyst, 2⅜" 95.00

Sandwich Ivy, sugar, crystal, 3¼" 75.00

Round oak table with claw feet, 23″ x 26″, with set of four press-back 31″ chairs, $1,650.00.

Children's Furnishings

Just about anything made for adults has been reduced to children's size. Early handmade items may be as primitive or as elaborate as their creator was proficient. Even later factory-made pieces are collectible. Baby rattles, highchairs, strollers, wagons, and sleds from the 1800s are especially treasured.

Bed, Country Sheraton, turned legs & posts, 29x48x31″ 215.00
Blanket chest, wood till-type hinge, old red pine, 12x25″ .. 125.00
Bookcase, cherry drop front desk type, 1870s 375.00
Chair, Mission, original finish .. 55.00
Cradle, cut-out walnut rockers with hand holds, 20x40″ . 165.00

Cupboard, handmade, step-back with glazed doors, 24½″ 130.00
Desk, rolltop with original swivel chair 275.00
Dresser-chest, walnut & maple, 4 feet 275.00
Fainting couch, leather, Victorian 350.00
Highchair, primitive arrow back, black with yellow striping, 32″ 70.00
Hobby horse, carved & painted, turned wooden trestle base, 45x50″ 350.00
Ice skates, clamp on, Winchester 38.00
Lamp shade, blue milk glass . 110.00
Loveseat, velvet upholstery, Victorian 565.00
Noah's Ark, wooden with original painted decor, 11 animals, 7¾″ 275.00

Rattle, Heinz, pink & blue .	5.00
Sailboat, North Star, wood, 17″	35.00
Sewing machine, Betsy Ross, metal, works, 5x7″	75.00
Sled, wood & iron, with painting of lake, 1860s, 32x12x11″	145.00
Swing & rocker, pressed oak in A-frame support, seat detaches	90.00
Table, pine, drop leaf	48.00
Tea kettle, tin, worn blue paint, 4″	95.00
Wash basin, double, with handle, china, transfers of children, 16″	225.00

Christmas

No other holiday season is celebrated to the extravagant extent as Christmas -- and vintage decorations provide a warmth and charm that none from today can match. Ornaments from before 1870 were imported from Dresden, Germany -- usually made of cardboard and sparkled with tinsel trim. Later, blown glass ornaments were made there in literally thousands of shapes such as fruits and vegetables, clowns, Santas, angels, and animals. Kugles, heavy glass balls (though fruit and vegetable forms are found on rare occasion) were made from about 1820 to late in the century in sizes from very small up to 14″. Early Santa figures are treasured, especially those in robes other than red. Figural bulbs from the twenties and thirties are popular, especially those that are character related.

Book, Santa Claus Visit, Donahue, 1905	12.50
Bulb, Betty Boop	45.00
Bulb, cat & fiddle	65.00
Bulb, Father Christmas	22.00

Ornament, cardboard candy holder, different scene on each of four sides and top, ca. 1910, 9″, $45.00.

Bulb, Santa holding sack, painted milk glass, 3″, M	20.00
Bulb, Santa's head, oval with holly, painted milk glass, 4″, M	24.00
Bulb, snowman	10.00
Bulb, woman in shoe	35.00
Christmas light, green hobnail pattern, 4″, pair	40.00
Fence, for tree, wicker & wood, 24x36″	70.00
Lights, complete set of comic character figurals	325.00
Lights, plastic stars, electric, 25 on card, 1950s	22.50
Ornament, angel, wax with original hair, fiberglass wings & dress, 4″	75.00
Ornament, baby on ball, blown, gold & red, 3¼″	65.00
Ornament, boot with painted Santa head, red, Italy, 5″	8.00

Ornament, bust of Indian, red & black paint, 4" 175.00

Ornament, cardboard houses, made in Japan, 12 in original box, set 25.00

Ornament, cat head figural, blown glass 65.00

Ornament, clown, blown glass 30.00

Ornament, cornucopia, gauze, with Santa die-cut on front, tinsel loop 15.00

Ornament, Daniel Boone, red glass gun, mask, coonskin cap, 1950s 35.00

Ornament, dog on ball, blown, 3½" 65.00

Ornament, Father Christmas head, blown glass 30.00

Ornament, Father Christmas holding tree, blown glass, early, 3½" 30.00

Ornament, foxy grandpa, blown legs 200.00

Ornament, gnome, blown, 4" . 60.00

Ornament, hot air balloon, glass & tinsel, with paper scrap Cupid 35.00

Ornament, ice skater, magenta costume trimmed in cotton & glitter, 6" 40.00

Ornament, icicle, silver with multicolored spirals & snow, 6", pair 15.00

Ornament, Man in Moon, blown glass 30.00

Ornament, mushroom, blown glass, clip on, early, 3¾" . 28.00

Ornament, peacock, blown glass, angel hair wings . 35.00

Ornament, pine cone, blown glass 6.00

Ornament, Santa, red blown glass, full figure 30.00

Ornament, tree top, tier: balls, tinsel, glitter bells, 12" . 45.00

Pitcher, china, Santa face on spout and handle 80.00

Santa, bisque candy cane holder, made in Japan, 4½" 15.00

Santa, candy bag, net & flannel, celluloid face, clay feet 85.00

Santa, cloth & chenille, compo head, hand painted, 6" .. 20.00

Figural lightbulbs, left to right: Betty Boop, $45.00; Minnie Mouse, $35.00; Mickey Mouse, $50.00; clown, $25.00.

Santa, fur beard, cardboard sleigh, German, small	55.00
Santa, holding small feather tree, German, 9″	90.00
Santa, nodder, all bisque, Germany	95.00
Santa, papier mache, sitting in decorated wreath	45.00
Santa, plaster face, early, 8″	65.00
Santa, red & blue robe, woven sleigh, celluloid deer, mounted	45.00
Santa, stand-up, with bag and bell, German embossed paper, 16″	55.00
Santa, tin windup, made in Great Britain, 4½″	50.00
Santa, vinyl face, hands & boots, red plush suit, 1940s, 24″	12.00
Santa face, wall plaque, pressed paper, chicken feathers, 20″	35.00
Santa mask, full head, 1920s	45.00
Shades, Barney Google and Snuffy Smith, for tree lights	20.00
Snowman, cotton, Occupied Japan, 6″	12.00
Stickpin, celluloid Santa, advertising	20.00
Tree, goose feathers, white with red berries, wooden pot, 15″	65.00
Tree, goose feathers, white with red berries, 29″	85.00
Tree stand, iron cylinder on wood board, picket fence, 7x12″	90.00
Tree stand, musical, revolves, clockwork, Victorian, German	375.00

Civil War Collectibles

Mementos from the great Civil War represent many things to many people -- the downfall of the antebellum grandeur of the South, the resulting freedom of the Black race, and the conflict itself that was the most personal tragedy America has ever known. In this context, collectors of Civil War memorabilia regard their artifacts with a softness of heart perhaps not present in those whose interests lie in militaria of the twentieth century.

Medal of Honor, inscribed, bronze, 4″, $1,600.00, in mint condition.

Anvil iron, hand forged, 4x14″	48.00
Artillery cannon primer hole clean-out pick, brass half cap	38.00
Belt & buckle, leather, 45″ long	35.00
Belt buckle, brass	120.00
Belt buckle, puppy paw, 'US'	75.00
Binoculars, brass, large	39.00
Book, The Rifled Musket, Fuller	12.00
Bridle rosettes, Cavalry, US brass, pair	45.00

Bridle rosettes, leather, twisted iron bit, Kennesaw, Georgia 39.00

Bucket, for artillery grease, chain handle, black sheet iron 350.00

Cannonball tongs, Federal Pennsylvania Foundry, large 78.00

Canteen, bull's eye, with cover 95.00

Canteen, wood, 9" diameter . 35.00

Cartridge pouch, US impressed, black leather 85.00

Commission case, officer's, maps, dispatches, 19" .. 125.00

Cup, pewter, folding, in tin container 22.00

Epaulets, officer's, gilt metal fishscales, pair 135.00

Epaulets box, black tole finish with gilt stripes, hinged lid 85.00

Fuse cutter 15.00

Gunner's gimlet 8.00

Horse bit, Cavalry, large mouth, smithy made ... 48.00

Horse brush, Cavalry 25.00

Identification bar 15.00

Instrument case, tin, ironmonger's brass label, 7x1" diameter 55.00

Kepi insignia, field artillery, crossed cannon, 2" 18.00

Map case, crudely tinner made, 30" long 32.00

Military paper, muster rolls, sick & prisoner lists 23.00

Mirror, Spotsylvania, 5th Infantry Star, pocket size . 45.00

Musket, contract 58 caliber rifle 400.00

Naval dividers tool, brass, 18" long 110.00

Naval utensils, knife, fork & spoon 100.00

Newspaper, Banger Jeffersonian, 1863 Battle of Gettysburg 34.00

Newspaper, common, no big battle described 4.50

Oil painting, of Lincoln, framed, 9x12" 110.00

Pass, railroad 15.00

Plumbob, engineer's, iron .. 48.00

Powder flask, pewter, plain, brass lid-measure 68.00

Shell loader, iron, wooden handles 15.00

Spurs 75.00

Sword, Ames M & Company, Chicopue, left handed ... 160.00

Sword, US Cavalry, with scabbard & curved steel blade, 35" 250.00

Telegram, civilian 6.00

Tumbler punch 5.00

Water keg, wooden with brass bands, 3 gallons 40.00

Clocks

Because many of the early clocks have handmade works, condition is important when you are considering a purchase. Repairs may be costly. Today's collectors prefer pendulum regulated movements from the 18th and 19th centuries, and clocks from the larger manufacturers such as Sessions, Ithica, Ingraham, Seth Thomas, Ansonia, and Waterbury.

A Smith, wooden water bracket with repousse brass reservoir, 27" 200.00

Alarm, Baby Ben, repeating alarm, black dial in nickel case 30.00

Alarm, Mr Peanut 60.00

Alarm, Old Reliable, 8-day, Wards 35.00

Alarm, WWII nostalgia piece, War Alarm, works 14.00

Animated, driver with whip, coach & horse, United Metal Goods 90.00

Animated, Kit-Kat Klock, eyes & tail move 35.00

Wm. Gilbert Clock Co. calendar school wall clock, octagonal, 24½", $125.00.

Animated, man at anvil, color	55.00
Animated, painted bird in cage, ball revolves, Japan .	200.00
Animated, racing car, man with flag, Jaz Clock	55.00
Ansonia, Diana	900.00
Ansonia, Patricia	750.00
Art Deco, glass, acid Greek columns, girl's head, wooden base, 8"	285.00
Art Nouveau, digital, Plato-type, woman atop, celluloid	120.00
Batman, talking figural . . .	18.00
Carriage, repeater, gold dial, 8-day, Corniche case	625.00
Cuckoo, hand carved figural mill with water wheel, weight driven	75.00
Cuckoo, house atop, trees at side & bottom, water mill, deer, 11"	125.00
Delft, mantel, porcelain, blue & white florals, 11¾" . . .	450.00
Dresser, brass, cupids on side & top, footed, 6"	28.00
Eli Terry, One Day Regulator, with alarm	100.00

Figural, Empire style, bronze female holding watch, 7" .	175.00
Florence Kroeber, iron front, 8-day time & strike	175.00
Germany, miniature kitchen with clock below, hand-made & painted	65.00
Germany, porcelain, hand painted windmill scenes, pendulum, 8-day	75.00
Germany, tin with porcelain face, brass works, lithograph house & lake .	55.00
Gilbert, gingerbread, oak Egyptian model, EX case .	160.00
Haig & Haig, wall, pendulum, illuminated, MIB	35.00
Hammond, electric, black bakelite Deco case, calendar windows	52.00
International Time Recording Company, time clock, oak case	350.00

Victorian walnut shelf clock, arched case with urn finial, drop finials at sides, mercury pendulum, stenciled door decoration, 19½", $300.00.

Left to right: Ansonia Brass and Copper Co. beehive shelf clock, eight day, strikes hour and half hour, rosewood case, stenciled door decoration, key and pendulum, 19″, $150.00; E.N. Welch kitchen shelf clock, eight day, strikes hour and half hour, gingerbread case, gilt door decoration, elaborate pendulum and key, 21″, $150.00.

Keebler, tiny house figural, pendulette, 6¼x3½″ 80.00
Kroeber, mantel cabinet, label, 8-day, time, strike & pendulum 100.00
Lendan, Nixon as Superman, 9″ diameter 75.00
Lux, Blue Bird 35.00
Lux, Bulldog with Kittens . 50.00
Lux, Lovebirds 55.00
Lux, Randolf 55.00
New Haven, banjo, mahogany with scenic decor, 29″ . . 60.00
Postal Telegraph, gallery wall, 1920s, large 35.00
Powder box, metal, musical with animated heartbeat, WWI 92.00
Self Winding Clock Company, metal gallery, pendulum driven 65.00
Sessions, B-hive Puritan mantel, 8-day strike, porcelain dial 75.00
Sessions, clipper ship, wooden, chrome electric, G 50.00

Sessions, Mission oak wall clock 70.00
Seth Thomas, pendulum, octagon top, 1885, 9″ 150.00
Seth Thomas, shelf, lyre movement, 8-day time & strike . 160.00
Seth Thomas, shell column, mirror, 30 hour 250.00
Seth Thomas, tambour, 8-day, striker, pendulum, 7½″ . 75.00
Shelf, 3 sections, mahogany veneer, gilt pilasters, reverse painted 195.00
Store, regulator, 8-day, cherry case 475.00
Terhune & Edwards, iron front, ornate design, 30 hour 130.00

E.N. Welch ogee shelf clock, ca. 1870, weight driven, strikes hour and half hour, thirty hour, brass works, rosewood case, elaborate stenciled decoration on door, two weights, key and pendulum, 26″, $250.00.

Terry & Andrews, shelf, 30
hour weight ogee 140.00
Treasure Isle, turtle shape,
clock under shell, brass
plated, Bentley 47.50
Wall, gilt wood, painted face
C Jerome, 19" diameter . 85.00
Waterbury, kitchen, ornate
oak, frosted white bird on
glass, 22" 80.00
Waterbury, mantel, Belfast,
arched pediment, square
base with scrolls 125.00
Welch, mantel, Ulmar, early
1900s, 5" dial 95.00
Welch, mantel, with lions on
each side 70.00
Wurttemberg, alarm, 30 hour,
horn on top, 7½" 90.00
Yale Company, miniature carriage, nickeled brass, 1881,
3" 80.00

New Haven Marine wall clock,
rosewood hexagonal case, calendar,
eight day, strikes hour and half hour,
second hand dial, key, 12¾", $250.00.

Cloisonne

Several types of cloisonne (a
method of decorating metal with
enameling) have been developed since
it was introduced in the 16th century

-- plique a jour (transparent enamel
work); foil cloisonne; wireless
cloisonne; or cloisonne on ceramic,
wood or laquer. The type you are most
likely to encounter at flea markets has
the pattern outlined with fine metal
wires, filled in with colored enamels.
The finest examples date from 1865
until 1900, though excellent work is
still being produced in China and
Taiwan.

Ash tray, pink & white
flowers, turquoise, black,
red 26.00
Bowl with lid & foot, scrolls,
vases with cherry
blossoms, 5x4½" 130.00
Box, apple; pink & yellow on
blue, clouds, scrolls, peony,
4x3½" 95.00
Cache pot, floral medallions,
jardinieres on blue, hex-
agon, 10" 300.00
Candlestick, rust color, 6",
pair 165.00
Charger, leaf border with
flowering branch, birds on
blue, 12" 175.00
Charger, lily pond, herons,
blue & red bands, 14½" . 350.00
Cigarette box, oyster, rust &
blue flowers, domed lid . 60.00
Ginger jar, scroll & lotus
decor, unmarked, 3x7"
diameter 225.00
Incense burner, gilt lions'
heads, 3 legs, 1700s, 8" . 450.00
Letter holder, scalloped front,
pointed back piece, 5" .. 150.00
Planter, flowers, scalloped rim
with short raised base,
3x6" diameter 160.00
Plate, birds & dragons in
reserves, flowers, blue,
11¾" 400.00
Rose jar, black, gold flecked,
butterflies, Japan, 1800s,
5" 125.00

Tazza, scaly dragons in multicolor on dark blue, 6″ x 8″, $325.00.

Salt & pepper, black, duck in white, green on blue, gold mesh 120.00

Smoke set, animal & floral decor, 3 piece 275.00

Teapot, butterflies, florets, silver flecked ground, bulbous, 3″ 90.00

Teapot, fancy spout & handle, flowers, Tao Tieh masks, 6¼x5″ 185.00

Toothpick holder, yellow, red & blue flowers, 1½″ 45.00

Tray, warrior's head in center, souvenir, 1906, 5¾x7″ .. 175.00

Urn, blue, phoenix birds at shoulder, domed top, 3 legs, 6½″ 250.00

Vase, bamboo motif base, silver rims, pigeon blood, ball shape, 3½″ 85.00

Vase, black, yellow dragon, 5″ 135.00

Vase, double gourd, bushes in reserve, flowers, fruit, 9½″ 365.00

Vase, emerald green fish scales, white & red stemmed roses, 7½″ 290.00

Vase, mica flecks in rust background, with bird and flowering wisteria branch, 15″, $500.00.

Vase, round & fan reserves, birds, flowers, light blue, 1880, 9½" 375.00

Vase, tree bark, flowers, butterfly, porcelain body, Japan, 5" 275.00

Vase, yellow, blue irises, 3¾" 250.00

Vase, 4 panels, goldstone, many colors, Japan, 6" . 175.00

Clothing and Accessories

Here's one collection you can enjoy by wearing, and many do! Victorian whites, vintage furs, sequined gowns, designer fashions -- whatever look you prefer is yours, at only a fraction of today's prices for modern copies. Alterations are possible, but unless done with tenderness and care may lessen the value. Fabrics may have become more delicate over the years, so very gentle cleaning methods are a must. Accessories are fun and hats, fur boas, belts, and shoes from the era of your outfit finish it off with a smashing authenticity.

Apron, appliqued sunbonnet ladies, embroidered 15.00

Bathing suit, man's, wool, 1920s 20.00

Bed jacket, turquoise, sheer silk chiffon, lace under yokes 25.00

Billfold, brown alligator ... 22.00

Bloomers, gym type, black . 18.00

Blouse, eggshell silk, cut work, hand embroidery . 40.00

Blouse, white embroidered, batiste, middy collar ... 25.00

Bodice, high collar, black lace, sequins, heavy beading, white lining 30.00

Bonnet, infant's, fine lace . 10.00

Bonnet, straw, braid trim, black with purple ribbon . 35.00

Bonnet, taffetta, lined, padded & layered, Godey type 35.00

Boudoir gown, chiffon & black lace, 1930s 40.00

Bunting, baby's, separate hood, pink satin, 1890s . 28.00

Caftan, silver & gold ornate embroidery, old Moroccan velvet 450.00

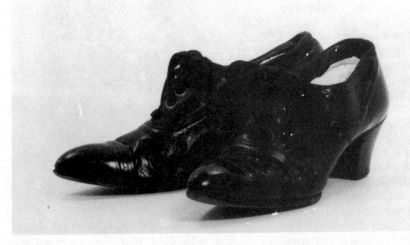

Day shoes, black leather lace-ups, early 1900s, $35.00.

94

Victorian brown taffeta dress, ca. 1865, two pieces, full skirt with train, velvet panel and hem, $100.00.

Camisole, batiste, button front, tucked, embroidered flowers	35.00
Cape, black velvet, long, 1930s	45.00
Cape, silk, bone buttons, braid trim, pointed collar, lined	15.00
Cardigan, orlon, pearls on front & collar, sequins, 1950s	25.00
Chemise, embroidered, white, 1900s	18.00
Cloak, flapper style, Dolman sleeves, silk velvet, marabou	200.00
Coat, evening; white knit, floor length, Woolf Brothers	75.00
Corset cover, pink knit, original label	7.00
Drawers, muslin, split, drawstring, embroidered ruffle on each leg	7.50
Dress, baby's, crocheted yoke & sleeve edge, dimity	15.00

Dress, bias lace, 3 piece, floor length, 1930s	75.00
Dress, chiffon with lace collar, floating panels, 1920s	60.00
Dress, flapper, low pleats, georgette with allover beading	85.00
Dress, wedding; blue wool, 3 piece, Amish	40.00
Dress, white, off-shoulder style, mid-1800s	50.00
Duster, auto	25.00
Duster, auto, child's, removable Bertha collar	55.00
Evening gown, crepe-back satin, rose, cranberry Harlequin effect	35.00
Fur boa, red fox	28.00
Fur coat, lady's, raccoon, 1930s	200.00
Fur collar, mink, 1930	30.00
Fur collar, silver fox	22.00
Fur scarf, brown fox	30.00
Gloves, knit, 1950s	2.50

Victorian blue silk dress, ca. 1895, two pieces, cobalt with white floral print, ribbed hem with train, leg-o'-mutton sleeves, $90.00.

95

Gloves, leather, rhinestones . 28.00
Hat, beret, straw, pink 8.00
Hat, black & purple velvet,
   black plumes, 1918 . . . . . 35.00
Jacket, smoking; silk lined,
   frog trim, black brocade . 36.50
Kimono, rayon, floral print,
   gold sleeve bands, 1920s . 20.00
Nightgown, peach satin, ecru
   lace, 1930s 22.00
Pajamas, satin, striped, fring-
   ed sash, 1930s 12.00
Pantaloons, eyelet trim, white
   cotton 14.00
Parasol, child's, bamboo &
   pink ruffled paper 10.00
Petticoat, cotton with open
   weave, embroidered,
   scalloped hem 20.00
Shawl, embroidered, extra
   long fringe, heavy, large . 85.00
Shoes, evening sandals, hand-
   lasted, silver, 1930s 16.00
Shoes, lady's, ties, brown
   leather, circa 1935 . . . . . 38.00
Slip, rayon, simple, long . . . 10.00
Teddy, crepe, satin straps,
   lace trim 15.00
Underpants, tucked, button-
   on, Hamburg lace trim . 7.50

Coca-Cola

Since it was established in 1891,
the Coca-Cola Company has issued a
wide and varied scope of advertising
memorabilia, creating what may well
be the most popular field of specific
product-related collectibles on today's
market. Probably their best known
item is the rectangular Coke tray,
issued since 1910. In excellent condition, some of the earlier examples may
bring prices of up to $500.00. Before
1910, trays were round or oval. The
1908 'Topless' tray is valued at around
$1,000.00. Most Coca-Cola buffs prefer
to limit their collections to items made
before 1970.

Bank, bottle vendor 95.00
Bank, vending machine that
   dispenses actual drink, late
   1950s 91.00
Blotter, 3 girls holding bottles,
   How About A Coke, 1944,
   NM 3.50
Blotter, 50th Anniversary,
   bottle center, 1936, M . . 36.50
Booklet, Truth About Coca-
   Cola, 1912 . . . . 19.50
Bottle, Christmas 1923, hob-
   ble skirt 5.00
Bottle opener, hand-held, iron 8.00
Calendar, girl with fox stole,
   1926 . . . . 250.00
Calendar, girl with skis, 1947 . 40.00
Calendar, Rockwell, boy
   fishing, 1935 . . . . 200.00
Calendar, Rockwell, boy with
   dog & bucket, 1932 . . . . 200.00

Sign, tin litho, 12″ x 31″, very fine condition, $70.00.

Left to right: tray, 1942, two girls and a car, excellent condition, $45.00; tray, 1941, ice skating girl, very fine condition, $50.00.

Calendar, 2 months on page, complete, 1950, M 28.00
Change purse, leather, Coke . 30.00
Cigar band, oval medallion with bottle, scroll decor, paper, M 56.00
Clock, dated 1953 .... 65.50
Clock, red & maroon, 18″ diameter 46.50
Cuff links, celluloid, Coca-Cola written out, pair, 1920s, NM 26.50
First day cover, Detroit, hand with bottle, 1939, NM .. 8.50
Matchbox, Yesteryear Model T, no box, M 47.50
Mini 6-pack with bottles, 1950, M 32.00
Pencil box, with ruler, eraser & pens, 1930s 29.00
Playing cards, girl holding bottle & card, 1961, MIB . 16.50
Playing cards, telephone operator, 1943, MIB 32.00
Pocket knife, Coca-Cola, 5¢ . 22.50
Postcard, Atlanta Bottling Plant with 5 scenes, 1920s, NM 75.00
Postcard, International delivery truck in color, 1930s, M 21.00
Safety lock, in original box, 1930 .... 20.00
Score keeper, Drink...Relieves Fatigue, 1906, EX 37.50

Sign, fishtail design, tin, 23x14″ 36.00
Sign, Victorian lady, plummage, small, 1911 ...... 56.50
Thermometer, Drink Coca-Cola in Bottles, 12″ diameter 27.50
Tip tray, girl holding glass looks over shoulder, oval, 1917, EX 91.00
Tray, Betty, rectangular, 1914, VG 66.00
Tray, birdhouse, rectangular, 1957, EX 46.50
Tray, flower cart, rectangular, 1958, NM 28.00
Tray, girl drinks with straw from bottle, rectangular, 1927, NM 100.00
Tray, girl holding bottle, rectangular, 1930, EX 105.00
Tray, girl in beret-type hat, rectangular, 1921, EX .. 237.00
Tray, girl looking over shoulder, rectangular, 1917, EX 100.00
Tray, girl sitting on diving board, rectangular, 1939, EX 41.00
Tray, girl talks to girl in convertible, rectangular, 1942, EX 45.00
Tray, girl with bottle, rectangular, 1948, NM 37.00

Sign, tin litho, bottle marked Pat'd Dec. 25, 1923, American Art Works, Inc., Coshocton, Ohio, 1936, 19″ x 27″, very fine condition, $135.00.

Tray, Hamilton King, girl with hat, rectangular, 1910, EX 325.00

Tray, Nordica with glass, oval, 1904, G 210.00

Tray, Rockwell scene of boy & dog, rectangular, 1931, M . 250.00

Tray, Santa at fireplace, rectangular, 1970, NM 28.00

Tray, seated girl with brimmed hat holds bottle, oblong, 1938 .... 40.00

Tray, table with sandwiches & bottles, rectangular, 1957, M 75.00

Water bottle, sailing ship .. 46.50

Yo-Yo, Coca-Cola 25.00

Coffee Grinders

In the days before packaged ground coffee was available, coffee beans were either ground at the local grocery or in the home. Now gone the way of the pickle barrel and Grandma's washboard, they are collected by those to whom visions of warm kitchens, rocking chairs, fresh baked bread, and the wonderful aroma of fresh ground coffee are treasures worth preserving.

Arcade #25, with glass jar & original top, M 75.00

Challenge Fast, table model . 67.50

Crystal, wall mount, glass jar 40.00

Crystal #3, cast iron base, 18″ 60.00

Daisy, miniature table model . 75.00

Delmew Coffee Mills, Simons Hardware, St Louis, wood 60.00

Elma, tin with bottom drawer 50.00

Everett, hand-held, 1890 .. 24.00

Favorite Mill Arcade Manufacturing Company, iron, ornate, table model . 75.00

Garant-Sewaarborge, Rock Hard, maple, spring-clipped drawer 25.00

Wilson's Improved Pat. Coffee Grinder, mounts on post, adjustable screw for various grinds, brass front plate, 6″ x 8″, $52.50.

Golden Rule	195.00
Grand Union Tea Company, red	85.00
Hobart, electric, aluminum hopper	150.00
Imperial, lap type, oak, cast iron top	70.00
Maple, dovetailed, with handle, tin tray & spout ...	55.00
Parker #60, tin & iron, mounted on wood	55.00
Peugeot Freres, wood, brass top, 8″	25.00
Swift Mill, Lane Brothers #13, commercial, patent 1885, 11″ wheels	40.00
Table top, with glass bean bin	30.00
Universal #110, tin with red decal	65.00
Wood & cast iron, open bowl, grooved construction, 5x7½x7¾″	80.00

Collector Plates

Two of the most well known manufacturers of collector plates are Bing and Grondahl, who issued the first of their famous Christmas plates in 1895, and the Royal Copenhagen Porcelain Manufactory whose first plate was released in 1908. In 1965 the Frankoma Pottery began production of plates with various themes, and since then have been joined in the field by well over one hundred manufacturers and marketing companies. As a general rule, first edition plates from a series appreciate in value more than those that follow, and are considered the best investment.

America the Beautiful, Monument Valley, 1972	40.00
America the Beautiful, US Capitol, 1969	40.00
American Commemorative, Southern Landmarks, Beauvoir, 1974	89.00

Bing and Grondahl, 1965, Bringing Home the Tree, $60.00.

American Commemorative, Southern Landmarks, Oak Hill, 1975	70.00
American Express, Four Freedoms/Rockwell, Freedom from Fear, 1976 .	38.00
American Express, Four Freedoms/Rockwell, Freedom of Worship, 1976	38.00
American Historical, Aviation, Amelia Earhart, 1972	58.00
American Historical, Bicentennial, A New Dawn, 1972	60.00
American Historical, General Douglas MacArthur, 1976	30.00
American Rose Society, All-American Rose, Color Magic, 1978	75.00
American Rose Society, All-American Rose, Double Delight, 1977	94.00
American Rose Society, All-American Rose, Prominent, 1977	95.00
Anri, Father's Day, Alpine Father & Children, 1974 .	85.00
Anri, Ferrandiz Birthday, Girl, 1973	150.00
Anri, Mother's Day, Alpine Mother & Children, 1972 .	50.00

Anri, Wedding, Wedding Scene, 1973 .... 90.00

Artists of the World, DeGrazia, Beautiful Burden, 1981 .... 170.00

Artists of the World, DeGrazia, Wondering, 1982 .... 140.00

Artists of the World, Don Ruffin, Child of the Pueblo, 1978 .... 78.00

Artists of the World, Don Ruffin, Colima Madonna, 1979 50.00

Artists of the World, Don Ruffin, Navajo Lullaby, 1976 . 88.00

Artists of the World, Larry Toschik, Mallards, Whistling In, 1971 .... 80.00

Bareuther, Christmas, Christkindlemarkt, 1969 . 26.00

Bareuther, Christmas, Kapplkirche, 1968 .... 36.00

Bareuther, Father's Day, Castle Pfalz, 1970 .... 18.50

Bareuther, Father's Day, Wurzburg Castle, 1974 . 38.50

Bareuther, Mother's Day, Mother & Children, 1971 . 20.00

Bareuther, Thanksgiving, First Thanksgiving, 1971 . 32.00

Belleek, Christmas, Celtic Cross, 1971 .... 52.00

Belleek, Irish Wildlife, A Leaping Salmon, 1978 .. 69.00

Belleek, Irish Wildlife, Hedgehog, 1980 .... 69.00

Bing and Grondahl, Christmas, Bringing Home the Tree, 1965 .... 60.00

Bing and Grondahl, Christmas, Churchgoers, 1926 . 82.00

Bing and Grondahl, Christmas, Frederiksberg Hill, 1904 .... 143.50

Bing and Grondahl, Christmas, Royal Guard, Amalienborg, 1936 ..... 90.00

Bing and Grondahl, Christmas, St Petri Church, 1908 .... 96.00

Bing and Grondahl, Christmas, Watchman, 1948 .. 90.00

Bing and Grondahl, Easter Plaque, 1912 .... 91.00

Bing and Grondahl, Easter Plaque, 1920 .... 75.00

Bing and Grondahl, Jubilee, Amalienborg Castle, 1970 . 35.00

Bing and Grondahl, Jubilee, Yule Tree, 1980 .... 60.00

Dave Grossman Designs, Margaret Keane, Bedtime, 1978 .... 25.00

Dave Grossman Designs, Margaret Keane, My Kitty, 1977 .... 30.00

Franklin Mint, Crystal; Crystal Annual, Snowflake, 1977 .... 200.00

Franklin Mint, Crystal; Rockwell Christmas, The Carolers, 1972 .... 166.00

Franklin Mint, Porcelain; Mark Twain, Stealing a Kiss, 1977 .... 46.50

Franklin Mint, Porcelain; Mark Twain, Trading Lives, 1977 .... 41.50

Franklin Mint, Porcelain; Mark Twain, Traveling the River, 1977 .... 44.00

Rosenthal, 1956, Christmas in the Alps, $180.00.

Goebel, Goebel Mother's
Series, Cats, 1976 ...... 45.00
Goebel, Goebel Wildlife Series,
Blue Titmouse, 1975 ... 46.00
Goebel, Goebel Wildlife Series,
Robin, 1974 .... 61.50
Goebel, Hummel Anniversary,
Hear Ye, 1972 .... 91.00
Goebel, Hummel Annual,
Singing Lesson, 1979 ... 71.00
Goebel, Hummel Annual, Um-
brella Boy, 1981 .... 100.00
Gorham, Boy Scout Plates,
Rockwell, A Good Sign,
1977 .... 32.50
Gorham, China Bicentennial,
1776 Bicentennial, 1976 . 32.50
Gorham, Christmas, Rock-
well, Good Deeds, 1975 . 65.00
Gorham, Christmas, Rock-
well, Tiny Tim, 1974 ... 72.00
Gorham, Moppets Christmas,
Bringing Home the Tree,
1975 .... 15.00
Gorham, Pewter Bicentennial,
Burning of Gaspee, 1971 . 36.50
Gorham, Presidential, Rock-
well, Eisenhower, 1976 .. 34.00
Gorham, Presidential, Rock-
well, Kennedy, 1976 .... 54.00
Haviland-Parlon, Christmas
Madonnas, Bellini, 1977 . 48.00
Haviland-Parlon, Tapestry I,
Start of the Hunt, 1972 . 74.50
Haviland-Parlon, Tapestry I,
Unicorn Surrounded, 1975 70.50
Knowles, Gone with the Wind
Collection, Ashley, 1979 . 126.50
Reco, World of Children, John
McClelland, When I Grow
Up, 1978 .... 81.50
Reco, World of Children, John
McClelland, You're In-
vited, 1979 .... 75.00
Reed & Barton, Audubon,
Red-Shouldered Hawk,
1971 .... 75.50
Rockwell Society, Christmas,
Golden Christmas, 1976 . 56.50

Rosenthal, Christmas,
Christmas Eve, 1954 ... 195.00
Rosenthal, Christmas, Nurn-
berg Angel, 1936 ...... 196.50
Royal Bayreuth, Christmas,
Snow Scene, 1973 ...... 22.50
Royal Bayreuth, Mother's
Day, Consolation, 1973 . 50.00
Royal Copenhagen, Christ-
mas, Fetching the Tree,
1964 .... 90.00
Royal Copenhagen, Christ-
mas, Hermitage Castle,
1934 .... 125.00
Royal Copenhagen, Christ-
mas, Our Saviour's Church,
1917 .... 96.50
Royal Copenhagen, Christ-
mas, The Last Umiak,
1968 .... 34.50
Royal Devon, Christmas,
Rockwell, Downhill Daring,
1975 .... 76.50
Royal Devon, Christmas,
Rockwell, One Present Too
Many, 1979 .... 32.00
Royal Devon, Christmas,
Rockwell, Puppets for
Christmas, 1978 .... 34.50
Royal Devon, Christmas,
Rockwell, The Christmas
Gift, 1976 .... 53.50
Royal Devon, Mother's Day,
Rockwell, Mother's Treat,
1980 .... 33.00
Royal Doulton, Commedia Del
Arte, LeRoy Neiman, Pier-
rot, 1976 .... 91.50
Royal Doulton, Mother's Day,
Edna Hibel, Kathleen &
Child, 1978 .... 86.00
Royal Doulton, Portraits of
Innocence, Masseria,
Adrien, 1981 .... 121.50
Schmid, B Hummel Christ-
mas, Angel, 1971 ...... 72.50
Schmid, B Hummel Christ-
mas, Angel with Fire,
1972 .... 38.50

Schmid, B Hummel Christmas, Sacred Journey, 1976 .... 51.50

Schmid, B Hummel Mother's Day, Bumblebee, 1974 .. 36.50

Schmid, B Hummel Mother's Day, Little Fisherman, 1973 .... 75.00

Schmid, Disney Christmas, Caroling, 1975 .... 20.00

Schmid, Disney Special, Happy Birthday Pinocchio, 1980 .... 18.00

Schmid, Peanuts Christmas, Christmas at Fireplace, 1974 .... 51.50

Schmid, Peanuts Mother's Day, Mom?, 1973 ...... 21.50

Schmid, Raggedy Ann Christmas, Decorating the Tree, 1977 .... 13.50

Schmid, Raggedy Ann Christmas, Raggedy Ann Skates, 1976 .... 23.50

Veneto Flair, Birds, Mallard, 1974 .... 62.50

Veneto Flair, Christmas, Christ Child, 1973 ..... 56.50

Veneto Flair, Christmas, Shepherds, 1972 .... 91.00

Comic Books

The 'Golden Age' is a term referring to the period from 1930 until 1950, during which today's most prized comic books were published. First editions or those that feature the first appearance of a popular character are the most valuable, and may bring prices of several hundred dollars -- some even more. Action #1, Superman's first, published in 1938 is worth $2,000.00 in excellent condition! Most early comics, however, are valued at less than $5.00 to $30.00. Remember, rarity, age, condition, and quality of the art work are factors to consider when determining value.

Airboy, Vol 9, #4, EX 5.00
All-American, #34, G 26.00
All-American, #60, Green Lantern, VG 28.00
Amazing Spider-Man, #13, NM 38.00
Amazing Spider-Man, #3, origin of Dr Octopus, EX . 82.00
Amazing Spider-Man, #4, by Ditko, EX 146.00
Amazing-Man, #24, VG ... 70.00
Avengers, #3, EX 49.00
Avengers, #7, NM 33.00
Batman, #87, VG 18.00
Best of Uncle Scrooge & Donald Duck, #1, Barks art, G 8.00
Beware, #10, Frazetta cover, EX 60.00
Big Chief Wahoo, #1, EX .. 40.00
Bill Barnes, #5, VG 13.00
Black Terror, #25, EX 18.00
Blondie, Feature B #47, EX . 8.00
Blue Beetle, #22, EX 14.00
Captain America, #20, EX . 120.00
Captain America, #30, NM . 85.00
Captain Marvel, #15, ... 28.00
Captain Marvel, #43, 1st appearance of Uncle Marvel, EX 26.00
Captain Marvel Junior, #18, VG 11.00
Conan King-Size, Barry Smith, NM 2.00
Creatures on the Loose, #10, 1st King Kull story by Wrightson, M 5.00
Crime Does Not Pay, #41, VG 10.00
Daredevil, #35, EX 11.00
Daredevil King-Size, #1, M . 4.00
Detective, #196, NM 30.00
Detective, #50, VG 70.00
Dick Tracy, #5, Dell, EX .. 21.00
Dickie Dare, #4, EX 15.00
Donald Duck, FC #223, VG . 60.00
Donald Duck, FC #263, G . 11.00
Famous Funnies, #214, Buck Rogers, Dickie Dare, M . 72.00
Famous Funnies, #41, NM . 19.00

Fantastic Four, #7, NM ... 79.00
Frontline Combat, #3, VG . 21.00
Green Hornet, #5 .... 41.00
Impact, #5, VG 10.00
Jingle Jangle, #6, G 2.00
Joe Palooka, #11, VG 8.00
Joker, #5, Wolverton, EX . 48.00
Journey into Mystery, #94,
EX 29.00
Krazy, #14, EX 4.00
Mad, #2, VG 33.00
Mad, #23, NM 31.00
Marvel Family, #74, EX ... 10.00
Mary Marvel, #17, EX 11.00
Mickey Mouse, FC #214, NM 10.00
Mickey Mouse, FC #261, VG . 15.00
Mystery Men, #31, VG 12.00
Our Gang, #24, VG 13.00
Phantom, #44, NM 13.00
Planet, #36, Lost World by In-
gels 44.00
Plastic Man, #5, by Jack Cole,
VG 27.00
Plastic Man, #62, VG 15.00
Pogo, #11, VG 12.00
Rangers, #15, G 5.00
Sensation, #32, Wonder
Woman, EX 35.00
Sheena, #9, G 14.00
Shock Suspenstories, #17, VG 14.00
Silver Streak, #23, EX 14.00
Skyrocket, #1, G 7.00
Sparkler, #3, VG 15.00
Speed, #2, Shock Gibson, VG 28.00
Spirit Sunday Sections,
Eisner art, EX 35.00
Sub-Mariner, #20, NM 69.00
Super Duck, #1, EX 22.00
Superman, #19, G 43.00
Superman, #19, VG 61.00
Superman, #49, VG 36.00
Superman, #91, VG 23.00
Target, Vol 3, #1, NM 75.00
Tarzan, #8, Dell, EX 22.00
The Funnies, #55, NM 39.00
Thrilling, #59, Ingels, VG . 8.00
Tillie the Toiler, FC #15, G . 5.00
Tip Top, #105, VG 7.00
Uncle Scrooge, #456, G 8.00

Weird, #6, EX 61.00
Weird Science, #11, EX ... 33.00
Whiz, #38, EX 29.00
Wings, #29, VG 19.00
Wonder Woman, #16, EX . 28.00
Wonderworld, #17, VG 22.00
World's Finest, #3, spine worn 96.00
Wow, #48, NM 10.00
2-Fisted Tales, #38, EX ... 17.00

Cookie Jars

The Nelson McCoy Pottery Co., Robinson Ransbottom Pottery Co., and the American Bisque Pottery Co., are three of the largest producers of cookie jars in the country. Many firms made them to a lesser extent. Today, cookie jars are one of the most popular of modern collectibles. Figural jars are the most common, made in an endless variety of designs. Early jars from the 1920s and '30s were often decorated in 'cold paint' over the glaze. This type of color is easily removed -- take care that you use very gentle cleaning methods. A damp cloth and a light touch is the safest approach.

Barrel, brown, 'Cookie Barrel'
on front, American Bisque,
USA 12.00
Bear with Cookie, Royalware 18.00
Bo-Peep, wears blue & white
hat, long braids, Napco . 13.00
Cheerleaders, megaphone
finial, Have A Cookie,
American Bisque 38.00
Churn, American Bisque .. 10.00
Clock, red & black trim,
Cookie Time, American
Bisque, unmarked 18.00
Clown, holding blackboard,
Don't Forget, American
Bisque, marked USA ... 20.00
Collegiate Owl, holds book
marked 'Cookies', Ameri-
can Bisque 22.00

Popeye, corncob pipe in mouth, $150.00.

Clown Bust, Brush McCoy Pottery Company, 1970, $25.00.

Cow, sitting with milk can between front legs, Doranne of California 25.00

Cup, lid is hot chocolate with marshmallows, American Bisque 14.00

Davy Crockett head, hat is lid, Regal China 58.00

Donald Duck & J Carioca, turn- about, marked Walt Disney USA 50.00

Duck, sitting with basket of corn between feet, Doranne of California 25.00

Elephant, standing on hind legs, green scarf at neck, unmarked 25.00

Elf Bakery Tree Stump, brown, elf in window, elf finial, Twin Winton 14.00

Fire Hydrant, red, Doranne of California 25.00

Granny, apron with black flowers, American Bisque, marked USA 25.00

Humpty-Dumpty, yellow pants, blue jacket, vest, Maddux of California ... 25.00

Igloo, with yellow & black door, figural seal lid, marked USA 30.00

Kittens, in old fashioned shoe, yellow, Maurice of California USA 15.00

Lion, red scarf around neck, licking his lips, Belmont . 22.00

Moon, ball shaped, with large cow finial, yellow & black, Doranne 35.00

Mouse, in sailor suit, brown with light blue trim, Twin Winton 25.00

Noah's Ark, Twin Winton . 17.00

Old Fashioned Telephone, wall type, black & white, Sierra Vista 25.00

Pelican, brown, with baby pelican on lid, unmarked California Original...... 15.00

Pig Chef, standing behind stove, wearing chef hat . 12.00

Poodle, sitting, blue bow at neck, American Bisque, marked USA 25.00

Red Riding Hood, Pottery Guild of America 35.00

Schoolhouse, elves in windows, red roof lid, California Originals 17.00

Snow White, dwarfs in circle around base, Walt Disney Productions 18.00

Soldier, standing in red & white striped doorway, American Bisque 25.00

Soldier, World War II, green uniform, Robinson Ransbottom 40.00

Tomato, red with green stem finial, Pantry Parade Co . 12.00

Left to right, chipmunk, $38.00; Coalby Cat, $28.00; puppy, $38.00; all manufactured by McCoy.

Turkey, with baby turkey
finial, unmarked Morton
Pottery 45.00
Winnie the Pooh, sitting with
blue honey pot between
legs, WDP 42.00
Yarn Doll, yellow long curls,
unmarked American Bis-
que 30.00
Yogi Bear, sign says 'Better
Than Average Cookies',
Hanna Barbera 30.00

Copper

Early copper items are popular
with those who enjoy primitives, and
occasionally fine examples can still be
found at flea markets. Check construction to help you determine the age of
your piece. Dovetailed joints indicate
18th century work; handmade seamed
items are usually from the 19th century. Tea kettles and small stills are
especially collectible.

Bedwarmer, wrought iron
handle, early 80.00
Bowl, hammered, old,
3½x12″ diameter 60.00
Chafing dish, strap knob
finial, 3 bronze rabbits form
holder 450.00
Footwarmer, Norway, dated
1818 on top, EX 135.00
Hand mirror, hammered, long
handle, signed, Arts &
Crafts 125.00
Haystack, measure; dovetailed, 1 gallon, Woods & Sons,
12″ 155.00
Kettle, no handles, rivets
down side, brass handle on
lid, 13x13″ 115.00
Kettle, polished, 22″ diameter 165.00
Ladle, hand forged hooked rat-
tail iron handle, circa 1800,
21″ 150.00
Pan, forged iron handle 12½″
long, mid-1800s, 5½x10″ . 110.00

Measures, copper with tin lining, 19th
century, $35.00 to $50.00.

Porringer, Balwin, English,
late 1700s, EX 125.00
Sauce pan, dovetailed construction, dated 1808, 19″
diameter 130.00
Still, with accessories, 4 feet . 650.00
Tea kettle, swing handle,
dovetailed, hammered, F
Wickman, 14″ 250.00
Tea kettle, swivel strap handle, dovetailed, 5″ recessed
base, 1850s 200.00
Teapot, delicate handle shape,
circular raised top with
finial, 1760s 140.00
Tray, round with handles,
hand wrought, G Stickley,
16″ 240.00
Vessel, applied handle, rolled
edge, burnished, signed,
1700s, 9½″ 130.00
Wash boiler, tin lid,
12x23x12½″ 50.00

Copper Lustre

Small pitchers and bowls in the
copper lustre glaze made by many of
the Staffordshire potteries in the
1800s are still very much in evidence
at even the smaller flea markets. They
may be had for around $30.00 to

Left to right: milk pitcher, white with swirling bands of cobalt and white alternating with iron red leaves, 10″, $70.00; Mug, beige with peach, yellow and green florals, beaded rim, $50.00; fruit bowl, turquoise band with pine trees, building and birds, 6½″, $50.00; creamer, floral band in yellow, 3½″, $30.00; creamer, turquoise with rose in relief, 4″, $40.00.

$50.00 in excellent condition, often even for less. Larger items are harder to find, and depending on the type of decoration may bring prices of $100.00 or more. Hand painted scenes and those with historical transfers are the most valuable.

Beaker, blue band, applied
   floral band, multicolor
   enameling, 3¼″ 45.00
Bowl, blue band, relief figures,
   footed, 2½x4½″ 30.00
Chalice, floral polychromed
   relief, blue band, 4″ 30.00
Creamer, embossed copper
   foliage, white band, blue
   stripes, 6¾″ 45.00
Creamer, green bands with
   florals, 4½″ 45.00
Goblet, peach color band, 2
   white reserves with enamel
   flowers 45.00
Master salt, lustre foliage,
   putty colored band, footed,
   2″ 45.00

Pitcher, coaching scene,
   Gray's Pottery, 2¼″ 12.00
Pitcher, rust band, embossed
   multicolor cherubs, ram,
   6¾″ 30.00
Pitcher, white reserves with
   people, canary lustre band,
   5″ 65.00

Coverlets

After the introduction of the Jacquard loom in America in the 1820s, weavers began to make the elaborate florals, pictorials and medallion patterns that in years previous were so tediously handwoven that they were reserved just for the rich. Dark blue and natural or white were colors most often used, but red and green were used with white, or several colors were used in combination. They were sometimes signed and dated in one corner; the name was either that of the weaver or the owner-to-be. Condition is very important; those with intricate patterns, dates, and signatures are most valuable.

Angels in spandrels, one piece single weave jacquard; red, green, blue, purple, lavender and white, some wear, 76" x 78", $300.00.

Bird & courthouse border, jacquard, 1860s, 80x84" ... 325.00
Child's, large leaf reserve, with geometric star, 1850 .... 200.00
Chintz, peacocks & roses, multicolor, knotted, 76x78" 300.00

Simple medallions, two piece double weave jacquard, blue and white, signed and dated, stains and wear, 72" x 82", $165.00.

Eagles, blue & white, signed, 1888 .... 765.00
Five patch squares, red, blue & white, 2 piece, 72x80" . 275.00
Floral border, central medallion, signed, 1 piece double weave 225.00
Goose Eye Twill, navy, light blue & red plaid, early, 80x84" 175.00
Hand woven, Dekalb County Indiana, 1859 .... 150.00
Hand woven, red, green & pink plaid, with fringe, 1870s, EX 300.00
Independence Hall, eagles, some wear, 1829 .... 400.00
Linear arrangement of floral medallions, 4 colors, worn, 1876 .... 115.00
Mirror image name border, 2 piece, blue & white, 83x90" 550.00
Overshot weave, green, gold, red, some wear, 1840s, 76x72" 175.00
Overshot weave, 2 piece, blue & white, 70x94" 135.00
Repeating device of 4 roses, mirror image bird border, 2 piece 250.00
Rose medallion, blue & white urns border, signed & dated corners, 1855 .... 325.00
Snowflake & pine tree, red, blue & white, double weave, 1820, 79x76" 200.00
Strawberry medallion, signed, dated corners, vintage & bird borders 275.00
Summer-Winter, blue & white eagles, signed, 1887 .... 750.00
Sunburst & Lily, with bird border, red, blue, green & beige 850.00
Tulip medallions, vining tulip border, 1852, 70x84" ... 350.00
4 rose & 4 thistle medallions, red, green, blue & white, 2 piece 425.00

Floral medallion, two piece single weave jacquard; red, green, blue and white; two signatures and date, 80" x 92", $395.00.

Cracker Jacks

The sugar coated popcorn confection created by the Ruekeim brothers in 1893 has continued to the present day to delight boys and girls with its crunchy goodness, and each 'toy inside every box' since 1916 has become a prized adult treasure. More than 10,000 different prizes have been distributed. The older ones, depending on scarcity, are usually worth in the $6.00 to $30.00 range, though some (the 2½" cast iron horse and wagon, for example) may fetch as high as $75.00. Early advertising and packages are also collectible.

Angelus truck, tin, ad on each side, CJ, 1½"	28.00
Book, drawing; paper, CJ	40.00
Bookmark, bulldog, paper, CJ	9.25
Books, miniature, Jackie's Friends, paper, CJ, each	38.00
CJ Band, gold or silver, tin, Hummer, 1¾" diameter	34.00

Dollhouse items, lantern, tray, mug, candle, cast metal, no mark	12.00
Fobs, alphabet letter, plastic, CJ	5.00
Horse & wagon, tin	15.00
Lunch box, tin	14.00
Model T Ford, New York, 1916, #999, tin, B&W, CJ, 2"	58.00
Pocket watch, silver & gold, tin, CJ, 1½"	32.00
Postcard, bear series, paper, 1907, CJ, each	14.00
Railroad train, engine & cars, plastic, 3-D, CJ, about 2"	9.50
Riddle cards, paper, CJ, series of 20	12.00
Spinner, with string & paper, rectangle, CJ	22.00
Sulky, tin, 2 wheels, 5" with stick, CJ	10.00
Tootsie Toy series, boats, cars, animals, cast metal, 1" to 3", CJ	8.25
Whistle, tin, 'lifesaver', CJ, 1¼" diameter	42.00

Box, red and blue lithograph on white cardboard, seventeen toys pictured on side, empty, 6½" x 2¾", $25.00.

Cruets

Used to serve vinegar, cruets were made during the 1800s through the early twentieth century in virtually every type of plain and art glass available. Nearly every early American pressed glass tableware line contained at least one style. Nice examples are still relatively easy to find, though some of the scarce art glass cruets are often valued at well over one hundred dollars.

Pigeon Blood, clear stopper and handle, 8½″, $195.00.

Alabama, with original stopper	55.00
Ashburton with Sawtooth, applied handle, no stopper	30.00
Beaded Grape, green, with original stopper	95.00
Block, with original stopper	20.00
Block & Fan, with original stopper	23.00
Block with Stars, with original stopper	16.00
Chrysanthemum Leaf, with faceted stopper	32.50
Cut Log, with original stopper, 5½″	45.00
Daisy & Button, blue paneled, with clear stopper	49.00
Daisy & Button with Crossbars, clear, with original stopper	28.00
Diamond Ridge, Duncan, clear, with original stopper	65.00
Flora, green with gilt trim, stopper not original	87.50
Forget-Me-Not, milk glass, with original stopper	55.00
Herringbone, blown, blue opalescent, with clear stopper	85.00
Hobnail, blue, old, with clear stopper	110.00
Hobnail with Bars, blue, with clear stopper	75.00
Inverted Thumbprint, blue, with blown clear stopper	95.00
Log & Star, amber, with original stopper	35.00
Peacock & Feather, with original stopper	25.00
Ribbed Thumbprint, green, with clear stopper	95.00
Star in Bull's Eye, with original stopper	20.00
Swirl, with original stopper	25.00
Teepee, (not Wigwam), with original stopper	35.00
Twist Oceanic, Sahara, Heisey, with original stopper	85.00

Cup Plates

It was the custom in the early 1800s to pour hot beverages into a deep saucer to cool. The cup plate was used under the cup in the same manner as we use coasters today. While

Sandwich was the largest manufacturer, mid-western glasshouses also made many styles. Condition is always an important factor, but because of the lacy nature of the patterns, it is common to find minor edge chips. Occasionally you may find an example where the mold did not completely fill out -- this was due to the primitive manufacturing methods used and the intricacy of the designs.

Collectors identify their cup plates by code numbers suggested in *American Glass Cup Plates* by Ruth Webb Lee and James A. Rose, a standard reference.

Lee & Rose 100-A	35.00
Lee & Rose 108, clear, rim chips, 3¾"	25.00
Lee & Rose 109	14.00
Lee & Rose 129, rim chips .	18.00
Lee & Rose 154-A, 3¼" . . .	27.50

Lee & Rose 172-B	20.00
Lee & Rose 176-A, 3¼" . . .	22.00
Lee & Rose 178-B, green tint .	24.00
Lee & Rose 187, rare	80.00
Lee & Rose 209, 3"	20.00
Lee & Rose 243, 3½"	22.50
Lee & Rose 25, rim flakes, 3½"	17.50
Lee & Rose 255	25.00
Lee & Rose 272, light opalescent, 43 scallops, 3½" . .	45.00
Lee & Rose 281-B, clear, 3" .	5.00
Lee & Rose 29, 1 scallop underfilled	26.00
Lee & Rose 313, green tint, rare	85.00
Lee & Rose 324	12.00
Lee & Rose 324, fiery opalescent	55.00
Lee & Rose 333	12.00
Lee & Rose 38, plume border, etc	35.00
Lee & Rose 41, clear, 3¼" .	27.00

Examples of cup plate designs, for specific examples and values, see the following listings.

Lee & Rose 440, unlisted, 51 even scallops, opalescent . 125.00

Lee & Rose 440-B, clear, 2 hearts & arrow, 3½" ... 15.00

Lee & Rose 440-B, sweetheart, cobalt, scarce 175.00

Lee & Rose 458, clear, 12 hearts, small edge chips, 3½" 12.50

Lee & Rose 476 .... 16.00

Lee & Rose 502, deep amethyst, rim flakes ... 250.00

Lee & Rose 502, sunburst, apple green, 3" 60.00

Lee & Rose 522, red amber, slight roughage 175.00

Lee & Rose 563 .... 10.00

Lee & Rose 565-A, Henry Clay, 3¾" 50.00

Lee & Rose 565-B 22.00

Lee & Rose 565-B, Henry Clay, electric blue, rim chips, 3½" 65.00

Lee & Rose 593, cabin, scarce, 3¼" 32.50

Lee & Rose 605-A, octagonal with ship, 3½" 65.00

Lee & Rose 610-A, ship, rim flakes, 3⅝" 20.00

Lee & Rose 640 .... 14.00

Lee & Rose 655, eagle, rim flakes, rare, 3" 45.00

Lee & Rose 661, eagle, 1831, rim chips, 3½" 12.00

Lee & Rose 667-A, eagle, rim flakes, 3" 17.50

Lee & Rose 670, eagle, rim flakes, 3½" diameter ... 22.50

Lee & Rose 680, eagle, 44 scallops, 3" 20.00

Custard Glass

Northwood was the first American glass house to produce custard glass, a luminous creamy ivory ware containing uranium salts, the ingredient responsible for the characteristic fiery glow. It was used for souvenir items as well as full lines of pressed glass tableware. Heisey, Fenton, McKee and Tarentum also manufactured it.

Tumbler, Diamond with Peg, enameled rose and gold trim, 4", $58.00.

Apple & Fan, creamer, tankard, souvenir, ½ pint 64.00

Argonaut Shell, creamer, excellent gold & enamel ... 130.00

Argonaut Shell, fruit bowl, 5x10½" 125.00

Argonaut Shell, master berry bowl 200.00

Argonaut Shell, spooner ... 100.00

Argonaut Shell, water pitcher 325.00

Beaded Cable, rose bowl ... 90.00

Beaded Circle, creamer & sugar 175.00

Beaded Swag, bowl, 4½" .. 32.00

Beveled Diamond, butter with cover, ruby stain 100.00

Butterfly & Berry, vase, pink decor, 9" 50.00

Cherry & Scale, butter dish, nutmeg stain 212.00

Chrysanthemum Sprig, berry, blue, small 100.00

Chrysanthemum Sprig, bowl, oval, footed 110.00

Chrysanthemum Sprig, compote, blue 400.00

Chrysanthemum Sprig, creamer, blue 360.00

Chrysanthemum Sprig, cruet with original stopper ... 255.00

Chrysanthemum Sprig, jelly compote, excellent gold & enamel 94.00

Chrysanthemum Sprig, sugar with lid 150.00

Chrysanthemum Sprig, toothpick, blue 400.00

Chrysanthemum Sprig, tumbler, blue, gold trim . 205.00

Cut Block, individual sugar . 35.00

Delaware, pin tray, rose decor 60.00

Delaware, ring tray, excellent blue enamel, 4" 70.00

Delaware, tumbler, blue decor 62.00

Diamond with Peg, creamer, tankard style, 6" 80.00

Diamond with Peg, cup, red rose & gold 34.00

Diamond with Peg, mug, red rose & gold, 3" 51.00

Diamond with Peg, pitcher, souvenir, Gettysburg, 5½" 75.00

Doric Column, candlestick, Cambridge, pair 123.00

Everglades, spooner 145.00

Everglades, tumbler, gold rim, excellent gold & enamel . 111.00

Festoon, water pitcher, Northwood 55.00

Fluted Scrolls, master berry bowl, gold decor, footed . 100.00

Geneva, butter with cover, excellent decor 125.00

Geneva, jelly compote 75.00

Geneva, master berry bowl, red & green decor, round . 123.00

Geneva, sauce, footed 32.00

Geneva, spooner, red & green decor 64.00

Georgia Gem, berry set, master & 6 sauces, very good gold 180.00

Georgia Gem, butter with cover 112.00

Georgia Gem, cruet with original stopper, green .. 165.00

Georgia Gem, hair receiver, souvenir 50.00

Georgia Gem, sugar with lid . 70.00

Grape, dish, basketweave exterior, fluted rim, 7½" .. 55.00

Grape & Cable, sauce, nutmeg stain, on pedestal 45.00

Grape & Cable, water set, nutmeg stain, 6 piece ... 700.00

Grape & Gothic Arches, table setting, 4 piece 200.00

Grape & Gothic Arches, water pitcher, nutmeg stain ... 215.00

Heart with Thumbprint, wine, Tarentum 94.00

Honeycomb, wine 74.00

Intaglio, cruet, gold, green enamel 274.00

Intaglio, salt shaker, gold & green decor 85.00

Intaglio, spooner, gold & green trim	95.00
Inverted Fan & Feather, jelly compote	252.00
Inverted Fan & Feather, punch cup	250.00
Inverted Fan & Feather, salt shaker	125.00
Inverted Fan & Feather, spooner	108.00
Inverted Fan & Feather, tumbler, excellent decor	84.00
Jackson, master berry bowl	75.00
Jackson, pitcher, 5½"	70.00
Jackson, shakers, goofus decor, pair	125.00
Jefferson Optic, butter dish	138.00
Lotus & Grape, bon bon, pink stain, 2 handles	32.00
Louis XV, banana boat	152.00
Louis XV, master fruit bowl	147.00
Louis XV, sugar with lid	108.00
Louis XV, water pitcher	177.00
Louis XV, water set, excellent gold, 7 piece	550.00
Maple Leaf, spooner, good gold	84.00
Maple Leaf, sugar with lid	150.00
Maple Leaf, tumbler	90.00
Peacock & Dahlia, plate, green stain	97.00
Peacock & Urn, individual ice cream bowl, nutmeg stain	65.00
Peacock & Urn, master ice cream bowl, nutmeg decor	115.00
Punty Band, creamer, souvenir, Heisey	34.00
Ring Band, butter with cover, excellent decor, Heisey	167.00
Ring Band, creamer, souvenir	30.00
Ring Band, salt shaker, old lid	47.00
Ring Band, sugar with lid, rose decor	124.00
Ring Band, syrup, rose decor	265.00
Sawtooth Band, custard cup, no handles, Heisey, 2¼x2½"	54.00
Sawtooth Band, match holder	41.00
Smocking, bell	40.00

Vermont, celery dish, floral center, blue trim	50.00
Victoria, spooner	60.00
Wild Bouquet, creamer	114.00
Winged Scroll, bowl, 8½"	174.00
Winged Scroll, cigarette holder, no gold	118.00
Winged Scroll, spooner, 2 handles, open	123.00
Winged Scroll, toothpick, gold decor	110.00
Winged Scroll, tray for cruet set, excellent rose decor	186.00
Winged Scroll, tumbler	88.00

Cut Glass

Although cut glass from the 'Brilliant Period,' about 1880 to 1915, is most popular with today's collectors, the first attempt at glass cutting in America was made in 1810. As the art developed, various patterns emerged. Gradually, deep cuttings and miters made it necessary to use a very heavy type of glass with a high grade of metal capable of withstanding the pressure involved in such a process. Because of this and the hand work involved, cut glass has always been expensive.

Punch bowl on stand, star and sunburst fan cuttings, 9" x 12", $400.00.

Bowl, berry; hobstar & fan with serrated rim, 8" ... 160.00

Bowl, butterfly & thistle, 10" 125.00

Bowl, floriform, Cosmos, 10" . 125.00

Bowl, flowers with 15 petals cutting, heavy, oval, 7½" . 45.00

Bowl, hobstar & caning, 8" . 52.50

Bowl, hobstar & wheat, 9" . 126.50

Bowl, sawtooth & pineapple plume, deep, 9" 150.00

Bowl, star cutting, 8" 110.00

Bowl, sunburst cutting, 9" . 180.00

Butter dish, allover cutting, hobstar 200.00

Candy dish, divided, with handles, bevels, prisms, hobstars, 9¼" 147.50

Carafe, stars, fans, bull's eyes, signed Clark, 8" 135.00

Celery dish, allover hobstars, 11½" long 81.50

Celery dish, brilliant cut, 5x11" 125.00

Compote, hobstar & diamonds, 12" 175.00

Compote, star cutting, 5x5½" 65.00

Compote, twisted stem, cranberry to clear with flowers & leaves, 8x7" .. 125.50

Creamer & sugar, hobstar & notched prisms, pair 90.00

Cruet, fan cutting, faceted stopper, 6" 61.00

Cruet, hobstars within pinwheels, crosshatching, ray base, 6" 45.00

Decanter, allover hobstars, fans, vesicas, faceted stopper, 9" 165.00

Dish, 4 part, leaves & 12 petal flower, double notched handles, 7" 61.50

Ferner, hobstars & fluted fans, 4x7¾" 85.00

Handkerchief box, intaglio flowers on hinged lid, square 312.00

Knife rest, barbell shape with stars on the end, 3½" .. 28.00

Lamp, leaf & diamond with brass fittings, electric, 14½" 225.00

Nappy, ring handle, crosshatching, fans, 7" diameter . 40.00

Nappy, 2 handles, salesman's sample, M 85.00

Perfume, double, lay-down with ornate sterling caps, 4½" 125.00

Pitcher, pinwheel & crosshatch, 7" 65.00

Pitcher, tankard; notched handle, pinwheels, rayed base, 9½" 95.00

Plate, signed Tuthill, 7" ... 89.00

Punch cup, Russian bowl with hobstar foot 90.00

Salt & peppers, panel & notch, pair 16.00

Sugar bowl, brilliant cut, Pitkin & Brooks 36.00

Tray, Harvard pattern, scalloped with intaglio cut flowers, 11x6½" 76.50

Tumbler, leaves & daisy ... 20.00

Tumbler, leaves & pinwheel . 20.00

Vase, sawtooth rim, crosshatched diamond, rib points, stemmed, 8" 100.00

Whiskey, floral, 2½" 16.50

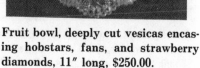

Fruit bowl, deeply cut vesicas encasing hobstars, fans, and strawberry diamonds, 11" long, $250.00.

Czechoslovakian Collectibles

Items marked Czechoslovakia are another of the more popular modern collectibles. Pottery, glassware, jewelry, etc., were produced there in abundance.

Bowl, with underplate, ruby
   cut to clear, vintage 25.00
Christmas ornament, red cone 4.00
Cigarette holder, hand painted
   cigarettes & stick matches,
   ceramic 25.00
Creamer, orange spotted cow
   figural 22.50
Dish, baby's; with children &
   animals, 5" 25.00
Figurine, boy holding heart &
   flowers with girl sitting, 6",
   pair 31.00
Figurine, miniature blue glass
   dog 15.00

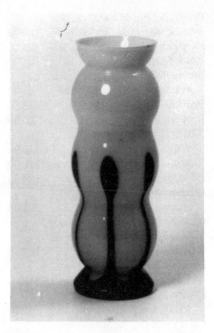

Vase, yellow and brown glass, 8", $42.00.

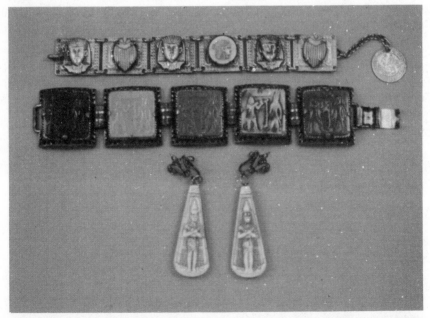

Jewelry, top: bracelet, Art Deco, German silver set with molded glass, $25.00; center: bracelet, Art Deco, copper over brass mounting set with molded glass, $35.00; bottom: earrings, Art Deco, 2" drops of molded glass, $30.00 for the pair.

Lustre, huge prisms, enameled green decor, large ...	323.00
Perfume, cut glass, with dropper, ornate, 6½x4½" ...	66.50
Pitcher, china Orphelia figural bird, red, black & ivory, 9"	27.50
Pitcher, cow	30.00
Pitcher, parrot	21.50
Planter, fat bald man	22.50
Salt & pepper, pink cut glass, large, pair	91.50
Vase, green overlay on white, clear with multicolor rigaree	48.00
Vase, hand figural, white cased glass, 9½"	17.50
Wall pocket, Amphora, 9" .	79.50
Wall pocket, owl	30.00
Wine set, amber, Deco, 7 piece	135.00

Decanters

The James Beam Distilling Company produced its first ceramic whiskey decanter in 1953, and remained the only major producer of these decanters throughout the next decade. By the late 1960s, other companies such as Ezra Brooks, Lionstone, and Cyrus Noble were also becoming involved in their production. Today these fancy liquor containers are attracting many collectors.

Beam, Club Series, Akron, 1973	24.00
Beam, Club Series, Milwaukee Stein, 1972	81.50
Beam, Convention Series, #3, Detroit, 1973	25.00
Beam, Convention Series, #5, Sacramento, 1975	15.50
Beam, Customer Series, Zimmerman, Two Handled Jug, 1965	97.50
Beam, Executive Series, Marble Fantasy, 1965	64.50
Beam, Executive Series, Royal Di Monte, 1957 ..	70.00
Beam, Foreign Series, Australia, Galah, 1980	18.00
Beam, Foreign Series, New Zealand Kiwi Bird, 1974 .	8.00
Beam, Opera Series, Madame Butterfly	563.00
Beam, People Series, Charlie McCarthy, 1976	35.50
Beam, Political, San Diego Elephant, 1972	21.00
Beam, Regal China, Antique Trader, 1968	5.00
Beam, Sport Series, Bing Crosby 29th, 1970	6.50
Beam, Sport Series, Hawaiian Open, Menehune, 1975 ..	13.00
Beam, State, Michigan, 1972 .	8.00
Beam, State, New Jersey, blue, 1963	62.50

Jim Beam decanters, Executive Series, left to right: Sovereign, 1969, hand painted yellow roses, Genuine Regal China; Charisma, 1970, 13"; Presidential, 1968, cobalt blue and gold, Genuine Regal China. Each is worth about $13.00.

Jim Beam decanters, Political Series, elephant and donkey footballs, 1972, $21.00 each.

Beam, State, Washington, 1975 .... 15.00

Beam, Trophy Series, Doe, 1963 .... 30.00

Beam, Trophy Series, Sailfish 31.00

Beam, Wheels Series, Bobby Unser Olsonite Eagle, 1975 42.00

Beam, Wheels Series, Ford Fire Chief 52.50

Beam, Wheels Series, Jewel Tea Van, 1976 .... 95.00

Beam, Wheels Series, Stutz Bearcat, 1977 .... 40.00

Brooks, Animal Series, Beaver, 1972 .... 8.00

Brooks, Animal Series, Clydesdale, 1972 .... 12.50

Brooks, Automotive Series, Ontario Racer #10, 1970 . 22.50

Brooks, Bird Series, Macaw, 1980 .... 51.00

Brooks, Bird Series, Owl #3, Snowy, 1979 .... 38.00

Brooks, Heritage China Series, Christmas Tree, 1979 .... 35.00

Brooks, Institutional Series, American Legion, Denver, 1977 .... 23.00

Brooks, Institutional Series, Fresno Grape, 1970 .... 8.00

Brooks, Institutional Series, Kachina #4, Maiden, 1975 . 26.00

Brooks, Institutional Series, Maine Lighthouse, 1971 . 21.00

Brooks, Institutional Series, NH Statehouse, 1969 ... 11.00

Brooks, Institutional Series, Slot Machine, 1971 ..... 21.00

Brooks, People Series, Betsy Ross, 1975 .... 12.00

Brooks, People Series, Clown #4, Keystone Cop, 1980 . 33.00

Brooks, People Series, Clown #6, Tramp, 1980 .... 36.00

Brooks, People Series, Dakota Cowgirl, 1976 .... 25.00

Brooks, People Series, Sea Captain, 1971 .... 11.00

Brooks, People Series, West Virginia Mountain Lady, 1972 .... 19.00

Brooks, Sport Series, Bluejay, Creighton University, 1975 20.00

Brooks, Sport Series, Gopher, Minnesota Hockey Player, 1975 .... 15.00

Brooks, Sport Series, Razorback Hog, 1969 .... 21.00

Brooks, Transportation Series, Train, Casey Jones #1, 1980 .... 44.00

Cyrus Noble, Animal Series, Beaver & Kit, Nevada edition, 1978 .... 38.00

Cyrus Noble, Animal Series, Elk & Bull, 1980 .... 50.00

Cyrus Noble, Animal Series, Mountain Lion & Cubs, Nevada edition, 1977.... 86.00

Cyrus Noble, Carousel Series, Horse & White Charger, 1979 .... 28.00

Cyrus Noble, Carousel Series, Tiger, 1979 .... 38.00

Cyrus Noble, Dancers, South of the Border, 1978 .... 26.00

Cyrus Noble, Mine Series, Blacksmith, 1974 ...... 41.00

Cyrus Noble, Mine Series, Landlady, 1977 .... 26.00

Cyrus Noble, Mine Series, Miner's Daughter, 1975 . 38.00

Cyrus Noble, Mine Series, Violinist, 1976 .... 34.00

Cyrus Noble, Olympic Skater, 1980 .... 41.00

Cyrus Noble, Sea Animal Series, Sea Turtle, 1979 . 53.00

Lionstone, Animal-Safari Series, Zebras, 1977, mini . 11.00

Lionstone, Bicentennial Series, George Washington, 1975 20.00

Lionstone, Bicentennial Series, Molly Pitcher, 1975 .... 20.00

Lionstone, Bird Series, Blue Bird, Eastern, 1972 .... 24.00

Lionstone, Bird Series, Blue Jay, 1971 .... 24.00

Lionstone, Bird Series, Capistrano Swallow with silver bell, 1972 .... 51.00

Lionstone, Bird Series, Owls, 1973 .... 35.00

Lionstone, Car Series, Turbo Car STP, red, 1972 ..... 25.00

Lionstone, Circus Series, Giraffe Necked Lady, 1973 14.00

Lionstone, European Workers Series, Silversmith, 1974 . 25.00

Lionstone, Firefighter Series, #4, Emblem, 1978 ...... 31.00

Lionstone, Old West Series, Belly Robber, 1969 ..... 16.00

Lionstone, Old West Series, Camp Follower, 1969 ... 20.00

Lionstone, Old West Series, Indian Weaver, 1976 ... 26.00

Lionstone, Old West Series, Judge Roy Bean, 1973 .. 28.00

Lionstone, Old West Series, Wells Fargo Man, 1969 . 15.00

Lionstone, Rose Parade, 1973 26.00

Lionstone, Sports Series, Basketball Players, 1974 . 24.00

Lionstone, Sports Series, Golfer, 1974 .... 25.00

McCormick, Bicentennial Series, John Paul Jones . 26.00

McCormick, Entertainer Series, Elvis #1, 1978 ..... 82.00

McCormick, Entertainer Series, Elvis-Aloha 111.00

McCormick, Football Mascots, Baylor Bears, 1972 ..... 28.00

McCormick, Football Mascots, SMU Mustangs, 1972 .. 25.00

McCormick, Frontiersman Series, Davy Crockett, 1975 .... 19.00

McCormick, Frontiersman Series, Kit Carson, 1975 . 18.00

McCormick, Lobsterman, 1979 .... 25.00

McCormick, Sports Series, Kansas City Chiefs, 1969 . 34.00

Ski Country, Bicentennial Series, Birth of Freedom, 1976 .... 87.00

Ski Country, Circus Series, Circus Lion, 1975 ...... 35.00

Ski Country, Circus Series, PT Barnum, 1976 .... 35.00

Ski Country, Customer Specialties Series/Mill River Country Club, 1977. 38.00

Ski Country, Fish Series, Muskie, 1977 .... 29.00

Ski Country, State Bird Series, Baltimore Oriole, 1975 .... 47.00

Ski Country, Waterfowl Series, Penguin Family, 1978 .... 41.00

Ski Country, Wild Life Series, California Condor, 1973 . 40.00

Ski Country, Wild Life Series, Mountain Goat, 1975 ... 44.00

Ski Country, Wild Life Series, Peregrine Falcon, 1980 . 67.00

Ski Country, Wild Life Series, Woodpecker--Gila, 1972 . 79.00

Decoys

Although ducks are the most commonly encountered type, nearly every species of bird has been imitated through decoys. The earliest were carved from wood by the Indians and used to lure game birds into the hunting areas. Among those most valued by collectors today are those carved by well-known artists, commercial decoys produced by factories such as Mason

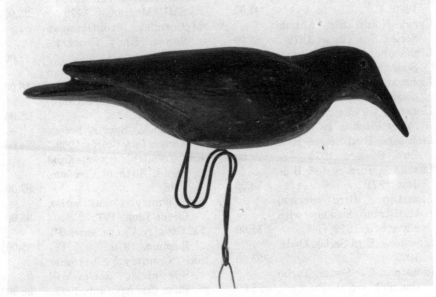

Crow, glass eyes, 17½" long, $195.00.

and Dodge, and well-carved examples of rare species. Many reproductions are on the market today that were produced for ornamental purposes only. Buyer beware!

Black Duck, oversize, turned head, original paint, Cramner, 20" 84.00

Black Duck, pine head, balsa body, worn original paint, 12" 45.00

Bluebill, carved eyes, original paint, primitive, folk art appeal, 11" 95.00

Bluebill Drake, glass eyes, repaint, Mason's Challenge, 14" 173.00

Bluebill Hen, glass eyes, balsa, worn original paint, Saginaw Bay, 14" 45.00

Bluebill Hen, glass eyes, original paint, bold stylized carving, 17" 51.00

Bluebill Hen, working repaint, St Clair, Michigan, 12½" . 40.00

Brandt, primitive, carved wood, worn original paint, 18" 155.00

Brant, belligerent, Nathan Cobb 2,800.00

Brant, hollow, Charles Birch . 3,300.00

Bufflehead Drake, original paint, AJ Mallory, 10½" . 96.00

Bufflehead Drake, worn original paint, Eastern Shore, Virginia, 11" 45.00

Canada Goose, glass eyes, original paint, mid-1900s, 23" 175.00

Canada Goose, laminated body, 1 piece carved head, Schmitz, 21" 76.00

Canada Goose, stuffed canvas, original paint, signed Don Shonk 3, 31" 200.00

Canvasback Drake, glass eyes, well carved, worn working repaint, 15" 65.00

Canvasback Hen, balsa body, wood keel, original paint, Wildfowler, 15" 41.00

Canvasback Hen, glass eyes, worn original paint, 1950s, Ackerman, 19″ 45.00

Coot, carved primary feathers, original paint 70.00

Coot, glass eyes, working repaint, Victor Animal Trap Co, 12″ 75.00

Crow, homemade laminated construction, 19″ 55.00

Duck, Mason Premier grade . 320.00

Eider Drake, glass eyes, original paint, contemporary, 14″ 83.00

Folding, original canvas bag, cardboard, wire rods, Johnson's 35.00

Goldeneye Drake, glass eyes, original paint, AJ Mallory, 15″ 41.00

Goldeneye Drake, original paint, laminated, New England 45.00

Goldeneye Hen, glass eyes, worn original paint, 13″ . 30.00

Goldeneyes, turned heads, pair, Ward Brothers 3,200.00

Loon, tack eyes, root head, old black repaint, 12″ 125.00

Loon, tack eyes, white spots, old repaint, 12½″ 35.00

Mallard, tack eyes, excellent original paint, third grade Mason 130.00

Mallard Drake, head to right, AE Crowell 200.00

Mallard Hen, worn original paint, glass eyes, 18″ ... 103.00

Mallards, Mason's Premier, pair 523.00

Merganser, contemporary, signed Marvin Schmitz, 7½″ 46.00

Merganser Drake, signed RD Laurie, 4″ 73.00

Pigeon, papier mache, old . 16.00

Pintail Drake, glass eyes, original paint, Victor Animal Trap Co, 17″ ... 50.00

Redhead Drake, glass eyes, canvas body, working repaint, Reeves, 15″ 93.00

Redhead Drake, pine head, balsa body, working repaint, Herter's, 15″ 24.00

Robin Snipe, glass eyes, original paint, Mason's, EX . 3,200.00

Ruddy Duck, original paint, Roy Bull, early 1940s, small 100.00

Ruddy Duck Drake, glass eyes, original paint, signed Dave Fried, 10″ 63.00

Scooter, black paint, white bill, primitive, 1 piece .. 48.00

Shorebird, folding wood, original paint, no rod, 10″ . 175.00

Snow Goose, glass eyes, original paint, Snow of Michigan, 16″ 54.00

Teal Duck, original paint, central Wisconsin, early 1900s, small 111.00

Depression Glass

Depression Glass, named for the era when it sold through dime stores or was given away as premiums, can be found in such varied colors as amber, green, pink, blue, red, yellow, white, and crystal. Mass-produced by many different companies in hundreds of patterns, Depression Glass is one of the most sought after collectibles in the United States today.

Adam, ash tray, pink 18.50

Adam, bowl, covered, pink, 9″ 35.00

Adam, butter dish & cover, pink 62.50

Adam, candy jar & cover, pink, 2½″ 47.50

Adam, coaster, pink, 3¾″ .. 14.50

Adam, pitcher, 32 ounce, pink, 8″ 25.00

Coronation. Cup and saucer $5.00; berry bowl $3.00; tumbler $8.00; luncheon plate $3.00; large berry bowl $7.00.

Adam, platter, pink, 11¾″ .	10.00		Anniversary, creamer, footed,	
Adam, salt & pepper, pink, 4″	39.50		crystal	3.50
Adam, sugar, pink	9.00		Anniversary, dinner plate,	
Adam, vase, pink, 7½″	107.50		pink, 9″	6.00
American Pioneer, bowl,			Anniversary, pickle dish,	
handled, green, 9″	14.50		crystal, 9″	3.50
American Pioneer, candle-			Aunt Polly, butter dish &	
sticks, green, 6½″, pair .	55.00		cover, blue	137.50
American Pioneer, cup, pink .	5.50		Aunt Polly, pickle bowl, handl-	
American Pioneer, sherbet,			ed, oval, green, 7¼″	8.50
pink, 4¾″	12.00		Aunt Polly, salt & pepper,	
American Pioneer, water			blue	137.50
goblet, green, 8 ounce, 6″ .	25.00		Avocado, creamer, footed,	
American Sweetheart, berry			green	27.50
bowl, flat, pink, 3¾″ . . .	21.50		Avocado, cup, footed, green .	27.50
American Sweetheart, cup,			Avocado, luncheon plate,	
monax	9.50		pink, 8¼″	11.50
American Sweetheart, pitcher,			Avocado, tumbler, pink . . .	67.50
pink, 80 ounces, 8″	300.00		Beaded Block, jelly bowl, 2	
American Sweetheart, salad			handled, opalescent, 4½″ .	12.50
plate, monax, 8″	6.50		Beaded Block, plate, round,	
American Sweetheart, tum-			opalescent, 8¾″	10.00
bler, pink, 10 ounces, 4½″	35.00		Beaded Block, sugar, pink .	9.50

Block Optic, butter dish & cover, green, 3x5″ 32.50

Block Optic, ice tub or butter tub, open, green 19.50

Block Optic, salt & pepper, footed, pink 40.00

Bubble, berry bowl, crystal, 4″ 3.00

Bubble, sugar, crystal 3.00

Bubble, water tumbler, blue, 9 ounce 6.00

Cameo, cake plate, 3 legs, green, 10″ 13.50

Cameo, candy jar & cover, green, 6½″ tall 89.50

Cameo, cookie jar & cover, green 35.00

Cameo, salt & pepper, footed, green, pair 47.50

Cameo, water goblet, green, 6″ 35.00

Cherry Blossom, Child's Junior Dinner Set, 14 piece, pink 175.00

Cherry Blossom, oval vegetable, pink, 9″ 17.50

Cherry Blossom, platter, oval, pink, 11″ 19.50

Cherry Blossom, sherbet, green 12.50

Cloverleaf, cereal bowl, yellow, 5″ 20.00

Cloverleaf, salt & pepper, yellow, pair 85.00

Cloverleaf, sherbet, footed, green, 3″ 4.50

Colonial, iced tea tumbler, pink, 12 ounces 18.50

Colonial, salt & pepper, green, pair 100.00

Colonial, soup bowl, low, pink, 7″ 25.00

Colonial Block, bowl, green, 7″ 10.00

Colonial Block, candy dish & cover, green, 8½″ 22.50

Colonial Block, creamer, green 7.50

Manhattan. Creamer $4.00; candlesticks $9.00 pair; tumbler $7.50; sugar $4.00; plate $7.50.

Mayfair "Open Rose". Tumbler $30.00 (pink); cereal bowl $15.00; cup and saucer $20.00; footed tumbler $28.00; luncheon plate $16.00; pitcher $65.00.

Colonial Fluted, cereal bowl, green, 6″	5.00	Diamond Quilted, candlesticks, 2 styles, blue, pair	22.50
Colonial Fluted, sherbet, green	4.00	Diamond Quilted, ice bucket, blue	55.00
Columbia, cup, pink	7.00	Diamond Quilted, iced tea tumbler, green, 12 ounces	7.00
Columbia, salad bowl, crystal, 8½″	6.50	Diana, cereal bowl, pink, 5″	3.50
Coronation, berry bowl, pink, 8″	7.00	Diana, salt & pepper, amber, pair	62.50
Coronation, sherbet, pink	3.00	Dogwood, cereal bowl, green, 5½″	17.50
Cube, butter dish & cover, green	47.50	Dogwood, creamer, thick, pink, 3¼″	13.50
Cube, candy jar & cover, pink, 6½″	19.50	Dogwood, luncheon plate, pink, 8″	4.75
Cube, salt & pepper, green, pair	25.00	Dogwood, pitcher, decorated, pink, 80 ounces, 8″	107.50
Cube, tumbler, pink, 9 ounces, 4″	20.00	Dogwood, sherbet, low footed, green	47.50
Daisy, dinner plate, amber, 9⅜″	6.00	Doric, butter dish & cover, pink	57.50
Daisy, oval vegetable, amber, 10″	12.50	Doric, creamer, green, 4″	8.50
Daisy, relish dish, 3 part, crystal, 8⅜″	8.00	Doric, salt & pepper, pink, pair	23.50

124

Doric, sherbet, footed, pink . 7.50

English Hobnail, celery dish, pink, 12″ 17.50

English Hobnail, cologne bottle, pink 22.50

Fire King Azurite, bowl, 8″ . 5.00

Fire King Azurite, mug, 8 ounces 5.00

Fire King Azurite, plate, 10″ . 3.50

Fire King Jadeite 'Alice', cup 1.00

Fire King Jadeite 'Alice', plate, 8½″ 3.00

Fire King Jadeite 'Alice', saucer .... .50

Fire King Jadeite 'Jane Ray', cup 1.00

Fire King Jadeite 'Jane Ray', oatmeal bowl, 5⅞″ 1.50

Fire King Jadeite 'Jane Ray', platter, 12″ 3.50

Fire King Jadeite 'Jane Ray', sugar & cover 3.50

Floragold, sherbet, low footed, iridescent 8.50

Floral & Diamond Band, butter dish & cover, green . 77.50

Floral & Diamond Band, candy jar & cover, pink 25.00

Floral & Diamond Band, pitcher, footed cone, green, 32 ounce, 8″ 25.00

Floral & Diamond Band, salt & pepper, pink, footed, 4″, pair 30.00

Floral & Diamond Band, sherbet, pink 4.50

Floral & Diamond Band, water tumbler, footed, green, 7 ounce, 4¾″ 13.00

Florentine Number 1, berry bowl, yellow, 8½″ 18.50

Florentine Number 1, pitcher, footed, yellow, 36 ounce, 6½″ 39.50

Miss America. Covered candy jar $47.50; salt and pepper $20.00 (pink); sugar $12.00 (pink); cup and saucer $28.00 (pink); platter $12.00.

Florentine Number 1, salad plate, green, 8½" 5.00

Florentine Number 1, salt & pepper, footed, yellow .. 40.00

Florentine Number 1, water tumbler, footed, green, 10 ounce, 4¾" 11.00

Florentine Number 2, butter dish & cover, green 77.50

Florentine Number 2, custard cup or jello, yellow 57.50

Florentine Number 2, iced tea tumbler, yellow, 12 ounce, 5" 24.00

Florentine Number 2, sherbet, footed, green 6.00

Forest Green, cup 3.00

Forest Green, dinner plate, 9¼" 9.00

Fortune, candy dish & cover, flat, pink 12.50

Fortune, juice tumbler, pink, 5 ounce, 3½" 3.00

Georgian, butter dish & cover, green 60.00

Georgian, creamer, footed, green, 4" 9.50

Georgian, tumbler, flat, green, 12 ounce, 5¼" 55.00

Heritage, cup, crystal 3.50

Heritage, dinner plate, crystal, 9¼" 6.00

Hobnail, decanter & stopper, crystal, 32 ounce 12.50

Hobnail, sherbet, crystal .. 2.00

Hobnail, wine tumbler, footed, crystal, 3 ounce 5.00

Holiday, candlesticks, pink, 3", pair 47.50

Holiday, dinner plate, pink, 9" 8.50

Holiday, sugar, pink 5.00

Holiday, sugar cover, pink . 7.50

Homespun, berry bowl, pink or crystal, 8¼" 8.50

Homespun, butter dish & cover, pink or crystal ... 39.00

Homespun, Child's Tea Set, 14 piece, pink or crystal . 185.00

Homespun, dinner plate, pink or crystal, 9¼" 8.50

Horseshoe Number 612, creamer, footed, yellow . 11.50

Horseshoe Number 612, dinner plate, yellow, 10⅜" . 14.50

Horseshoe Number 612, relish, footed, 3 part, green 12.00

Horseshoe Number 612, tumbler, footed, yellow, 9 ounce 13.50

Horseshoe Number 612, vegetable bowl, oval, green, 10½" 12.50

Iris & Herringbone, berry bowl, ruffled, iridescent, 8" 8.50

Iris & Herringbone, butter dish & cover, crystal ... 27.50

Iris & Herringbone, candlesticks, iridescent, pair .. 22.50

Iris & Herringbone, sherbet plate, crystal, 5½" 5.00

Iris & Herringbone, sugar, iridescent 6.50

Iris & Herringbone, tumbler, footed, crystal, 7" 13.50

Lorain, cereal bowl, yellow, 6" 37.50

Lorain, dinner plate, yellow, 10¼" 39.00

Lorain, sugar, footed, green . 12.50

Lorain, tumbler, footed, green, 9 ounce, 4¾" 13.50

Madrid, berry bowl, amber, 9⅜" 13.50

Madrid, candlesticks, amber, 2¼", pair 15.00

Madrid, cookie jar & cover, amber 30.00

Madrid, cream soup bowl, amber, 4¾" 9.50

Madrid, hot dish coaster, green 27.50

Madrid, jello mold, amber, 2⅛" high 8.00

Madrid, juice pitcher, amber, 36 ounce, 5½" 27.50

Madrid, salt & pepper, flat, amber, 3½" 37.50

Madrid, tumbler, footed, amber, 10 ounce, 5½" .. 18.50

Mayfair, butter dish & cover, blue 197.50

New Century Sugar and creamer $20.00; ashtray/coaster $25.00; sherbet $6.00; plate $10.00.

Mayfair, candy dish & cover, blue 127.50

Mayfair, cookie jar & lid, pink 27.50

Mayfair, decanter & stopper, pink, 32 ounce 79.50

Mayfair, dinner plate, blue, 9½″ 39.50

Mayfair, grill plate, pink, 9½″ 22.50

Mayfair, salt & pepper, flat, pink, pair 39.50

Mayfair, sandwich server, center handle, blue 42.50

Mayfair, sugar, footed, pink . 15.00

Mayfair, vase, sweet pea, pink 82.50

Mayfair, vegetable bowl, blue, 7″ 30.00

Mayfair, vegetable bowl, oval, pink, 9½″ 15.50

Mayfair, water tumbler, blue, 9 ounce, 4¼″ 60.00

Mayfair Federal, cream soup bowl, amber, 5″ 13.50

Mayfair Federal, platter, oval, green, 12″ 14.50

Mayfair Federal, tumbler, green, 9 ounce, 4½″ 14.50

Miss America, bowl, incurvate rim, crystal, 8″ 27.50

Miss America, candy jar & cover, crystal, 11½″ 47.50

Miss America, creamer, footed, pink 11.50

Miss America, cup, crystal . 7.50

Miss America, dinner plate, crystal, 10½″ 9.50

Miss America, pitcher with ice lip, pink, 65 ounce, 8″ .. 87.50

Miss America, sherbet, pink . 12.50

Moderntone, butter dish with metal cover, cobalt 57.50

Moderntone, cream soup bowl, amethyst, 4¾″ 9.50

Moderntone, salt & pepper, amethyst, pair 27.50

Queen Mary. Cup and saucer $7.00; salt and pepper $15.00 (crystal); sugar and creamer $8.00; plate $8.00.

Newport, creamer, cobalt . .	9.00
Newport, salt & pepper, amethyst	32.50
Normandie, berry bowl, pink, 8½″	10.00
Normandie, cup, amber	5.50
Normandie, iced tea tumbler, pink, 12 ounce, 5″	29.50
Normandie, pitcher, amber, 80 ounce, 8″	45.00
Normandie, salt & pepper, pink, pair	42.50
Old Cafe, cup, red	5.50
Old Cafe, dinner plate, pink, 10″	12.50
Old Cafe, water tumbler, red, 4″	7.00
Open Lace, candy jar & cover, ribbed, pink	32.50
Open Lace, cookie jar & cover, pink	35.00
Open Lace, grill plate, pink, 10½″	11.50

Open Lace, tumbler, footed, pink, 10½ ounce, 5″	35.00
Oyster & Pearl, candle holder, pink, 3½″, pair	15.00
Oyster & Pearl, fruit bowl, deep, red, 10½″	30.00
Parrot, berry bowl, green, 8″ .	45.00
Parrot, butter dish & cover, amber	557.50
Parrot, dinner plate, green, 9″	25.00
Parrot, sherbet, footed, cone, amber	12.50
Parrot, tumbler, green, 10 ounce, 4¼″	60.00
Patrician, cookie jar & cover, green	177.50
Patrician, cream soup bowl, amber, 4¾″	10.00
Patrician, cup, amber	7.50
Patrician, salt & pepper, green, pair	45.00
Petalware, cream soup bowl, monax, 4½″	7.50

Petalware, creamer, footed, monax 4.50

Petalware, dinner plate, pink, 9″ 3.50

Petalware, platter, oval, pink, 13″ 5.50

Pineapple & Floral, cream soup, amber 17.50

Pineapple & Floral, creamer, diamond shaped, crystal . 6.50

Pineapple & Floral, relish platter, divided, crystal, 11½″ 15.00

Pineapple & Floral, sandwich plate, crystal, 11½″ 12.50

Princess, cake stand, green, 10″ 14.50

Princess, candy dish & cover, pink 35.00

Princess, platter, closed handles, pink, 12″ 10.00

Princess, sugar, green 8.00

Princess, tumbler, footed, pink, 10 ounce, 5¼″ 15.00

Rock Crystal, cake stand, crystal, 2¾x11″ diameter 15.00

Rock Crystal, candlesticks, low, pink, 5½″, pair 27.50

Rock Crystal, cup, pink, 7 ounce 12.50

Rock Crystal, parfait, crystal, low foot, 3½ ounce 8.00

Rock Crystal, pitcher, large, pink 117.50

Rock Crystal, relish bowl, 2 part, crystal, 11½″ 10.00

Rock Crystal, sundae, low footed, pink, 6 ounce ... 15.00

Rock Crystal, vase, pink, footed, 11″ 37.50

Rosemary, cup, green 6.00

Rosemary, dinner plate, green 10.00

Rosemary, sugar, footed, amber 6.00

Rosemary, vegetable bowl, oval, amber, 10″ 8.50

Royal Lace, candlesticks, straight edge, blue, pair . 72.50

Royal Lace, creamer, footed, blue 27.50

Royal Lace, pitcher, straight sides, blue, 54 ounce ... 80.00

Royal Lace, salt & pepper, pink, pair 37.50

Royal Lace, tumbler, pink, 13 ounce, 5⅜″ 19.50

Royal Ruby, creamer, footed, red 6.50

Royal Ruby, cup, round or square, red 3.50

Royal Ruby, dinner plate, red, 9″ or 9¼″ 6.50

Royal Ruby, saucer, round or square, red 1.50

Royal Ruby, vegetable bowl, oval, red, 8″ 11.50

Royal Ruby, water tumbler, red, 10 ounce 4.50

Sandwich, Hocking, butter dish, low, crystal 30.00

Sandwich, Hocking, cookie jar & cover, crystal 27.50

Sandwich, Hocking, custard cup, green 1.50

Sandwich, Hocking, pitcher with ice lip, green, ½ gallon 162.50

Sandwich, Indiana, berry bowl, pink, 4¼″ 3.00

Sandwich, Indiana, creamer & sugar on diamond shaped tray, crystal 12.00

Sandwich, Indiana, sandwich server, center handle, pink 25.00

Sharon, berry bowl, pink, 8½″ 15.50

Sharon, cake plate, footed, amber, 11½″ 14.50

Sharon, candy jar & cover, amber 32.50

Sharon, cheese dish & cover, pink 525.00

Sharon, cream soup bowl, amber, 5″ 15.00

Sharon, sherbet, footed, amber 8.50

Sharon, tumbler, thick or thin, pink, 9 ounce, 4⅛″ 19.50

Sierra, butter dish & cover, pink 42.50

Royal Ruby. Cup and saucer $5.00; tumbler $5.00; sherbet $6.00; dinner plate $6.50; salad plate $3.00.

Sierra, salt & pepper, pink, pair	25.00	Swirl, cup, pink	4.00
Starlight, creamer, oval, crystal	3.00	Swirl, tumbler, footed, ultramarine, 9 ounce	16.50
Starlight, dinner plate, pink, 9″	6.00	Tea Room, candlestick, low, green, pair	27.50
Strawberry, berry bowl, deep, pink or green, 7½″	13.50	Tea Room, creamer & sugar on tray, pink, 3½″	40.00
Strawberry, compote, pink or green, 5¾″	12.50	Tea Room, tumbler, footed, green, 9 ounce	17.50
Strawberry, sugar, large, pink or green	12.00	Waterford, creamer, oval, crystal	2.50
Sunflower, ash tray, center design only, pink or green, 5″	7.00	Waterford, dinner plate, pink, 9⅝″	9.50
Sunflower, creamer, pink or green	8.50	Waterford, sherbet, footed, crystal	2.50
Sunflower, cup, pink or green	7.50	Windsor, butter dish, crystal	22.50
Sunflower, dinner plate, pink or green, 9″	9.00	Windsor, candy jar & cover, pink	18.50
Swirl, console bowl, footed, ultramarine, 10½″	18.00	Windsor, cup, crystal	2.50
		Windsor, pitcher, pink, 16 ounce, 4½″	77.50
		Windsor, sherbet, footed, pink	5.50

Doll Furniture

Every little girl has her favorite doll, and like all good mothers, wants her loved one to have all the 'necessities' of life! Thus a vast array of doll-size furniture can be found, ranging from the most elaborate to those homemade items of simple design.

Armchair, ladderback, primitive, turned finials, splint seat, 12″ 65.00

Bed, armoire, dresser & chair, Victorian, paper litho on wood 180.00

Bed, canopy; metal 27.00

Bed, half crown, Victorian, 23″ long 140.00

Bed, Murphy; chestnut, 2 doors with 2 drawers in wardrobe, 15x10½″ 225.00

Bed, spool, complete with roping, 9x13″ 25.00

Buffet, mirror, pressed carved, original pulls, oak, 22x16″ 135.00

Buggy, Wyandotte, white tires, metal, 6¾x9″ 35.00

Cabinet, 2 drawers below 2 doors, dated 1909, 9½″ . 75.00

Carriage, brown wicker, all original 115.00

Carriage, painted wood, 4 wheels, fringed canopy, 27″ 275.00

Cart, wicker, 2 wheels, long handle 75.00

Chair, spindle back with original red paint & yellow striping, 10″ 25.00

Chair, wicker, high back, 8x10″, EX 40.00

Chair, wood with paper litho, Bliss, 12″ 125.00

Chest, Empire, curly cherry & walnut with scrolled feet, 12½x11″ 375.00

Chest, oak, 5 long drawers with pilasters on each side, 13″ 155.00

China closet, oak with brass hardware, 21″ x 11″, $85.00.

Chest, primitive, 3 drawers & 6″ original mirror, brass pulls, 16″ 65.00

Cradle, pine, original green paint; black, red & yellow striping, 21″ 75.00

Cradle, pine, original paint with stenciled stag, worn, 11½″ 155.00

Cradle, poplar with worn original oak graining, 19½″, G 55.00

Cupboard, kitchen; 2 doors with 2 drawers below, old, 9½x7½x4″ 75.00

Cupboard, 3 open shelves with 2 base doors, primitive, 23x12″ 100.00

Desk, mahogany with slant top, 7½x7″ 14.50

Desk, roll top; oak & chestnut with 6 drawers, 15x18x9″ . 275.00

Dresser, pine, 1 drawer with 2 doors & mirror, dated 1905 125.00

Dresser, 3 drawers & mirror,
original red paint, 18″ .. 40.00
Highchair, Pla-Doll 45.00
Highchair, with tray, old,
18x7x9″ 85.00
Ironing board, oak, 13x16½″ 26.00
Sled, wooden with original
floral stencil, curved iron
runners, 1885 .... 225.00
Stroller, Paris Manufacturing,
all original, early 365.00
Table, turtle top, carved skirt
& bow legs, Victorian, 5″ . 90.00
Trunk, steamer with original
labels, 1930s, 14x8″ 25.00
Trunk, wooden with tray &
domed top, old, 16″, VG . 75.00
Washstand, painted tin,
serpentine legs, bottom
shelf, 10¾″ 18.00
Washstand, 1 drawer with 2
doors below, towel bar, old,
16x13x6″ 195.00

Dollhouse Furnishings

Collecting antique dollhouses and building new ones is a popular hobby with many today, and all who collect houses delight in furnishing them right down to the vase on the table and the scarf on the piano! Flea markets are a good source of dollhouse furnishings, especially those from the 1940s through the '60s made by Strombecker or Renwal, or the Petite Princess line by Ideal.

Armchair, turned legs, fabric
upholstery, 4x2″ 10.00
Basket, woven, mini 1.00
Bathinette, Renwal 15.00
Bathroom set, painted wood,
curved tub, toilet, 2″
pedestal sink, 1920..... 12.00
Bathtub, lavender, Tootsie
Toy 12.50

Petite Princess Occasional Table Set #4437-0100, made in 1964 by Ideal Toy Co., $17.50, MIB.

Bed, twin; chest & mirrored
vanity, Renwal 17.00
Bedspread, Skipper's 8.50
Bureau, stencil design, brown,
Renwal, 3¼" 8.50
Chair, brown, Tootsie Toy . 7.00
Chair, parlor; white with floral
stencil, overstuffed, Ren-
wal, 2¾" 7.00
Clock, Grandfather; Strom-
becker 7.00
Dresser set, celluloid, original
box 24.00
Highchair, Renwal 10.00
Phonograph, Tootsie Toy .. 10.50
Piano, baby grand; brown,
white & brown keys, Ren-
wal 10.00
Plant stand, wood, base shelf,
2" diameter top 8.50
Radiator, cast iron, 8 ribs,
2½x2" 34.00
Rocker, padded seat, oak,
4¾" 9.00
Rug, hooked, 3" diameter .. 5.00
Scales, bathroom; Strom-
becker 4.50
Sink, bathroom; white with
black faucet, Renwal ... 6.00
Slide, Renwal 9.50
Sofa, slanted arms, curved
back, painted cast iron,
3¾" long 29.00
Sofa, stencil decor, Empire
style, Biedermeyer 98.00
Step stool, green, Tootsie Toy 8.50
Stove, kitchen; cast metal, Ar-
cade 25.00
Stroller, Ideal 7.50
Table, end; Shoenhut 6.00
Table, library; tan, Tootsie
Toy 10.50
Tea cart, Strombecker 8.50
Telephone, Renwal 9.00
Toilet set, porcelain, hand
painted, basin, pitcher, pail,
pot, 1800s 300.00
Tray, serving; mahogany,
galleried edge, 1½x2¼" . 4.50

Tricycle, red & yellow, moving
parts, Renwal 8.00
Vacuum cleaner, Renwal .. 8.50
Victrola, top lifts, four legs,
Tootsie Toy, 2" 9.00
Washboard, Rub-A-Dub ... 2.50
Washer, Renwal 14.00
Waste basket, dustpan,
broom, Strombecker 7.50

Dolls

Doll collecting is no doubt one of
the most popular fields today. Antique
as well as modern dolls are treasured,
and limited edition or artist's dolls
often bring prices in excess of several
hundred dollars. Investment potential
is considered excellent in all areas.
Dolls have been made from many
materials -- early to middle 19th century dolls were carved of wood, poured
in wax, and molded in bisque or china.
Primitive cloth dolls were sewn at
home for the enjoyment of little girls
when fancier dolls were unavailable. In
this century, from 1925 to about 1945,
composition was used. Made of a mixture of sawdust, clay, fiber and a binding agent, it was tough and durable.
Modern dolls are usually made of vinyl
or molded plastic.

Learn to check your intended purchases for damage which could jeopar-
dize your investment. Bisque dolls
may have breaks, hairlines, or eye
chips; composition dolls may sometimes become crazed or cracked.
Watch for ink or crayon marks on
vinyl dolls. Original clothing is important, although on bisque dolls replacement costumes are acceptable as long
as they are appropriately styled.

Armand Marseille

A 1 M, socket head, closed
dome, 11" 275.00

A 4/0 M, marked Made in Germany, shoulder plate, turned, ·16½" 275.00

A 8/0 M, marked Made in Germany, shoulder plate, 24" . 495.00

A 8/0 M, socket head, sideglance eyes, 13" 1,100.00

Alma/10/0/Germany, shoulder plate, 18" 295.00

AM DEP/Germany/9, shoulder plate, 26" 450.00

Baby Gloria/Germany 3, shoulder plate, 16" 600.00

Beauty/Made in Germany, shoulder plate, 1898, marked AM, 12" 195.00

Dutch couple, painted bisque, original costumes, 6", pair 150.00

Floradora/A 3/0 M, socket head, marked MIG/Armand Marseille, 18" 325.00

Floradora/A 6M/DRGM 3748 30, shoulder plate, marked 1374, 26" 550.00

Indian, AM/7/0, marked Germany, socket head, 9½" . 365.00

Indian, marked AM/Germany 4/0, socket head, 11" ... 425.00

Kiddiejoy, AM 375/6, 1918, o/m, Germany, 9" 265.00

Lilly/3/0/Germany, shoulder plate, 12" 175.00

Lilly/3/0/Germany, shoulder plate, 26" 450.00

Mabel/0, marked Germany, shoulder plate, 18" 275.00

My Playmate, closed dome & mouth, 1903, 18" 500.00

Puppet baby in blanket, marked AM, 8" 225.00

Queen Louise/7/Germany, socket head, 1910, 30" .. 850.00

Special/Germany, socket head, 1904, 12" 195.00

The Dollar Princess/Germany/A 3½ M, socket head, 26" 725.00

1894 AM/8/0 DEP/MIG, shoulder plate, 1910, 17" . 350.00

3200/AM 10/0x DEP, musical jestor, 1900, 10" 350.00

341, My Dream Baby, flange or socket head, closed mouth, black, 21" 825.00

352/Germany, marked AM, socket head, 1914, 18" .. 400.00

353 12/OK, marked Am/Germany, Oriental, socket head, 12" 795.00

353 12/OK, marked Am/Germany, Oriental, socket head, 9" 550.00

370, kid body, open mouth, shoulder plate, 21" 325.00

390, open mouth, socket head, 12" 175.00

390, open mouth, socket head, 30" 895.00

390N, open mouth, socket head, 11" 185.00

560/DRGM 232, toddler, socket head, 1924, 15" .. 475.00

640/A`3 M/Germany, painted eyes, shoulder plate, 1909, 22" 650.00

975 M/Germany, baby, socket head, marked Armand Marseille, 25" 1,200.00

Barbie Collectibles

Barbie, #1, brunette, holes in feet for holder, 1959 .... 850.00

Barbie, #3, blonde ponytail & curly bangs, blue eyeliner, 1960 .... 110.00

Barbie, #5, various color ponytail & bangs, hollow body, 1961 .... 80.00

Barbie, any color of hair with swirl ponytail, 1964 .... 90.00

Barbie, Ballerina, 1st issue, hair pulled back 30.00

Barbie, Ballerina Barbie On Tour, reissue, 3 costumes, 1978 .... 30.00

Barbie, Busy Barbie With Holdin' Hands, 1972 ... 80.00

Left to right: 1959 #2 Barbie doll, blonde, MIB, $400.00; 1959 #2 Barbie doll, brunette, MIB, $450.00.

Barbie, Deluxe Quick Curl, 1976 .... 25.00

Barbie, Gold Medal, Olympic Sports, 1975 .... 25.00

Barbie, Hair Happenin's, Sears limited edition, rare, 1971 .... 250.00

Barbie, Malibu, 1971 ...... 20.00

Barbie, Spanish Talking, 1968 100.00

Barbie, stand, #3 .... 40.00

Barbie, Sun Valley, ski costume, 1974 .... 45.00

Barbie, Talking Barbie, 1969 . 75.00

Barbie, Twist 'N Turn, 1966 . 50.00

Barbie, With Growin' Pretty Hair, 1972, rarer than 1971 issue 100.00

Barbie & Francie Color Magic Fashion Set 110.00

Barbie Baby-Sits, #953 (1962 booklet) 125.00

Barbie Queen Size Bed, by Suzy Goose 30.00

Barbie Sports Car, Irwin Corporation 60.00

Barbie's Dining Room Furniture Set, Go Together Furniture 50.00

Barbie's Mountain Ski Cabin, #4283, Sears Exclusive . 15.00

Barbie's New Restyled Dream House, #4092 .... 50.00

Brad, bendable leg, 1971 .. 40.00

Cara, Ballerina, 1976 ...... 30.00

Chris, Bendable Posable, 1967 40.00

Christie, Twist, 1969 ...... 50.00

Clothes, Barbie in Japan, #0821, (1963 booklet) ... 50.00

Countess Dagmar, parian, blue enamel paperweight eyes, cloth body with parian limbs, 20″, $425.00.

Clothes, Business Appointment, #1424	65.00
Clothes, Campus Sweetheart, #1616	45.00
Clothes, Drum Major, #0775, (1963 booklet)	25.00
Clothes, Ken in Mexico, #0820, (1963 booklet)	35.00
Clothes, Nighty-Negligee, #965, (1958 booklet)	20.00
Clothes, Poor & Rich Cinderella, #6872, (1963 booklet)	40.00
Clothes, Wedding Day Set, #972, (1961 booklet)	45.00
Curtis, Free Moving, only issued for 1 year, 1975	40.00
Francie, Busy Francie With Holdin' Hands, 1972	80.00
Francie, Twist 'N Turn, 1970	55.00
Jamie, Walking, 1970	75.00
Kelley, Quick Curl, 1973	50.00
Ken, Malibu, 1971	15.00
Ken, painted hair, 1962	50.00
Ken, Sun Valley, with ski outfit, 1974	50.00
Ken, Super Star Ken, 1st issue, with extra gift ring, 1976	20.00
Ken, Talking, 1969	45.00
Ken, Walk Lively, 1972	65.00
Midge, closed mouth, blonde, brunette, or red hair, 1963	55.00
Miss America, Blonde Quick Curl, from Canada	45.00
PJ, Malibu, 1972	20.00
PJ, New 'N Groovy Talking, 1969	70.00
Pretty Pairs, Lori 'N Rori, 1970	90.00
Skipper, Growing Up, 1975	20.00
Skipper, Twist, 1970	45.00
Skipper, Twist 'N Turn, 1968	45.00
Skipper, 1st bendable leg, 1965	55.00
Skipper On Wheels Gift Set, #1032 (1964 booklet)	225.00
Stacey, Talking, 1968	50.00
Steffie, Busy Talking Steffie With Holdin' Hands, 1972	100.00
Talking Barbie Pink Premier Gift Set, #1596, (1969 booklet)	275.00
Todd, Bendable Posable, 1967	40.00
Tutti, Me & My Dog play set, 1966	150.00
Tutti, Night Night Sleep Tight set, European reissue, 1975	45.00
Tutti, Walking My Dolly play set, 1966	75.00
Tutti Playhouse, doll included, #3306 (1966 booklet), M	50.00
Twiggy, Casey with more make-up, short hair & twist waist, 1967	75.00

Bru

Closed mouth, all-kid body, bisque lower arms, Bru, 16″	6,500.00
Closed mouth, all-kid body, bisque lower arms, Bru, 21″	8,300.00

Closed mouth, bisque lower
arms, kid with wood body,
Bru Jne, 14" 6,600.00
Closed mouth, bisque lower
arms, kid with wood body,
Bru Jne, 25" 14,500.00
Closed mouth, circle dot,
marked Bru, 16" 7,400.00
Closed mouth, circle dot,
marked Bru, 26" 16,000.00
Closed mouth, socket head on
composition body, Bru, R,
17" 5,000.00
Open mouth, composition
walker's body, throws
kisses, 18" 3,000.00
Open mouth, nursing (Bebe),
high color, late SFBJ, 12" . 1,800.00
Open mouth, nursing Bru
(Bebe), early, EX bisque,
12" 4,500.00
Open mouth, socket head on
composition body, Bru, R,
14" 2,500.00
Open mouth, socket head on
composition body, Bru, R,
17" 3,200.00
Open mouth, socket head on
composition body, Bru, R,
25" 5,800.00

Effanbee

Airman, 1919, 16" 100.00
Americana Collection, 1975-
1977, each 55.00
Anne Shirley, 1935-1939, 15" 100.00
Babette, 1980 .... 45.00
Baby Blanche, 1918, 15" .. 100.00
Baby Bright Eyes, 1916, 11" . 85.00
Baby Catherine, 1918, 12" . 125.00
Baby Daintie, 1918, 16" ... 96.00
Baby Peaches, 1965, 15" .. 44.00
Babyette, 1942, 10" 135.00
Beautee-Skin Baby, 1944, 17" 66.00
Betty Bounce, 1913-1915, 11" 78.00
Blue Danube, 1978 .... 76.00
Bobby Bounce, 1913, 11" .. 76.00
Bubbles, Walking, 1926, 14" . 178.00
Buttons Monk, 1923, 12" .. 96.00

Cherries Jubilee, 1979 ..... 75.00
Cinderella for Disney, 1977-
1978 .... 105.00
Country Bumpkin Collection,
1977, each 55.00
Cupcake, 1963, 12" 26.00
Dolly Dumpling, 1918, 14" . 126.00
DyDee Kin, 1933-1940, 13" . 76.00
Emily Ann, 1937, 14" 96.00
Frontier Women, 1977-1979 . 66.00
Ginger Curls, 1938, 21" ... 154.00
Half Pint, 1966-1980, 11" .. 47.00
Honey, 1950s, 18" 105.00
Hourglass Look, 1978-1979 . 65.00
Jack, 1979-1981 .... 65.00
Judy, 1928, 18" 85.00
Lamkin, 1930, 16" 276.00
Lili, 1980 .... 46.00
Little Lady, 1939-1946, 27" . 300.00
Love & Learn Set, 1965, 22" . 65.00
Lynn, 1969, 14" 45.00
Maid Marion, 1978 .... 105.00
Marvel-Tot, 1934, 16" 98.00
Mary Sue, 1927, 26" 155.00
Miss Glamour Girl, 1942, 21" 155.00
Naughty Eyes, 1927, 16" .. 95.00
Over the Rainbow, 1973, each 55.00
Patsy, 1926, 1930s, 1940s, 14" 195.00
Peaches & Cream, 1965, each . 55.00
Poochie, 1937, 14" 125.00
Rainbow Parfait Collection,
1979, each 45.00
Romper Babies, 1918, 15" . 98.00
Skippy, Limited Edition ... 176.00
Suzette, 1939, 11" 102.00
Three Pigs, 1934, 10", each . 150.00
Toddle Tot, 1958-1970, 13" . 26.00
WC Fields, 1929, 18" 327.00
Yesterday's Collection, 1977,
each 45.00

Half Dolls

Arms away, rose in hand,
#5237, 4½" 165.00
Bisque, arms away, #3705,
4⅛" 110.00
Colonial lady, arms away,
molded bust & tiny waist,
3¼" 145.00

Half Doll, **arms away from body, brown hair and blue ribbon,** 3½", $185.00.

Flapper, blue & white dress, gloves & necklace, German #6716, 4" 160.00

Flapper, blue dress, gray lid lines, German #74507, 4" . 85.00

Flapper, large rose at side with hands at waist, pink bodice, 3¼" 35.00

Flapper, orange lustre dress, green hat, German #14506, 3¾" 100.00

Green picture hat, 1 open arm & 1 away, #14910, 3¾" . 85.00

Japanese lady on base, blue & white hat, hands to chest, dressed, 5" 40.00

Lady & fan, 1 hand to face, blonde with blue headband, Japan, 3¼" 30.00

Open arms behind head, mohair hair, German, 2¼" 110.00

Red hat with blue plume, holds fan, German #345, 3¾", VG 35.00

Heubach

Black boy, closed mouth, teeth, kinky molded hair, 12" 1,200.00

Boy, #6-6894, closed mouth, intaglio eyes, molded hair, sailor, 19" 2,200.00

Googly glass eyes, 5 piece papier mache, watermelon mouth, 7" 1,600.00

Nurser baby, #7770 with 14k pacifier, 14" 1,400.00

Ideal

Bam Bam, 16" 15.00

Bonnie Braids, hand painted with vinyl head, braided saran hair, 1951 .... 43.00

Bozo, cloth with early vinyl head, painted features, 1950s, 18" 20.00

Dianna Ross, 18" 25.00

Evel Knievel & rescue set, 7" . 12.00

Fanny Brice as Baby Snooks, replaced outfit, 1939 ... 130.00

Look Around Crissy, black . 50.00

Mortimer Snerd, all original, 12½" 250.00

National Velvet, marked Metro-Goldwyn-Mayer Inc/Ideal, 38" 750.00

Patsy, original clothes, EX . 195.00

Peter Playpal, rooted hair, open close eyes, vinyl, 1961, 36" 185.00

Talking Crissy 20.00

Jumeau

Closed mouth, marked EJ (incised) Jumeau, 10" 3,000.00

Closed mouth, marked EJ (incised) Jumeau, 14" 4,000.00

Closed mouth, marked Tete Jumeau, 10" 2,200.00

Closed mouth, marked Tete Jumeau, 16" 2,800.00

Closed mouth, marked Tete Jumeau, 23" 3,700.00

Closed mouth, marked Tete
Jumeau, 30″ 5,500.00
Depose/Tete Jumeau, ear
rings, long curls, swivel
head, 18″ 3,700.00
E 6 J/Jumeau, inset eyes, kid
body, swivel head, 16″ ..4,500.00
EJ/Depose Brevete, inset
eyes, 'mama/papa', swivel
head, 16″ 4,500.00
Open mouth, marked Tete
Jumeau, 10″ 750.00
Open mouth, marked Tete
Jumeau, 16″ 1,400.00
Open mouth, marked Tete
Jumeau, 23″ 2,300.00
Open mouth, marked Tete
Jumeau, 30″ 3,000.00
Open mouth, marked 1907
Jumeau, 17″ 1,200.00
Open mouth, marked 1907
Jumeau, 28″ 2,500.00
Phonograph in body, open
mouth, 20″ 2,400.00
Portrait Jumeau, closed
mouth, 16″ 4,500.00
1907, open mouth, open close
eyes, pierced ears, swivel
head, 23″ 1,800.00

Kammer and Reinhardt

#101, boy or girl with glass
eyes, 12″ 2,000.00
#101, boy or girl with glass
eyes, 20″ 4,500.00
#101, boy or girl with painted
eyes, 16″ 1,900.00
#109, rare, 18″ 10,000.00
#109, with glass eyes, rare, 15″
...................7,500.00
#114, with glass eyes, rare, 15″
...................5,200.00
#115, closed mouth, 15″ ..2,500.00
#115, open mouth, 15″ 1,400.00
#115a, closed mouth, 15″ ..2,500.00
#115a, open mouth, 15″ ...1,400.00
#116, closed mouth, 15″ ...2,000.00
#116, open mouth, 15″ 1,000.00

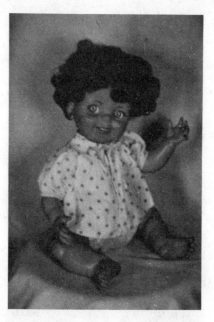

Baby Giggles, plastic and vinyl, raise
arms and head tilts, eyes flirt and she
giggles. Marked 1966/Ideal Toy
Corp/BG-18-H-118 on head, 1968/Ideal
Toy Corp/BG-16 on hip, $38.00.

Kestner

A, shoulder head, open mouth,
MIG/Kestner, 19″ 358.00
B/6, socket head, jointed composition, open mouth, 2
teeth, set eyes 425.00
Century Doll Company, flanged closed dome, closed
mouth, 15″ 700.00
G/8, turned shoulder head,
open mouth, MI/JDK, 19″ 395.00
H/12, socket head, open closed mouth, 1892, 23″ 1,500.00
J/13, socket head, open mouth,
1896, 27″ 600.00
L/3, shoulder head, open closed mouth with molded
teeth, 23″ 1,300.00
10, socket head, bisque
shoulder plate, closed
mouth, 21″ 1,700.00

139

13, socket head, open mouth,
JDK/MIG, 18″ 425.00

147, turned shoulder head,
open mouth, JDK, 25″ .. 495.00

16, socket head, open mouth,
JDK/MIG, 21″ 475.00

168, socket head, open mouth,
MID/G7, 26″ 650.00

171, shoulder head, open
mouth, INCIDFIN F ½,
G/10½, 20″ 485.00

180 12/Ox/Crown seal, socket
head, open mouth, 16″ .. 375.00

245, socket head, 5 piece baby,
G/MIG/11/JDK Jr/1914
Hilda, 14″ 2,395.00

257, socket head, 5 piece baby,
open mouth, G/JDK, 10″ . 350.00

639, turned shoulder head,
closed dome, closed mouth,
G/6, 18″ 995.00

Madame Alexander

African, hard plastic,
1966-1971, 8″ 350.00

Alice in Wonderland, hard
plastic, with trousseau,
Maggie, 14″ 700.00

Amish Boy or Girl, Wendy
Ann, hard plastic, 1966-
1969, 8″ 450.00

Babs Skater, Margaret, hard
plastic, 18″ 385.00

Baby Clown, Wendy Ann,
hard plastic, painted face,
1955, 8″ 1,200.00

Bad Little Girl, cloth, blue
dress, 1964, 16″ 125.00

Belgium, Tiny Betty, composition, 1935-1938, 7″ 145.00

Blue Boy, cloth, 16″ 350.00

Bonnie Toddler, cloth, hard
plastic head, vinyl limbs,
1951, 18″ 200.00

Bridesmaid, Elise, hard
plastic, 1957, 16½″ 265.00

Butch McGuffey, composition
& cloth, 1940 .... 175.00

Carreen, Wendy Ann, com-
position, 1937, 14″ 200.00

Cherub Babies, cloth 350.00

Cinderella, Lissy Classic, hard
plastic, 1966, 12″ 1,400.00

Cornelia, cloth & felt, 1930s . 425.00

Curly Locks, Wendy Ann,
hard plastic, 1955, 7½″ . 600.00

David Copperfield, cloth
Dicken's character, 16″ . 500.00

Dearest, 12″ Baby 125.00

Dionne Quints, cloth body,
composition, 14″, each .. 450.00

Dressed for Opera, Margaret,
hard plastic, 18″ 700.00

Egyptian, Little Betty, composition, 1936, 9″ 250.00

Emily, cloth & felt, 1930s . 375.00

Fairy Queen, Margaret, hard
plastic, 18″ 450.00

Flowergirl, Cissy, hard plastic,
1954, 15″ 250.00

Garden Party, Margaret, hard
plastic, 1953, 18″ 700.00

Glamour Girls of 1953,
Margaret-Maggie, hard
plastic, 18″ 700.00

Godey Lady, Margaret, hard
plastic, 14″ 700.00

Goldilocks, Tiny Betty, composition, 1938, 7″ 185.00

Graduation, Lissy, hard
plastic, 12″ 650.00

Groom, composition, 18-21″ . 495.00

Hello Baby, 22″ 125.00

Hilda, Margaret, composition,
1946, 18″ 650.00

Ice Skater, Wendy Ann, hard
plastic, 1954-1956, 8″ ... 275.00

Jack & Jill, Little Betty, composition, 1939 only, 9″ .. 250.00

Judy, Jacqueline, hard
plastic vinyl arms, 1962,
21″ 950.00

Kate Greenaway, Princess
Elizabeth, composition, 13″ 350.00

Little Colonel, composition,
1953, 13″ 475.00

Mama Kitten, 18″ 125.00

Mary Cassatt Baby, cloth & vinyl, 1969, 14″ 185.00

McGuffey, Ana; Princess Elizabeth, composition, 1937, 25″ 425.00

Milly, Polly, plastic & vinyl, 1968, 17″ 275.00

Pamela, Lissy, hard plastic, takes wigs, 1962, 12″ ... 300.00

Picnic Day, Margaret, hard plastic, 18″ 750.00

Prince Charming, Margaret, composition, 1947, 16″ .. 500.00

Rainy Day, Wendy Ann, hard plastic, 1955, 8″ 275.00

Riley's Little Annie, Mary Ann, plastic & vinyl, 1967, 14″ 600.00

Ruth, Tiny Betty, composition, 1935-1939, 7″ 145.00

Shari Lewis, 1959, 14″ 325.00

Sleeping Beauty, 1959, 21″ . 500.00

Southern Belle, Lissy, hard plastic, 1963, 12″ 1,400.00

Sweet Violet, Cissy, hard plastic, 1951-1954, 18″ .. 325.00

Tippy Toe, cloth, 16″ 350.00

White Rabbit, cloth & felt . 350.00

SFBJ

Celestine, bisque socket head on mache, open mouth, inset eyes, 18″ 900.00

11, composition with bisque swivel head, closed mouth, inset eyes, 16″......... 700.00

223, bisque, closed dome, open mouth with eight teeth, molded hair, 17″ 1,500.00

227, closed dome, open mouth, painted hair, inset eyes, 15″1,800.00

229, wood walker, open closed mouth, inset eyes, 18″ .. 1,850.00

235, closed dome, molded hair, open closed mouth & eyes, 8″ 750.00

239, Poulbot, urchin, red wig, closed mouth, 14″......3,900.00

247, toddler, open closed mouth with 2 inset teeth, 16″ 2,000.00

252, character, mache body, pouty, closed mouth, inset eyes, 18″ 3,000.00

301, bisque socket head on composition, open mouth, inset eyes, 16″ 595.00

60, Kiss-Blower, cryer walker, 22″ 1,450.00

60, socket head, composition, straight legs, open mouth, 15″ 500.00

Shirley Temple

Look-alike, all composition, tin eyes, teeth, long curls, 24″, VG 200.00

Outfit, #9540, pants, jacket, straw hat, 1950s, MIB .. 35.00

Outfit, #9750, shirt & shorts, MIB 20.00

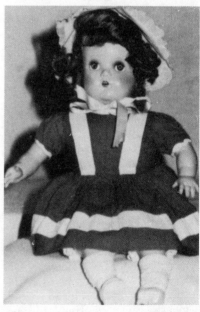

Betty Ann, cloth body with hard plastic head, arms and legs, open mouth, eye shadow. Marked Horsman Doll on head, 1951, $18.00.

11" composition, original dress, wig, undies, flirty eyes, EX 595.00

13" composition, all original, in Shirley trunk 500.00

13" composition, tagged blue & white dress with pin, original, 1930s 360.00

16" composition, Our Little Girl, with pin, tagged, all original, M 500.00

17" composition, copy of Curly Top, EX 575.00

18" composition, with pin, all original 550.00

19" composition, all original, EX 575.00

25" composition, sailor suit, EX 725.00

7" composition, Japan, M . 100.00

8" vinyl, Stowaway, Ideal, 1982 .... 30.00

Simon and Halbig

Baby Blanche, socket head, open mouth baby, S&H, 21" 695.00

CM Bergmann, socket head, open mouth, S&H6, 1897, 12" 175.00

CM Bergmann, socket head, open mouth, Simon & Halbig, 3½, 18" 450.00

Handwerck, socket head, open mouth, 1893, 16" 375.00

S&H3, all bisque, closed mouth, inset eyes, molded-on shoes, 6" 285.00

10, socket head, open mouth, G/Halbig/S&H, 22" 500.00

101, socket head, closed mouth, Simon & Halbig/ K*R, 16" 1,900.00

114, socket head, closed mouth, Simon & Halbig K*R/L, 20" 4,400.00

115a, socket head, closed mouth pouty, K*R/Simon & Halbig, 15" 2,500.00

116a, socket head, closed mouth, K*R/Simon & Halbig, 17" 2,500.00

117a, socket head, closed mouth, K*R/Simon & Halbig, 16" 3,300.00

120, socket head, open mouth, SH, 28" 2,500.00

121, socket head, open mouth, K*R/Simon & Halbig, 1920, 19" 525.00

126, socket head, open mouth, Simon & Halbig/K*R, 19" 575.00

1296, socket head, FS&Co/ Simon & Halbig, 1911, 14" 475.00

156, socket head, S&H, 1925, 22" 500.00

191, socket head, open mouth, Bergmann/CB, 18" 450.00

282, socket head, open mouth, S H, 14" 375.00

383, socket head, flapper body, S H, 14" 900.00

403, socket head, open mouth, walker, K*R SH, 21" ... 750.00

409, socket head, open mouth, S&H, 24" 550.00

50, socket head, closed mouth, Simon & Halbig, 16" ... 950.00

530, socket head, open mouth, G/Simon & Halbig, 21" . 450.00

570, socket head, open mouth, Halbig S&H/G, 18" 475.00

670, socket head, open mouth, Simon & Halbig, 16" ... 400.00

739, socket head, closed mouth, brown, S 5 H DEP, 14" 1,400.00

769, socket head, S&H DEP, 17" 1,600.00

929, socket head, closed mouth, S&H, DEP, 25" . 2,800.00

939, socket head, closed mouth, S 11H DEP, 23" . 2,500.00

Vogue

Brooke Shields 12.00

E Wilkens Baby Dear, 12", MIB 25.00

Ginny, bent knee, vinyl head, heart dress, hard plastic, 1963 .... 80.00

Ginny, Davy Crockett, bent leg walker, 1955 .... 85.00

Ginny, Majorette, bent leg walker, 1956 .... 100.00

Ginny, Spanish outfit, red & black, purple box, 1970s . 20.00

Sassoon Ginny, blonde, 1981 . 12.00

Welcome Home Baby Turns Two, MIB 85.00

Doorstops

Doorstops, once called door porters, were popular from the Civil War period until after 1930. They were used to prop the doors open during the hot summer months so that the cooler air could circulate. Though some were made of brass, wood, and chalk, cast iron was by far the most preferred material, usually molded in amusing figurals -- dogs, flower baskets, frogs, etc. Hubley was one of the largest producers.

Bear, fuzzy cover over chalkware 17.50

Cat, Hubley, sitting, full figure, original paint, 9", M 165.00

Cornucopia, with fruit, repainted cast iron, 7½" .. 45.00

Covered wagon, with oxen, cast iron, 16x18" 95.00

Deer, full antlers, flat back, on base 125.00

Dog, Boston Bull, black & white, 5", VG 65.00

Dog, Fox Terrier, smooth hair, flat back on base 50.00

Dog, puppy, bee on thigh, worn original black paint, 4¾" 30.00

Dog, Scotty, full figure facing front, 8½x10½", EX ... 110.00

Dog, Setter, original paint, 3x4½", EX 40.00

Drum major, full figure, 12½" 165.00

Elephant, full figure with trunk up, tusks, 8", M .. 90.00

Flower basket, flat back, original paint, 3", M ... 35.00

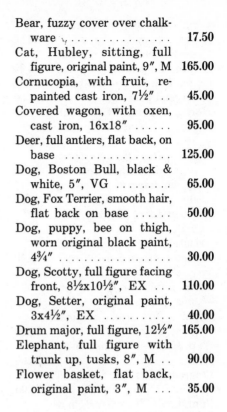

English Setter, cast iron with original paint, 9½" x 15", $65.00.

Frog, cast iron, dark green, very heavy 60.00

General Robert E Lee, cast iron, old paint, 7¼" 75.00

Golfer, in knickers, flat back, original paint 175.00

Horse, Hubley, #345, full figure, original paint, 10½", M 135.00

House, cottage figural on base with original blue coloring 65.00

Lady, holding hat & flowers, flat back, 11", EX 85.00

Organ grinder & monkey, iron, 9½" 85.00

Oriental baby on pillow, full figure, original paint, 6¼" 70.00

Peacock, cast iron 100.00

Peter Rabbit, red sweater, blue pants, 8¼" 80.00

Poppies, flat back, original paint, Hubley #330, 7" .. 50.00

Ship, signed 1928, flat back, 4" 12.00

Stagecoach, flat back, original paint, 7", G 50.00

Sunbonnet Baby, original paint, EX 42.50

Turtle, cast iron 60.00

Windmill, flat back, original paint, M 65.00

Witch, riding on broomstick, brass 150.00

Farm Collectibles

Farming memorabilia is a specialized area of primitives that is of particular interest to those interested in preserving the memory of farm life when horses drew the plow, and steam engines ran the thrashers . . . when 'hands' were called to noon 'dinner' by the ringing of the dinner bell, and work days began at three in the morning. Today, cast iron implement seats make stools for the family room bar; and scythes, wagon wheels, and oxen yokes are almost commonplace on restaurant walls.

Apple butter stirring stick, 36" long 12.50

Auger, hollow, Stearns & Company, 6¾" long blade 25.00

Auger, wood handle, good, 14" long 15.00

Barley fork, four tines, wide spaced 14.00

Basket, pea-picking, wood, 20" long 70.00

Bell, for animal, cast brass, 3" bell mouth diameter 18.00

Bench, splayed legs, old gray paint, 49x19" tall 55.00

Birdhouse, wren's, hanging, cream-glazed pottery, 11" tall 89.00

Cheese tester, tapered steel blade, wood handle, 15" long 42.00

Chicken snatcher, long wire with hook end, wood handle, homemade 13.00

Churn, plunger, wood-strip bands, early 105.00

Cleaver, cast steel blade, hardwood handle, 13" long .. 17.50

Corn planter, wood handle, 32" 16.00

Divider, brass joint, cast iron, 10" high 12.50

Engine, gasoline, used on spray rigs, Fairbanks-Morse, circa 1918 ...... 148.00

Farm wagon, sideboards with stencils, original equipment 175.00

Feed box, cast iron, for stall corner, 16" wide 26.00

Flashlight, cardboard tube, convex lens, 8" long 15.00

Grain measure, double, wood-staved, ½ & 1 peck sizes . 68.00

Grain shovel, all wood, 46" . 125.00

Hand seeder, cast iron gears, no straps 36.00

Spray rig, horse drawn, cast iron axles, cast and forged wheels, ca. 1890, $100.00.

Hatchet, broad, marked blade, label on handle	23.50
Hay fork, all wood, 60″ long .	90.00
Hoe, hand forged iron head, old handle, 5 feet long ..	13.00
Horse anchor, iron block, original brass studded leather strap	44.00
Horse collar, leather, weathered	17.00
Horse tether, beehive configuration, unusual	47.50
Milk jug, heavy tin, bail, brass bands, Shaker type	65.00
Parts list, Oliver Tractor Implements	21.00
Reins keeper, sticking type, blacksmith-made, 7″ long .	27.50
Saw, rectangular heavy blade, hand forged, wood handles	60.00
Tinder box, strike-a-light, flint & tinder, very old	112.00
Tongs, grooved tips, 21″ handles	9.50
Yoke, adjustable bentwood collars, large iron ring, 32″ long	38.00

Fiesta

For over ten years now, since it was discontinued by Homer Laughlin China, Fiesta has been collected with a passion by those who succumbed to its clean lines, timeless style, and beautiful colors. Its popularity continues to grow, and its value continues to climb. Still, except for the scarce items (such as the red 12″ vase which may bring $250.00 and up), table settings can be reassembled without too much difficulty or strain on one's budget. It is usually marked except for the flat jiggered pieces such as plates, saucers, and platters, since these were hand stamped without much consistency. Hollow ware items are signed with the indented mark which was made into the mold itself, though some were too small to accomodate it. Rarely are tea cups, demitasse cups, salt and pepper shakers, etc. ever marked. Red is usually more expensive, though medium green, dark green, gray, rose and chartreuse are often just as high,

Demitasse or after dinner set: pot, $85.00 in dark blue; cup and saucer, $75.00 in red, dark green, rose, chartreuse, or gray, $24.00 in other colors.

because of scarcity and popular demand.

Ash tray, original colors ...	22.00
Ash tray, red & '50s colors .	28.00
Bowl, dessert, 6″; '50s colors .	16.00
Bowl, dessert, 6″; original colors	12.50
Bowl, dessert, 6″; red	20.00
Bowl, footed salad; original colors	100.00
Bowl, footed salad; red	135.00
Bowl, fruit, 11½″	80.00
Bowl, fruit, 4¾″; '50s colors .	10.00
Bowl, fruit, 4¾″; medium green	30.00
Bowl, fruit, 4¾″; original colors	8.00
Bowl, fruit, 4¾″; red	12.00
Bowl, fruit, 5½″; medium green	18.00
Bowl, fruit, 5½″; red & '50s colors	13.00
Bowl, individual salad	35.00
Bowl, individual salad; medium green	40.00
Bowl, unlisted; yellow	35.00
Cake plate, Kitchen Kraft, other than red	24.00
Cake plate, Kitchen Kraft, red	30.00
Candle holders, bulb; original colors	30.00
Candle holders, bulb; red ..	40.00
Candle holders, tripod; original colors	95.00
Candle holders, tripod; red .	125.00
Carafe, red	90.00
Casserole, French; yellow ..	120.00
Casserole, individual; Kitchen Kraft, other than red ...	50.00
Casserole, individual; Kitchen Kraft, red	65.00
Casserole, medium green ..	85.00

Casserole, red & '50s colors . 58.00

Casserole, 7½"; Kitchen Kraft, other than red ... 55.00

Casserole, 7½"; Kitchen Kraft, red 65.00

Casserole, 8½"; Kitchen Kraft, other than red ... 60.00

Casserole, 8½"; Kitchen Kraft, red 70.00

Coffee pot, '50s colors 70.00

Coffee pot, demitasse; original colors 85.00

Coffee pot, demitasse; red . 100.00

Coffee pot, original colors . 45.00

Coffee pot, red 58.00

Comport, sweets; original colors 20.00

Comport, sweets; red 32.00

Comport, 12"; original colors . 42.00

Comport, 12"; red 60.00

Creamer, individual; red ... 50.00

Creamer, individual; yellow . 27.50

Creamer, original colors ... 6.50

Creamer, red, medium green & '50s colors 12.00

Creamer, stick handle; original colors 12.00

Creamer, stick handle; red . 15.00

Cup & saucer, demitasse; '50s colors 75.00

Cup & saucer, demitasse; original colors 24.00

Cup & saucer, demitasse; red . 32.50

Cup & saucer, original colors . 15.00

Cup & saucer, red & '50s colors 18.50

Egg cup, '50s colors 40.00

Egg cup, original colors ... 20.00

Egg cup, red 30.00

Fork, Kitchen Kraft 30.00

Gravy boat, original colors . 16.00

Gravy boat, red & '50s colors 20.00

Jar, large; Kitchen Kraft, other than red 125.00

Jar, large; red 135.00

Jar, medium; Kitchen Kraft, other than red 110.00

Jar, medium; Kitchen Kraft, red 130.00

Jar, small; Kitchen Kraft, other than red 100.00

Jar, small; Kitchen Kraft, red 125.00

Jug, Kitchen Kraft 135.00

Marmalade, original colors . 70.00

Marmalade, red 85.00

Metal handle for 13" chop plate 25.00

Metal holder for marmalade . 25.00

Mixing bowl, #1, original colors 25.00

Mixing bowl, #2, original colors 23.00

Mixing bowl, #3, original colors 27.00

Mixing bowl, #4, original colors 29.00

Mixing bowl, #6, original colors 40.00

Mixing bowl, #7, original colors 45.00

Mixing bowl, #8, any color . 85.00

Mug, original colors 22.50

Mug, red, medium green & '50s colors 45.00

Mustard, original colors ... 50.00

Mustard, red 80.00

Nappy, 8½"; original colors . 13.00

Nappy, 8½"; red & '50s colors 18.50

Nappy, 9½"; original colors . 18.00

Nappy, 9½"; red 23.00

Pie plate, 10"; Kitchen Kraft, in frame 50.00

Pie plate, 10"; Kitchen Kraft, other than red 28.00

Pie plate, 10"; Kitchen Kraft, red 35.00

Pie plate, 9"; Kitchen Kraft, other than red 25.00

Pie plate, 9"; red 32.00

Pitcher, disc; chartreuse ... 55.00

Pitcher, disc; original colors . 28.00

Pitcher, disc; red 38.00

Pitcher, disc; rose, dark green & gray 45.00

Pitcher, ice lip; original colors 32.00

Pitcher, ice lip; red 50.00

Pitcher, jug, 2 pint; original colors 23.00

Pitcher, jug, 2 pint; red & '50s colors 32.00
Plate, chop, 13"; '50s colors . 22.00
Plate, chop, 13"; original colors 12.50
Plate, chop, 13"; red 16.00
Plate, chop, 15"; '50s colors . 26.00
Plate, chop, 15"; original colors 15.00
Plate, chop, 15"; red 20.00
Plate, compartment, 10½"; '50s colors 20.00
Plate, compartment, 10½"; original colors 12.00
Plate, compartment, 10½"; red 17.50
Plate, compartment, 11½" . 22.00
Plate, deep; original colors . 11.50
Plate, deep; red & '50s colors . 18.00
Plate, 10"; medium green .. 22.00
Plate, 10"; original colors .. 9.50
Plate, 10"; red & '50s colors . 14.00
Plate, 6"; original colors ... 3.00
Plate, 6"; red, medium green & '50s colors 4.50
Plate, 7"; original colors ... 4.50
Plate, 7"; red, medium green, & '50s colors 6.00
Plate, 9"; original colors ... 6.00
Plate, 9"; red, medium green & '50s colors 10.00
Platter, Kitchen Kraft, in frame 70.00
Platter, Kitchen Kraft, without frame 50.00
Platter, original colors 11.50
Platter, red & '50s colors .. 20.00
Relish, multicolored 57.50
Salt & pepper, Kitchen Kraft, other than red, pair 40.00
Salt & pepper, Kitchen Kraft, red, pair 50.00
Salt & pepper, original colors, pair 10.00
Salt & pepper, red & '50s colors, pair 16.00
Server, Kitchen Kraft 38.00
Soup, cream; '50s colors ... 22.00
Soup, cream; original colors . 15.00

Soup, cream; red 20.00
Soup, onion; original colors . 130.00
Soup, onion; red 150.00
Spoon, Kitchen Kraft, other than red 30.00
Spoon, Kitchen Kraft, red . 38.00
Sta Brite tableware, 6 place settings 45.00
Stack set, Kitchen Kraft .. 80.00
Stack set, Kitchen Kraft, lid only 25.00
Sugar, with lid, '50s colors . 14.50
Sugar, with lid, original colors 9.50
Sugar, with lid, red & medium green 20.00
Syrup, original colors 80.00
Syrup, red 120.00
Teapot, large; original colors . 50.00
Teapot, large; red & '50s colors 70.00
Teapot, medium; medium green 125.00
Teapot, medium; red & '50s colors 56.00
Tom & Jerry, white with lettering 13.50
Tray, figure-8; cobalt 30.00
Tray, figure-8; turquoise ... 50.00
Tray, figure-8; yellow 65.00
Tray, utility; original colors . 13.00
Tray, utility; red 20.00
Tumbler, juice; original colors 13.50
Tumbler, juice; rose & red . 15.00
Tumbler, red 28.00
Tumbler, 10 ounce; red 28.00
Tumbler, 10 ounce; regular colors 21.50
Vase, bud; original colors .. 24.00
Vase, bud; red 35.00
Vase, 10"; original colors . 175.00
Vase, 10"; red 225.00
Vase, 12"; original colors .. 190.00
Vase, 12"; red 250.00

Fire Fighting Collectibles

Fire fighting squads from the early 19th century were made up of volunteers whose only pay was reward money donated by the home owner whose property they had saved. By 1860, cities began to organize municipal fire departments. Much pomp and ceremony was displayed by the brigade during parade festivities. Fancy belts, silver trumpets, and bright-colored jackets were the uniform of the day. Today these are treasured by collectors who also search for fire marks, posters, photographs of engines and water wagons, and equipment of all types.

Leather helmet with eagle and leather shield, in good condition, $110.00.

Alarm, cast iron, Automatic Sprinkler Company, 15″ .	34.00
Axe holder, brass	56.00
Booklet, Firehouse History 1775-1975, Elsie Lowe & David Robinson	25.00
Bucket, leather, black paint with red interior, pair ..	225.00
Certificate, unframed, Worcester Fire Dept Co, Winthrop Morre, 1839	125.00
Chalice, coin silver, scene with fire engine, Curry, 9″ ...	400.00
Extinguisher, The Improved Emergency Fire Extinguisher	25.00
Fire mark, Aetna, tin, United States	131.00
Fire mark, Royal Exchange, lead, English	81.00

Fire mark, Sun, copper, English	41.00
Fire mark, United Firemen's Insurance Company, cast iron, 9½x12″	123.00
Gong, small alarm in oak case, nickel plated gong	125.00
Grenade, amber, Hazelton's High Pressure Chemical Fire Keg	115.00
Hand rattle, wooden, 8½″ long	63.50
Helmet, leather, High Eagle, 'Captain-NH Foster-Beverly'	175.00
Helmet, leather, low profile, 'Ladder 1 CFD'	43.00

Trumpet, tin painted red with gold trim, used to decorate fire station, 68″, $250.00.

Lantern, tubular, clear globe,
Dietz Fire Dept, patent Jan
1, 1889 .... 85.00
Nozzle, brass & copper play
pipes, Boston Corysling Co,
31″, pair 125.00
Panel, red glass etched 'BFD',
with bezel, 6¼″ diameter . 85.00
Parade belt, black with red &
white trim, 'Nashua-VET',
1891 .... 65.00
Parade torch, oil burning,
wood hdl, marked Fire
King 65.00
Program, first annual parade,
Boston Fire Dept, Sept 17,
1856 .... 30.00
Sign, enamel, Fire Chief Tex-
aco 12.50
Sign, tin, Holyoke Mutual
Fire Insurance Co, Salem,
Mass, Est 1843 .... 55.00

Fireplace Accessories

From the primitive cooking utensils of the early years of our country,
to the elegant Federal brass andirons,
fireplace accessories, while rarely collected in that particular context, are
purchased for reasons as varied as the
items themselves. Screens, fire
fenders, bellows, and the like, may be
needed to furnish a period room, while
simple items like gypsy pots, trivets,
and firebacks may be put to a
decorative use for which they were
never intended.

Andirons, brass, lemon finials,
restored iron log rests,
1700s 338.00
Andirons, brass, spur on legs,
turned with ball finials,
1700s, 18″ 250.00
Andirons, cast iron ring top,
14½″ 23.00

Toaster, hand wrought iron, revolving,
early to mid-19th century American,
11″ x 7″ x 3¾″, $175.00.

Andirons, figural form, portly
gentlemen, painted cast
iron, 21″ 108.00
Bellows, brass nozzle, top
split, original painted shell,
foliage, 18″............ 102.00
Bellows, stenciled, tin spout,
old leather, old repaint, 21″ 66.00
Coffee bean roaster, iron
rotating ball, 8½″
diameter 198.00
Crane, wrought iron, mounting brackets, 25″ 36.00
Fender, engraved brass bow
front, George III, early
1800s, 54″ long 348.00
Fire board, pine with worn
paint, stenciled basket,
27x38″ 371.00
Fire dog, wrought iron, dog
form with four legs, 1700s,
7x12″ 174.00
Fireplace front, ornate cast
iron, Victorian, 27x18″ .. 41.00
Floor rack, with cross bars, for
baking potatoes, iron,
15x14″ 130.00
Fork, wrought iron, Neptune . 62.00
Fuel box, tole chinoiserie
decor, 6 winged animal-paw
feet, 21″ 112.00
Grate, floral molded back
plate, serpentine fire box,
steel, cast iron........ 652.00

Griddle, cast iron, wrought iron overhead handle, hanging loop, 3 feet......... 117.00

Kettle tipper, wrought iron, 19" 86.00

Lid lifter, thimble ferrule, wood handle, 4½" hook, 5½" handle 51.00

Mantle, country, pine, simple pilasters, shelf, stripped, 54" wide 86.00

Screen, walnut, adjusts, 17th century tapestry base, 30x22" 148.00

Sling, for pan or kettle, 1700s 89.00

Toaster, flip style, 12" across, 21" handle 90.00

Tongs, wrought iron, 25" long 27.00

Trivet, cast iron, 3 footed, 5½x7½" diameter 50.00

Fishing Collectibles

Very much in evidence at flea markets these days, old fishing gear is becoming a popular collectible. Because the hobby is newly established, there are some very good buys to be found. Early 20th century plugs were almost entirely carved from wood, sprayed with several layers of enamel, and finished off with glass eyes. Molded plastics were of a later origin. Some of the more collectible manufacturers are James Heddon, Shakespeare, Rhodes, and Pflueger.

Book, Determined Angler, pocket volume, 1900 .... 18.00

Chix Bait, in box 21.00

Creel, leather strap, tight woven wicker, bait tray, EX 80.00

Cricket box, perforated lid, belt extension, painted tin, 3½" 20.00

Decoy, Northern Pike, tin fins & tail, painted wood body, 1930s, 9" 60.00

Decoy, pike, carved wood, metal fins, original paint, modern, 11" 39.00

Decoy, tack eyes, painted, jigsaw cut-out, lead weight, 9" 36.00

Decoy, tin tail, 2 large fins, glass insert eyes, painted dots, 8" 45.00

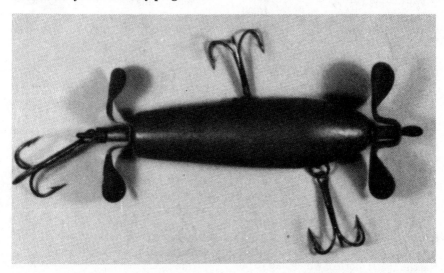

Decker Underwater Lure, two spinning metal propellers, 3" long, $25.00.

Decoy, wood with 4 tin fins, 1920s, 10″	47.00
Fish spear, iron, 3 barbed prongs, no handles	31.00
Float ball, amber, 5¼″	23.00
Float balls, blown, assorted colors, 24 for	350.00
Gig, wood handle, handmade 1 piece iron spear, brass ferrule, 1700s	70.00
Hook maker, iron block, shapes wire to curve, snell & eye, 8″	143.00
Lure, frog or silver finish, Arbogast, Weedless Kicker, 1929	15.00
Lure, ice fishing, wood, Torpedo Ray	12.00
Lure, plastic, Arbogast, Jitterbug, circa 1937	60.00
Lure, The Prez	3.00
Mold, cast iron, for making lead sinkers, hinged	26.00
Plug, Game Fisher	14.00
Plug, Heddon Triple Teaser .	19.00
Reel, Frost's Auto Fly, original box, EX	45.00
Reel, Horricks Ibson Shark .	13.00
Reel, Meisselbach Takapart #481, 100 yard, VG	21.00
Reel, Pflueger Trump 1943 .	16.00
Reel, Ramsbottom, VG	184.00
Rod, bamboo, Winchester .	87.00
Rod & reel, Winchester	139.00
Rod basket, wicker, oval, hinged, Victorian, 40″	71.00
Scale, Sportsman's Chattilion, February 13, 1912, much brass	23.00
Speargun head, bronze, 5″ arrow with upward flair tail .	18.00

Flatirons

The iron evolved from the smithy-made flatiron, to the improved patented models with hand shields of the the 1870s (both of which had to be heated on a hot range), to box irons (which held heated slugs), charcoal irons, gas irons, and finally to electric models. Fluting irons, pleating irons, and tailor's irons did little to make ironing day easier, but nevertheless performed specialized jobs efficiently. Thank goodness for perma-press!

Left to right: #12 Ober Pat. Pend., open holes in handle for cooling, $15.00; Enterprise Mfg. Co., Phila., U.S.A., patd October 1, '87, with fluted handle, $35.00.

AC Williams, Ravenna, Ohio, #1, 2 or 3, one handle, 3 base irons	32.00
Acme Carbon Iron, patent March 15, 1910	38.00
Asbestos, nickel plated, detachable cover & handle, 4¾″	35.00
Charcoal, cast iron, with chimney	35.00
Chinese, brass with ivory handle, charcoal	54.00
Davis, natural gas, wood handle, metal hose, signed in oval	48.00
Dover, child's #22, 4¾″ . . .	20.00
Eclipse, coal burning, attached wood handle	25.00
Enterprise, #3, no handle . .	14.00
Enterprise, 3 irons & one handle	35.00
Fluting, hinged, one piece .	52.00

Gas, blue granite	25.00
Geneva, fluting, dated 1866 .	43.00
Geneva, pleating, 1871	40.00
Miniature, swan, 2½"	28.00
Mrs Potts No 3, detachable wood handle, 1870-1871 .	20.00
Sterno, miniature, collapsible trivet base, wood handle .	30.00
Syracuse, pleating machine, board, rods & label complete	36.00
Wright's Patent, gas, wood handle, nickel plated ...	23.00

Fountain Pens

Fountain pens have been manufactured commercially since the 1880s. Today's collectors value those made by well-known companies such as Waterman, Parker, and Sheaffer's, or those made of gold or set with jewels. Various types of pumping mechanisms were employed; abbreviations used here are: AF -- aeromatic filler; BF -- button filler; ED -- eyedropper filler; and TD -- touchdown filler.

Parker, 1913 Black Giant, black hard rubber, ED ..	995.00
Parker, 1924 Lucky Curve P3X, black hard rubber, BF	49.00
Parker, 1928 Duofold St, mandarin yellow, BF	575.00
Parker, 1929 Lady Duofold, red hard rubber, BF	69.00
Parker, 1929 Pastel, magenta moire	65.00
Parker, 1930 Duofold, black hard rubber, BF	45.00
Parker, 1932 Lucky Curve, black, BF	25.00
Parker, 1950-51, beige, lustraloy cap, chrome plated trim, AF	25.00
Parker, 1962 VP, black, lustraloy cap, AF	125.00

Sheaffer's, 1905 Aiken Lambert #8 Dip	35.00
Sheaffer's, 1916 #34, black chased hard rubber, nickel plated trim	55.00
Sheaffer's, 1926 Lady Lifetime, green jade marbled	39.00
Sheaffer's, 1939 #875 Lifetime, emerald striped .	29.00
Sheaffer's, 1939 Eagle, silver streaked scarlet	20.00
Sheaffer's, 1939 Lifetime, emerald striped	39.00
Sheaffer's, 1951 #33, black, TD	10.00
Sheaffer's, 1951 Feather Touch, green, TD	12.00
Sheaffer's, 1953 #5 Snorkel, maroon, TD	18.00
Wahl-Eversharp, 1918 Tempoint, black chased hard rubber	35.00
Wahl-Eversharp, 1931 Silver Seal Personal Point Doric, cathay, rare	725.00
Wahl-Eversharp, 1932 Doric, burgundy marbled	125.00
Wahl-Eversharp, 1943 Fifth Ave Ladies, maroon, gold filled cap	39.00
Wahl-Eversharp, 1946 Presentation Skyline, blue, gold filled cap	29.00
Waterman's Ideal, 1901 #22 Taper, black chased hard rubber, ED	175.00
Waterman's Ideal, 1918 #44 Safety, black chased hard rubber, ED	195.00
Waterman's Ideal, 1918 #45 Safety, black chased hard rubber, ED	250.00
Waterman's Ideal, 1922 #452, sterling filigree, sterling trim	195.00
Waterman's Ideal, 1924 #0552, Gothic gold filled metal	140.00

Waterman's Ideal, 1925 #452, pansy panel sterling, initialed 175.00

Waterman's Ideal, 1925 #52½ V, Rose Ripple, marbled . 29.00

Waterman's Ideal, 1925 #58, Rose Ripple, marbled ... 795.00

Waterman's Ideal, 1932 Patrician, green & gold marbled 640.00

Waterman's Ideal, 1943 100 Year, solid 14 karat gold, rare 925.00

Waterman's Ideal, 1947 Stateleigh Taperite, black, gold filled cap 65.00

Waterman's Ideal, 1949, black, chrome cap 25.00

Franciscan

Dinnerware has been made by Gladding McBean and Company from 1934 until the present day. Their earlier lines have become popular collectibles, especially Swirl or Coronado ware, which was made in more than sixty shapes and fifteen solid colors; and Apple, the ivory line with the red apple on the branch whose design was purchased from the Weller Pottery. During the 1930s the ware was marked with a large 'F' in a double-walled square; a two-line mark was used in the 1940s, and after 1947, a circular mark identified their product.

Apple, bowl, soup or cereal . 7.50

Apple, creamer 10.00

Apple, cup & saucer, demitasse 8.50

Apple, dinner plate 11.00

Apple, egg cup 7.50

Apple, open sugar 9.50

Apple, platter, 12″ 19.00

Apple, saucer 4.00

Coronado, carafe, orange .. 12.50

Coronado, gravy boat, attached underliner, ivory 16.00

Coronado, jam jar, square . 7.50

Water set, maroon and gray, 9″ pitcher, $30.00; 5½″ tumblers, $12.50 each.

Coronado, serving plate, coral, 11½"	10.00
Coronado, sherbet, ivory	4.50
Coronado, sugar, open, yellow	6.50
Coronado, teapot, yellow	34.00
Desert Rose, ash tray, rose petal, small	10.00
Desert Rose, butter, oblong, ¼ pound	17.00
Desert Rose, cigarette box	38.00
Desert Rose, relish, 3 part	18.00
Desert Rose, soup cup, with liner, large	19.50
Desert Rose, tidbit, 3 tier	34.00
Desert Rose, tumbler, 14 ounce	11.50
El Patio, cream soup, lettuce green, handled	9.50
El Patio, cup & saucer, demitasse; pretzel handle, original label	11.50
El Patio, plate, lettuce green, 9¼"	5.00
El Patio, platter, lettuce green, oval, 13"	14.00
Heritage, butter dish with lid	21.00
Heritage, creamer & sugar	32.50
Heritage, divided relish	27.50
Heritage, divided vegetable	32.00
Heritage, salad plate	11.50
Heritage, salt & pepper, pair	21.00
Indigo, bread & butter plate	14.00
Indigo, cup & saucer	25.00

Frankoma

Since 1933, the Frankoma Pottery Company has been producing dinnerware, novelty items, vases, etc.; and in 1965 became the first American company to produce a line of collector plates. The body of the ware prior to 1954 was a honey tan color. A brick red clay was used from then on, and this and the colors of the glazes help determine the period of production.

Candle holder, double, Brown Satin, #304, pair	12.50

Wall pocket, Billikin figural, green glaze with brown shading, 7", $65.00.

Chocolate set, Mayan, ivory, signed, pitcher, six 8 ounce cups, 1930s	117.00
Christmas card, 1949	56.00
Christmas card, 1954	66.50
Christmas card, 1959	66.00
Christmas card, 1966	44.50
Christmas card, 1971	26.00
Cookie jar	12.50
Cornucopia, Prairie Green, #222	25.50
Creamer & sugar, Wagon Wheel, old mark	10.50
Donkey mug, 1975, Autumn Yellow	14.50
Donkey mug, 1978, Woodland Moss	9.50
Elephant mug, 1968, white	74.00
Elephant mug, 1971, black	49.00
Elephant mug, 1975, Autumn Yellow	10.00
Flower arranger, Gracetone #68, Brown Satin, 4½" cube	9.50
Honey pot, beehive with bee finial, Desert Gold, 4½"	21.00

Bottle vase, collectors' series, blue glaze, V2N-4800, 12½″, $60.00.

Mug, Uncle Sam toby, Bicentennial Blue, #600, 1976	13.00
Pitcher, juice; Prairie Green, with lid & 2 cups, #93	10.50
Planter, black foot, #55, 4″	16.00
Plate, Bible Teenagers, 1972, Jesus the Carpenter, Desert Gold	20.50
Plate, Bible Teenagers, 1976, Dorcas the Seamstress, Desert Gold	36.00
Plate, Bible Teenagers, 1978, Martha the Homemaker, Desert Gold	21.00
Plate, Bible Teenagers, 1982, Mary the Mother, Desert Gold	15.50
Plate, Bicentennial, 1974, Battle for Independence, white	25.50
Plate, Christmas, 1971, No Room In The Inn	21.00
Plate, Mason's commemorative, 1849-1949, 10″	23.50

Plate, Wildlife series, set of 7, complete	155.00
Sculpture, coyote	16.00
Sculpture, gardener girl, 5¾″	82.00
Sculpture, puma, reclining, white	14.50
Trivet, Bicentennial Liberty Bell, dates on face, White Sand, 6″	11.00
Tumbler, juice; Prairie Green, white clay, 3″, set of 4	24.50
Vase, collector; V-10-B, Morning Glory Blue, signed JF, 11½″	24.00
Vase, collector; V-12, black with terra cotta, 1980, signed JF, 13″	31.00
Vase, collector; V-2, turquoise blue, 1970, signed John Frank, 12″	49.00
Vase, collector; V-5, Flame, black base, white interior, G Lee, 13″	59.00
Vase, collector; V-8, Freedom Red & white, red stopper, JF, 13″	61.00
Vase, cylinder, black with combed effect, 8″	16.00
Vase, snail, #31, Osage Brown	12.50
Wall mask, Indian, black	8.50
Wall pocket, Peter Pan, #100	24.50
Wall pocket, Phoebe, red, #130	26.50

Fruit Jars

Some of the earliest glass jars used for food preservation were blown, and corks were used for seals. During the 19th century, hundreds of manufacturers designed over 4,000 styles of fruit jars. Lids were held in place either by a wax seal, wire bale, or the later screw-on band. Jars were usually made in aqua or clear, though other colors were also used. Amber jars are popular with collectors, milk glass jars are rare, and cobalt and black glass jars often bring $500.00 and up if they can be found! Condition, age, scarcity and unusual features are also to be considered when evaluating old fruit jars.

Left to right: Atlas Mason's Patent, 1900-1910, zinc lid, aqua quart, $5.00; Ball Perfect Mason No. 2, 1900-1910, zinc lid, pint and cup measuring lines, amber, $30.00.

ABC, aqua, pint	344.00
Almy, aqua, quart	102.00
American Fruit Jar, eagle & flag, green, quart	118.00
Atlas, E-Z Seal, blue, half pint	9.50
Atlas, Good Luck, clear, half pint	13.00
Atlas Strong Shoulder Mason, light blue, pint	10.50
Ball, Perfect Mason, amber, half gallon	24.50
Ball Mason, yellow green, erased root, quart	20.50
Baltimore Glass Works, stopper neck, aqua, quart	250.00
Banner in Banner, clear, quart	12.50
Blown, wide mouth, pontil, light green, 13x6″	69.00
Canadian King, glass lid & full wire bail, clear, quart	6.50
Clarke Fruit Jar Company, aqua, half gallon	61.00
Crown with crown, amber, quart	49.50
Darling, ADM, aqua, quart	31.00
Dexter, aqua, half gallon	35.50
DG Company, intertwined, aqua, quart	41.00
Doolittle, Patented Dec 3, 1910 on lid, pint	66.00
Erased Western Pride, aqua, quart	33.00
FB Company, yellow amber, quart	126.00
Flaccus Company, EC Trade Mark, elk & floral design, milk glass	90.50
Fruit Keeper, GC Company, aqua, pint	43.00
Globe, amber, half gallon	54.00
Hahne & Company, Newark NJ, with star, pint	45.50
Helmes Railroad Mills, amber, quart	12.50
Hilton's Pat Mar 10th 1868, aqua, quart	285.50

Ideal Imperial, aqua, quart	24.50
Improved Jam, LG Company, aqua, pint	102.00
Johnson & Johnson New Brunswick NJ USA, amber, quart	23.50
LaFayette, in script, aqua, quart	95.00
Marion Jar, The; aqua, quart	9.00
Mason, KBG Co Nov 30th, 1858, aqua, quart	14.50
Mason's, sheared top, black, 7¼″	252.00
Mason's CFJ Nov 30th, 1858, amber, quart	136.00
Meyer's Test Jar	96.50
Millville Atmospheric Fruit Jar, aqua, pint	39.00
Ohio Quality Mason, clear, pint	21.00
Queen, aqua, quart	14.50
Schaffer Jar, Rochester NY, aqua, half gallon	185.50
Smalley Full Measure AGS Quart, amber, quart	51.00
Telephone jar, full wire bail, glass top, green, quart	18.50
Trade Mark Climax Registered, blue, pint	5.50
Trade Mark Lightening, amber, half gallon	49.00

Empire, 1860s, glass lid with wire bale, deep blue quart, $55.00.

Trade Mark Lightening Reg US Patent Office, cornflower blue, pint	39.00
Woodbury, aqua, quart	25.50
Yeoman's Fruit Bottle, wax seal, small mouth, aqua, 1855-1870	35.50

Furniture

Golden oak continues to be a favorite of furniture collectors; Victorian, Country, and Mission Oak are also popular, and flea markets are a good source for all these styles. After the industrial revolution, mail order furniture companies began to favor the lighter weight oak over the massive rosewood and walnut pieces, simply because shipping oak was less costly. This type of furniture retained its popularity throughout several decades of the 20th century. Mission was a style developed during the Arts and Crafts movement of the late 1900s. It was squarely built of heavy oak, with extreemly simple lines. Two of its leading designers were Elbert Hubbard and Gustav Stickley. Country furniture is simply styled, often handmade, and generally primitive in nature. Recently, good examples have been featured in magazine articles on home decorating.

Armchair, arrow back, worn original grainpaint with foliage & stripes	275.00
Armchair, child's; arrow back with painted & stenciled decor, low seat.........	75.00
Armchair, Country, maple, turned legs, three-slat back, caned seat	75.00
Armchair, ladderback, turned posts & finials, four slats, splint seat	385.00

Oak side-by-side curio cabinet, curved glass door, three drawers and mirror with double doors below, carved feet, 75″ x 47″, $1,000.00.

Jenny Lind maple double bed, twelve spindle footboard, arched headboard, turned posters and legs, $250.00.

Armchair, oak, made by Limbert, rush seat, #1721½ in catalog, 39″ . 175.00

Armchair, oak, Stickley, V-shaped back, leather seat, #354½, 38″ 275.00

Armchair, Victorian, open arms, cartouch back with grape crest 350.00

Armchair, Windsor, brace back & saddle seat, re-painted, from RI 500.00

Bed, metal, floral cartouch on head & footboard, ball finials 1,200.00

Bed, oak, plain with applied carving & wood rails, 48″ headboard 125.00

Bed, poster; pine & maple, single type, baluster & lobe-turned posts 275.00

Bed, rope; 'hired man's', single size, turned posts & shaped headboard........... 425.00

Bench, kneeling; pine with bootjack foot & beaded apron, painted, 44″ 50.00

Bench, Mammy's; arrow back, scrolled arms & rockers, re-painted, 55″ 430.00

Bench, primitive plank seat with two-chair base & spindle back, 53″ 190.00

Blanket chest, pine, three dovetailed overlapping drawers, till, 50″ 700.00

Blanket chest, poplar, dovetailed, turned foot, till, grainpaint, 39″ 575.00

Bookcase, oak, stacking, curved top trim with beading, 3 parts 385.00

Bookcase, oak, two double-supported shelves, trestle foot, Roycroft 275.00

Bureau, walnut, Victorian, marble top, mirror, shelves & glove drawers........ 900.00

Cabinet, china; oak, mirrored back, 3 convex glass panels, 65″ 275.00

Cabinet, china; oak, mirrored back, 3 convex glass panels, 87″ 795.00

Cabinet, Hoosier; oak, roll-up door, pull-out metal bin, glazed panels.......... 800.00

Cabinet, kitchen; oak, spice drawers, bin, glazed top doors, 75x48″ 950.00

Cabinet, spool; oak, lift top, 4 drawers, leather top, brass pulls 375.00

Cabinet with yellow and brown grain-painting, early 1800s, 29″ x 32″ x 14½″, $525.00.

Candlestand, birch & cherry, two-board top, snake feet & turned column 250.00

Candlestand, walnut, Country Hepplewhite, spider leg, spade 125.00

Card table, Victorian, octagonal flip top, four paw feet 200.00

Chair, corner; Country, turned posts & stretchers, cut-out arms 400.00

Chair, ladderback; original Shaker label #6, in original finish 650.00

Chair, oak, saddle seat, cartouch Autumn Face, 36x26" 250.00

Chair, secretary's; oak with slat back & seat, swivel type 85.00

Chair, side; Country Queen Anne, Spanish feet, turned legs & rush seat 200.00

Chair, side; oak, pressed border on headpiece, caned seat 125.00

Chair, side; rosewood, Victorian, cartouch back & seat, cabriole legs 200.00

Chair, side; Windsor fan back, country style, turned legs, saddle seat 950.00

Chair set, kitchen, press-back oak, cane seat, spindle back, 4 for 500.00

Chest, chestnut, 2 short & 3 long drawers, fancy brass pulls, ca 1930 .... 200.00

Chest, flame grain mahogany, Chippendale, 3 cockbeaded drawers, 29x31" 450.00

Chest, lingerie; oak, 5 drawers, door compartment, applied carvings 795.00

Chest, oak, Mission, 5 drawers with recessed panel sides, 50x35" 135.00

Chest, pine, hinged lift top, 42x18x15" 250.00

Chest, pine, square posts, cut-out foot, 6 dovetailed drawers, 48" 250.00

Chest, pine, 2 short & 2 long drawers, old brasses, painted, small 600.00

Chest, walnut & poplar, line inlay, 3 short & 4 long drawers 375.00

Chiffonier, oak, harp framed beveled mirror, 5 long serpentine drawers 395.00

Church pew, oak, plain cut, circa 1920, 48" long 325.00

Cupboard, apothecary; pine, open shelves, 12 dovetailed drawers 1,100.00

Cupboard, corner; cherry, 2 glazed doors over 2 paneled base doors 200.00

Cupboard, corner; walnut, 2-pc, 12-pane door over 2 in base, 88" 1,250.00

Cupboard, grainpainted poplar, 2-pc stepback, 2 doors top & base, 73" .. 525.00

Cupboard, hanging; pine, base & cornice molding, paneled door, 29" 365.00

Cupboard, jelly; ash, primitive 1-board door, dry sink & shelf, small 250.00

Cupboard, jelly; grainpainted poplar, 2 drawers, 2 paneled doors, 45" 325.00

Cupboard, pine, primitive, board & batten door, dry sink & shelf 800.00

Cupboard, pine, 2-pc, dentil molded cornice, repainted, 90x44" 900.00

Cupboard, pine & poplar, 1-panel door, molded cornice, 60" 300.00

Day bed, maple with spool turnings, upholstered cushion, 24x60x25" 380.00

Oak chiffoniere with mirror, ogee colonades, two short drawers over four, $245.00.

Day bed, oak, made by Stickley, angled headrest, caning replaced 500.00

Desk, cylinder roll; oak, brass pulls, ca 1870, 42x38" .. 950.00

Desk, lady's; oak, drop front, machine carvings, mirror gallery 375.00

Desk, oak, made by Stickley, slat top, double drawer with medial shelf....... 550.00

Desk, oak drop front, 2 glazed doors, drawer & base shelf, Crafters 200.00

Desk, partner's; oak, Victorian, leather top, 2 pedestals, 48" 1,400.00

Desk, pine, Country, lift top, fitted interior, old finish, 35x29" 135.00

Desk, pine, primitive, 3 drawers, 16 interior pigeon holes, 49x37" 400.00

Desk, rolltop; oak, pull-out shelf each side, 44x48x28"1,650.00

Dresser, oak, beveled mirror, serpentine front, 4 drawers, large 500.00

Dresser, oak, large mirror, 5 drawers, applied carvings, 81x48" 450.00

Dresser, oak, 2 short & 2 long drawers, wishbone mirror holder, 70" 400.00

Dry sink, pine & poplar, primitive, 2 doors, cut-out ends, gallery 650.00

Dry sink, pine & poplar, 2 panel doors, 2 drawers, open well, graining...... 650.00

Dry sink, 2-pc, gallery & 2 doors in top, grainpainted, 76x40" 500.00

Drying rack, swivel fold-down rack, 4 bars, 57" 135.00

Foot stool, oak, made by L & JG Stickley, leather surface, 19" long 425.00

Foot stool, oak, made by Stickley, catalog #302, 5x12" 175.00

Foot stool, poplar, bootjack ends, scalloped apron, old red finish 185.00

Hall tree, oak, hour glass shaping, applied carvings & pediment, seat 645.00

Hall tree, oak, large beveled mirror, lift seat, ornate carving, 84" 950.00

Highboy, oak, beveled mirror, hat cabinet, 3 short & 2 long drawers 395.00

Highboy, oak, 5 drawers, simple styling, small 200.00

Hutch table, pine, lift-lid seat, wide board top, good finish, 36x59″ 525.00

Hutch table, pine, square top, worn grainpaint, 32x48″ . 850.00

Magazine rack, oak, Mission, 1 angled & 3 flat shelves, 27″ 175.00

Pie safe, hanging, compass star punched tin, repainted, 35x26″ 600.00

Pie safe, pine, original punched tin sides & front, 48″ . 395.00

Pie safe, poplar, gallery top, 2 dovetailed drawers, punched tin 400.00

Rocker, bentwood, caned seat & oval medallion in back, ca 1800s 200.00

Rocker, child's; bentwood, oak, 3-spindle back, handmade, ca 1890s 110.00

Rocker, Mission type, shaped back splat, upholstered seat 200.00

Rocker, oak, 7-spindle pressed back, caned seat, spindle arms 300.00

Rocker, quarter-sawn & plain oak, curved seat, spindle back & sides 325.00

Rocker, Shaker, with arms & spindle back, tape seat, #7, Bro Gregory 225.00

Rocker, walnut, Victorian, upholstered back & seat, scrolled arms 200.00

Secretary-bookcase, oak, French Revival, mirrors, drop front, 66″ 595.00

Settee, bentwood, 3 caned medallions in back, caned seat, 56″ 245.00

Settle-rocker, Federal, scroll arms, 12-spindle back, youth rail 500.00

Sewing stand, mahogany, Federal, 2 drawers, pull-out basket 350.00

Pine cupboard in restored paint, two hinged paneled doors with shelves, bracket feet, repaired, ca. 1835, 48″ x 47″ x 19″, $660.00.

Sideboard, oak, applied carvings, beveled shelf divided mirrors, 82″ 950.00

Sideboard, oak, serpentine drawers, applied carving, 40x44″ 275.00

Sideboard, oak, solid & quarter-sawn, simple, scrolled feet, 38x42″ 285.00

Sideboard, oak, Stickley, 46x48x19″ 450.00

Sideboard, oak & tiger veneer, flower shaped & carved stiles, mirror 350.00

Stand, birch, Country Sheraton, reeded legs, 2 drawers, 1-board top ... 400.00

Stand, butternut & ash, turned column with 3 turned feet, 30″ 150.00

Stand, curly maple, turned legs, dovetailed drawer, refinished 350.00

Stand, pine, country Hepplewhite, dovetailed drawer, refinished 160.00

Stool, piano; oak, reeded splay legs & center post, revolving seat 125.00

Table, center; rosewood, Victorian, marble top, well carved 1,200.00

Table, dining; oak, lion's heads & feet, beaded edge, 42″ diameter 1,400.00

Table, dining; oak, paw & claw feet, quarter & plain cut, 48″ diameter 900.00

Table, dining; oak, round base, curved legs, 2 leaves, 42″ diameter 400.00

Table, dining; oak, square, leaves store, 5 round legs, ball feet, 48″ 850.00

Table, drop leaf; birch & pine, Country, 10″ leaves, 18x36″ closed 250.00

Table, drop leaf; cherry, Federal, square legs, 42x38″ open 325.00

Table, oak, made by Stickley, trestle base with medial shelf, 72″ 300.00

Table, parlor; oak, cannonball turnings, brass claw & glass ball feet 375.00

Table, parlor; oak, scalloped 28″ square, flat button-turned legs 145.00

Table, pembroke, mahogany, Empire, 1 drawer, pineapple carved legs 375.00

Table, pine, Country, 18x25″ breadboard top, two drawers, refinished 550.00

Table, tavern; maple, Country Queen Anne, 2-board curly maple top 3,000.00

Table, tavern; pine, English, triangle base with shelf, round top 275.00

Walnut, Victorian, marble top with 3 graduated drawers, 48x34″ 350.00

Wardrobe, pine & poplar, cut-out base, applied mouldings, grainpaint 300.00

Wardrobe, walnut, turned feet, paneled door with arch inserts, 85x66″ 500.00

Washstand, butternut, burl door panels, marble gallery with shelves 500.00

Washstand, oak, hand carved, wishbone towel bar holder, brass draws 750.00

Washstand, oak, towel bar, tilting mirror, applied machined carvings 600.00

Washstand, pine, English, grainpaint & inlay, gallery, drawer, 30x24″ 200.00

Washstand, rosewood, Victorian, marble top, drawer & 2 doors, 32x36″ 600.00

Gambling Devices

Though Lady Luck still attracts her share of eager partakers at the games of chance, today those interested in vintage gambling devices can be confident of gaining rather than loosing, by making wise selections on their investments. Especially valued are cheat devices, layouts, and items that can be authenticated as having been used in the 'Floating Palace' riverboats, or in the early days of the famous casinos of the West.

Arrow-spinner wheel, marked Mason, New Jersey, small 276.00

Bingo outfit, ballboard, cage, balls, cards 44.50

Book, Card Mastery, MacDougall, 202 pages, 1944 . 15.50

Book, Foster's Practical Poker, Foster, 253 pages, 1905 . . . . 24.00

Book, Round the Green Cloth, Chester, 254 pages, 1928 . 20.50

Card case, holds 2 decks, wood covered with paper 22.50

Card press, for 6 decks, marked George Mason, Denver . 276.00

Dice cage, ends covered in calfskin, with two trips and rubber bumper, large 21" x 9" size, $300.00.

Chip rack, stainless steel, removable bill box, 14 rows, M 65.50

Dealer's apron, with letter of explanation, used to steal chips, 1920 .... 76.50

Dealing box, side squeeze, gaffed, German silver, Ball Brothers 596.00

Dice, red celluloid, SBM Lowes Monte Carlo, ¾", 5 in case 8.50

Dice caliphers, marked Will & Finck, pair 124.50

Dice cup, leather embossed 'Pour La Robless', 4", NM 42.00

Dice jiggler, pull dome down then jiggle trapped dice, 3½x2" 25.50

Dice stick, wood, combination pull & card flip tool, 3 pieces, 36" 32.50

Gambling license from Virginia City, 1885 ..... 196.00

Lotto, boxed set with all cards, markers & buttons . 25.00

Poker chip, brass, embossed with 'Recreation' on both sides 2.50

Postcard, cowboys gambling, going for guns, color, circa 1900 .... 21.00

Roulette ball, regulation size, ivory 35.50

Roulette cloth, unmounted, hand painted numbers, 54x37" 105.00

Roulette wheel, painted wood, 48" 151.00

Sign, Betting or Gambling of Any Description Strictly Prohibited 102.00

Woodcut, Gambling at Pike's Peak, 1864 .... 40.00

Roulette wheel, made by JOSA Games, bakelite with cast aluminum center, 10", $50.00.

Games

Before the turn of the century, several large companies began to produce parlor games; among them were Milton Bradley and Parker Brothers, both of whom still exist and continue to distribute games that delight young and old alike. These early games make wonderful collectibles; especially valuable are those dealing with a popular character, transportation theme, Black theme, or other areas of special interest. Condition of both game pieces and the box is important.

Wonderwood, color cover illustration signed Norman Price, box measures 10″ x 15″, $50.00.

Barney Google & Spark Plug, Milton Bradley, 1923 . . .	75.00
Bob Feller Big League Baseball	22.00
Buster Brown, Necktie Party Game, in original box, 1915	125.00
Checkerboard, wooden with red & blue paint, primitive, 12x12″	100.00
Cinderella, card game with color lithograph cards, 1895 .	27.00
Corner Grocery, Parker Brothers, 1887	75.00
Dominoes, ivory & ebony, mahogany case with chip carving, 2¾x5″	35.00
Gee-Whiz Horse Racing, 1920s, 29″	88.00
Humpty Dumpty, with gun, Parker Brothers, 1924, MIB	35.00
Jack Sprat & His Merry Wife, Parker Brothers, 1880s .	35.00
Magic box, 2 dice within, only 1 removes, old paint, 6½″	100.00
Marble, spiral groove on wooden rod with king's head carving, 9″	175.00
Movie Sticks, with colored sticks, Parker Brothers, 1937	18.00
Parcheesi, 1918	10.00

Pretty Village, boathouse set, McLaughlin Brothers . . .	40.00
Progressive Angling, comes with poles, hooks & fish in box, 1886	85.00
Radio Questionnaire, in original box, patent 1928 .	15.00
Tiddleywinks, ivory discs, Milton Bradley	9.00
Uncle Wiggly, paper litho hat game, EX	40.00
20th Century Limited, train on box lid, Parker Bros .	65.00

Moon Mullins' Automobile Race, Milton Bradley, cartoon art on box top and game board, incomplete, 7½″ x 13½″, $50.00.

Gas Globes and Panels

Globes that once crowned gasoline pumps are today being collected as a unique form of advertising memorabilia. There are basically four types: plastic frames with glass inserts from the 1940s and '50s; glass frames with glass inserts from the '30s and '40s; metal frames with glass inserts from the '20s and '30s; and one-piece glass globes (no inserts) with the oil company name etched, raised or enameled onto the face from 1914 to 1931. There are variations.

Atlantic, glass frame, glass inserts, 1930s-40s	135.00
Atlantic, very rare, 1-piece glass globe w/company name	1,200.00
Cities Service, clover shape, glass frame, glass inserts, 1930s-40s	350.00

Cities Service, very rare,
1-piece glass globe w/company name 1,300.00
Crowns, 1-piece glass globe
w/company name 200.00
Esso, metal frame, glass inserts, 1920s-30s 200.00
Gulf, 1-piece glass globe
w/company name 400.00
Hudson, plastic body, glass inserts, 1940s-50s 120.00
Kanotex Aviation, glass inserts, glass frame, 1930s-40s 350.00
Koolmotor, metal frame, glass
inserts, 1920s-30s 300.00
Marathon, man, plastic body,
glass inserts, 1940s-50s . 100.00
Marathon, plastic body, glass
inserts, 1940s-50s 60.00
Mobilgas, metal frame, glass
inserts, 1920s-30s 200.00
Monamotor, rare, 1-piece glass
globe w/company name . 800.00
Musgo, 1-piece glass globe
w/company name 1,500.00
Old Dutch, rare, plastic body,
glass inserts, 1940s-50s . 125.00
Pan Am, metal frame, glass inserts, 1920s-30s 300.00
Pendrake, glass frame, glass
inserts, 1930s-40s 300.00
Penzoil, glass frame, glass inserts, 1930s-40s 200.00
Penzoil, scarce, 1-piece glass
globe w/company name . 900.00
Phillips, glass frame, glass inserts, 1930s-40s 150.00
Phillips 66, plastic body, glass
inserts, 1940s-50s 65.00
Phillips 77, rare, plastic body,
glass inserts, 1940s-50s . 125.00
Polly-Gas, very rare, glass inserts, metal frame, 1920s-30s 1,500.00
Red Crown, metal frame, glass
inserts, 1920s-30s 400.00
Shell, 1-piece glass globe
w/company name 175.00

Sinclair Aircraft, 1-piece glass
globe w/company name . 1,200.00
Sinclair Dino, plastic body,
glass inserts, 1940s-50s . 40.00
Sinclair Gas, 1-piece glass
globe w/company name . 700.00
Sinclair H-C, glass frame,
glass inserts, 1930s-40s . 180.00
Sinclair H-C, plastic body,
glass inserts, 1940s-50s . 155.00
Socony, very rare, 1-piece
glass globe w/company
name 1,400.00
Sohio, glass frame, glass inserts, 1930s-40s 125.00
Sunoco, metal frame, glass inserts, 1920s-30s 220.00
Sunray, plastic body, glass inserts, 1940s-50s 150.00
Texaco, glass frame, glass inserts, 1930s-40s 150.00
Texaco, plastic body, glass inserts, 1940s-50s 100.00
Texaco, rare, metal frame,
glass inserts, 1920s-30s . 350.00
Texaco, 1-piece glass globe
w/company name 500.00

Geisha Girl China

Dinnerware and novelty items
made in Japan depicting geisha girls
in various pursuits have recently been
attracting collectors who usually
prefer to match border colors -- red,
yellow, blue, green, and rust -- when reassembling a table service.

Bowl, dessert; blue, 5¼", set
of 6 .... 35.50
Bowl, fruit; blue, 10" 25.50
Cracker jar, blue 45.50
Cup, chocolate; rust 5.50
Cup & saucer 7.50
Hair receiver, rust 26.00
Match safe, hanging 25.50
Mustard, rust, 3 piece 34.50
Nut cup, footed 5.50

Cup & saucer, $12.00; chocolate pot, $75.00.

Pitcher, bulbous melon shape, rust, small	21.00
Powder jar, rust	25.50
Shaker, red border, tall, pair	12.50
Tea set, gold blossom design in relief, 11 piece	176.00
Toothpick holder, rust	16.50

Goofus Glass

Produced in the early part of the twentieth century, 'goofus' glassware was pressed with designs in very high relief, and painted on the reverse with metallic lustres. Lamps, pickle jars, vases and trays are easy to find. Flea markets are often a good source, but watch for flaking paint. Careful cleaning is a must to prevent paint loss.

Bowl, Daisy & Plume, opalescent, 3 short feet, original paint, 9″	52.00
Bowl, La Belle Rose, original paint, 2x5½″ square	35.00
Bowl, Pinecones & Leaves, shallow, original paint, 10″, M	47.50
Compote & saucer, Poppy, crackle glass, original paint, 6″ diameter	23.00
Decanter w/stopper, La Belle Rose, turned amethyst, 9″	42.50

Fairy lamp, roses, flash-fired green, 3 holes in top for smoke, 7″	30.00
Jewel box, Basketweave, original paint, rare, 4″ diameter	47.00
Lamp base, Poppy, Gone with the Wind, includes chimney, 15″	55.00
Lamp, Cabbage Rose, includes chimney, turned amethyst, rare, 15″	88.00
Picture frame, Cabbage Rose, blue glass, 6½x10½″	40.00
Powder box, Basketweave, single rose on side & top, 7 sided, 3½″	65.00
Powder box, Puffy Rose, original paint, 3x5″ diameter	40.00
Salt & pepper, Dogwood, original paint & tops, 4″	37.50
Salt & pepper, Poppy, original paint turned amethyst, rare, 3″	30.00
Sauce dish, Rose, original paint, 5½″ diameter	23.50
Vase, Cabbage Rose, Poppy, original paint, 7″, pair	40.00
Vase, Dogwood Blossom on satin glass, flower on front & back, 5½″	8.00
Vase, Four Poppies, original paint, 12″	30.00

Fruit bowl, fruit decoration, 4″ x 7″, $35.00.

Water bottle, Grape, crackle glass, rare, 7½″ 42.00

Water bottle, white background, red rose, 10″ ... 43.00

Graniteware

A collectible very much in demand by those who enjoy the 'Country' look in antiques, graniteware (also called enameled ware) comes in a variety of colors, and color is one of the most important considerations when it comes to evaluating worth. Purple, brown, or green swirl pieces are generally higher than gray, white, or blue -- though blues and blue swirled examples are popular. Decorated pieces are unusual, as are salesman's samples and miniatures, and these also bring top prices.

Angel food cake pan, gray mottled & fluted, 11″ diameter 25.00

Bowl, gray, 7″ diameter ... 22.00

Bread box, white with 'Bread' in black 38.00

Butter bucket, gray & oval, tin handle & lid finial ... 65.00

Chamber pot, blue & white swirl, with lid 25.00

Child's cook set, mottled turquoise & white, 8 piece . 110.00

Colander, gray mottled, footed, with handles, 10″ diameter 13.00

Cream pitcher, white, light blue speckles, pewter trim, Lion mark 125.00

Dishpan, blue & white marbleized, with handles, 20″ diameter 19.50

Double boiler, blue marbleized, with lid 27.50

Egg separator, cobalt & white marbleized, 3¾x6″ 85.00

Ice cream scoop, gray speckled, with wooden handle . 12.00

Kerosene heater, sky blue, bail handle, 22″ 45.00

Lunch bucket, plain blue, bail handle, tin lid 22.00

Miniature cup, blue with white ribbon trim, 1½″ 6.00

Mold, melon shape, gray, tall sides, 5″ 75.00

Muffin tin, blue and gray mottled 28.00

Pie plate and coffee pot, in unused condition with original labels, mottled gray enamel, pot: $65.00, pie plate, $20.00.

Tube pan, blue with white speckles, 9″ diameter, excellent condition, $34.00.

Napkin holder, white	28.00
Plate, red & yellow paper label with anvil	22.00
Potty, child's, side handle, blue & white marbleized, white interior	35.00
Salt box, blue & white splash, 'Seife' lettered on front	42.00
Sign, white with 'Receiving' in blue, 2½x10″	12.00
Soap dish, cream & green, hanging type	22.50
Stew pot, sky blue, pour spout, bail handle, 8″ diameter	21.50
Tea kettle, brown & white swirl, with lid, 13″	40.00

Teapot, medium blue with Foval glass top insert, 8½″, $75.00.

Tea set, child's, white with black rim, painted flowers, 11 piece	85.00
Teapot, cobalt and white marbled, tin lid, gooseneck, 6½″	45.00
Tumbler, gray, rough	10.00
Wall rack, for cup & soap, white	55.00
Wash basin, blue marbleized, 6¾″	12.00

Guns, Antique

Muskets, large-bore shoulder arms, were among the earliest forms of firearms. They fired black powder; some ignited the charge by flintlock or caplock. Later types used a firing pin with a metallic cartridge. Early pistols were single shot or had multiple barrels. Any type of firearm made before the turn of the century is considered antique. Condition is extremely important; guns with all their original parts and with a good original finish are worth much more than repaired or restored guns.

Allen & Thurber, harpoon gun, 1840-1860s	450.00
Allen's Patent 31 caliber 6 shot pepperbox, with casing, flask & mold	1,200.00
American Arms pistol with double swivel barrel, 1866	125.00
Bacon Mfg Co pocket revolver, 1860s	85.00
Blake, English manufacturer, blunderbuss with straight brass barrel	600.00
Chicago Firearms palm pistol, The Protector, 32 caliber rimfire	200.00
Colt Army 44 caliber percussion revolver, 1860, with original holster	1,100.00
Colt Cloverleaf 4 shot revolver, 41 caliber, nickel plate & pearl	225.00

Colt Model 1862 Police revolver, 4½" barrel 175.00

Gibbs Tiffany Co bootleg pistol, 31 caliber, engraved eagle, 8" 125.00

Hutchinson Dublin 70 caliber flintlock pistol, brass & silver, pair 900.00

J Nadler & Peruel plains rifle, 1840-1855 .... 350.00

K&P Pat 1861 trap pistol, percussion 180.00

Kentucky percussion pistol, curly maple with silver inlay, 1835 .... 550.00

Manhattan Firearms pepperbox, 31 caliber 3 shot, 1860 150.00

New England Militia percussion musket, Ashmore lock 195.00

Parker Snow & Co rifled musket with Miller conversion 250.00

Purdey percussion double-barrel shotgun, engraved lock, 1800s 200.00

Quackenbush boy's rifle, 22 caliber single-shot, 1900. 65.00

Remington Model 1 Smoot revolver, dated 1874 .... 275.00

Remington New Model 44 revolver, percussion, 1858 . 225.00

Remington single-action revolver, 44-40 caliber, 1874 . 700.00

Samuel E Robins, Richard Lawrence; pepperbox with ring trigger 150.00

Smith & Wesson Double Action revolver, 32 caliber, 1800 .... 125.00

Springfield Arms pocket revolver, 30 caliber 6 shot, 1850s 75.00

Stevens 22 caliber rimfire single-shot pistol 150.00

Tower militia musket with bayonet, early 1800s ... 225.00

Winchester rifle, full octagon barrel, 38-55 caliber, 1894 . 425.00

Winchester rifle, octagon barrel, 32-40 caliber, 1894 .. 1,300.00

Winchester Saddlering 30-35 caliber carbine, ca 1892 . 400.00

Guns, Modern

Modern guns from the twentieth century vary in value because of quantities produced, markings, special finishes (such as engraving and inlays), historical value, and factory options. Geographical preference and market popularity are also considerations. Of course, condition is of prime importance.

Handguns

American, 25 Automatic, 25 ACP caliber, semi-automatic, 8-shot clip 142.00

Bauer, Stainless, 25 ACP caliber, semi-automatic, concealed hammer 136.00

Charter Arms, Explorer II, 22 long rifle caliber, semi-automatic 99.00

Colt, Model 1900, 38 ACP caliber, semi-automatic, 7-shot clip 950.00

Detonics, Combat Master, Mark I, 45 ACP caliber, semi-automatic 610.00

Llama, Model I, 32 ACP caliber, blow-back type, semi-automatic 140.00

Colt Government Model #1911A1 45 ACP semi-automatic, exposed spur hammer, seven-shot clip, checkered walnut grips, 5" barrel, in excellent condition, $400.00.

Ruger, Bearcat, 22 short caliber, single, 6-shot, alloy frame 150.00

Savage, Model 1905, Military type, 45 ACP caliber, semi-automatic 2,000.00

Smith & Wesson, Model 25-5, 45 Colt caliber, double, solid frame 409.00

Star, Model 1919 Pocket, 25 ACP caliber, semi-automatic, 8-shot clip 150.00

Stevens, Single-shot Target, 22 long rifle caliber, single shot 265.00

Walther, Model 1 Vest Pocket, 25 ACP caliber, semi-automatic, 6-shot 265.00

Webley, 1906 Model Vest Pocket, 25 ACP caliber, 6-shot clip 180.00

Rifles

Colt, Colteer 1-22, 22 caliber, bolt action, hammerless, single shot 65.00

Harrington & Richardson, Fieldsman 852, 22 short caliber, bolt action 70.00

Johnson, MMJ Spitfire, 223 caliber, semi-automatic . 215.00

Marlin, Model 37, 22 short caliber, slide action, exposed hammer 200.00

Marlin, Model 39, 22 long caliber, lever action, exposed hammer 225.00

Marlin, Model 65, 22 long rifle caliber, bolt action, single shot 50.00

Mauser, Model MM 410, 22 long rifle caliber, bolt action, repeating 325.00

Remington, Model 510 Targetmaster, 22 long caliber, bolt action 80.00

Ruger, Mini 14, 223 Commercial caliber, gas-operated semi-automatic 304.00

Savage, Model 840, 222 Remington caliber, bolt action, repeating 120.00

Smith & Wesson, Model A, 22-250 caliber, bolt action, repeating 275.00

Universal, 440 Vulcan, 44 magnum caliber, slide action, hammerless 210.00

Winchester, Model 52, 22 long rifle caliber, bolt action, repeating 360.00

Shotguns

Baikal, Model MC-8, 12 gauge, box lock, top lever, over & under 800.00

Beretta, Model 410, 10 magnum, box lock, hammerless, top lever 950.00

Browning Automatic 5 Standard Grade, 12 gauge, semi-automatic, 4-shot .. 430.00

Browning Double Automatic Standard, 12 gauge, 2-shot, semi-automatic 350.00

Charles Daly Hammerless Double, 10 gauge, box lock, top lever, Empire 1,200.00

Ithaca, Model 66, Supersingle, 20 gauge, lever action, exposed hammer 55.00

Mauser, Model 580, 12 gauge, side lock, top lever, break-open 825.00

Hartford Automatic Target, 22 long rifle caliber, semi-automatic, concealed hammer, ten shot clip, 6¾″ barrel, 10¾″ overall, in excellent condition, $275.00.

New Haven, Model 600, 410 gauge, slide action, hammerless, repeating 215.00

Noble, Model 80, 410 gauge, semi-automatic, hammerless, 5-shot tubular 200.00

Remington, Model 31, 16 gauge, slide action, hammerless, side ejection.... 290.00

Savage, Model 220, 28 gauge, top lever, break-open, single shot 70.00

Stevens, Model 330, 20 gauge, top lever, break-open, hammerless 185.00

Winchester, Model 370, 410 gauge, top lever, break-open, box lock 65.00

Zoli, Silver Snipe, 20 gauge, box lock, top lever, break-open 450.00

Hall

Most famous for their extensive lines of teapots and colorful dinnerwares, the Hall China Company still operates in East Liverpool, Ohio, where they were established in 1903. For listings of their most popular dinnerware line, see Autumn Leaf.

Advertising, ash tray, Birch Camp, Higgins Lake, turquoise & gold 15.00

Advertising, sugar bowl, Lipton, black 8.50

Ash tray, with match stand, black 9.00

Blue Bouquet, jug, Colonial . 10.00
Blue Bouquet, pretzel jar .. 68.00
Blue Bouquet, salad bowl .. 12.00
Cameo Rose, cup 4.00

Cameo Rose, oval vegetable bowl 10.00

Cameo Rose, plate, 9" 5.00

Cameo Rose, vegetable dish with cover 38.00

Casserole, Basketweave, pink 15.00
Chinese red, ball jug, #2 ... 15.00

Twin Tee teapot with forget-me-not decoration, on partitioned tray, $75.00.

Chinese red, beanpot, tab handle 35.00

Chinese red, casserole, tab handle 15.00

Chinese red, doughnut jug . 20.00

Chinese red, jug, Sani-Grid, large, 7½" 15.00

Coffee mug, Irish; black ... 8.00

Coffee pot, Enterprise Drip-O-Lator, Panel, with flowerpots 10.00

Coffee pot, floral, on Parade shape 30.00

Colonial, jug, Delphinium .. 20.00

Colonial, jug, pink mums decal, 5" 15.00

Cookie jar, Banded, Indian Red 45.00

Crocus, bowl, 5½" 6.00

Crocus, casserole with cover, Sunshine 25.00

Crocus, mixing bowl, 6" ... 9.00

Crocus, plate, Sprig decal, D-Shape, platinum trim, 6" . 3.50

Crocus, sauce dish, Sprig decal, D-Shape, platinum lines, 6" 2.50

Crocus, sugar bowl 8.00
Daffodil Squiggle, salad bowl 5.00
Flare Ware, casserole 19.00
Flare Ware, coffee pot 45.00
Gold Dot, cookie jar with lid . 22.00
Heather Rose, cup & saucer . 6.00
Heather Rose, plate, 6½" .. 1.50
Monticello, plate, 10" 3.50

Mt Vernon, cup & saucer ..	7.50	Teapot, Boston, beige & gold, 6 cup	24.00
Mt Vernon, plate, 9¼″	6.00	Teapot, Boston, Daffodil, 6 cup	25.00
Orange Poppy, bowl, deep, 10″ diameter	12.00	Teapot, Boston, Orange Poppy	45.00
Orange Poppy, condiment set	30.00	Teapot, Cozy, Daffodil	20.00
Orange Poppy, cup & saucer .	10.00	Teapot, Disraeli, aqua, 6 cup .	25.00
Orange Poppy, mustard & plate	9.50	Teapot, Forman, tip pot, turquoise, with holder & candle	93.50
Orange Poppy, sugar with lid	8.00	Teapot, French, Dresden, gold flowers, 8 cup	30.00
Orange Poppy, teapot, Melody	57.00	Teapot, Globe	93.50
Primrose, jug, 5¾″	15.00	Teapot, Hook Cover, cobalt with gold	40.00
Red Poppy, creamer	10.00	Teapot, Hook Cover, Emerald	35.00
Red Poppy, mixing bowl, set of 3	35.00	Teapot, Illinois	104.50
Red Poppy, saucer	2.50	Teapot, Inverted Spout, cobalt with gold	65.00
Refrigerator Ware, Aristocrat, butter	12.00	Teapot, Joe Thorley design, white with gold grapes & jewels	45.00
Refrigerator Ware, King, roaster, open, Canary, Westinghouse	5.00	Teapot, Lipton, light blue .	15.00
Refrigerator Ware, Patrician, water server, Delphinium Blue	28.00	Teapot, Lipton, Mustard Yellow	15.00
Rose Parade, bean pot, 2 quart	22.50	Teapot, McCormick, dark green, with infuser, 6 cup .	24.00
Rose Parade, mixing bowl, large	12.00	Teapot, Melody, red	50.00
Rose Parade, shakers, Sani-Grid, pair	15.00	Teapot, Moderne, cobalt ...	55.00
Rose White, covered drip jar .	15.00	Teapot, Nautilus, Canary Yellow with gold, 6 cup .	90.00
Sani-Grid, salt & pepper shakers, plain handle, blue, pair	15.00	Teapot, New York, green & gold, 6 cup	24.00
Springtime, gravy boat ...	12.00	Teapot, Philadelphia, cobalt & gold decor, 4 cup	26.00
Springtime, plate, 6¼″	3.00	Teapot, Philadelphia, cobalt with allover gold, with sugar & creamer	45.00
Springtime, soup bowl, 8½″ .	7.00		
Taverne, butter top	50.00	Teapot, Saf-Handle, Warm Yellow with gold leaves .	50.00
Taverne, fruit bowl, 5⅝″ ..	10.00	Teapot, Star, dark green ..	25.00
Taverne, pretzel cookie with cover	70.00	Teapot, Surfside, turquoise .	83.50
Taverne, tankard mug	30.00	Teapot, Trackulator, red ...	25.00
Teapot, Airflow, cobalt, gold decor, 6 cup	45.00	Teapot, Twinspout, black ..	40.00
Teapot, Aladdin, Chinese Red, 6 cup	35.00	Teapot, Windshield, Camellia with gold, 6 cup	25.00
Teapot, Aladdin, Delphinium Blue, with infuser, 6 cup .	25.00	Teapot, Windshield, maroon & gold, 6 cup	25.00
Teapot, Automobile, black & silver	440.00		

Tulip, breakfast plate	8.00
Wild Rose, cereal bowl	3.50
Wild Rose, custard, Sunshine	4.00
Wildfire, Aladdin pot with infuser	28.50
Wildfire, cereal bowl, 6″ ...	3.50
Wildfire, custard cup	3.25
Wildfire, grease pot, Big Lip .	15.00
Wildfire, shakers, loop handle, pair	20.00
Zeisel, celery, red & black flower	12.00
Zeisel, cookie jar, pink basket	35.00
Zeisel, gravy, red & black flower	12.00

Harlequin

Made by the Homer Laughlin China Company who also produced the popular Fiesta, Harlequin was a light weight dinnerware line made in several solid glaze colors. It was introduced in 1938, and was marketed mainly through Woolworth stores. During the early forties, the company made a line of Harlequin animals: a fish, lamb, cat, duck, penguin and donkey.

Ash tray, basketweave	20.00
Baker, oval, 9″	6.50
Candle holders, pair	32.00
Cream soup	7.00
Creamer, novelty	6.50

Service water jug in gray, chartreuse, dark or medium green, $30.00, in other colors, $17.50; tumblers, $20.00.

Cup, large tankard	40.00
Deep plate	10.00
Demitasse cup & saucer ...	20.00
Fruit, 5½″	4.50
Marmalade	42.00
Nappy, 9″	9.00
Plate, 10″	5.50
Plate, 7″	3.00
Platter, 11″	6.50
Relish tray, 5 piece	45.00
Salt & pepper shakers, pair .	7.00
Sauceboat	7.00
Saucer	1.50
Saucer/ash tray	25.00
Spoon rest	95.00
Sugar with lid	5.00
Syrup	85.00
Teacup	4.50
Tumbler, water	17.50
Tumbler, with car decal ...	22.50

Hatpin Holders

Made from many materials, hatpin holders are most often encountered in china decorated by hand painting or floral decals. Glass hatpin holders are rare, especially those of slag or carnival glass.

Carnival glass, purple, Grape & Cable, Northwood	200.00
Clown figural, 1 leg forward, bisque, 5½″	38.00
ES Prussia, rose decor, 7″ .	37.50
Geisha Girl, flared bottom, 4″	30.00
German, white with gold scalloped top & base ...	25.00
Jasperware, green Kewpies in relief, signed O'Neill, Germany	250.00
Nippon, attached dish, gold with florals, 4½″	120.00
Nippon, scenic with white slip, blue leaf mark	80.00
Pickard, with saucer, hand painted florals, signed ..	150.00
Rosenthal, gold & pale green with pink roses	40.00

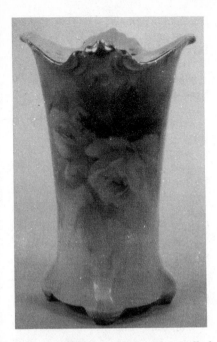

**R.S. Prussia, four-sided with scrolled top, rose decoration, mold #727, 4½",
$300.00.**

Royal Bayreuth, figural Dachshund, blue mark . .	400.00
Royal Rudolstadt, wild roses, signed Hahn	52.00
RS Prussia, 3 handled, with ring tray, unmarked	120.00
Silver plate, Egyptian decor with 3 ball feet, Karnak Brass, 4½"	48.00
Willets, belleek, allover silver scrollwork	58.00

Hatpins

Hatpins range in length from about 4" to as long as 12", depending upon the fashion of the day. The longer type were required to secure the large bonnets that were in style from 1890 to 1914. Many beautiful examples exist -- some with genuine or manufactured stones, some in silver or brass with relief-molded Art Nouveau

motifs, others of hand painted porcelains, and 'nodder' types.

Art Nouveau, sterling with enameled floral motifs . .	45.00
Arts & Crafts elongated kite shape, marked sterling, 2¾"	45.00
Billiken, sterling figural, signed, 1x1½"	75.00
Bird figural, 4½" sterling head with stone eyes, 8" pin	95.00
Bohemian, blown glass, 1¼" hand painted head, 4½" pin	25.00

Left to right: Art Nouveau gilt over brass with enameling, $65.00; Art Deco plastic with brass scarab, molded plastic insert with pharaoh, $110.00.

Damascene, floral motif with
1¾" head, 11" pin 45.00
Egyptian motif, molded plastic disc with rising sun .   20.00
Gift boxed hatpins, 1¼" enameled head, hallmarked,
pair 150.00
Golf club figurals, sterling,
8¼" overall length 22.00
Jet, with japanned frame &
pin, hand set with riveted
stones 95.00
Mercury glass, cased, elong-
ated teardrop, 2¼" 65.00
Mosaic, multicolored florals
on 1" brass button mount .   55.00
Nodder, 7" gilt, pin, figural
butterfly mount 35.00
Peacock eye, 1" oval head on
7½" steel pin, circa 1905 .   40.00
Satsuma, 2 birds in relief,
enamel florals, 1½", 8¾"
steel pin 95.00
Satsuma, 2 Oriental ladies,
ball shape 95.00
Sporting activity, sterling
silver 25.00
Tortoise, elongated teardrop
with tiny gold bead trim,
1¼" 85.00
Vanity heads, compact, rouge
rag, straight pin holder .   95.00

Historical Blue Ware

Made by many Staffordshire potteries from as early as 1820 for export
to America, this type of transfer
printed earthenware was decorated
with views of American landmarks to
assure its acceptance in this country.
Early wares were dark blue on white;
later, light blue, green, black, red, and
pink transfers were used, but these are
not as valuable today. Some views are
rarely found, and naturally these bring
top prices. In addition to color, condition of the glaze and brilliance of the
print are important.

Bidet, blue transfer, Moore &
Company 385.00
Bowl, Columbus Discovering,
oval, green with minor
wear, 11" 155.00
Bowl, Near Hudson, Junction
of Scandaga, Hudson,
brown, 8¾" 150.00
Bowl, Winter View, Pitts-
burgh, dark blue, Clews,
worn, 7x9½" 275.00
Coffee pot, Lafayette at
Franklin's Tomb, dark
blue, high dome lid 1,350.00
Compote, Windsor Castle,
squared with sloping sides   400.00
Creamer, LaFayette at Frank-
lin's Tomb, dark blue,
Wood 450.00
Creamer, Mt Vernon, Seat of
the Late General Washing-
ton, dark blue, M 600.00
Cup & saucer, Boston State
House, medium dark blue,
Rogers, EX 225.00
Cup & saucer, handleless; Ab-
bey Ruins, red, T&J Mayer   40.00
Cup & saucer, LaFayette at
Franklin's Tomb, dark
blue, Wood, NM 275.00
Cup plate, Battery, dark blue,
trefoil border, Wood, 3⅝"   250.00
Cup plate, Large Cottage with
People, dark blue, Adams,
3⅞" 75.00
Cup plate, Oriental Scenes,
purple, 4" 20.00
Dish, vegetable with lid; Mt
Vernon, dark blue,
Ridgway 750.00
Foot bath, Catskill Moss,
American scene, blue &
white, 8x19x13" 400.00
Ladle, dark blue, Stevenson's
wild rose border, 12" . . .   250.00
Pitcher, Albany, light blue,
8¾", EX 180.00
Pitcher, American Naval
Heroes, dark blue, 6" . . .   700.00

Pitcher, New York City Hall & Hospital, Stevenson, 6" . 550.00

Pitcher, Water Girl, dark blue, Clews, 5¾" 265.00

Plate, America & Independence, dark blue, states rim, 8¾" 250.00

Plate, Arms of New York, dark blue, Mayer, 10", EX 500.00

Plate, Baltimore & Ohio, dark blue, Wood, 9" 465.00

Plate, Battery & C, green, Jackson, American Scenery, 7¾" 75.00

Plate, Catskill House, Hudson, dark blue, Wood, 6½" 350.00

Plate, Columbian Star, brown, 1840, Ridgway, 8¾" 110.00

Plate, Dr Syntax Painting a Portrait, dark blue, small nick, 10" 165.00

Plate, Eashing Park, Surrey, medium dark blue, R Hall, 7½" 45.00

Plate, Highlands, North River, eagle border, Stubbs, 10", M 850.00

Plate, Landing of LaFayette, dark blue, Clews, 9", EX . 200.00

Plate, Landing of the Fathers at Plymouth, medium blue, Wood, 8½" 65.00

Plate, Landing of the Fathers at Plymouth, medium dark blue, Wood, 10" 140.00

Plate, Mahomedan Mosque & Tomb, dark blue, Hall, Oriental, 9" 75.00

Plate, Monuments & Urns, black, 8¾" 65.00

Plate, Near Sandy Hill, Hudson River, purple, 7¾", M 45.00

Plate, Pass in the Catskills, dark blue, Wood, 7½", EX 325.00

Plate, Pittsfield Elm, dark blue, 6¾" 230.00

Plate, St Paul's School Regents Park, dark blue, Adams, 7½" 85.00

Plate, Landing of LaFayette, dark blue on white, marked Clews, 10", in mint condition, $250.00.

Plate, Table Rock, Niagara, dark blue, Wood, 10" . . . 275.00

Plate, Union Line, dark blue, 9¼" 325.00

Plate, View Near Conway, New Hampshire, pink, Adams, 9" 65.00

Plate, West Point, Hudson River, black, Clews, 8" . . 75.00

Platter, Alms House, New York, dark blue, Ridgway, 16½", M 530.00

Platter, Dorney Court, reticulated lattice border, Wood, 8x10" 265.00

Platter, Landing of LaFayette, dark blue, 17" 690.00

Platter, Palestine, blue & white, floral border, 15" . 80.00

Platter, Pennsylvania Hospital, dark blue, Ridgway, 10", EX 645.00

Platter, Teresa Panza & the Messenger, dark blue, 14¾", M 445.00

Punch bowl, Pagoda Scene, dark blue, 11" 450.00

Relish dish, Don Quixote, green, Brameld, 11½", EX 95.00

Sauce tureen, lid, ladle, undertray, Hudson Views, light blue, Clews 450.00

Soup, Albany, Cities Series, dark blue, Clews, 9¾" .. 250.00

Soup, Baltimore & Ohio, dark blue, Wood, 10" 565.00

Soup, Castle Views, Gates of Sebastion, medium blue, Spode, 9¾" 55.00

Soup, Chauteau Ermenonville, dark blue, Wood, 10¼" . 150.00

Soup, Millenium, medium blue, 10½", M 65.00

Sugar bowl, Cupid Imprisoned, beehive finial, barrel form, 4" 325.00

Sugar bowl, Wadsworth Tower, Connecticut, dark blue, Wood 450.00

Sugar bowl, Washington with Scroll in Hand, dark blue, Wood 550.00

Teapot, LaFayette at Franklin's Tomb, dark blue, hairline 475.00

Tray, handles, Boston From... Dorchester, light blue, Meigh, 11½" 150.00

Tureen, with ladle, Yorkshire, dark blue 250.00

Wash bowl, LaFayette at Franklin's Tomb, Wood, 4½x11" 252.00

Hull

Established in Zanesville, Ohio, in 1905, Hull manufactured stoneware, florist ware, art pottery, and tile until about 1935, when they began to produce the lines of pastel matt glazed artware which is today very collectible. The pottery was destroyed by flood and fire in 1950. The factory was rebuilt and equipped with the most modern machinery which they soon discovered was not geared to duplicate the matt glazes. As a result, new lines -- Parchment, Pine and Ebb Tide, for example -- were introduced. During the forties and into the fifties, their Red

Riding Hood kitchenware and novelty line was very successful. Collectors of character memorabilia, Hull collectors, and kitchenware collectors alike vie to own these endearing figural charmers -- match safes, banks, canisters, salt and pepper shakers, etc. -- dressed in the traditional red cape and hood, and carrying a basket to Grandma's house.

Bank, Corky Pig, no mark, brown, 5" 10.00

Basket, #56, 6¼" 20.00

Blossomflite, basket, ruffled oval, T-8 .... 35.00

Blossomflite, console set, T-10 bowl, T-11 candle holders . 45.00

Bow Knot, console set, B-16, 13½" bowl & pair of candlesticks 90.00

Bow Knot, cornucopia, B-5, 7½" 40.00

Bow Knot, vase, B-2, 5" ... 30.00

Bow Knot, vase, B-4, 6½" .. 38.00

Bow Knot, vase, B-7, 8½" .. 48.00

Bow Knot, vase, B-8, 8½" .. 45.00

Bow Knot, wall pitcher, B-26, 6" 40.00

Chinaman wall pocket, 8¼", $24.00.

Butterfly, basket, blue lining, tri-handle, 10½" 65.00

Butterfly, cornucopia, B-2, 6¼" 12.50

Butterfly, pitcher, 5" 10.00

Calla Lily, vase, #501-33, 6½" 35.00

Coffee server, yellow & brown, #32, 11" 24.00

Dogwood, basket, #501, 7½" 55.00

Dogwood, bowl, #521, 7" .. 38.00

Dogwood, candle holders, #512, 3¾", pair 35.00

Parchment and Pine ewer, S-7, 14½", $40.00.

Early Art, vase, brush-stroke decor, #32, 8" 25.00

Ebb Tide, candle holder, E-13, 2¾", pair 20.00

Iris, candle holder, #411, 5", pair 40.00

Iris, ewer, #401, 13½" 125.00

Iris, rose bowl, #412, 7" ... 36.00

Iris, vase, #403, 4¾" 19.00

Magnolia, glossy; console set, H-23 & 24, 13" bowl & candlesticks 38.00

Magnolia, glossy; pitcher, H-3, 5½" 18.00

Magnolia, glossy; vase, H-2, 5½" 15.00

Magnolia, matt; tea set, #23, 24 & 25, 6½", 3 piece ... 85.00

Magnolia, matt; vase, #9, 10½" 37.50

Mardi Gras, ewer, #66, 10" . 32.00

Open Rose, basket, #107, 8" . 65.00

Open Rose, swan, #118, 6¼" 30.00

Open Rose, vase, #131, 5" . 20.00

Orchid, low bowl, #321, 7" . 40.00

Parchment & Pine, cornucopia, S-2, 7¾" 20.00

Parchment & Pine, tea set, green, original carton ... 75.00

Planter, dachshund, brown, 14" long 40.00

Planter, duck, #104, 10½" . 20.00

Planter, poodle, green, #114 . 20.00

Planter, swan basket, #413, 10" 23.00

Red Riding Hood, bank, standing 195.00

Red Riding Hood, creamer . 35.00

Red Riding Hood, match holder 395.00

Telephone planter, $15.00.

Red Riding Hood biscuit jar, 8″, $135.00.

Red Riding Hood, milk pitcher	100.00
Red Riding Hood, salt & pepper, large	30.00
Red Riding Hood, salt & pepper, small	20.00
Red Riding Hood, syrup pitcher, large	100.00
Red Riding Hood, wall pocket	175.00
Rosella, ewer, R-11, 7″	35.00
Rosella, pitcher, R-9, 6½″	30.00
Rosella, wall pocket, R-10, 6¼″	35.00
Serenade, pitcher, S-21	40.00
Sunglow, basket, #84, 6½″	17.50
Sunglow, pitcher, 24 ounce, pink with yellow flowers	15.00
Sunglow, wall pocket, whiskbroom	20.00
Tokay, candy on stem, covered, 8½″	25.00
Tulip, basket, #102-33, 6″	57.50
Tulip, jardiniere, #117-30, 5″	30.00
Tulip, vase, #107-33, 6″	32.50
Vase, #108, 8″	16.00
Wall pocket, goose, gold trim	25.00
Water Lily, cornucopia, L-7, with label, 6½″	65.00

Water Lily, ewer, L-3, 5½″	27.50
Water Lily, planter with saucer, L-25, 5½″	50.00
Water Lily, vase, L-4, 6½″	25.00
Wildflower, basket, W-16, 10½″	85.00
Wildflower, console bowl, W-21, 12″	42.00
Wildflower, vase, W-6, 7½″	27.50
Woodland, glossy; console bowl, W-29	42.00
Woodland, glossy; double bud vase, W-15, 8½″	25.00
Woodland, glossy; teapot, W-26	45.00
Woodland, matt; cornucopia, W-5, 6½″	20.00
Woodland, matt; wall pocket, shell shape, W-13, 7½″	40.00

Water Lily, vase L-12, 10½″, $55.00.

Hummel

Figurines, plates and plaques produced since 1935 by Franz Goebel of West Germany are today highly collectible, often bringing prices several times that of their original retail value. They can generally be dated by their marks, each variation of which can be attributed a production period: (1) Crown mark, 1935-1950 (2) Full Bee mark, 1950-1959 (3) Stylized Bee mark with variations, 1957-1970 (4) Three-Line mark, 1964-1972 (5) Goebel Bee mark, 1972-1979 (6) Current mark, no bee, 1979 to the present.

Accordion Boy, Stylized Bee, #185 .... 100.00

Apple Tree Boy, Stylized Bee, #142/3/0, 4" 70.00

Ash tray, Happy Pastime, Stylized Bee, #62 ...... 90.00

Band Leader, Stylized Bee, #129 .... 125.00

Barnyard Hero, hands spread, 3-line, #195/2/0 .... 85.00

Bird Duet, Full Bee, #169 . 135.00

Birthday Serenade, 3-line, #218/2/0, 4" 95.00

Boots, Stylized Bee, #142/0, 5" 85.00

Boy with Toothache, 3-line, #217 .... 75.00

Calendar, 1960s 35.00

Candle holder, Herald Angels, Stylized Bee, #37, 2¾x4" . 90.00

Chick Girl, Goebel Bee, #57/I, 4¼" 70.00

Chimney Sweep, Goebel Bee, #12/I, 6" 50.00

Christmas Song, Current mark, #343, 6" 90.00

Cinderella, Goebel Bee, #337, 4¾" 110.00

Congratulations, Full Bee, no socks, #17 .... 180.00

Cow, Stylized Bee, #214/K, 3½" 45.00

Crossroads, Last Bee, #331 . 155.00

Culprits, eyes open, hollow, Crown mark, #56., decimal number 375.00

Daisies Don't Tell, Goebel Bee, #380, 6" 90.00

Doll Bath, 3-line, #319, 5" . 115.00

Doll Mother, Stylized Bee, #67 110.00

Donkey, Stylized Bee, #214/J, 5" 45.00

Farewell, Stylized Bee, #65/I, 4¾" 130.00

Farm Boy, Stylized Bee, #66, 5" 145.00

Feeding Time, Stylized Bee, old style, #199/I 150.00

Flower Madonna, small Stylized Bee, white, #10/I, 8" . 100.00

Flying Angel, 3-line, #366, 3½" 75.00

For Father, Goebel Bee, #87, 5" 55.00

Going to Grandma's, Stylized Bee, #52/0 .... 130.00

Good Friends, Stylized Bee, old style, #182, 4¾" 90.00

Good Shepherd, Full Bee, #42/0 .... 130.00

Happy Birthday, US Zone Germany, #176, 5¾" ... 600.00

Happy Pastime, Stylized Bee, #69, 3½" 100.00

Hear Ye, Hear Ye, Crown mark, brown mittens, #15/I, 6½" 200.00

Postman, current mark, 5½", $85.00.

St. George and the Dragon, **current mark**, 6½″, $145.00.

Heavenly Angel, Goebel Bee, #21/0/1/2, 6½″ 50.00

Hello, Goebel Bee, #124/0, 6½″ 95.00

Home From Market, Crown mark, plain number, #198, 6″ 200.00

Just Resting, Stylized Bee, #122/3/0, 4″ 85.00

King, Stylized Bee, kneeling, #214/N, 4″ 125.00

Lamb, Stylized Bee, #214/0, 2″ 20.00

Letter to Santa, 3-line, #340, 7″ 325.00

Little Drummer, 3-line, #240 . 55.00

Little Fiddler, small Stylized Bee, #2/I, 7½″ 175.00

Little Gardener, Stylized Bee, raised flower oval base, #74, 4½″ 125.00

Little Goat Herder, Full Bee, old style, #200/0 .... 210.00

Little Helper, Stylized Bee, #73, 4″ 65.00

Little Pharmacist, Vitamins, 3-line, #322, 6″ 115.00

Lost Sheep, 3-line, #68/2/0, 4″ 60.00

Mail Coach, Goebel Bee, #226 180.00

Meditation, Goebel Bee, #13/II, 7″ 125.00

Mother's Darling, small Stylized Bee, #175 ..... 120.00

Mountaineer, Goebel Bee, #315, 5″ 75.00

Not For You, 3-line, #317 .. 95.00

Photographer, Full Bee, #178, 5″ 165.00

Plaque, Mail Coach, small Stylized Bee, #140 ..... 110.00

Postman, Crown mark, #119, 5″ 200.00

Puppy Love, Goebel Bee, #1 . 80.00

School Boy, Stylized Bee, #82/2/0, 4″ 75.00

Signs of Spring, Goebel Bee, #203/2/0, 4″ 65.00

Singing Lesson, small Stylized Bee, #63, 3″ 80.00

Skier, Crown mark, wooden poles, #59, 5¾″ 200.00

Soloist, Full Bee, #135 .... 105.00

Stitch in Time, 3-line, #255, 7″ 100.00

Sweet Music, Goebel Bee, #186, 5½″ 55.00

Telling Her Secret, Stylized Bee, #196/0 .... 180.00

Trumpet Boy, Full Bee, #97 . 125.00

Umbrella Boy, small Stylized Bee, #152/II, 8″ 525.00

Volunteers, small Stylized Bee, #50/2/0, 5″ 85.00

Indian Artifacts

Anything made by or related to the American Indian is of interest to collectors, whether it be a simple utilitarian tool or an object of art. Often each tribe exhibited certain characteristics in their work which help collectors determine the origin of their treasures. Some of the tribes are best known for their expertise in a particular craft. For instance, Navajos were weavers of rugs and blankets, the Zuni excelled in petit-point and inlay jewelry, and the Hopi made beautiful kachina dolls. Ceremonial items, fine beaded clothing and bags, and antique rugs are among the most valuable examples of Indian art.

Awl, bone, 4¼" 20.00
Axe, dark gray stone, grooved, 5 pounds 50.00
Axe, 6 pounds, 8" 150.00
Bag, Nez Perce, fully beaded cloth, 10x8¾" 155.00
Bag, Northern Blackfeet, fully beaded cloth, florals, 12x9¼" 135.00
Bag, parfleche, painted decor with some wear, 14x25" . 45.00
Bag, Sioux, drawstring velvet with full beading on 1 side, 11x14" 75.00
Bag, Stony, fully beaded cloth with chief, butterfly & diamond, 11x10" 135.00
Basket, Apache, twined with trade cloth center, 1890, 9½" diameter 75.00
Basket, Chemehuevi, terraced rectangular band, 1x3½" . 150.00
Basket, Hopi, coiled plaque with black, yellow & white, 15½" 125.00
Basket, Jicarilla Apache, polychrome, 4x14", EX 400.00
Basket, Klamath, oval, 4x10½ x11½", EX 175.00
Basket, Papago, black vertical terraces, 5¾x5¾" 35.00
Basket, Papago, brown & natural designs, flat, 11" . 35.00
Belt, Blackfeet, fully beaded, leather, rectangular panels, 40" long 125.00
Belt, Navajo, link style button conchos, 27" 175.00
Blade, draw; gray with blue flint 10.00
Blade, shouldered & stemmed with brown chert, 3" ... 7.00
Blanket, Navajo, eyedazzler, circa 1890s, 49x88", EX . 1,500.00
Bowl, Acoma, polychrome, 1940s, 5¼x8" 65.00

Hopi kachina doll, The Owl, 28", $250.00.

Bowl, San Ildefonso, polychrome, signed Blue Corn, 2x2¾" 250.00
Box, Navajo, stamped silver, with lid, Knife Wing Dancer, 3" 100.00
Bracelet, Navajo, hand stamped, ¾" triangle turquoise cabachon 105.00
Bracelet & ring, Navajo, total of 8 coral cabachons 150.00
Case, Crow, painted parfleche, circa 1890, 11x26" 185.00
Collar & necktie, Crow, hide with multicolored beading, 19" long, EX 85.00
Doll, Kachina, Hopi, Antelope & Deer, 15" 175.00
Doll, Kachina, Hopi, crosslegged, AKA Bluebird Snare, 9½" 25.00
Doll, Kachina, Hopi, Hopi Cloud Man, 12" 95.00

Hopi coiled polychrome basket with lid by Mary Jane Batala, 10″ x 10″, $450.00.

Doll, Sioux, male, hide with cloth clothing & beaded decor, 14″, EX 90.00

Drill, chipped, hafted base, reworked point, 2¼″ 35.00

Earrings, Zuni, petit point, 23 turquoise with wagon wheel motif 100.00

Flute, Plains, 2 piece wooden V-shape with cord & string decor 27.50

Headband, Plains, reptile with fully beaded arrow motif, 1880, 18″ 75.00

Jar, Acoma, polychrome, intricate designs, 1930s, 10x12″ 200.00

Jar, Acoma, 4 colors, 1930s, 6½x7¾″, EX 125.00

Knife, 1 curved & 1 straight edge, striated flint, 4″ .. 18.00

Leggings, Cree, cloth with beading, metal sequins with yarn ties, 16″ 135.00

Moccasins, Cheyenne, partially beaded, marked Red Shield, worn 85.00

Moccasins, Sioux, lazy stitch beading, bands, pointed toe 200.00

Necklace, 43 nuggets strung with shell heshi, 13″ 175.00

Pipe, Chippewa, stone with pewter inlay & nude male stem, 2½″ 150.00

Pipe, Sioux, Dakota, catlinite, carved florals, pierced stem 205.00

Pouch, Crow, fringed, checkerboard beading, 6″ 60.00

Pouch, Plains, beaded each side with leaf, flower & geometrics, 4½″........ 125.00

Pouch, tobacco; Plains, fringed, 5 color beading, losses, 21″ 175.00

Ring, Navajo, oval, ½x¾″, #8 spiderweb cabachon 65.00

Roach, dyed horsehair, recent 20.00

Rug, Navajo, gray, tan, dark brown & white geometrics, 50x82″ 450.00

Rug, Navajo, optical decor in rust, tan & white, 16x24″ . 30.00

Sheath, knife; Sioux, partial beading, 1920, 7″ 35.00

Skull cracker, grooved, round, 3 pounds 15.00

Spade, tan, polished, flared, 8″ 200.00

Spear, buffalo; gray flint with full base, 5″ 25.00

Watercolor, buck & doe, Quincy Tahoma, Navajo, 12x10″ 675.00

Navajo sand painting, 'Yeibichai' by Nelson Lewis, in frame, 24″ x 24″, $275.00.

Inkwells

Since about 1835, when ink was refined, there has been a market for inkwells. Today collectors appreciate them for their beauty, ingenuity, rarity, and styling. They are found in abundance in art glass of all types, brass, bronze, cast iron, wood with glass liners, natural stones, pottery, and pewter.

Cast iron rose with gilt paint, $45.00.

Advertising, Carter's Fountain Pen Liquid, embossed glass	60.00
Amber glass, enamel florals, 8 sides, prism-cut base, hinged	125.00
Art Nouveau, brass holder with glass insert	17.50
Bottle, 12 sides, green, 'Ink', rough pontil, 2″	16.00
Brass, 2 pottery inkwells, snakeskin covered, 13¾″	160.00
Bronze, double, 3 figures of Dutch children	450.00
Copper, hinged lid, 3½″ diameter	45.00
Copper pyramid, hinged cover, glass liner, MF & Company, Artmetal	130.00
Cranberry, double, plated holder	265.00
Crystal, 4 sides, sterling silver top	95.00
Cut glass, Harvard, no insert	80.00
Daisy & Button, cat on hamper, blue	120.00
Glass, aqua, Carter's Raven Black, original labels, 1882, 2½″	10.00
Glass, clear, with swirl design, 2x4″ diameter	30.00
Glass, flint, clover design, pressed base, cut top, 4x2½″ square	45.00
Glass, sapphire blue, hinged, 3¾″	150.00
Golf ball, metal with green glass insert	30.00

Horseshoe with horse figural, single glass insert & top	55.00
Letter scale figural, brass, Victorian, English, 9½x4½″	350.00
Limoges, double well	30.00
Loetz, green insert, brass lid, pewter lily pad frame, 3x2½″	180.00
Mephistopheles, bronze figural, face is cover, 6″	85.00
Pewter, cylinder with hinged lid, marked SO & crown, 3¼″ diameter	120.00
Phrenology, impressed 'F Bridges, Phrenologist,' 1850, rare	350.00

Metal pencil holder rack, three wells, and perpetual calendar, 5″ x 5½″, $65.00.

Reindeer & sleigh, brass & copper, 6x11" 135.00

Silver embossed metal, low flared feet, pen holders, swirled wells 60.00

Tea kettle, cobalt glass, 8 sides, brass hinged spout . 235.00

Traveling, gutta percha, square with 2 round screw lids, EX 95.00

Yellowware, with gold lustre double well, grape leaf tray, mark #12 .... 145.00

Insulators

After the telegraph was invented in 1844, insulators were used to attach the transmission wires to the poles. With the coming of the telephone, their usefullness increased, and it is estimated that over 3,000 types were developed. Collectors today value some of them very highly -- the threadless type, for example, often bring prices of several hundred dollars. Color, rarity, and age are all important factors to consider when evaluating insulators. In the 1960s, N.R. Woodward developed a standard system of identification using numbers with a 'C.D.' prefix.

CD #102, Brookfield #9, aqua   3.00

CD #102, Diamond, pale lavender 10.00

CD #102, Hawley, aqua ...   9.00

CD #104, New England Telegraph & Telephone Company, light aqua ...   8.00

CD #105, American Ins Co, aqua 45.00

CD #106, Diamond, lemon .   9.00

CD #106, Hemingray #9, clear 5.00

CD #106, Maydwell #9, light purple 12.00

CD #106, Maydwell #9, smoke   5.00

CD #106, McLaughlin #9, light green 5.00

CD #106, PSSA #9, yellow-green 8.00

CD #106, Star, green 4.00

CD #107, Hemingray #9, clear   4.00

CD #112, Lynchburg #31, light aqua 5.00

CD #113, Hemingray #12, clear 4.00

CD #121, AGEE, greenish aqua 10.00

CD #121, California, blue .. 10.00

CD #121, Canada, purple .. 13.50

CD #121, Hemingray #16, green 5.00

CD #121, McLaughlin #16, dark green 9.00

CD #121, WGM Co, purple . 12.00

CD #121.2, AGEE, purple . 15.00

CD #122, McLaughlin #16, light green 3.00

CD #122, VMR Napoli, light aqua 6.00

CD #124.6, AGEE, light purple 18.00

CD #124.7, CCG, light straw . 10.00

CD #126, Brookfield, aqua . 15.00

CD #126, Brookfield, yellow-green 30.00

CD #127.5, Brookfield, aqua frost 7.00

CD #128, Hemingray CSA, clear 4.00

CD #128, Pyrex, clear 3.00

CD #129, Armstrong, TS, clear 4.00

CD #129, Hemingray, TS, clear 2.00

CD #133, BGM, amethyst . 30.00

CD #133, City Fire Alarm, aqua 30.00

CD #133, ER, aqua 7.00

CD #134, CEL, aqua 20.00

CD #134, Good, light aqua . 7.00

CD #143, Canadian-Pacific, purple 14.00

CD #143, Canadian-Pacific Ry Co, ice blue 4.00

CD #143, Dwight Pattern, aqua 20.00

CD #145, American, sky blue . 10.00
CD #145, Brookfield, light
    aqua 5.00
CD #145, California, pale
    green 25.00
CD #145, GTP Tel Co, bright
    aqua blue 10.00
CD #145, NEGM Co, greenish
    aqua 5.00
CD #145, Postal, green 6.00
CD #145, Star, green 10.00
CD #151, HG Co Petticoat,
    aqua 5.00
CD #152.9, AGEE, purple . 20.00
CD #154, Dominion #42, light
    green 4.00
CD #154, Maydwell #42, clear 5.00
CD #162, California, light
    green 5.00
CD #162, Hemingray #19,
    emerald green 15.00
CD #162, Lynchburg #36,
    green 8.00
CD #162, McLaughlin #19,
    light green 4.00
CD #162, McLaughlin #19,
    steel blue 8.00
CD #162, Whitall Tatum #4,
    clear 6.00
CD #164, Brookfield, green . 10.00
CD #164, Hemingray #20,
    clear 4.00
CD #164, McLaughlin #20,
    light green 4.00
CD #205, Gayner #530, aqua . 10.00
CD #205, Lynchburg #530,
    aqua 15.00
CD #252, Maydwell, light pur-
    ple 20.00
CD #257, Hemingray #60,
    clear 8.00
CD #272, Armstrong #511A,
    dark amber 5.00
CD #275, Locke, #21, green . 20.00

Ironstone

    There are many types of decorated ironstone available today, but the most sought-after is the simple white dinnerware sometimes decorated in relief with fruit, grains, and foliage, ribbing and scallops. It was made by many English potters from the last quarter of the 18th century until well into the 1900s.

Bedpan 26.50
Bowl, fruit; Bellflower, Ed-
    wards, small 12.50
Bowl, scalloped, large 30.00
Bowl, vegetable with cover,
    Paris, EM & CF, 6x9" . . 24.00
Bowl, vegetable with cover,
    Sydenham, Boote 145.00
Brush vase, Hawthorn 60.00
Cake plate on pedestal,
    Grenade, Boote, 1850s . . 65.00
Chamber pot, ornate lid finial,
    Meakin 73.00
Chamber pot, vertical flutes &
    ribs, white 35.00
Coffee pot, Baltimore,
    Brougham Mayer, 1850s . 115.00
Coffee pot, Corn & Oats,
    white, large 170.00
Creamer, Memnon, Meir, 1857 50.00
Creamer, President Edwards . 57.00
Cup, Corn & Oats 15.00
Ewer, Scalloped Decagon, J
    Wedgwood 134.00
Gravy boat, white, Meakin . 21.50
Nappy, oval, Alfred Meakin,
    5x6½" 8.50
Pitcher, milk; Paneled Grape,
    Meakin 65.00
Pitcher, milk; TR Boote, 8½" 53.00
Pitcher, Oriental, Mason's Pa-
    tent, 4½" 70.00
Pitcher, snake handle,
    Mason's, 5½" 105.00
Pitcher, water; with ice lip . 45.00
Plate, Clipper Ship, Mason, 8" 9.50
Plate, Corn & Oats, Daven-
    port & Wedgwood, dinner . 17.00
Plate, Wheat, Meakin, 8½" . 14.50
Platter, French Ironstone,
    11x16" 21.50
Platter, Meakin, 8x11" 15.50

Pudding mold, Corn, medium	55.00
Pudding mold, Grape, medium	40.00
Relish, Lily-of-the-Valley ..	36.00
Sauce boat, Ceres, Forester .	60.00
Shaving mug, Lily-of-the-Valley	42.00
Sugar bowl, Gothic, Ridgway	60.00
Sugar bowl, Pacific, Tunstall, 5″	61.50
Syrup pitcher	38.00
Teapot, Corn & Oats	75.00
Teapot, St Louis, Edwards, 1850s	95.00
Toothbrush holder, Wheat & Blackberry	44.00
Tureen, Atlantic, Boote, 1858, 4 piece	375.00
Tureen, flower lid finial, pedestal foot, white, J Wedgwood	85.00

Jewelry

Today, anyone interested in buying gems will soon find out that the antique stones are the best values. Not only are prices from ⅓ to ½ less than on comparable new jewelry, but the craftsmanship and styling of modern-day pieces are lacking in comparison. Costume jewelry from all periods is popular, especially Art Nouveau and Art Deco examples. Signed pieces are particularly good, especially those by Miriam Haskell, Georg Jensen, David Anderson, and other well-known artists.

Beads, amber colored glass with double drop, 21″ ..	25.00
Beads, double strand of rock crystals	65.00
Beads, sterling, graduated sizes	25.00
Bracelet, amber & black plastic strung on elastic bands, circa 1930	35.00
Bracelet, gilt on brass, hinged, engraved, circa 1850, ½″ wide	90.00

Bookchain necklace set with amethysts and pearls, gold filled, 10½″ long, $225.00.

Bracelet, gold filled ribbon weave, Etruscan work on drop, circa 1850	50.00
Bracelet, hinged, yellow gold filled with pink & green gold designs	150.00
Bracelet, hinged bangle type, gold filled, ca 1940s, ¾″ wide	95.00
Bracelet, Italian mosaics, 12 gold washed links	12.00
Bracelet, yellow gold filled, jointed, engraved, ¼″ wide	85.00
Bracelet, 3 strands of imitation pearls, fancy clasp, gold over brass	8.00
Bracelet, 4 rows of rose-cut garnets, ½″ wide	300.00
Brooch, Art Nouveau, marked sterling, heart shape with female head, 1″........	125.00
Brooch, Art Nouveau, silver over copper, grapes & child's face, 2″	125.00
Brooch, Art Nouveau, sterling & German silver, female with flowers	150.00
Brooch, Bohemian garnets, butterfly mount, gold over brass, 1⅛″	125.00
Brooch, Bohemian garnets, star-like arrangements, brass mount, 1¾″	125.00
Brooch, gilt mountings, enameled leaves, molded cameo, circa 1840	55.00
Brooch, gold filled with garnet colored stones, 1860s, 2¾x1¾″	95.00

Brooch, gold over brass mounting, flower mosaic set in black onyx, 1″ 30.00

Brooch, gutta percha, figural relief, circa 1850, 1¾x2″ . 90.00

Brooch, jet with seed pearl set in 15k center mount, 1½x⅝″ 150.00

Brooch, 15k, rock crystal over hair flowers, 2 rows of pearls, 1800s 390.00

Brooch, 18k mounted lava cameo, 1¾x2″ 750.00

Brooch-pendant, 10k gold with shell cameo, early 1900s . 450.00

Brooch-pendant, 14k mounting, shell cameo with 2 diamonds, 2¼″ 625.00

Brooch-pendant, 900 silver with shell cameo & marcasites, 1¼x1½″........ 125.00

Buckle, Art Nouveau, sterling, relief nude decor, 1½x2¾″ 125.00

Cameo, jet, surrounded by rose-cut jet, circa 1860, 1½x1½″ 80.00

Chatelaine, sterling with simple design, 5 piece 300.00

Comb, amber with black bars, set with green brilliants, 8½x9½″ 75.00

Comb, simulated tortoise, intricate filigree, 21 teeth . 15.00

Comb, tortoise shell, solid top with gold floral filigree, 6″ 75.00

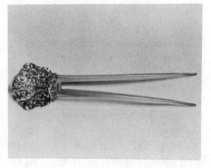

Hair ornament, 10k gold and blonde tortoise shell, 4½″, $125.00.

Glass fruit necklace, multicolor, $18.00.

Cross, gilt on brass with gold ornaments, circa 1850, 1½x2⅜″ 60.00

Cross, gutta percha, molded in relief, 1½x2½″ 95.00

Earrings, copper, 4 studded squares, sterling screws, ca 1940 .... 8.00

Earrings, faceted crystal teardrops, ca 1920s 28.00

Earrings, gold filled with blue molded glass, Czechoslovakia 48.00

Earrings, rolled gold, paste emerald drops, Victorian mounting 12.00

Lavalier, Art Nouveau, 14k with peridot & seed pearls, 2″ 295.00

Lavalier, 18k gold, paste stones, circa 1890 ...... 120.00

Locket, composition, floral relief, circa 1860, 1½x2″ . 75.00

Locket, gilt over brass, glass insets, with tintype, circa 1840, ⅞″ 125.00

Locket, gold filled with mosaic bird, gold filled bookchain, 1860s 250.00

Locket, pinchbeck, bouquet made of hair, circa 1840s, ¾x1″ 125.00

Choker necklace, blue glass and metal filigree stations, blue glass rectangular drop in floral accented frame, $38.00.

Locket, yellow gold with 5 pearls, circa 1840, ⅝″x⅜″″ ... 125.00

Locket, 10k gold, engraved, circa 1850 .... 130.00

Necklace, Art Deco, sterling with hemetite & marcasites, triangle drop.... 200.00

Necklace, bookchain, gold filled, stone cameo drop, 19″ . 125.00

Necklace, bookchain, gold over brass, ⅛″ flat links, ¾″ drop 85.00

Necklace, carved plastic 'ivory' beads, ca 1925, 16″ 16.00

Necklace, glass, amethyst & crystal, 1928, 15″ 55.00

Necklace, hand carved bone, circa 1920 .... 38.00

Pendant, pinchbeck with hinged beveled glass, 1800s, 1⅝″ 225.00

Pin, Art Deco, black jet flower, 3½″ 9.00

Pin, sterling & marcasites, Art Deco greyhound, 2¼″ long 75.00

Pin, sterling filigree with enameled butterfly 8.00

Pin, sterling florals, signed Georg Jensen 58.00

Ring, Art Deco, 14k & platinum, carved onyx, 28 small diamonds 500.00

Ring, marked silver, marcasites, ½x⅜″ 95.00

Ring, sterling with marcasites around enameled center, 1930s 250.00

Ring, wedding band, marked silver, set with marcasites 75.00

Ring, 14k fitting on ⅛″ wide hair weaving, circa 1850 . 95.00

Ring, 15k gold, diamond shaped lapis lazuli cabachon 95.00

Ring, 15k with oval coral cabachon 50.00

Watch chain, gold filled, ¼x20½″ 70.00

Watch chain, gold fittings with woven hair chain, circa 1840, 8½″ 95.00

Watch chain, silver with tassel, 8½″ 50.00

Kewpies

Since first introduced through the pages of *The Ladies' Home Journal*, Rose O'Neill's Kewpies have continued to work their charms on us all. Collectors today treasure dolls with the original O'Neill label -- anything decorated with Kewpies is considered very collectible.

Advertising sheet, Kellogg's Toasted Corn Flakes, O'Neill baby 18.00

Bell, brass Kewpie 45.00

Box, blue and white heart shape, 3 Kewpies on bench, signed 246.00

Calendar, 1975, Kewpie ... 19.00

Card holder, figural kewpie . 41.00

Chocolate mold, Kewpie, marked Reich, 5x3¾″ ... 52.00

Cup & saucer, 8 action Kewpies, Royal Rudolstadt . 96.00
Egg, bisque with hand painted Kewpie, signed Wilson, rare 197.00
Kewpie, bisque, fully signed, 9" 289.00
Kewpie, bisque, molded blue pants, white shirt & cap, 4½" 760.00
Kewpie, bisque, reclining with cheek on hand, winks eye, 3½" 45.00
Kewpie, bisque, suitcase & umbrella, signed, #8/4859 . 167.00
Kewpie, brass 67.50
Kewpie, celluloid, 2¼" 28.00
Kewpie, chalkware, 12½" . . 31.00
Kewpie, glass, 4" 46.00
Kewpie, red cloth, signed, 12" 86.50
Kewpie Doodle Dog, bisque, marked O'Neill, 1¾" . . . 295.00
Kewpie Gal, Little Dottie Darling, MIB 52.50
Kewpie Scootles, MIB 77.00
Kewpie Sleeper, Cameo, MIB 60.00
Letter opener, pewter, figural Kewpie, 6¼" 47.00
Paperweight, Kewpie decor, Purdue Foundry pot metal 25.50
Place card, little girl Kewpie, roses on dress & curls, with purse 5.50
Plate, action Kewpies, O'Neill, Rudolstadt, Prussia, 7½" 115.00
Plate, deep; Action Kewpies, Royal Rudolstadt, 7¾" . 126.00
Postcard, Kewpie Christmas, 1923 cancelation 26.50
Poster, suffrage, Get Mother The Vote, Kewpies march, 30x45" 326.00
Song book, Safety, circa 1937, 71 pages, illustrated by O'Neill 34.00
Thimble, metal Military Kewpie, marked Kewpie . 41.00
Tobacco felt, Kewpie soldier, signed 25.00

Tray, cloverleaf shape, Jasper, green with 5 action Kewpies in pink 190.00
Whistle, brass figural Kewpie 19.00

Kitchen Collectibles

From the early patented apple peelers, cherry pitters and food choppers to the gadgets of the twenties and the thirties, many collectors find a special appeal in kitchen tools.

Adjustable wire tongs for removing pies from oven, 20", tongs only, $27.00.

Apple corer, tin with wood handle, Boye Needle Company, patent 1916 . . . . . . 4.00
Apple parer, cast iron, CL Hudson, Rocking Table, patent 1882 . . . . 26.00
Apple parer, homemade, wooden, red paint, clamps on table, mid-1800s 73.00
Beater jar, blue & white stripes, with eggbeater . 35.00
Cake knife, steel blade, cast iron handle, Christy, patent 1889 . . . . 9.00
Cherry pitter, cast iron, New Britain 45.00
Chopping knife, hand forged crescent blade, bentwood handle, 6" long 65.00
Churn, Red Wing stoneware, 5 gallon 40.00
Churn, tin, small 9" cylinder . 35.00
Coffee grinder, wood with iron hopper, 19th century . . . 75.00
Coffee mill, cast iron, double-wheel store model, Enterprise #12 . . . . 320.00

Coffee pot, red enamelware,
nickel plated lid, gooseneck   25.00
Colander, pierced tin, footed,
ear handles, circa 1890-
1910, 12″ 16.00
Colander, sheet iron in good
condition, 10″ 30.00
Cookie cutter, tin eagle, flat
back 30.00
Corn popper, wire & mesh,
wood handle, sliding metal
lid, circa 1910 ....   12.50
Crimper, cast aluminum,
1920s or 1930s, 4¾″ long .   8.00
Crimper, turned maple with
bone wheel, 19th century,
4½″ long 35.00
Double boiler, gray graniteware 20.00
Doughnut cutter, tin, strap
handle, 1920s to 1940s ..   6.50

**Glass butter churn with wooden pad-
dles, 9½″ x 5″ x 5″, $55.00.**

Drink mixer, metal shaker
with lid, Ovaltine 18.00
Dry measure, bentwood with
old red paint, bail handle .   15.00
Egg scale, metal, Toledo ..   16.00
Egg timer, wood, old red
paint, 19th century 20.00

**White Mountain apple parer, Goodell
Company, $38.00.**

Eggbeater, iron & wire, A&J,
patent 1923, 11″ long ..   12.00
Fish scaler, cast iron, CD Ken-
ny, 19th century 20.00
Flour bin, white enameled tin   28.00
Food grinder, cast iron, granite-
ware hopper, 1880s 43.50
Food mold, individual alumi-
num fluted molds, 4x3½″,
set of 8 ....   12.00
Food mold, tin, fish shape, 9″
long 85.00
Frying pan, cast iron, footed,
10½″ diameter 20.00
Grater, stamped & punched
tin, circa 1910, 9½″ long .   8.00
Ice pick, Arcade 10.00
Measuring cup, green glass,
Kellogg's 9.50
Mixing bowl, yellowware with
brown bands, 9″ diameter .   20.00
Muffin pan, cast iron, shell
design 45.00
Nut grinder, cast iron & tin,
Climax 35.00
Pastry blender, heavy nickeled
iron, wood handle, 9¼″
long 6.50
Pie pan, cobalt blue & white
agateware, 10″ diameter .   12.50
Rolling pin, red & blue spatter
glass 150.00
Sausage grinder, iron, hangs
on wall, patent 1885, 27″
long 28.50
Stove tongs, wrought iron,
Shaker, 16″ long 50.00

Sugar nippers, iron, hand held,
very simple, 19th century . 50.00
Tea kettle, mottled green
agateware, some flaking . 26.00
Vegetable slicer, Universal,
turn-of-the-century 26.00
Waffle iron, cast iron, hearts
& stars, Griswold, 1920 . 52.50

Knives

Collectors of pocket knives look for those with bone handles in mint unsharpened condition, those with pearl handles, Case doctor's knives, and large display models.

Case, #2202½, marked XX,
black composition, 2 blades 70.00
Case, #31212½, marked
Tested, cream composition,
4″ 145.00
Case, #3165, marked Tested,
yellow composition, 5½″ . 205.00
Case, #3201, marked Dots,
yellow composition, 2
blades, 2⅝″ 12.00
Case, #3207, marked Tested,
yellow composition, 2
blades, 3½″ 85.00
Case, #4100SS, marked USA,
white composition, 5½″ . 58.50
Case, #51050SAB, marked
Tested, genuine stag, 5⅜″ 412.50
Case, #5165, marked XX,
stag, 5½″ 205.00
Case, #61048SP, marked XX,
bone handle 27.50
Case, #61049, marked Tested,
green handle, 4″ 115.00
Case, #6116SP, marked Tested,
green bone, 3⅜″ 85.00
Case, #6165SAB, marked XX,
laminated wood, 5½″ ... 51.50
Case, #62009, marked Tested,
brown bone, 2 blades, 3¼″ 85.00
Case, #6205, marked Tested,
green bone, 2 blades, 3¾″ 170.00
Case, #6205, marked XX,
green bone, 3¾″ 51.50

Case, #6208, marked XX,
green bone, 2 blades, 3¼″ 42.00
Case, #62109X, marked XX,
rough black, 2 blades, 3⅛″ 42.00
Case, #6213, marked Tested,
green bone, 2 blades, 4″ . 205.00
Case, #6216, marked XX,
bone, 2 blades, 3 3/8″ ... 33.50
Case, #6216½, marked USA,
bone, 2 blades, 3⅜″ 27.50
Case, #62210, marked Tested,
green bone, 2 blades, 3⅜″ 170.00
Case, #82001R, marked Tested,
pearl, 2 blades 75.00
Case, #82101R, marked Tested,
pearl, 2 blades, 2¼″ 58.00
Case, #9200, marked Tested,
imitation pearl, 2 blades,
3⅞″ 220.00
Case, #9201, marked USA, im-
itation pearl, 2 blades, 2⅝″ 17.00
Case, leg knife, marked Tested,
Christmas tree, 2 blades . 170.00
Cattaraugus, #10484, white
fiberloid, 1 blade, 3¾″ .. 50.00
Cattaraugus, #11486, black
fiberloid, 1 blade, 4½″ .. 50.00
Cattaraugus, #12144, red
fiberloid, 1 blade, 5″ 40.00
Cattaraugus, #12839, stag, 1
blade, 5⅜″ 700.00
Cattaraugus, #20232, French
pearl, 2 blades, 3″ 30.00
Cattaraugus, #206, Shrine
emblem, 2 blades, 3¼″ .. 40.00
Cattaraugus, #206, 32nd
emblem, 2 blades, 3¼″ .. 40.00
Cattaraugus, #20673, mother
of pearl, 2 blades, 3″ ... 40.00
Cattaraugus, #21229, stag, 2
blades, 3½″ 60.00

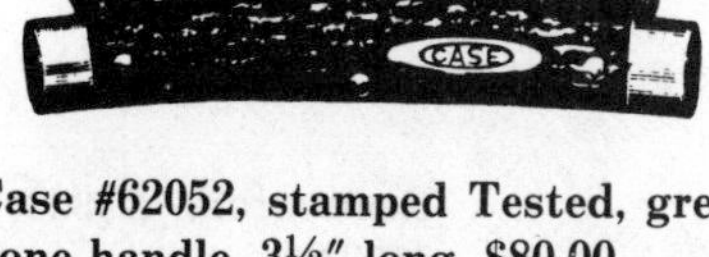

Case #62052, stamped Tested, green bone handle, 3½″ long, $80.00.

Cattaraugus, #2139, bone, 2 blades, 3⅜″ 100.00

Cattaraugus, #2149, bone, 2 blades, 3⅜″ 108.50

Cattaraugus, #21809, stag, 2 blades, 3⅛″ 40.00

Cattaraugus, #22053, mother of pearl, 2 blades, 3¼″ .. 40.00

Cattaraugus, #22109, stag (round bolsters), 2 blades, 4½″ 147.50

Remington, RA1, cocobola, 1 blade, 3½″ 67.50

Remington, R01, redwood, 1 blade, 3⅜″ 40.00

Remington, R33, stag, 2 blades, 3⅜″ 53.50

Remington, R355, pyremite, 2 blades, 3¾″ 82.50

Remington, R392, black, 2 blades, 3¾″ 87.50

Remington, R423, stag, 2 blades, 3¾″ 72.50

Remington, R453, stag, 2 blades, 3½″ 57.50

Remington, R473, stag, 2 blades, 3½″ 87.50

Remington, R52, black, 2 blades, 3⅜″ 83.50

Remington, R523, stag, 2 blades, 3½″ 82.50

Remington, R525, pyremite, 2 blades, 3½″ 77.50

Remington, R551, redwood, 2 blades, 3¼″ 67.50

Remington, R82, black, 2 blades, 3⅜″ 67.50

Russell, #0360, model stag, 3 blades, 3⅝″ 265.00

Russell, #053, model stag, 2 blades, 3⅜″ 232.50

Cattaraugus #22919, stag handle, two blades, 4¼″ closed, $150.00.

Russell, #1118, iron, 1 blade, 3½″ 132.50

Russell, #1119, iron, 2 blades, 3½″ 160.00

Russell, #15, iron, 1 blade, 2¾″ 196.50

Russell, #222, cocobola, 2 blades, 3⅜″ 217.50

Russell, #313, ebony, 1 blade, 2⅞″ 110.00

Tree Brand, #201, composition, 1 blade, 3⅜″ 8.00

Tree Brand, #6514, nickeled silver, 2 blades, 3″ 10.00

Tree Brand, #6697, celluloid, 1 blade, 3¼″ 8.00

Tree Brand, #6703, stag, 1 blade, 4¼″ 13.00

Tree Brand, #9301, stag, 2 blades, 3⅝″ 13.00

Winchester, #2051, celluloid, 2 blades, 2⅝″ 123.00

Winchester, #2053, celluloid, 2 blades, 3⅜″ 143.50

Winchester, #2111, celluloid, 2 blades, 3½″ 77.50

Winchester, #2112, celluloid, 2 blades, 3½″ 93.50

Winchester, #2612, cocobola, 2 blades, 3⅝″ 108.50

Winchester, #2613, cocobola, 2 blades, 3⅝″ 108.50

Remington, R3933, stag handle, three blades, $170.00.

Winchester, #2701, bone, 2
blades, 3½" 208.50
Winchester, #2853, stag, 2
blades, 3⅜" 167.00

Labels

The colorful lithographed labels
that were once used on wooden pack-
ing crates are being collected for their
artwork and advertising appeal. Clever
association between company name or
location and depicted themes are common; particularly good examples of
this are usually most desirable. For instance, Santa Paula lemon labels show
a jolly Santa Claus, and Red Cat
oranges have a cat mascot.

Acropolis, scene of ruins of ancient Athens 7.00
Bajazzo, jester dressed in
blue, looking in mirror .. 8.00
Bessie Green, classy woman,
wears green hat 5.00
Cardinal, 2 cardinals on branches with heavy leaves . 8.50

Chicago Club, monogram in
front of spider web, bronze
& tan 5.00
Cuban, Cuban man in blue
coat smoking cigar, scene
of plantation 4.00
Flor Fina, woman framed in
oval, embossed & bronzed
pattern 6.00
Frisco, Salinas, California,
railroad station, clock
tower, vegetables 2.50
Index, La Habra, California,
hand points to brand name,
lemons 6.00
La Duena, lady seated in chair
reads book 6.00
Lochinvar, San Bernadino,
California, armored knight,
lady, oranges 6.00
Monday, military portrait of
Civil War hero 7.50
Morjon, San Francisco, boy
blows horn, 2 large apples . 3.00
Nelly, woman sits on bale of
cotton, holds box of cigars 6.00
Onze Buitenhuizen, scene of
big European estate 8.00

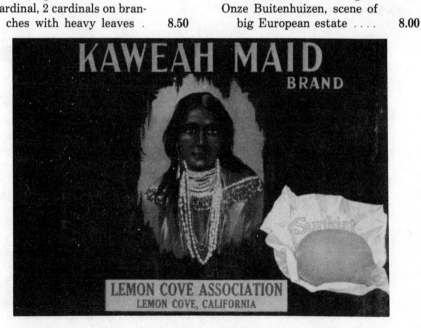

Kaweah Maid Sunkist, Lemon Cove Association, valued at $1.00-$5.00.

Oribit, Exeter, California, orange is head of streaking comet 7.00

Pioneer Orchard, Medfork, Oregon, oxen pull Conestoga wagon, pears 4.00

Russel Young, portrait of politician in front of Capital 8.00

San Francisco, car decals, Chinatown, Golden Gate Bridge, 1940 .... 1.00

Selva, Fillmore, California, Selva Canyon, lemons .. 3.00

Sir David, bust of man of 18th century 10.00

Soda pop, lot of 50 obsolete . 3.00

Thendora, woman looks at pink rose 3.00

Travel, USA & Foreign, lot of 50 .... 7.50

Triton, Seattle, Washington, Neptune sits by ocean holding apples 7.00

Victorian lady, embossed, 1911, 3x4" 1.00

Victory, scenes from Roman gladiator event 3.00

Wines, discontinued Valley of the Moon, set of 18 .... 2.25

Yakima Chief, Yakima, Washington, bust of Indian chief, apples 5.00

Lace & Linens

Crocheted and tatted lace are varieties of handwork most often encountered at flea markets today, and collectors can still appreciate the tedium, expertise and eyestrain that went into their making. If your treasured laces are yellowed or stained, an instant tea bath can be used to obtain a natural ecru look, and is far less damaging to the old threads than using bleach to whiten them. Doilies are often framed and hung in groupings on bedroom walls or used to top throw pillows. From remnants of lace trims, you can create your own Victorian 'waist' -- either trim a ready-made or sew one up using a basic pattern. Machine washing is not recommended.

Oxnard, Ventura County Lemons Sunkist, $1.00-$5.00.

Embroidered and drawnwork tablecloth, 72″ square, $175.00.

Tablecloth, heavy floral embroidery, 4″ crochet edge, 42″ diameter 85.00

Trapunto pillow cover, basket of flowers with feather quilted wreath and initials, very good condition, 24″ x 32″, $400.00.

Banquet set, Swiss Appenzelle embroidery, cloth & 12 napkins 225.00

Bedspread, crocheted, scalloped, 94x66″ 50.00

Bedspread, crocheted, tight stitch, cotton, 120x90″ . 195.00

Crochet, bird on limb with flowers, 3″ fringe, dated 1897, 21x25″ 70.00

Crochet, two horses design, 14x25″ 40.00

Dresser scarf, crocheted Colonial man & lady each end, 16x58″ 48.00

Needlework on satin, florals, French, 5x6½″ 50.00

Needlework on silk, memorial scene, French, 8½x10½″ . 225.00

Needlework on silk, oval with girl & floral border, 1700s, 16x13½″ 160.00

Picture, needlework, Biblical scene, English, 1800s, 26x19″ 50.00

Picture, needlework, flower arrangement, bird's eye frame, 12x15″ 80.00

Punched paper, cross-stitch, old gilded frame, signed, 4x4½″ 20.00

Tablecloth, crochet, Pinwheel & Spider Web, 45x82″ .. 145.00

Tablecloth, crochet, 4 petal rosette medallions, 56x79″ 125.00

Lamps

From the primitive rush light holder and Betty lamp to Tiffany's elaborate stained glass lamps, lighting devices have evolved with the style of the times and the development of better lighting methods. Depending on the taste of the collector, there are many types that are especially desirable. Miniature figural and art glass lamps are popular, and often bring prices of several hundred dollars.

Fairy lamps, Gone-with-the-Wind lamps, and pattern glass lamps of many types are also treasured. Aladdin lamps are the most popular kerosene lamps; they have been made since 1908 by the Mantle Lamps Company of America in over eighteen models and more than one hundred styles. Emeralite lamps, identified by their green cased glass shades, are also highly collectible. They were made from about 1909 into the forties by the H.G. McFaddin Company in a variety of styles.

Lamp with gilt-metal base, glass shade painted with four parrots in pine boughs, ca. early 20th century, $880.00.

Aladdin, Beehive B-80, crystal, with burner 85.00

Aladdin, Beehive B-82, red, with original shade holder, complete 450.00

Aladdin, Cathedral B-110, white moonstone with burner 170.00

Aladdin, Corinthian B-105, clear with green foot, with burner 57.50

Aladdin, hanging lamp, #9, with shade 225.00

Aladdin, Hopalong Cassidy night lamp, gun in holster, Alacite 85.00

Aladdin, Quilt B-86, green moonstone, without burner 90.00

Aladdin, Simplicity B-30, white, with burner 120.00

Aladdin, Tall Lincoln Drape B-75, Alacite, with burner . 75.00

Argand, brass standard, long prisms, clear shade with cut floral, 32″ 265.00

Banquet lamp, blown-out lions' heads, enameled desert scene, 28″ 295.00

Betty lamp, tin with crimped edge pan top, high sided saucer, 8″ 215.00

Betty lamp, wrought iron with hanger & wire link wick pick, 4¼″ 115.00

Boudoir lamp, Emeralite, Jr . 225.00

Bracket lamp, Plume & Attwood Unique, kerosene burner, dated 1877 ..... 175.00

Chandelier, walnut, 5 spindles with drip pans, brass tack trim, 27″ 200.00

Chandelier, 8 light, gilt metal & crystal with prisms, 24x21″ 400.00

Coin Dot, oil burner font, clear opal glass on clear Herringbone base 95.00

Crusie, double, tin with simple tooling on medallion, 9″ . 80.00

Desk lamp, Emeralite, brass base with green cased glass shade 275.00

Fairy lamp, blue frosted opal swirl on matching ruffled base, 5¾″ 550.00

Fairy lamp, burmese, ruffled & reversible, Clarke cup, Webb, 6¾″ 600.00

Fairy lamp, burmese with ivy leaf decoration, ruffled base, Webb, 12″ 2,000.00

Fairy lamp, clear ribbed font with milk glass ribbed shade 400.00

Fairy lamp, cranberry Diamond Quilted, clear Clarke base, 3½″ 95.00

Fairy lamp, green & white satin stripe, clear base, Stevens & Williams..... 175.00

Fairy lamp, Burmese glass, signed Webb, three pieces, 5¾", $450.00.

Fairy lamp, Mother of Pearl Diamond Quilted, blue, signed Clarke base 150.00

Fairy lamp, overlay glass with pink striped dome, ruffled, 3 part, 5" 365.00

Fairy lamp, spangled glass on clear Clarke's Cricklite base 150.00

Finger lamp, blue Bristol glass with enameled flowers, 9½" 135.00

Finger lamp, blue ribbed glass with bulge at waist, flat base 95.00

Finger lamp, Centennnial 1876 American shield design around font 30.00

Finger lamp, Excelsior pattern, applied handle, flint glass 95.00

Finger lamp, Guardian Angel pattern in amber, all original 95.00

Finger lamp, Lincoln Drape pattern in cobalt glass, pedestal base 195.00

Finger lamp, Peanut pattern in emerald green glass .. 65.00

Finger lamp, Prince Edward pattern in green glass, pedestal base 135.00

Gone-With-The-Wind, hand painted roses, 27" 500.00

Gone-With-The-Wind, red satin glass with blown-out lions' heads, 24" 700.00

Gone-With-The-Wind, red satin glass with blown-out Regal Iris design 625.00

Hall lamp, pull-down, cranberry glass, oil burner 175.00

Hand lamp, Coolidge Drape pattern 100.00

Hand lamp, Peanut pattern in clear glass 55.00

Hand lamp, Prisms with Plain Band pattern in clear glass, flat base 65.00

Hand lamp, Snowflake pattern in clear opalescent glass, pedestal base 250.00

Hand lamp, Thousand Eye pattern in clear glass ... 120.00

Hand lamp, Zipper & Rib pattern in clear glass 65.00

Hanging lamp, blown glass, birds, shells & flowers on brass trim, 22" 575.00

Hanging lamp, pull-down, red satin glass with blown-out poppies, 12" 345.00

Lace maker's lamp, cranberry overshot glass shade, brass base, 16" 375.00

Marriage lamp, blue opalescent glass, patented DC Ripley & Co 1,500.00

Miniature lamp, Acorn pattern, opalescent stripe .. 130.00

Miniature lamp, Beaded Drape pattern with white satin glass shade 75.00

Miniature lamp, Buckle pattern, electric blue, original & complete 150.00

Miniature lamp, Christmas Tree, milk glass with gilt trim 200.00

Miniature lamp, Embossed Flowers pattern, milk glass 175.00

Miniature lamp, Greek Key pattern in clear glass ... 75.00

Miniature lamp, Maltese Cross pattern, milk glass . 165.00

Miniature lamp, Moon & Star pattern, acorn burner, glass shade 75.00

Miniature lamp, Nellie Bly pattern, pink forget-me-not trim 200.00

Miniature lamp, Panel & Drape pattern in clear glass, 6½" 50.00

Miniature lamp, Princess Feather pattern in cobalt glass 225.00

Miniature lamp, Thumbprint & Zipper panels in clear glass, 2 part, 6" 125.00

Miniature lamp, Uncle Sam's Night Lamp, milk glass, by Gillinder 300.00

Oil burner, marble base, brass stem & honeycomb font, 9" 45.00

Owl, bisque figure with glass eyes, candle burner, 3½" . 145.00

Owl, porcelain figure, glass eyes, embossed swirled satin glass shade 425.00

Peg lamp, blown glass, 3 applied spouts, brass base ring, 5" 200.00

Peg lamp, cranberry with gold decoration on fonts & fluted shades, 13"...... 600.00

Peg lamp, tin with handle, 2 tube whale oil burner & petticoat base 65.00

Rayo, oil burner, brass standard & burner 65.00

Remember the Main, brass bullet figural on iron crossed cannon base 195.00

Sewing lamp, Greek Key pattern, very large 75.00

Stand lamp, Beveled Blocks pattern in clear glass ... 145.00

Stand lamp, Riven Ribs pattern in clear glass 145.00

Student lamp, brass, cylinder reservoir & counter balance, CH Covell 450.00

Student lamp, brass, original green overlay shade, marked Manhattan 495.00

Student lamp, brass, peacock blue glass font, marked Perfection, '81 .... 400.00

Student lamp, brass with white shade, Kaiser, German Student Lamps Co . 175.00

Table lamp, chipped ice 18" shade with sailboats, by Classique 1,650.00

Table lamp, Dewdrop & Petal pattern in clear glass ... 60.00

Table lamp, Erin Fan pattern in green glass 160.00

Lamp with leaded glass shade and patinated-metal base, ca. early 20th century, 22¾", $935.00.

Table lamp, Fishscale pattern in clear glass 65.00

Table lamp, leaded glass 16" rose design shade with painted-on leaves 550.00

Table lamp, leaded glass 16" shade with brickwork top, leaf border 400.00

Table lamp, leaded glass 21″ Deco shade with panels & foliate devices 700.00

Table lamp, New York pattern, peacock blue base with amber font 175.00

Table lamp, reverse painted landscape, glass panels in metal frames 180.00

Table lamp, reverse painted scenic, bronzed metal standard, Jefferson 1,100.00

Whale oil burner, brass, stacked disk font & stem, Empire style, 9″ 300.00

Whale oil burner, brass apple font, 9″ 350.00

Whale oil burner, pewter, signed with Gleason touch mark, 9″ 295.00

Law Enforcement

Memorabilia having to do with law enforcement, especially related to the early days of our country, is attracting a following of interested collectors who search for posters, handcuffs, jail keys, etc. Law officers' badges are listed in section titled 'Badges.'

Belt buckle, pre-1900 ..... 75.00

Book, Twentieth Century Souvenir, 1901 Boston Police 50.00

Call box, Gamewell, complete, late 1920s 100.00

Club, mahogany, carved handle, cord & tassel, San Francisco, 1900s 75.00

Handcuffs with key, ca. 1900, $75.00.

Keys, jail 25.00

Lantern, Little Supreme #150, Boston Police Dept, carrying, 1890s 115.00

Magazine, Arizona Sheriff, The; December, 1971 ... 2.50

Painting, on wooden board, old-time policeman, one of a kind, 22x11″ 100.00

Print, Harper's Weekly, March 27, 1897 .... 40.00

Sculpture, pewter, Sheriff by Philip Kraczkowski, circa 1975, 5½″ 100.00

Stamp, Law & Order, 6 cents, 1968 .... 1.50

Suspenders, 'Police' on slide adjustors, engraved with police club 25.00

Whistle, tubular or drum style 15.00

Group of shoulder patches of various agencies, valued from $1.00-$3.00.

Letter Openers

Made from wood, ivory, glass, and metals, letter openers are fun to collect without being expensive. Generally

Brass with figural nude handle, marked 1945, Naples, 9½", $10.00.

the most valuable are advertising openers and figurals made of brass, bronze, copper or iron.

Alligator swallowing Black
man, figural 22.00
Coes Wrench Company,
celluloid, shaped like
monkey wrench 16.00
Egyptian figure handle, carv-
ed ivory, 3" figure 41.50
Elephant head, hollow
celluloid 16.50
Garden of Gods, Pikes Peak,
carved ivory 18.00
Girl's head figural, Art
Nouveau, pewter 19.00
Owl family figural, copper
plated iron, 8½" 11.00
Rat figural, on ear of corn,
brass 61.00
Souvenir, Kennedy Space
Center, Florida 16.50
Sword, with brass scabbard,
9" 25.00
Welsbach Lights, eagle &
lamp, advertising 26.50
Wrought iron, allover engrav-
ed ring handle terminal . 33.00

Locks

Among the most collectible locks on the market today are those made by Yale, Sargent, Winchester, and Keen Kutter. When evaluating the value of locks consider construction, condition, and rarity. Generally, brass and bronze locks outsell those made of steel or iron. Some railroad locks are included here, also see section on Railroadiana.

ALPHA, embossed iron, with
key, VG 51.00
American Keyless, brass, pa-
tent 4/11/08, EX 15.00
Brass, 1882, miniature 6.50
Browne & Sons, London Lock
Smith, brass, 6-lever, mark-
ed WF Company 40.00
Cast iron, very ornate front &
back, with key, 4x2½" .. 66.00
Corbin, brass, incised KCT Ry
Union Station 60.00
Corbin, iron, 6-lever, Iron
Clad, with key, EX 8.00
Detroit Brass Works, brass,
iron double hasp, 1867 .. 80.00

Ward locks, left to right: Fraim, Auto, $20.00; Fraim Slaymaker, Neplus Ultra, $15.00; Eagle Invader, $15.00; Fraim, $20.00.

Eagle, 6-lever pancake push key	14.00
Elbow box, wrought iron, brass plate on exterior level, 4x4½″	65.00
Fraim, iron, 6-lever, for double barrel key, no key, EX	8.00
Fraim Slaymaker, pin tumbler push key, Blue Grass, #44	20.00
Good Luck, horseshoe shaped, brass, 1870	100.00
Harvard, brass, 4-lever, push key	35.00
Loxem, iron, warded, round, with key, VG	15.00
Missouri Pacific Lines Maintenance-way, brass, embossed	65.00
Navy embossed on nickel plated cast iron	21.00
Our Very Best, HSB Company, Chicago	102.00
Reg'd US Mail, brass, counter on side, very good	75.00
Rugby, embossed iron, no key	8.00
Sargent, iron, brass shackle, pin tumbler, push key missing	15.00
Scandinavian, iron, with key, 3½″	20.00
Slaymaker, brass, one seal	50.00
Star, jail lock, with key, 4½″	91.00
Switch, brass, heart, embossed SAFE, with key	20.00
Western Union Telegraph Company embossed on brass, heart shape	28.00
Winchester, with key	150.00
Yale, brass, 6-lever, push key missing	30.00

Lu Ray Pastels

Introduced in the 1940s by Taylor, Smith and Taylor of East Liverpool, Ohio, Lu Ray Pastels is a line that has become popular with today's collectors of American dinnerware. It was made in solid colors: Windsor Blue, Gray, Persian Cream, and Sharon Pink.

Bowl, fruit; 5½″	4.50
Bowl, mixing; rare	30.00
Bowl, oval vegetable	7.00
Bowl, soup; tab handle	10.00
Butter dish, ¼ pound	17.50
Casserole, covered	21.00
Coffee pot, demitasse; with lid, ovoid	25.00
Coffee pot, demitasse; with lid, straight sides	40.00
Creamer, demitasse; ovoid	10.00
Creamer, demitasse; straight sides	16.00
Cup & saucer, demitasse	10.00
Egg cup	13.00
Muffin cover, with 8″ underplate	45.00
Pitcher, juice; ovoid	26.50
Pitcher, syrup; rare, M	40.00
Pitcher, water; footed	25.00
Plate, cake	15.00
Plate, calendar; 1959	10.00
Plate, grill	11.00
Plate, serving; tab handle	15.00
Plate, 10″	6.00
Plate, 7″	3.00
Plate, 8″	4.00
Salt & pepper, pair	10.00
Sugar, with lid, demitasse; ovoid	10.00
Sugar, with lid, demitasse; straight sides	20.00
Teapot, with lid	26.00

Water pitcher, 8″, $25.00.

Tidbit, 2 tier, signed	18.00
Tumbler, juice	10.00
Tumbler, water	13.50

Lunch Boxes

In the early years of this century, tobacco companies often packaged their products in tins that could later be used for lunch boxes. By the 1930s oval lunch boxes designed to appeal to school children were produced. The rectangular shape that is now popular was preferred by the 1950s. Character lunch boxes decorated with the faces of TV personalities, super heroes, Disney and cartoon characters are especially sought after by collectors today.

Children's lunch box with decal of trains and airplanes, ca. 1930s, 4″ x 7¾″ x 5½″, $35.00.

Adam 12, 1972	5.00
American Tobacco Company, 3 states, Kentucky, Virginia, Louisiana	45.00
Batman, 1966	8.00
Cameron & Cameron, red, humidor top	125.00
Custom House, cigar tin ..	85.00
Dixie Kid, 4x7½x4″	225.00
Edwin B Simpson, yellow .	19.00
Family Affair, 1969	8.00
Green Turtle Cigars	150.00

Joe Palooka	40.00
Mother Goose characters, tin litho, candy box	125.00
Peter Rabbit	77.00
Postmaster, cigar tin, orange	30.00
Summer Time, pail	40.00
The Big Show, shows circus parade	32.00
Thermos, Barbie, Midge, Skipper, black background ..	15.00
Tindeco, blue, Santa	45.00
Union Leader, EX	74.50
Welcome Back Kotter	8.00
Woody Woodpecker, 1972 .	6.00

Magazines

Magazines are collected for both their contents and their covers, often signed by well known illustrators. Their values hinge on the type and quality of the advertising they contain, their cover illustrations, age, rarity, and condition.

American, 1930, May	16.50
American, 1935, January, Rockwell illustration, M .	9.00
Boy's Life, 1936, February, Rockwell cover, NM	21.00
Boy's Life, 1937, July, Howard Chandler Christy cover	12.00
Boy's Life, 1965, February, Rockwell cover	15.00
Century, 1904, Parrish prints	25.00
Collier's, 1908, June 6, Parrish cover	35.00
Collier's, 1933, June 10, Chicago World's Fair cover	5.00
Country Life, 1919, August, Parrish tire ad	35.00
Harper's Bazaar, 1895, Parrish cover	50.00
Harper's Monthly, 1893, July, Remington illustrations .	5.00
Hearst's, 1922, Parrish ad .	35.00
Ladies' Home Journal, 1896, May	10.00

QUEEN MARIE · A. H. Z. CARR · ISAAC DON LEVINE

Saturday Evening Post, April 14, 1934, $7.50.

Ladies' Home Journal, 1925, July, Parrish, Broadmoor Hotel, G 25.00

Ladies' Home Journal, 1942, April 4.00

Life, 1937, May 3, Harlow in Hollywood, M 15.00

Life, 1939, Bette Davis cover . 15.00

Life, 1945, December 3, Spencer Tracy, Rockwell back cover 10.00

Life, 1958, February 3, Shirley Temple cover 8.00

Look, 1961, September 12, Kennedy One Year Later, VG 7.00

McCall's, 1936, August, full page color Coke ad, VG . 3.00

National Geographic, Volume 1, #4, complete, VG 900.00

National Geographic, Volume 5 (1893/94), #1 .... 150.00

National Geographic, Volume 6, #1, complete, VG 200.00

National Geographic, 1915, May, American Wild Flowers 7.00

National Geographic, 1920-1930, Volume 1, #628, 204 pages 20.00

National Geographic, 1921, January 9.00

Outer's Recreation, 1922, August 5.00

Playboy, 1969, April, Bardot Pictorials, EX 8.00

Saturday Evening Post, 1913, November 22 .... 10.00

Saturday Evening Post, 1916, August 5, Rockwell cover, EX 60.00

Saturday Evening Post, 1922, December 2, Rockwell cover, VG 55.00

Saturday Evening Post, 1924, December 27, Parrish ad . 12.00

Saturday Evening Post, 1930, September 13, Rockwell cover, G 15.00

Saturday Evening Post, 1934, December 15, Rockwell cover, NM 30.00

Saturday Evening Post, 1934, June 30, Rockwell cover, VG 35.00

People's Home Journal, January, 1928, $5.00.

Saturday Evening Post, 1935, November 16, Rockwell cover, EX 18.00

Saturday Evening Post, 1936, March 7, Rockwell cover, NM 22.00

Saturday Evening Post, 1939, December 16, Rockwell cover, NM 41.00

Saturday Evening Post, 1942, March 21, Rockwell cover . 15.00

Saturday Evening Post, 1943, May 29, Rockwell cover, NM 18.00

Saturday Evening Post, 1946, March 2, Rockwell cover, EX 12.00

Saturday Evening Post, 1950, August 19, Rockwell cover 10.00

Saturday Evening Post, 1954, March 6, Rockwell cover, EX 27.00

Saturday Evening Post, 1956, October 6, Rockwell cover . 8.00

Saturday Evening Post, 1958, November 8, Rockwell, Elect Casey 18.00

Saturday Evening Post, 1958, September 20, Rockwell cover, NM 14.00

Saturday Evening Post, 1964, March 21, Beatles cover & story 7.50

Woman's Home Companion, 1938, August 4.00

Youth's Companion, 1916, August 3, with Rockwell ad, NM 10.00

Youth's Companion, 1917, June 14, Rockwell illustration, M 10.00

Youth's Companion, 1923, November 1, Rockwell ads, NM 15.00

Youth's Companion, 1924, January 3, Parrish ad .. 42.00

Youth's Companion, 1925, March 13, with Rockwell ad, M 8.00

Majolica

The type of majolica earthenware most often encountered was made during the 1800s, reaching the height of its popularity in the Victorian period. It was made abroad and in this country as well. It is usually vividly colored and nature themes are the most common decorative devices. Animal and bird handles and finials, and dimensional figures in high relief were used extensively.

Basket, bird in low relief, ribbon tied handle, 10″ long . 175.00

Biscuit jar, cobalt & floral, French, later period 85.00

Bowl, floral, scalloped, turquoise, 4x9″ diameter ... 173.00

Bowl, vegetable; bird & fan, footed, Wardle & Co, England, 10″ long 110.00

Bread tray, floral & butterfly decor 175.00

Bread tray, Waste Not-Want Not, butterfly, 13½″ ... 140.00

Butter dish, sunflower with fly, green, 6¾″ diameter . 122.50

Butter pat, shell & seaweed, copy of Wedgwood version 20.00

Cigarette urn, match holder and striker, figural frog, 6″ x 7″, $125.00.

Cake plate, brown basket-
weave, open handles   35.00
Cake plate, shell & seaweed,
Etruscan, 12" 250.00
Cake stand, pink with green
leaves, tree base, Etruscan,
9½" 65.00
Cake stand, shell & seaweed,
2¼x8½" diameter 110.00
Chocolate pot, creamer &
sugar, 4 mugs, brown &
yellow with orchids 85.00
Compote, grape leaf, copy of
Wedgwood   pattern,
4½x8½" diameter 122.00
Compote, pineapple, yellow,
green base, blue inside,
4¾x9" diameter........   130.00
Creamer, bow & leaf, English
registry mark, 3¼" 60.00
Creamer & sugar, blue floral,
brown branch-like handles,
3" & 4", pair..........   65.00
Cup & saucer, shell & seaweed,
Etruscan, 6" diameter
saucer 165.00
Cuspidor, flowers on each side,
square, blue & yellow, 5½"   145.00
Jardiniere, pond lily, 8" ...   180.00
Match holder, man & woman
figurals, 6½", pair 95.00
Mug, picket fence & floral,
3¾" 55.00
Pitcher, floral, square topped,
blue & white, brown han-
dle, 6" 55.00
Pitcher, pelican figural,
pelican head handle, 9" .   225.00
Plaque, chalet, scenic in relief,
pierced, Zell, 9¼" 55.00
Plate, wild rose, blue trim,
8¾" diameter 50.00
Platter, begonia on bark, 2
handles, 12¼" 110.00
Platter, blackberry, Clifton
Decor mark, 13" 127.00
Sardine box, swan preening
feathers finial, dolphin feet,
5¾" long 250.00

Sardine   box,   yellow
basketweave, fish figural
on lid, 5½" long 145.00
Sugar, bird & fan, cobalt
ground, 4½" 105.00
Sweetmeat, figural deer's
head, 4½" 240.00
Syrup, bow & floral, 8¼" tall   135.00
Syrup, high dome top, Morley   175.00
Teapot, cobalt with blue birds,
rectangular 200.00
Teapot, drum shape, white,
white red-tipped flowers,
green handle, 9" 175.00
Toothbrush holder, New
England aster, footed ...   72.00
Tureen, fish figural, 8x18"
long 75.00
Urn, griffin handles, 4 panels,
lizards & vines, impressed
O with X 350.00
Vase, 3 lion feet, cobalt
ground, 9" 125.00

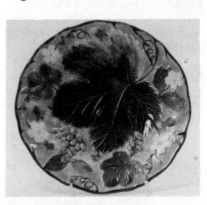

**Plate, grapes, leaves and blossoms,
Wedgwood, 8¾", $65.00.**

Marbles

Because there are so many
varieties of marbles that interest today's collectors, we suggest you study
a book on that specific subject, such
as the one recently published by Collector Books. The larger marbles, 1½"
to 2¼", are the most expensive,

especially the Lutz type with gold flaking, the Onionskins, Micas, and some of the rarer Sulfides (clear glass marbles with figures inside). Condition is extreemly important. Chips commonly occurred and though some may be ground down and polished, the values of both badly chipped and repolished marbles are low.

Advertising, Poll Parrot Shoes, 5 marbles in box .	19.00
Agate	13.00
Bennington, ½"	4.50
Clambroth, black & white, ⅝"	60.00
Comic strip, Annie	35.00
Comic strip, Kayo	41.00
Comic strip, Moon Mullins .	86.00
Comic strip, Skeezix	40.00
Coreless, pink cast, 1¼" ...	66.00
End of Day, average size, M .	13.00
End of Day, red, white, & blue, 1⅞"	60.00
Indian Swirl, average size, M .	35.00
Latticinio Core Swirl, average size	25.00
Lobed Core, polished, 1½" .	80.00
Lutz type, 1⅞", M	500.00
Mica, clear, ⅝"	8.50
Mica, one pontil, green, rare, large chip, 2⅛"	260.00
Open Core, 4 color center, 4 multicolor bands, 1½" ..	75.00

Ribbon Core Swirl, 1⅜", $75.00.

Peppermint Swirl, ½"	21.00
Slag, green, single pontil mark, ⅞", M	10.00
Slag, purple, single pontil mark, 1¼"	20.00
Solid Core Swirl, average size	23.00
Solid Core Swirl, 2"	95.00
Sulfide, #2, 1⅝"	175.00
Sulfide, camel, 1½"	90.00
Sulfide, dog, begging, 1½" .	80.00
Sulfide, goat, 1½", EX	51.00
Sulfide, lion, 1½", NM	650.00
Sulfide, pig, standing, 2¼" .	160.00
Sulfide, rabbit, 1½"	60.00
Sulfide, razorback pig, 1¼" .	60.00
Sulfide, rooster, silver figure, 1¾"	110.00
Tiger Eye, brown, average size	25.00
Vaseline, ¾"	15.00

Match Holders

Because early matches were easily combustible, they were stored in match holders, usually wall-hanging or table-top models. Though the safety match was invented in 1855, the habit was firmly entrenched, and match holders remained popular well into the 20th century.

Alligator, black, white, & red painted cast iron, back opens, 12x4"	70.00
Angel, kneeling with match holder on back, hand decorated, china	44.00
Boy, kneeling by basket, lamb stands beside him, porcelain	75.00
Boy, sitting on stone wall, basket on ground, bisque, 3½x3"	43.00
Cone, ceramic & silver, striker, embossed hunt & tavern scene, 3¾"	49.00
Daisy & Button, sapphire blue, striker across front, 4x3"	65.00

Clown bust, painted plaster of Paris, 1800s, 3¾", $35.00.

Eagle, wings spread, gilt & black painted cast iron, wall hanging, 5" 55.00

Flemish Art, Dutch girls with buckets, double pocket . 16.00

Girl, bow in hair, striker in back, bisque 36.00

Good Luck, mother owl with young, horseshoe, easel, metal die-cut 46.00

Hanging game, leaves on top, 2 pouches below, brass, 7½" 55.00

Leaf shape, acorn pocket in relief, brass 36.00

Lucas Paint, advertising, VG 55.00

Porcelain box, applied flowers, striker under lid, 3x2" .. 75.00

Skull, composition, with striker, early 1900s 65.00

Toleware, crimped crest, worn brown japanning, 4½x7½" 55.00

Treenware, footed, 4" 16.50

Wilson Brothers Grinding Mills, advertising, ornate embossed cast iron..... 49.00

Worn-out shoe, painted well carved wood, 6x2½x2½" . 31.00

Match Safes

Before cigarette lighters were invented, matches were carried in pocket-size match safes, as simple or elaborate as the owner's financial status and flair for fashion dictated.

Art Nouveau, woman's head, sterling 65.00

Brass, with old matches, patent 1884 .... 40.00

Diamond Match Company, advertising, tin, small .. 15.00

Dog, stands on hind legs, silver, red stone eyes, 3" . 210.00

Golfer, sterling repousse silver, dated 1900 ...... 275.00

Horse in horseshoe, Art Nouveau, silver plated, 2" . 32.00

Nude, dancing, draped flowers & scrolls, Gorham sterling 95.00

O'Conner & Wittner, Syracuse, New York, embossed stag, patent 1904 ...... 50.00

Pig, figural, hinged top, striker base, silver plated, 1½x1x2¾" 75.00

Rooster head, mechanical .. 185.00

Sterling silver with Art Nouveau female head in relief, $65.00.

McCoy

A popular collectible with flea market goers, McCoy pottery has been made in Roseville, Ohio, since 1910. They are most famous for their extensive line of figural cookie jars, more than two hundred in all. They also made amusing figural planters, etc., as well as dinnerware, and vases and pots for the florist trade. Though some pieces are unmarked, most bear one of several McCoy trademarks.

Bank, hobo, #609	20.00
Basket, oak leaf & acorn	15.00
Bean pot, brown stoneware, with lid, 2 quart, #2	22.00
Bud vase, lily	10.00
Caddy, dog with shoe spoon tail	18.00
Chuck wagon with wheels, El Rancho Bar-B-Que	65.00
Cookie jar, Animal Crackers	32.00
Cookie jar, Bananas	32.00
Cookie jar, Barnum's Animals	35.00
Cookie jar, Caboose	50.00

Windmill cookie jar, $40.00.

Cookie jar, Clown in Barrel	30.00
Cookie jar, Coffee Grinder	17.50
Cookie jar, Cookie Boy, aqua	75.00
Cookie jar, Cookstove	20.00
Cookie jar, cylinder, with red flowers	12.50
Cookie jar, Drum	32.00
Cookie jar, Dutch Girl, boy on reverse	50.00
Cookie jar, Early American Chest, Chiffonier	50.00
Cookie jar, Engine	50.00
Cookie jar, Globe	35.00
Cookie jar, Hamm's Bear	40.00
Cookie jar, Hillbilly Bear	150.00
Cookie jar, Indian	125.00
Cookie jar, Kittens on Ball of Yarn	34.00
Cookie jar, Liberty Bell	20.00
Cookie jar, Mac Dog	30.00
Cookie jar, Mother Goose	75.00
Cookie jar, Pelican	60.00
Cookie jar, Pirate's Chest	22.00
Cookie jar, Quaker Oats	30.00
Cookie jar, Spaceship, Friendship	38.00
Cookie jar, Tepee	95.00
Cookie jar, Turkey	75.00
Cookie jar, Upside Down Bear, panda	12.00
Cookie jar, WC Fields	65.00
Cookie jar, Wishing Well	18.00
Cookie jar, Yosemite Sam	16.00
Creamer, dog figural, blue glaze, 1950s	15.00
Decanter, Apollo Series, astronaut	35.00
Fern box, Butterfly line	6.00
Grease jar, cabbage figural	20.00
Iced tea server, El Rancho Barb-B-Que	45.00
Lamp, black panther	22.00
Mixing bowl, yellowware with 3 wavy lines, wide lip, small	5.00
Oil jar, classic shape, shoulder handles, maroon glaze, 16"	50.00
Pitcher, elephant figural, foot on drum, trunk handle, white	30.00

Ivy tea set, $45.00.

Pitcher, tankard; Buccaneer, green stoneware	30.00		Pretzel jar, green stoneware, 'Pretzels'	35.00
Planter, carriage, removable umbrella	50.00		Shoes, twin	7.00
Planter, dog with cart	9.00		Teapot, Sunburst Gold	25.00
Planter, gondola	12.00		Vase, aqua green semi-matt, lizard handle, 10″	25.00
Planter, old mill	12.00		Vase, urn; Onyx, berries & leaves in relief, blue, 6″	18.00
Planter, rabbit & stump	9.00		Wall pocket, banana	12.00
Planter, rolling pin with Blue Boy	20.00		Wall pocket, grapes on leaves	17.50
Planter, Springwood, footed	12.00		Wall pocket, lily	12.00
Planter, zebra mother & young	14.00		Wall pocket, owls on trivet	18.00
			Wall pocket, pear	12.00

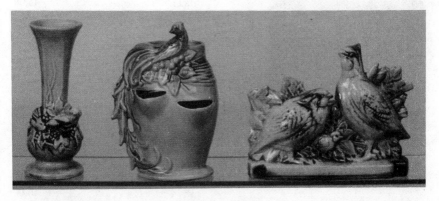

Left to right: bud vase, 1950s, $8.00; strawberry jar with bird, 1950s, $15.00; quail planter, 1955, $18.00.

Medical Collectibles

What used to be of interest to those in the medical profession only, is today regarded as a significant part of the early American way of life, and as such is being collected by many. Especially fascinating are the 'quack' devices that used violet ray and electricity to 'cure' a variety of aches and pains.

Alcohol burner, folding tin, 3x2" 25.00
Applicator, knife shape, 'Apply Antiphogistine...', aluminum 4.50
Book, Practical Obstetrics, TW Eden, 1915, 700 pages 5.00
Booklet, Swaim's Panacea, 1873, 42 pages, 4x6" . . . 8.50
Bottle, Shaker label, open pontil 70.00
Box, mahogany, hinged top, 2 doors, fitted within, brass handles, 11" 600.00
Catalog, Porcelain Teeth, SS White Company, 1905, 195 pages 50.00
Enema kit, mahogany box . 177.00
Fleam, 3 blades in brass folding case, no mark . . . 25.00

Machine, Master Violet Ray, in original case, $38.00.

Hypodermic, Codman & Shurteff, in case, 1¾x3½" 105.00
Irrigation syringe, bone, circa 1790, 5½" 352.00
Lancet bleeder, brass & steel, original box, 8" 85.00
Machine, Davis & Kidder's Magneto Electric for Nerves, patented 1854 . . 100.00
Medicine spoon, Gibson Castor Oil, pewter, circa 1837 . . . . 425.00
Microscope, binocular, single scope, Enst Leitz, Wetzlar, 12" 180.00
Print, engraving, open cadaver, organs showing, German, 1825 . . . . 20.00
Tongue depressor, hinged . . 40.00
Tooth extractor, 4½" 30.00
Trocar, Weiss, sterling 86.50

Milk Glass

Milk glass has been used since the 1700s to make tableware, lamps, and novelty items such as covered figural dishes and decorative wall plaques. Early examples were made with cryolite and ring with a clear bell tone when tapped.

Banana stand, openwork base & rim, triple split stem, 8x11" 45.00
Battleship, no name, rare size, 6" 75.00
Bowl, Basketweave with Lattice, reticulated, 6½x9½" . 23.00
Butter dish, Blackberry . . . 75.00
Butter dish, Oak Leaf, acorn finial 75.00
Candlestick, crucifix, 7" . . . 15.00
Compote, Jenny Lind, 7½x8½" diameter 150.00
Creamer, Basketweave, embossed Patented June 30, 1874 . . . . 45.00
Creamer, Owl, glass eyes, detailed feathers, 3½" . . 25.00

Dish, covered; robed Santa on sleigh	90.00
Dresser bottle, 10x6″	25.00
Egg cup, Blackberry	50.00
Goblet, Blackberry, HB & Company, set of 6	540.00
Humidor, monk on front, pipe on back, brown, metal lid, Austria	45.00
Master salt, Birch Leaf	23.00
Napkin ring	35.00
Pickle dish, Fish, 1872, 4x11″	30.00
Plate, Arch Border, blue, 8″	35.00

Plate, three cats in relief, hand painted floral, 8″, $22.50.

Sauce, Basketweave, flat, 4″	9.00
Shaving mug, bearded man's head in relief, dated 1867	38.00
Spooner, Birch Leaf, flint	35.00
Spooner, Swan	20.00
Sugar, Blackberry, corner & lid beading, berry finial	60.00
Syrup, Fishnet & Poppies	125.00
Tray, Blackberry	12.00
Tray, Child & Shell	127.00
Tumbler, Netted Oak	41.00
Vase, hand painted roses with gold trim, cylinder shape, signed, 9″	85.00
Vase, Moose Head, brown tone	22.00
Wall pocket, heart shape	25.00

Molds

The two most popular types of molds with collectors are chocolate molds and ice cream molds. Chocolate molds are usually quite detailed, and are usually made of tin or copper. While some are flat backed, others make three dimensional molds. Baskets, Santas, rabbits and those with holiday themes are abundant. Ice cream molds are usually made of pewter and come in a wide variety of shapes and styles.

Blackpool tower, tin, 4 part, marked FW Kutscher Schwarzenberg	26.00
Chicks, 3 wearing bonnets, hinged, overall 9x5″	42.00
Cross, 3 with flowers, hinged, overall 4½x8″	29.00
Easter mixture, flat, egg, hen on nest, chicken & rabbit, 13x28″	66.00

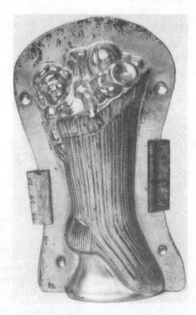

Stocking, two-piece, marked 59+ 4271, Larosh Schw. Gmund., $125.00.

Easter mixture, tin, 2 piece, heavy frame, attached clips 38.00

Halloween mixture, flat, jack-o'-lantern, owls & witches, 13x28" 66.00

Hen on nest, 2 part with base, marked Germany, 5¾" .. 50.00

Lambs, 2 jumping over fence, hinged, overall 5x9½" .. 40.00

Pelicans, 2, hinged, overall 6½x10" 40.00

Puppy, tin, 2 part, 3x5" ... 16.00

Rabbits, Disney's Thumper, 2 in mold, tin, hinged, overall 7x12" 40.00

Rabbits, embossed on each of 6 eggs, made in Germany, 6½" 20.00

Rabbits, pair on nest holding hands, tin ½ mold, 5x7" . 24.00

Roosters, 2 with hats, hinged, overall 6x8½" 40.00

Santa, standing, flat sheet, 7 rows with 15 each, overall 13x28" 66.00

Santa head, flat sheet, 4 rows with 4 each, stick indent, 13x28" 70.00

Valentine mixture, flat, hearts, arrows & cupids, 105 figures 66.00

Ice Cream

Ace of Clubs, E908 .... 32.50
Ace of Spades, #444 ...... 32.00
Airplane, E1132 .... 40.00

American Flag, E1075 .... 38.00
American Legion Emblem, E1119 .... 33.50
Apple, E240 .... 30.00
Baby Cradle, #344, 3 piece . 31.00
Ball, E936 .... 21.00
Banana, #157 .... 32.00
Battleship, #513 .... 43.50
Bell, #404 .... 31.00
Bunch of Grapes, E278 ... 28.00
Cat, E644 .... 30.00

Chick-in-Egg, E600 .... 35.00
Cooing Doves, E665 ...... 30.00
Cupid, #492 .... 38.50
Daisy, #363 .... 29.50
Easter Lily, E354, 3 piece . 32.50
Egg, E907 .... 24.50
Engraved Wedding Ring, E1142 .... 30.00
George Washington Bust, E1084 .... 50.00
Goose Egg, #298 .... 29.50
Harp, #361 .... 36.50
Horseshoe, 'Good Luck', #183 30.00

Liberty Bell, July 4, 1776, #473 .... 40.00
Masonic Emblem, Shrine, E1081 .... 31.00
Melon, E204 .... 26.50
Mutton Chop, E961 ...... 30.50
Peach Half with Stone, E206 . 29.00
Pear, #151 .... 26.00
Petunia, #238 .... 31.00
Pumpkin, #309E 27.00
Santa, E991 .... 39.00
Slipper, #570, 3 piece 27.50
Wedding Ring, #608 ...... 30.00

Engine and coal car #477 and #478, $75.00 each.

Movie Memorabilia

Anything connected with the silver screen and movie stars in general is collected by movie buffs today. Posters, lobby cards, movie magazines, promotional photos, souvenir booklets, and stills are their treasures. Especially valuable are items from the twenties and thirties that have to do with such popular stars as Jean Harlow, Bella Lugosi, Carol Lombard, and Gary Cooper. Elvis Presley and Marilyn Monroe have devoted fans who often limit their collections to them exclusively.

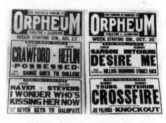

Posters, lot of six (only two shown), featuring old favorites, each 17″ x 24″, $75.00.

Campaign sheet, Blood & Sand, Tyrone Power, 1941, 2 sided 10.00

Cel, Sleeping Beauty, Walt Disney, 1959, full color, 5½x6¼″ 79.00

Lobby card, Desire, Marlene Dietrich with Cooper, 1936, center photo 275.00

Lobby card, Hazard, Paulette Goddard, #5, 1948 ..... 10.00

Lobby card, High Noon, Gary Cooper, #3, 1952 .... 25.00

Lobby card, Never Let Me Go, Clark Gable, #2, 1953 ... 10.00

Lobby card, Operation Petticoat, Cary Grant, #5, 1959 .... 5.00

Lobby card, Ruthless, Sydney Greenstreet, #5, 1948 ... 10.00

Lobby card, Suddenly, Last Summer, Montgomery Clift, #7, 1960 .... 10.00

Lobby card, Sunnyside, Charles Chaplain, 1919, center photo 400.00

Lobby card, The Harvey Girls, Judy Garland, #7, 1945 . 25.00

Lobby card, The White Cliffs of Dover, Irene Dunne, 1944 .... 10.00

Magazine, Modern Screen, Bette Davis, October, 1940 20.00

Magazine, Modern Screen, Judy Garland, June, 1941 . 15.00

Magazine, Modern Screen, Olivia DeHaviland, September, 1937 .... 15.00

Magazine, Movie Mirror, Errol Flynn, January, 1940 . 15.00

Magazine, Movie Mirror, Jean Harlow, July, 1937 ..... 20.00

Magazine, Movie Pix, Carole Lombard & Fred McMurray, February, 1938 .... 12.00

Magazine, Movie Pix, Katherine Hepburn, March, 1938 .... 20.00

Magazine, New Movie, Katherine Hepburn, September, 1935 .... 12.00

Magazine, Screen Guide, Rita Hayworth, June, 1940 .. 12.00

Magazine, Screen Guide, Rock Hudson, July, 1938 .... 15.00

Poster, Abbott & Costello Meet Dr Jekyll & Mr Hyde, 1953, 22x28″ 60.00

Poster, Alias a Gentleman, Wallace Beery, 1948, 14x36″ 25.00

Poster, And the Angels Sing, Dorothy Lamour, 1944, 14x36″ 40.00

Poster, Black Magic, Orson Welles, 1949, 27x41″ ... 40.00

Poster, Daddy, Jackie Coogan, top trimmed, 1923, 14x22″ 75.00

Myrna Loy publicity photo, $7.50.

Poster, Dangerous When Wet,
Esther Williams, 1953,
14x22″ 25.00
Poster, Ganster's Boy, Jackie
Cooper, 1938, 22x28″ . . .   50.00
Poster, I Was a Male War
Bride, Cary Grant, 1949,
14x22″ 35.00
Poster, Las Vegas Nights,
Tommy Dorsey, 1941,
center photo 65.00
Poster, Miss Sadie Thompson,
Rita Hayworth, 1954,
41x81″ 50.00
Poster, Over My Dead Body,
Milton Berle, 1942, 14x36″   40.00
Poster, Passport to Alcatraz,
Jack Holt, 1940, 41x81″ .   85.00
Poster, Safari, Douglas Fair-
banks, Jr, 1940, center
photo, 27x41″ 75.00
Poster, The Fan, Jeanne
Crain, 1949, 27x41″ 25.00
Poster, Voodoo Island, Boris
Karloff, 1957, 27x41″ . . .   60.00
Pressbook, Beachhead, Tony
Curtis, 1954, 12 pages . .   10.00

Pressbook, College Swings,
Burns & Allen, 1938, 34
pages 65.00
Pressbook, One, Two, Three,
James Cagney, 1961, 12
pages 15.00
Pressbook, The Big Broadcast
of 1938, WC Fields, 1938,
34 pages 150.00
Pressbook, The Boy from
Oklahoma, Lon Chaney, Jr,
1954, 12 pages 10.00
Pressbook, This Way Please,
Fibber McGee & Molly,
1941, 6 pages 150.00
Sheet music, A Night at the
Opera, Alone, Marx
Brothers, 1935 . . . .   45.00
Sheet music, High Society,
True Love, Bing Crosby,
1956 . . . .   15.00
Sheet music, Love Affair,
Wishing, Irene Dunne,
1939 . . . .   10.00
Sheet music, Untamed, That
Wonderful Something,
Joan Crawford, 1929 . . .   35.00
Still, On Our Merry Way,
Paulette Goddard, 1948,
black & white 3.50
Still, The Immortal Sergeant,
Henry Fonda, 1943, black
& white 4.00
Title card, To the Ends of the
Earth, Dick Powell, 1947 .   25.00

Music Boxes

Early music boxes were made in
models that play either a disc or a
cylinder. Some were housed in ornate
inlaid cases, sometimes with extra
features such as bells or mechanical
birds. The largest manufacturers of
music boxes were Regina, Polyphon,
and Symphonion; these are treasured
by today's collectors. Condition is
always an important factor; well
restored examples bring the best
prices.

Bremond Bells in View, 15″ cylinder, 10 airs, 9 bells, 26″ 2,090.00

Capital Cuff, Style A 3,000.00

Helvetia, 12″ disc, stripped of veneer 1,000.00

Keywind, 13″ cylinder, brass bedplate, side door, 3 levers 1,600.00

Mermod Freres, four 13″ 8 tune cylinders, inlaid case . 2,600.00

Mermod Freres Ideal Sublime Harmonie, 4 cylinders .. 2,200.00

Mojon Manger Soprano Bells in View, 13″ cylinder, 12 air 990.00

Nicole Freres Piano Forte, cylinder, restored, M ... 2,900.00

Pillard Vaucher Fils, 13″ cylinder, 10 airs, zither, 22″ 600.00

Polyphon #42D, 11″ double comb, inlaid lid, restored, M 1,800.00

Polyphon Excelsior, 15½″ disc, single comb 2,000.00

Ragina Hexaphone, #104, mahogany case, all original 5,050.00

Regina, #11, 15½″ disc, carved mahogany case & stand, 42″ 2,200.00

Regina, #19, carved walnut, double comb, with records, NM 2,850.00

Regina, #26, mahogany with cupola, 20¾″, zither, M . 4,900.00

Regina, 27″ fold top, rare .. 4,500.00

Swiss, bell & drum, 10 tunes, inlaid case, brass handles . 3,600.00

Swiss, rosewood with inlay, 15″ cylinder, 12 airs, lever wind 800.00

Swiss, rosewood with inlay, 4½″ cylinder with 6 airs, 13″ 450.00

Swiss, rosewood with marquetry, 10 air 11″ cylinder 400.00

Symphonion, upright, glass door, coin operated, 13½″ disc 2,650.00

Symphonion, upright table, coin-operated, 19⅛″ disc, 40x22″ 4,000.00

Symphonion, walnut case, 12″ discs 300.00

Regina music box, mahogany case, copyright 1896, with ten 15″ discs, case: 12″ x 21″ x 18″, $2,500.00.

Napkin Rings

Figural silver plated napkin rings were popular in the late 1800s, and today's collectors enjoy the hundreds of different designs. Among the companies best known for their manufacture are Meriden, Wm. Rogers, Reed and Barton, and Pairpoint (who made some of the finest). Kate Greenaway figurals, those with Kewpies or Brownies, and styles with wheels that turn are especially treasured.

Angel, pushes ring, butterfly on top 160.00

Angel, writes on heart 95.00

Bambi, embossed, marked WDP 800 .... 42.00

Boy with mouse, silver plated, 4″, $235.00.

Barrel, branch & leaf feet	45.00
Barrel, footed, engraved 'Comin' Thru the Rye'	40.00
Bear, pushing ring with large bee, palm leaf base	135.00
Beaver & branch on ring, leaf base, Toronto SP Company	90.00
Bird, by bud vase	150.00
Bird, perched on top of triangular ring	39.00
Birds, facing, on top of oval ring, engraved, marked Gorham, 1865	196.00
Boy, pulling boot	120.00
Boy, pulling cart, wheels revolve	191.00
Boy, stands with ring on shoulder, Rogers Brothers	165.00
Boy, with cookie on footed oval base, signed, 3″ figure	105.00
Boy, with drumstick, marked Pairpoint	191.00
Branch, flowers & leaves at top, holds ring, Meriden	65.00
Bug, by ring, Shiebler	75.00

Bulldog, right paw up, by hammered ring	51.00
Bulldog, running, ring on back, large	86.50
Bulldog, sits chained to doghouse, Simpson, Hall & Miller	275.00
Cat, on back legs, one paw on ring, Knickerbocker	135.00
Cherries & leaves hang from ring, leaf base, ball feet, gold	165.00
Cherub, fancy filigree ring	100.00
Cherub, plays mandolin, 6¾″	75.00
Cherub, with cymbals upon triangular ring	86.00
Cherubs, each side of ring, Victor Silver Company	60.00
Chick, on wishbone, 'Best Wishes', Derby	72.00
Child, astride decorated ring, pedestal base, Rogers	70.50
Corset shape, satin, brite-cut	36.50
Cow, next to ring, round base	185.00
Cupid, leans on ring with fancy branch & flower	115.00
Cupid, on top of ring, dog with front paws on ring	125.00
Cupid, stands by ring	125.00
Dog, chases bird on ring	80.00
Eagles, carrying ring, Rogers Brothers, 2″	65.00
Eagles, two on rectangular base, Meriden	46.00
Fawn, with garland, decorated ring, square footed platform	146.00
Giraffe, beside ring, fancy leaf base	223.00
Girl, in pigtails, pushes ring, William Rogers	127.00
Goat, pulls cart of flowers, Meriden	147.00
Good Luck horseshoe on large leaf base, finger-grip handle	75.00
Hen, beside ring, Meriden, #268	98.00
Horse, prancing on back legs, pulling elaborate sulky	166.50

Kangaroo, next to ring, EX . 75.00
Kate Greenaway, boy holds
ring with right hand ... 185.00
Kate Greenaway, girl pulls
ring with wheels 176.50
Kate Greenaway, girls in coats
with hats & muffs, backs to
ring 245.00
Kittens, each side of ring,
Reed & Barton 51.50
Koala bear figural, Australia,
2x3" diameter 65.00
Kookaburra bird figural, 2½" 75.00
Lady, with tennis racket .. 126.50
Leaf, with frog & fly 87.00
Lily bud, with ring on leaf
base, Meriden 60.00
Lion, pulls ring on cart, wheels
turn 227.50
Lion, rampant, on base mark-
ed Rogers, 3¼" 125.00
Miner of the West 46.50
Monkey, dressed, missing
cane 135.00
Ostrich, with kangaroo and
boomerang, resilvered,
marked 85.50
Parakeet, on stem, large leaf
base, Meriden 86.50
Peacock, on perch, each side of
ring, fancy base, no mark . 115.00
Peasant girl, hands on hips,
bare feet, rectangular base,
signed 151.00
Rabbit, stands by ring 75.00
Seal, next to ring 95.00
Shaker, open salt & napkin
ring on footed stand with
handle 137.00
Soldiers, with bugles each side
of ring 95.00
Squirrel, decorated rectangular base, Southington .. 87.50
Squirrel, on back legs with
large tail, beside ring,
Wilcox 115.00
Turtle, with fancy floral ring
on back 66.50

Nazi Collectibles

An area of militaria attracting a growing following today, Nazi collectibles are anything related to the Nazi rise and German participation in World War II. There are many facets to this field; among the items hunted most enthusiastically are daggers, medals, badges, patches, uniforms, and toys with a Nazi German theme.

Arm Band, Hitler Youth .. 15.00
Arm Band, NSDAP, swastika
on red band 15.00
Arm Band, Volkstrum 10.00
Badge, General Assault ... 20.00
Badge, Luftwaffe Airgunner . 150.00
Badge, Luftwaffe Ground
Assault 40.00
Badge, Navy Auxiliary Cruiser 150.00
Badge, Navy Destroyer ... 75.00
Badge, Navy E-Boat, 1st pat-
tern 250.00
Badge, Navy U-Boat 125.00
Badge, Panzer Assault 30.00
Badge, Wound, gold 30.00
Bayonet, Infantry & Artillery,
single etched 105.00
Bayonet, Luftwaffe, etched 175.00
Dagger, Hitler youth knife,
motto on blade, with scab-
bard 65.00
Dagger, Luftwaffe Officer's,
1st model, chain hanger . 250.00
Dagger, Red Cross Officer's . 350.00
Dagger, SA, brown wooden
handle, brown scabbard . 130.00
Dagger, SS, black wooden
handle, black scabbard .. 300.00
Helmet, Army 70.00
Helmet, Luftschutz 40.00
Helmet, Navy 150.00
Helmet, Police 60.00
Helmet, Waffen SS 50.00
Medal, Army Long Service, 4
year, with ribbon 25.00
Medal, Iron Cross 2nd Class,
with ribbon 25.00

Medal, Russian Front, with ribbon 15.00

Medal, War Merit Cross 2nd Class, with ribbon 15.00

Sword, Army Officer's, lion-head pommel, etched blade, with scabbard 350.00

Sword, Army Officer's, lion-head pommel, plain blade, with scabbard 150.00

Sword, Navy Officer's, with scabbard 350.00

Visor cap, Army Officer's, silver chin cords, complete 165.00

Visor cap, Luftwaffe Officer's, silver chin cords, complete 175.00

Visor cap, Naval Officer's, black leather chin cords, complete 250.00

Visor cap, Waffen SS Enlisted, black leather chin cords, complete 300.00

Luftwaffe Cape Eagle, $125.00; Luftwaffe cloth German Cross, $50.00; display ribbon bar, $25.00.

Netsukes

The netsuke is a button or a toggle that is worn on the waist cord with a kimono. They are carved by hand from a variety of materials, but ivory is the one most often encountered. Figural forms are common and are preferred by collectors. Workmanship is important, and pieces signed by noted artists command the best prices.

Actor, next to drum hiding child, polychrome, signed . 76.50

Badger, with young on back, signed, 1¾″ 100.00

Basket, upside down, 2 mice on top 41.50

Boy, holds pup 152.00

Cicada, rests on persimmon, tea stained, signed 69.00

Devil head, pop eyes, 2½″ . 143.50

Dog, surmounted by rat ... 51.00

Dragon 95.00

Elephant, trumpeting, mouse on back, 1¼″ 103.00

Father & child, seated, playing, polychrome, signed . 77.50

Father Time, with pitchfork & incense burner, polychrome, 2″ 51.00

Frog, on leaf, turtle climbing on his back, signed 83.50

Horse, recumbent, 2″ 42.00

Hotei, traveling, polychrome, signed 100.00

Karakos, prepares fish at table, polychrome, signed . 75.00

Man, holds lantern, 2″ 41.50

Man, holds up hatchet, revolving face, signed, 2″ 62.50

Man, mounting horse, 2″ .. 40.00

Man, sitting, beating drums with drumsticks 40.50

Mice, playing in rice bale, 1800s, EX 200.00

Monkey, mother with baby on back, 1¼″ 100.00

Monkey, sitting on ball ... 97.00

Ivory carving of mother hen with chicks and eggs, signed, $55.00.

Mythical dog, 2½" 140.00
Mythical lion & dog, 2½" .. 147.00
Octopus, with 3 turtles & rat,
   2½" 300.00
Pig, signed, 1¼" 113.00
Puppeteer, standing, signed . 52.00
Rabbits, two, one coming out
   of basket, 2½" 125.00
Shoki the Demon Queller,
   Baishodo Yasufusa, 1900s,
   1¾" 1,100.00
Sumo wrestler, polychrome,
   2½" 115.00
Turtle, good carving, poly-
   chrome, signed, 1¾" 100.00
Water buffalo, recumbent,
   1800s, 2¼" long 450.00
Wild boar, 2" 52.50
Woman, feeding Kiwi, stands
   on wicker basket, 2" ... 41.50

Niloak

Produced in Arkansas by Charles Dean Hyten from the early 1900s until the mid-1940s, Niloak (the backward spelling of kaolin, a type of clay) takes many forms -- figural planters, vases in both matt and glossy glazes, and novelty items of many types. The company's most famous product and their most collectible is their swirl or Mission Ware line. Clay in colors of brown, blue, cream, red, and buff are swirled within the mold, and the finished product left unglazed on the outside to preserve the natural hues. Small vases are common; large pieces or unusual shapes, and those with exceptional coloration are the most valuable.

Ash tray, Mission Ware ... 29.50
Bowl, Mission Ware, 2½x5" . 22.00
Clown, with drum 25.50
Ewer, blue glaze, 6¾" 20.00
Ewer, high gloss brown, relief
   mark, 6½" 19.50
Jar, with lid, Mission Ware,
   browns, original label, 4" . 40.00

Mug, Mission Ware, 4½" .. 95.00
Pitcher, light blue, stylized
   flowers in relief, square
   body, 7" 21.00
Planter, parrot, 6" 20.50
Planter, squirrel 26.50
Planter, swan, blue, 4½" .. 13.00
Vase, Mission Ware, blue, red,
   white, brown; blue speckled
   inside, 4" 42.50
Vase, Mission Ware, blue &
   cream, large mouth with
   lip, 6" 42.00
Vase, Mission Ware, cream,
   blue, light & dark brown,
   ogee sides, 10" 86.00
Vase, Mission Ware, top folds
   in, paper label, 7" 50.00
Vase, scalloped with melon rib
   base, spiral neck, wing handle, 6½" 13.50
Wall pocket, Mission Ware . 65.50

Nippon

In complying with American importation regulations, from 1891 to 1921 Japanese manufacturers marked their wares 'Nippon', meaning Japan, to indicate country of origin. The term is today used to refer to the highly decorated porcelain vases, bowls, chocolate pots, etc., that bare this term within their trademark. Many variations were used. In the following listings marks are indicated by numbers: #1, China E-OH; #2, M in wreath; #3, Rising Sun; and #4, Maple Leaf.

Ash tray, figural boy sits on
   edge 400.00
Ash tray, kingfisher sits on
   rim, mark #2, 6½" wide . 850.00
Berry set, windmill scene in
   lavenders, gold decor, 7
   piece 85.00
Boat dish, flowers with moriage decor, mark #3 ..... 40.00

Bowl, bird of paradise, pastels & black, with handles, 9" . 65.00

Bowl, flowers, gold beading, 3 handles, 8" 30.00

Bowl, moriage, nuts & leaves in relief, 7" 81.00

Bowl, peanut, walnut, acorn, leaves on scenic background, 10" 80.00

Bowl, scenes in brown & lavender, mark #1, 9½" diameter 45.00

Bowl, scenes with walnut relief, jeweled handles, diamond shape, 10" 75.00

Cake plate, cobalt & gold border, open handles, scenes of sailboats 235.00

Cake plate, plain, beaded handles & trim, bisque . . 30.00

Cake plate, small roses, heavy gold relief, 10" 58.00

Candlestick, Arab on camel, 8" 135.00

Candy dish, clover shape, elk in lake 35.00

Celery dish, multicolor wild roses, mark #2, 12" 40.00

Chocolate pot, Deco design, gold trim, 10" 142.00

Chocolate pot, jeweled, 8½" . 150.00

Compote, scenic, pedestal base, gold handles, mark #2, 9½" diameter 75.00

Compote, traced pink roses in red reserves, with handles . 90.00

Cracker jar, cobalt & roses, heavy gold decor 275.00

Creamer, Wedgwood type, pedestal base, cut-out decor on handle, 3¼" 30.00

Creamer & sugar, melon ribbed, large pink roses, white beading 46.50

Cup & plate, blown-out child's face 65.00

Cup & saucer, Oriental decor . 22.00

Dresser set, floral decor, gold beaded, 6 piece 95.00

Mission Ware vase, 3½", $40.00.

Dresser set, tray, powder box, hair receiver, pink & gold florals 140.00

Egg cup, rose & lattice 20.00

Ferner, Egyptian people . . . 183.00

Hatpin holder, gold & pink florals, gold trim & beading, mark #2 . . . . 40.00

Humidor, man on camel, bisque, 7" 250.00

Humidor, 7 ducks on shore, swirling sky & water, Art Nouveau 325.00

Inkwell, Egyptian scene . . . 165.00

Jug, bisque, windmill, brown & gray, 9½" 475.00

Jug, chickens beside water, blue moriage wreath, 6½" 400.00

Lamp base, scenic, 5" 30.00

Mug, barrel shape, allover scenic, jeweled handle, 5" . 165.00

Mug, man on camel, moriage trim, 4¾" 240.00

Napkin ring, figural owl on stump, 4" 450.00

Nappy, flowers & gold design, 3½" 13.50

Nut dish, & 2 salts, black tree silhouette, scenic, footed 85.00

Nut set, ivory, gold flowers, footed, 6" diameter, 5 piece 65.00

Pancake server, white, pink & blue flowers, 8¾" dia. . . . 100.00

Patch box, light green, gold
  beading, pink trumpet
  flowers, 1⅞" 20.00
Pitcher, leaves, fall colors,
  heavy outline beading,
  5½" 80.00
Planter, Deco design, 8" long . 127.00
Plaque, flowers & fruit in
  wicker basket, gold rim,
  11½", pair 275.00
Plate, cobalt, heavy gold rim
  design & center accent,
  mark #2, 9" 125.00
Plate, fish decor, gold border,
  8½" 105.00
Plate, roses, red & brown
  shading, 10 sided, mark #2,
  11" 52.00
Powder box, green with pink
  flowers 45.00
Reamer, allover gold,
  multicolor flowers, gold
  handle & top 125.00
Reamer, flowers with gold
  trim, mark #2 .... 155.00

Vase, blue to caramel with gold traced
coralene florals, gold throat, base and
handles, 11", $475.00.

Relish, trees, 2 houses, center
  handle, crown mark, 8" . 25.00
Ring tree, beading, gold
  swags, 2½" 55.00
Shaving mug, Indian in canoe,
  4" 167.00
Spittoon, lady's; violets, turquoise beading, moriage . 275.00
Spooner, scenic on bisque,
  jeweled handles 75.00
Sugar, house on lake, jeweled
  handles, with lid 25.00
Sugar shaker, Gaudy, flowers
  on green, gold trim &
  beads, mark #4, 5" 92.00
Tea set, moriage dragon, 17
  piece 165.00
Tea set, white, bands of gold
  & blue flowers, 15 piece . 150.00
Teapot, white with gold
  overlay, pedestaled 62.50
Toothpick, barrel shape,
  scenic 30.00

Vase, marked Royal Nippon, 12½",
$65.00.

Toothpick, 3 gold handles & rim, mark #3 .... 25.00

Tray, lake, trees & boat scene, satin finish, 9½x11″ 150.00

Urn, with lid, cobalt with allover beading, mums, 2 handles, 11x9½″ 450.00

Vase, allover gold, green, scenic reserves front & back, 14″ 385.00

Vase, blown-out acorns & leaves, green & gold, 7″ . 635.00

Vase, brown bark ground, red cloisonne flowers, 8″ ... 325.00

Vase, Egyptian decor, triangular, mark #2, 5″ 125.00

Vase, medallion, 2 deer in moriage leaves, handles, 7½″ 200.00

Vase, poppies, daisies, gold filigree top & base, 3 feet, handles, 14″ 400.00

Vase, violets, much gold & green, slender form, 12″ . 100.00

Noritake

Since the early 1900s the Noritake China Company has been producing fine dinnerware, occasional pieces, and figural items decorated by hand in delicate florals, scenics, and wildlife studies. One of their most popular dinnerware lines was Azalea; see also Azalea.

Left to right: vase, house framed by leafage, gold handles and shoulder decoration, 6″, $135.00; ewer, windmill in gold reserve, gold top, base, and handle, 8″, $175.00.

Ash tray, Tree in Meadow, nested, green wreath mark, pair 35.00

Basket, #16034, White & Gold; ruffle border, green wreath mark 65.00

Bowl, blown-out peanuts within, 3 ball feet, 5 sides, 7″ wide 50.00

Bowl, nut; footed, florals in basket, wide blue lustre band, 3¾″ 10.00

Bowl, nut; 3 dimensional nuts, green ferns 65.00

Bowl, wood scene, allover gold, 8½″ diameter 65.00

Bud vase, tree stump with butterflies 95.00

Candle holder, scenic, raised gold, pair 60.00

Candy dish, tan lustre rim, center handle, pearlized, tulips 30.00

Celery dish, celery stalks mold 25.00

Chocolate set, white with floral decor, 9 piece, 9½″ pot 192.00

Creamer, Del Monte 15.00

Creamer & sugar, Tree in Meadow 25.00

Creamer & sugar shaker, house by lake pattern .. 40.00

Cup & saucer, #5693 ...... 3.50

Cup & saucer, Grasmere ... 10.00

Dealer's sign 50.00

Egg cup, small floral design, double, 3½″ 25.00

Ferner, floral decor, triangular, 6″ wide 92.00

Figurine, maiden with bundle of sticks on head, white, 9″ 95.00

Gravy boat with attached underplate, Lares 22.50

Humidor, blown-out lion & python 625.00

Humidor, cigar painted on side 90.00

Inkwell, owl figural 210.00

Lemon dish, ring handle, house by lake pattern .. 10.00

Lemon tray, Tree in Meadow . 12.50
Luncheon set, scenic, green
    wreath mark, 18 piece .. 240.00
Mustache cup with saucer,
    scenic decor, 5¾" diameter
    saucer 70.00
Plate, Venetian scene, 9½" . 14.00
Punch bowl, Oriental scene, red
    ground, 16" diameter ... 375.00
Salt & pepper, Tree in the
    Meadow, pair 15.00
Spooner, #16034, White &
    Gold; green wreath mark . 50.00
Spooner, Deco design, 8" long 35.00
Sugar shaker, Tree in Meadow 25.00
Tea caddy, scenic decor, 3¾" 160.00
Toast rack, 2 slice 25.00
Vase, gold trim & florals, 11" . 135.00
Vase, jack-in-the-pulpit shape,
    7¾" 95.00
Waffle set, Tree in Meadow . 50.00
Wall pocket, bird decor, 8½"
    long 45.00
Wall pocket, geometrics &
    flowers 25.00

Nutcrackers

Of most interest to collectors are nutcrackers marked with patent information, or those made in the form of an animal or bird. Many manufacturers chose the squirrel to model their nutcrackers after; dogs were also popular. Cast iron examples are most often encountered, but brass, steel, even wood was also used.

Alligator, cast iron, wood
    base, Blake's Nut Cracker,
    10½" 45.00
Antelope head, glass eyes,
    solid wood, hand carved,
    9x3½" 70.00
Bear, sitting, hand carved
    wood, glass eyes, German . 95.00
Dog head, dated 1820 ..... 62.00
Lady's legs, cast iron 75.00
Nude, carved wood 15.00

Cast and machined brass ship's wheel, wood base, ca. 20th century, 4½", $20.00.

Rabbit head, glass eyes, hand
    carved wood, German .. 95.00
Rooster head, brass, large . 15.00
St Bernard, iron, EX 65.00
Wizened old man with night-
    cap, wooden, 10¾" 35.00

Occupied Japan

Items with the 'Occupied Japan' mark were made during the period from the end of World War II until April, 1952. Porcelains, novelties, paper items, lamps, silver plate, lacquer ware, and dolls are some of the areas of exported goods that may bear this stamp. Because the Japanese were naturally resentful of the occupation, it is felt that only a small percentage of their wares were thus marked. Although you may find identical items marked simply 'Japan,' only those with the 'Occupied Japan' stamp are being collected.

Ash tray, with Black boy .. 22.00
Boot, yellow trim, hand
    painted flowers, 3" 7.50
Bowl, lacquer, Yoshida, 9¾"
    diameter 22.00
Cigarette lighter, Buick ... 25.00

Cup & saucer, dragon, translucent, demitasse 20.00

Cup & saucer, green leaves,
pink dogwood, gold trim . 28.00

Demitasse pot, blue base &
rim, hand painted roses,
scrolled spout 15.00

Dinner set, china, service for
6, with serving pieces . . 170.00

Doll, bisque baby, clothed,
2¾" 20.00

Figurine, angel, sits with book
in lap, yellow frock, gold
trim, 2x2" 7.50

Figurine, bird, crane, blue &
yellow wings stretched up-
ward, 3¾" 7.50

Figurine, cat playing saxophone, bisque, 5" 25.00

Figurine, couple dancing, lady
in yellow dress, man in red
pants 12.50

Figurine, Dutch pair, man has
basket, girl has milk pail at
feet, 4" 12.00

Figurine, lady, plumed hat,
flowered petticoat, holds
goblet, 8¼" 18.00

Aladdin lamp cigarette lighter on tray,
silver metal, $20.00.

Incense burner, Indian, 4" . 15.00

Jewelry casket, enamel top
with pheasant 20.00

Leaf dish, hand painted lake
scene, gold trim, 5" 9.00

Match holder, pastels, hand
painted, Chase, 6¾x4¾" . 45.00

Match holder, 2" Colonial man
sitting by vase, with striker 12.00

Pencil box, wood with
multicolor decor 22.50

Pincushion, shoe, china, 2½" 6.00

Pitcher, windmill, 4" 15.00

Planter, duck, black bonnet,
floral decor, horseshoe
mark, 6½" 12.00

Shakers, dog figural, pair . . 9.00

Left to right: Colonial man, tri-corner hat, 11", $30.00; lady with horn, 11", $35.00;
lady with accordian, 10", $27.50.

226

Shakers, with holder, 2 pigs in
sty, feet on railing 15.00

Shelf sitter, boy, blue sweater,
plays harmonica, 3x4½″ . 9.00

Tape measure, cat figural,
celluloid, 2½″ 20.00

Tea set, Cottage, sugar,
creamer, large teapot, T-in-
circle mark 45.00

Tea set, tomato figural, 7
piece, large size 60.00

Toby mug, full figure,
gentleman, 2″ 9.00

Toothpick holder, dog with
basket, 2¾″ 10.00

Tray, lacquer, gold decor,
16x22″ 58.00

Tray, lacquer, metal, hand
painted bamboo on red,
Maruni, 7½x5½″ 10.00

Vase, reticulated neck, full-
figure peacock on side,
6½″ 22.00

Wall plaques, Colonial figures,
pair 30.00

Old Sleepy Eye

The Sleepy Eye Milling Company
and the town where it was located in
Minnesota both took their name from
the Sioux Indian Chief who was born
there in 1789, Old Sleepy Eye. In the
early 1900s, the milling company con-
tracted with the Weir Pottery Co. to
make four pieces of blue and gray
stoneware -- a salt bowl, butter crock,
vase and stein -- each decorated with
the likeness of the old chief. One of
these pieces were given as a premium
inside each barrel of their flour. Weir
was one of six companies that in 1906
merged to form the Western
Stoneware Company. There the line
was produced in blue and white and
several more items were added. These
early pieces, along with advertising
items such as pillow tops, postcards,
match holders, signs, labels, etc., are
today highly collectible.

Calendar, 1906, M 250.00
Cookbook, loaf of bread ... 185.00
Egg carton, paper, 'We Sell
Sleepy Eye Flour' 175.00
Fan 165.00
Letter opener, bronze 900.00
Mirror, advertising, 1940s . 15.00
Mug, blue & white, convention
issue, dated 125.00
Mug, blue & white, 5″, M . 200.00
Mug, brown, 1952 .... 400.00

**Postcards, Monument; Chief Sleepy Eye Welcomes Whites; Sun Never Sets
on Users of Sleepy Eye Flour; Mark of Quality; each $60.00.**

Paperweight, bronze plated, rare 450.00
Pillow top, colorful picture of large trademark head in center 550.00
Pillow top, Monroe at Washington 550.00
Pitcher, #1 .... 175.00
Pitcher, #2 .... 200.00
Pitcher, #3 .... 225.00
Pitcher, #4 .... 250.00
Pitcher, #5 .... 295.00
Salt crock, M 500.00
Sign, tin, 19x13¼" 1,000.00
Stein, all blue 750.00
Stein, blue & gray 450.00
Stein, blue & white 500.00
Sugar bowl 500.00
Thimble 350.00
Vase, blue & white 350.00

Mug, 4¼", $150.00.

Opalescent Glass

Pattern molded tableware and novelty items made from glassware with a fiery opalescence became popular around the turn of the century. It was made in many patterns by several well known companies.

Barber bottle, Swirl, blue, polished pontil 145.00
Berry set, Beatty Honey-comb, clear, 5 piece 130.00

Berry set, Everglades, blue, 7 piece 395.00
Berry set, Palm Beach, blue, 7 piece 285.00
Berry set, Tokyo, blue, 7 piece 285.00
Berry set, Wild Bouquet, green, 7 piece 325.00
Bowl, Abalone, green 18.00
Bowl, Astro, ruffled, blue .. 40.00
Bowl, Beaded Cable, ruffled, green, 3 feet 22.50
Bowl, Blocked Thumbprint & Beads, blue, 5" 15.00
Bowl, Fluted Scrolls, blue, 7" 29.50
Bowl, Intaglio, master berry, blue 150.00
Bowl, Intaglio, ruffled, footed, vaseline 45.00
Bowl, Jewel & Fan, oval, green, 7" 25.00
Bowl, Meander, deep, 3 legs, blue 40.00
Bowl, Pearl Flowers, footed, green 25.00
Bowl, Roulette, footed, green, 8½" 25.00
Bowl, Shell & Wild Rose, blue, 8½" 13.00
Butter dish, Argonaut Shell, blue 275.00
Butter dish, Circled Scroll, green 175.00
Butter dish, Diamond Spearhead, vaseline 175.00
Butter dish, Fluted Scroll, vaseline 165.00
Butter dish, Guttate, clear with some gold 95.00
Butter dish, Idyll, blue 275.00
Butter dish, Regal, green .. 135.00
Candy dish, Jackson, footed, clear 28.00
Celery tray, Alaska, vaseline . 185.00
Celery vase, Diamond Spearhead, blue 110.00
Celery vase, Ribbed Lattice, cranberry 85.00
Compote, Circled Scroll, blue . 125.00
Compote, Everglades, blue . 50.00

Spanish Lace butter dish, blue, 8″, $200.00.

Compote, jelly; Intaglio, blue	15.00
Compote, jelly; Iris with Meander, vaseline	30.00
Compote, jelly; Swag with Brackets, open, blue	40.00
Compote, Maple Leaf, green	50.00
Compote, Regal, blue	63.00
Creamer, Alaska, blue	75.00
Creamer, Diamond Spearhead, green, individual size	45.00
Creamer, Fluted Scroll, clear	20.00
Creamer, Jewelled Heart, blue	60.00
Creamer, Scroll with Acanthus, blue	55.00
Creamer, Shell, clear	30.00
Cruet, Reverse Swirl, vaseline	165.00
Doughnut stand, Tokyo, apple green	48.00
Master salt, Beatty Rib, blue	40.00
Nappy, Sea Spray, handled, green	25.00
Olive dish, Sea Spray, handled, green	25.00
Pitcher, water; Alaska, vaseline	285.00
Pitcher, water; Coin Spot, amberina, clear reeded applied handle	325.00
Pitcher, water; Coin Spot, cranberry, ruffled top	145.00
Pitcher, water; Daisy & Fern, clear	120.00
Pitcher, water; Fluted Scroll, vaseline	195.00
Pitcher, water; Palm Beach, blue	395.00
Pitcher, water; Reverse Swirl, tankard, clear	85.00
Pitcher, water; Swirl, cranberry, square top	210.00
Punch cup, Chrysanthemum Base Swirl, clear	25.00
Rose bowl, Beads & Bark, vaseline, open	25.00
Rose bowl, Button Panels	45.00
Sauce, Drapery, blue	13.00
Sauce, Everglades, blue	30.00
Sauce, Everglades, vaseline	35.00
Sauce, Intaglio, footed, blue	22.50
Spooner, Dolly Madison, green	45.00
Spooner, Everglades, vaseline, with gold trim	75.00
Spooner, Fluted Scroll, blue	50.00
Spooner, Gonterman Swirl, clear with amber rim	110.00
Spooner, Hobnail & Paneled Thumbprint, blue	65.00
Spooner, Iris with Meander, green	85.00
Spooner, Jackson, blue	23.00
Spooner, Leaf with Basketweave, blue	115.00
Spooner, Shell, blue	85.00
Spooner, Wild Bouquet, green	65.00
Sugar, Jewel & Flower, clear with gold & red	35.00
Sugar, Sunburst on Shield, blue, breakfast style	25.00
Sugar, Tokyo, blue	125.00
Table set, Circled Scroll, blue, 4 piece	750.00
Table set, Hobnail & Paneled Thumbprint, vaseline, 4 piece	385.00
Table set, Intaglio, clear, 4 piece	245.00
Table set, Palm Beach, blue, 4 piece	650.00
Table set, Wooden Pail, vaseline, 4 piece	200.00
Toothpick, Iris with Meander, green	55.00

Regal water set, pitcher and six tumblers, blue, $900.00.

Tumbler, Baby Coinspot, blue
crackle glass 45.00
Tumbler, Buttons & Braids,
blue 25.00
Tumbler, Daisy & Fern,
cranberry 45.00
Tumbler, Everglades, blue . 65.00
Tumbler, Fluted Scroll,
vaseline 40.00
Tumbler, Poinsettia, green . 30.00
Tumbler, Reverse Swirl,
cranberry 40.00
Tumbler, Ribbed Spiral, blue . 75.00
Tumbler, Wreathed Shell, blue 32.00
Water set, Circled Scroll, blue,
7 piece 700.00
Water set, Inverted Fan &
Feather, gold trim, 7 piece 450.00

Paper Dolls

Though the history of paper dolls can be traced even farther back, by the late 1700s they were being mass produced. A century later, paper dolls were being used as an advertising medium by retail companies wishing to promote sales. The type most often encountered are in book form -- the dolls on the cardboard covers, their wardrobe on the inside pages -- published since the 1920s. Those representing famous people or characters are popular; condition is very important. Those in original, uncut folders are most valuable.

Baby Jane, Gertrude Breed,
1927 .... 17.50
Baby Sparkle Plenty, boxed
set, Saalfield, #5160, 1948 . 15.00
Betty & Dick Tour the USA,
Standard Toykraft, #D100,
1940 .... 17.00
Betty Grable, Merrill
Publishing, #2552, 1953 . 35.00
Betty Marie, Londy Card Cor-
poration, #5F, 1932 .... 5.00
Bible Land Children, Near
East Foundation, 1934 . 8.00
Bible Think & Do, CR Gibson
Company, #4936 .... 3.00
Big Sister, Londy Card Cor-
poration, #5J, 1932 ..... 5.00
Birthday Party, National Syn-
dicate Displays, Inc, #77-2,
1944 .... 8.00
Boarding School, Merrill
Publishing, #3492, 1942 . 15.00
Bob & Nan, MA Donahue &
Company, #80A 20.00
Bobby, Doll to Dress, MS
Publishing Co, #900 .... 20.00
Bride & Groom Military Wed-
ding Party, Merrill
Publishing, #3411, 1941 . 20.00

National Art Co., Mother Goose Cut-Out Picture Book, $20.00.

Carmen Miranda, Saalfield, #2723, 1952 . . . . 25.00

Children of the War Zone, Central Committee on Foreign Missions, 1916 . . . . 15.00

Circus Twins, National Paper Box Company, Inc, #12-29 5.00

Coke Crowd, The; Merrill Publishing, #3445, 1946, teens with Cokes 12.00

Coronation, Saalfield, #4312, 1953 . . . . 15.00

Cutie Paper Dolls, Milton Bradley Company, #4053 . 15.00

Daisy Dolly, Goldsmith Publishing Company, #516, 1922 . . . . 17.00

Daisy Mae & Li'l Abner, Saalfield, #2360, 1941 . . 20.00

Dancing Priscilla, Gertrude Breed, 1927 . . . . 17.50

Deanna Durbin, Merrill Publishing, #3480, 1940 . 60.00

Dearie Dolls, Charles E Graham & Company, front & back cover, #0212 . . . . 15.00

Dolls We Love, Merrill Publishing, #3416, 1936, 5 children & nurse 30.00

Dress-Up, Reuben H Lilja & Company, Inc, #905, 1947 . 10.00

First Lady, Magic Wand Corporation, Jackie Kennedy, #204, 1963 . . . . 25.00

Fun Farm Frolics, International Paper Goods, #60, 1932 . . . . 35.00

Funny Bunnies, McLoughlin Bros, #553, 1938 . . . . 35.00

Glenn, Janex Corporation, #2002, 1971 . . . . 5.00

Gloria Jean, Saalfield, #1664, 1941 . . . . 40.00

Gone with the Wind, Merrill Publishing, #3405, 1940 . 90.00

Happi Time Dressmaker Kit, Cardinal Games 15.00

Happy Birthday, Merrill Publishing, #3466, 1939 . 25.00

Children's Press, Inc., Around the World with Bob and Barbara, 1946, $15.00.

Heavenly Blue Wedding, Merrill Publishing, #2580, 1955 7.00

Hedy Lamarr, Saalfield, #2600, 1951 . . . . 25.00

Hollywood Fashion Dolls, Saalfield, #2242, 1939 . . 10.00

Housekeeping with the Kuddle Kiddies, Saalfield, #2140, 1936 . . . . 20.00

Ivy, Janex Corporation, #2001, 1971 . . . . 5.00

Jack & Janet Paper Dolls, MH Leavis 12.00

Jackie & Caroline, Magic Wand Corporation, #107 . 20.00

Jane Russell Paper Dolls & Coloring Book, Saalfield, #4328, 1955 . . . . 25.00

Johnny Jones, Goldsmith Publishing Co, #516, 1922 . 17.00

Kewpies, Saalfield, #1332, 1963 . . . . 15.00

Kiddie-Kolored-Kut-Outs, Charles E Graham & Company, #0219 . . . . 15.00

Linda the Ballerina, Avalon Industries, Inc, #701-1 . . 4.00

Little Audrey's Dress Designer Kit, Saalfield, #6042, 1962, in box 15.00

Little Ballerina, Merrill Publishing, #1542, 1953 . 5.00

Little Princess, Merrill Publishing, #3405, 1936 . 30.00

Little Sister, Dandyline Company, 1918 . . . . 18.00

Lucille Ball, Saalfield, #2475, 1944 .... 40.00

Magic Mary, Milton Bradley Company, #4010, 1955 .. 7.00

Magic Mary Ann, Milton Bradley Company, #4010-2, 1966 .... 5.00

Mark Antony, Blaise Publishing Company, 1963 15.00

Martha Washington Doll Book, Howell Soskin Publishers, 1945 .... 30.00

Mary Martin, Saalfield, #2427, 1942 .... 45.00

Moderne Sewing for Little Girls, American Toy Works, #417 .... 10.00

My Baby Dress-Up Kit, Color-forms, #176, 1964 ...... 6.00

My Fair Lady, Avalon Industries, Inc, #401 ..... 18.00

My Little Margie, Saalfield, #2737, 1945 .... 20.00

Nancy & Jane, Howell Soskin Publishers, 1945 .... 15.00

New Baby, Merrill Publishing, #4827, 1943 .... 12.00

Ozzie & Harriet, Saalfield, #4319, 1954 .... 20.00

Pansy Prattle, Goldsmith Publishing Company, #516, 1922 .... 17.00

Patti Page, Samuel Lowe Company, #2406, 1957 .. 25.00

Pink Prom Twins, Merrill Publishing, #2583, 1956 . 5.00

Piper Laurie, Merrill Publishing, #2551, 1953 . 35.00

Pixie Doll & Pup, Samuel Lowe Company, #2764, 1968 .... 3.00

Polly Patchwork & Her Friends, Samuel Lowe Company, #1024, 1942 .. 15.00

Princess Paper Doll Book, Elizabeth & Margaret, Saalfield, #2216, 1939... 55.00

Quintuplets, Saalfield, #1352, 1964 .... 6.00

Raggedy Ann & Andy, Saalfield, #2497, 1944 .. 15.00

Rita Hayworth in the Loves of Carmen, Saalfield, #2712, 1948 .... 20.00

Robin Hood & Maid Marian, Saalfield, #2748, 1956 .. 12.00

Shirley Temple, Saalfield, #4435, 1958 .... 15.00

Shirley Temple Standing Doll, Saalfield, #1719, 1935, in box 35.00

Sister Helen, Kaufmann & Strauss Company, #12, 1915 .... 40.00

Smile Dress-Up Set, Color-forms, #581, 1971 ...... 3.00

Sonja Henie, Merrill Publishing, #3418, 1941 . 55.00

Story Princess, Saalfield, #2761, 1957 .... 18.00

Sue & Sal, The Snap-on Sisters, Novel Products Corporation 10.00

Sunny the Wonder Doll, Milton Bradley Company, #4236 .... 8.00

Susan Dey, Saalfield, #4218, 1972 .... 5.00

Television Dolls, Milton Bradley Company, #4425 . 12.00

The Animated Goldilocks Doll, Milton Bradley Company, #4101 .... 15.00

The Twins, Round About Dolls, Milton Bradley Company, #4447, 1935 ...... 10.00

Tiny Tears, Magic Wand Corporation, #112 .... 6.00

Toni, Merry Manufacturing Company, #6501 .... 6.00

Tressy, Magic Wand Corporation, #111, 1964 .... 6.00

Tricia--Welcome to the White House, Saalfield, #4248, 1970 .... 5.00

Two-Gun Pete, Milton Bradley Company, #4042, new in 1950 .... 8.00

Tyrone Power & Linda Darnell, Merrill Publishing, #3438, 1941 .... 70.00

Uncle Sam's Little Helpers, Saalfield, #2450, 1943 .. 25.00

Velva Doll, My Name is Jill, Kingston Products Corporation, D20, 1932 .... 15.00

Victory Volunteers, Merrill Publishing, #3424, 1942, dolls & uniforms 18.00

Watch Me Grow, Merrill Publishing, #4857, 1944 . 15.00

Wedding Belles, Dot & Peg Productions, 1945 ...... 15.00

Young American Designer, Dot & Peg Productions, 1941 .... 18.00

Ziegfeld Girl, Merrill Publishing, #3466, 1941 . 90.00

Pattern Glass

As early as 1820 glassware was being pressed into patterned molds to produce tablewares and accessories. The process was perfected, and by the latter part of the century, dozens of glass houses were making hundreds of patterns. This type of glassware retained its popularity until about 1915. Two types of glass were used: flint, the early type made with lead to produce a good clear color and resonance; and non-flint, the later type containing soda lime. Generally, flint glass is the more expensive.

Actress, bread platter 55.00
Actress, cake stand 150.00
Actress, cheese dish 195.00
Actress, compote, covered, 7″ 110.00
Actress, compote, open, low standard, 6″ 55.00
Actress, jam jar with lid .. 85.00
Alaska, creamer 20.00
Alaska, creamer, green 35.00
Alaska, sauce, green, enameled forget-me-nots & leaves 45.00
Alaska, sugar with lid 40.00

Amazon, spooner, etched .. 29.00
Amazon, sugar with lid ... 55.00
Amazon, wine 22.00
Arched Ovals, creamer 30.00
Arched Ovals, goblet 18.00
Arched Ovals, wine 25.00
Ashburton, ale glass, flint, 6½″ 55.00
Ashburton, claret, low stem, flint 40.00
Ashburton, egg cup, barrel . 23.00
Ashburton, egg cup, flared . 23.00
Ashburton, goblet, etched grapes, leaves & tendrils, flint 175.00
Ashburton, honey dish, flint, 3½″ 8.00
Atlas, cake stand, 8″ 18.00
Atlas, goblet 28.00
Atlas, toothpick 18.00
Atlas, wine 18.00
Banded Portland, butter with cover, maiden blush 165.00
Banded Portland, cologne with original stopper, 9½″ 45.00
Banded Portland, dresser jar, with gold trim 27.00
Banded Portland, jelly compote with cover 24.50
Banded Portland, relish, maiden blush, 6½″ 15.00
Banded Portland, shakers, pair 30.00
Banded Portland, vase, 6″ . 15.00
Basketweave, goblet 23.00
Basketweave, goblet, vaseline 25.00
Basketweave, pitcher, amber 45.00
Basketweave, water tray, with scenic center, vaseline .. 50.00
Beaded Grape, bread tray, green 45.00
Beaded Grape, butter with cover, green with gold trim 110.00
Beaded Grape, cake stand, green 75.00
Beaded Grape, creamer, green 25.00
Beaded Grape, pitcher, green 135.00
Beaded Grape, wine, green with gold trim 65.00

Beaded Swirl, berry set, green
with gold trim, 7 piece .. **175.00**

Beaded Swirl, creamer, green
with gold trim **60.00**

Beaded Swirl, tumbler, ruby
stained, rare **45.00**

Beaded Swirl, wine **30.00**

Bellflower, bowl, scalloped
rim, footed, flint, 8″ **35.00**

Bellflower, champagne, flint . **75.00**

Bellflower, goblet, fine rib,
banded, flint, amethyst
tinted **75.00**

Bellflower, honey dish, flint . **12.00**

Bellflower, sugar, double vine,
flint, no lid **46.00**

Bellflower, wine, flint **65.00**

Bird & Strawberry, compote,
open, scalloped, ruffled rim,
6x8″ **110.00**

Bird & Strawberry, table set . **335.00**

Bird & Strawberry, water pitcher **185.00**

Bird & Strawberry, wine .. **40.00**

Block & Lattice, butter with
cover, amber stain **85.00**

Block & Lattice, creamer,
ruby stained **55.00**

Block & Lattice, sugar with
lid, amber stained **70.00**

Block & Lattice, water set,
amber, tankard pitcher, 5
piece **175.00**

Broken Column, basket with
applied handle **160.00**

Broken Column, butter with
cover **45.00**

Broken Column, cruet **65.00**

Broken Column, jam jar with
cover **57.00**

Broken Column, oval relish,
7½x4″ **20.00**

Broken Column, tumbler .. **45.00**

Button Arches, creamer, ruby
stained **40.00**

Button Arches, milk pitcher,
ruby stained **55.00**

Button Arches, spooner, clear
with gold band **25.00**

Button Arches, spooner, ruby
stained with clear band . **25.00**

Cabbage Rose, celery **39.00**

Cabbage Rose, creamer **52.00**

Cabbage Rose, spooner **32.00**

Cathedral, compote with
scalloped top, blue, 9½″ . **65.00**

Cathedral, spooner **24.00**

Cathedral, sugar with lid, ruby
stained **65.00**

Cathedral, wine **29.00**

Cherry with Thumbprint,
berry bowl **15.00**

Cherry with Thumbprint,
celery vase, tall **87.00**

Cherry with Thumbprint,
spooner **32.50**

Cherry with Thumbprint,
tumbler **30.00**

Cherry with Thumbprint,
water pitcher **110.00**

Colorado, berry set, green
with gold trim, 7 piece .. **165.00**

Colorado, butter with cover,
blue with gold trim **225.00**

Colorado, card tray, green,
footed **19.00**

Colorado, creamer, green,
small **25.00**

Colorado, creamer, green with
gold trim, table size **60.00**

Colorado, sherbet, blue with
gold trim **35.00**

Colorado, water pitcher, dark
blue, no gold **115.00**

Columbian Coin, berry set, 7
piece **295.00**

Columbian Coin, creamer .. **150.00**

Columbian Coin, spooner .. **75.00**

Columbian Coin, syrup **145.00**

Columbian Coin, table set,
with gold trim, 4 piece .. **350.00**

Croesus, berry bowl, purple
with gold trim **35.00**

Croesus, jelly compote,
amethyst **250.00**

Croesus, relish, amethyst .. **75.00**

Croesus, sugar, green with
gold trim, breakfast style . **65.00**

Croesus, sugar with lid, green
with gold trim 135.00
Croesus, tumbler, green with
gold trim, set of 4 ..... 200.00
Crystal Wedding, banana
stand 160.00
Crystal Wedding, compote,
covered, clear & frosted,
9¾x6″ square 65.00
Crystal Wedding, saucer, 3″ . 14.00
Crystal Wedding, tumbler . 35.00
Cupid & Venus, butter with
cover 50.00
Cupid & Venus, champagne . 85.00
Cupid & Venus, compote,
open, low standard, 8½″
wide 25.00
Cupid & Venus, goblet 52.00
Cupid & Venus, milk pitcher . 45.00
Cupid & Venus, sauce, footed,
3½″ diameter 7.50
Currier & Ives, compote, open 50.00
Currier & Ives, goblet 24.00
Currier & Ives, tray, Balking
Mule on Railroad Tracks,
12″ 68.00

**Currier & Ives, tray, Balky Mule,
$40.00.**

Currier & Ives, water pitcher,
Bellair, circa 1890 ...... 75.00
Cut Log, celery 40.00
Cut Log, compote, open, 10″
diameter 30.00

Cut Log, master berry bowl,
large 25.00
Cut Log, nappy 17.00
Cut Log, relish 20.00
Daisy & Button, butter with
cover, amber top, clear
base, square 35.00
Daisy & Button, creamer, ap-
plied handle, 4″ 15.00
Daisy & Button, ice cream
bowl, vaseline 65.00
Daisy & Button, spooner, with
amber panels 40.00
Daisy & Button, water tray,
handled, triangular, vas-
eline 46.00
Dakota, cake stand, etched,
10″ 85.00
Dakota, goblet 30.00
Dakota, jelly compote 35.00
Dakota, spooner, etched ... 33.00
Dakota, wine, ruby stained . 50.00
Delaware, butter with cover,
green 125.00
Delaware, custard cup, rose
with gold trim 20.00
Delaware, master berry bowl,
green with gold trim ... 65.00
Delaware, tankard pitcher,
rose with gold trim 175.00
Delaware, tumbler, green with
gold trim 30.00
Diamond Medallion, butter
with cover 45.00
Diamond Medallion, goblet . 18.00
Diamond Medallion, spooner . 22.50
Diamond Medallion, wine .. 35.00
Diamond Quilted, champagne 21.00
Diamond Quilted, goblet, blue 35.00
Diamond Quilted, mug,
amethyst 30.00
Diamond Quilted, sauce,
pedestal, vaseline 22.00
Diamond Quilted, wine 19.00
Diamond Quilted, wine, light
blue 38.00
Feather, cruet 30.00
Feather, relish, oval, with
amber trim, 8¼″ long .. 45.00

Feather, wine	35.00
Feather Duster, water pitcher	45.00
Fine Cut & Block, celery dish	26.50
Fine Cut & Block, creamer, with pink blocks	65.00
Fine Cut & Block, egg cup .	25.00
Fine Cut & Block, sauce, footed, with amber trim .	16.00
Fishscale, butter with cover .	45.00
Fishscale, compote, open . .	25.00
Fishscale, milk pitcher	28.00
Fishscale, sauce	6.00
Heart with Thumbprint, card tray, folded sides, gold trim	20.00
Heart with Thumbprint, creamer, individual	18.00
Heart with Thumbprint, goblet, gold trim	45.00
Heart with Thumbprint, master berry bowl	28.00
Heart with Thumbprint, plate, 6″	25.00
Holly, butter dish	150.00
Holly, egg cup	65.00
Holly, table set, 4 piece . . .	450.00
Holly, water pitcher	170.00
Honeycomb, goblet, flint . .	25.00
Honeycomb, spooner, flint .	20.00
Honeycomb, whiskey, handled, flint	45.00
Honeycomb, wine, non-flint .	16.00
Horseshoe, celery	40.00
Horseshoe, goblet, ornate stem	35.00
Horseshoe, oval vegetable bowl, large	16.00
Horseshoe, pitcher, large . .	110.00
Horseshoe, pitcher, milk . . .	58.00
Horseshoe, waste bowl	40.00
Hummingbird, butter with cover	60.00
Hummingbird, creamer, blue .	40.00
Hummingbird, milk pitcher .	49.00
Hummingbird, water pitcher, blue	95.00
Inverted Thumbprint, creamer, amber, 4x4″	20.00
Inverted Thumbprint, tumbler, cranberry	32.00
Inverted Thumbprint, wine, apple green	40.00
Inverted Thumbprint, wine, blue with clear stem	22.00
Inverted Thumbprint, wine, vaseline	40.00
Jacob's Ladder, compote, open, low standard, 10″ .	30.00
Jacob's Ladder, creamer . . .	32.00
Jacob's Ladder, pickle dish .	15.00
Jacob's Ladder, wine	31.00
Kansas, goblet	38.00
Kansas, master berry bowl .	42.00
Kansas, milk pitcher	48.00
Kansas, sauce	15.00
King's Crown, cake stand, 9″	85.00
King's Crown, goblet, citrine rim	32.00
King's Crown, goblet, purple eyes	28.00
King's Crown, salt dip, individual; rectangular . . .	12.00
King's Crown, wine	14.00
Lattice & Oval Panels, butter with cover	95.00
Lattice & Oval Panels, creamer, applied handle .	125.00
Lattice & Oval Panels, sauce .	9.00
Lattice & Oval Panels, sugar with lid, high standard, flint	125.00
Leaf Medallion, berry set, cobalt with gold trim, 5 piece	250.00
Leaf Medallion, creamer, amethyst with gold trim, Northwood	75.00
Leaf Medallion, jelly, green with gold trim	65.00
Leaf Medallion, master berry bowl, green with gold trim	85.00
Leaf Medallion, spooner, amethyst with gold trim, Northwood	65.00
Leaf Medallion, water set, cobalt with gold trim . . .	750.00
Lion, celery, frosted	75.00
Lion, compote, oval, frosted & clear, 8″ high	115.00

Lion, goblet, frosted 65.00
Lion, sauce, frosted, footed . 8.50
Loop & Dart with Round Ornament, creamer, applied handle 45.00
Loop & Dart with Round Ornament, goblet, non-flint . 30.00
Loop & Dart with Round Ornament, spooner 24.00
Loop & Dart with Round Ornament, wine, barrel shape 35.00
Mascotte, butter with cover, etched 48.00
Mascotte, spooner 20.00
Mascotte, sugar with lid, etched 38.00
Mascotte, water pitcher, tankard 35.00
Medallion Sunburst, berry set, 8 piece 120.00
Medallion Sunburst, bowl, 9¼" 30.00
Medallion Sunburst, cake stand, 10½" 35.00
Medallion Sunburst, goblet . 22.00
Medallion Sunburst, punch cup 9.00
Medallion Sunburst, vase, 9½" 32.50
Michigan, butter with cover, maiden blush with gold trim 90.00
Michigan, compote, open, 9¼" diameter 65.00
Michigan, creamer, maiden blush with gold trim ... 50.00
Michigan, souvenir water set, clear with pink carnation, 5 piece 235.00
Michigan, sugar, open, maiden blush with gold trim ... 50.00
Michigan, water pitcher, 8" . 50.00
New England Pineapple, creamer, applied handle, flint 155.00
New England Pineapple, master salt 45.00
New England Pineapple, spooner 35.00

New England Pineapple, wine 150.00
New Hampshire, creamer, small 30.00
New Hampshire, syrup with pewter top 25.00
New Hampshire, water pitcher, with ice lip 40.00
New Hampshire, wine 16.00
New Jersey, creamer & open sugar 38.00
New Jersey, jelly dish, open . 16.00
New Jersey, sugar with lid, gold flashed 35.00
New Jersey, water pitcher, with gold trim 80.00
New Jersey, wine 41.00
Oriental, butter with cover . 58.00
Oriental, table set 125.00
Oriental, tumbler 20.00
Oriental, 3 legged creamer & open sugar 70.00
Panelled Forget-Me-Not, cake stand 35.00
Panelled Forget-Me-Not, compote, covered, high standard 52.00
Panelled Forget-Me-Not, sauce, footed 12.00
Panelled Forget-Me-Not, spooner 22.00
Pavonia, cake stand, 9" ... 35.00
Pavonia, goblet, etched 32.00
Pavonia, tumbler, maple leaf etching 20.00
Pavonia, water pitcher, tankard, etched 63.00
Pavonia, wine, etched 35.00
Pennsylvania, creamer 27.00
Pennsylvania, goblet 16.00
Pennsylvania, syrup 42.00
Pennsylvania, wine, green . 37.50
Pillow Encircled, creamer, ruby stained 30.00
Pillow Encircled, master berry bowl, ruby stained 45.00
Pillow Encircled, spooner, ruby stained 55.00
Priscilla, berry bowl, straight sides, small 10.00

Priscilla, doughnut stand, 9x5¾" 60.00
Priscilla, sauce, flared sides . 6.00
Priscilla, table set, 4 piece . 185.00
Red Block, creamer, individual 35.00
Red Block, goblet 35.00
Red Block, sugar with lid . 75.00
Red Block, water set, ruby stained, 7 piece 245.00
Rose in Snow, compote, covered, low base 75.00
Rose in Snow, double pickle dish 75.00
Rose in Snow, plate, 6" ... 17.50
Rose in Snow, relish, 8½" . 15.00
Rose in Snow, tumbler 35.00
Rose Sprig, cake stand, high standard, square, blue .. 47.50
Rose Sprig, compote, covered, high standard, large 75.00
Rose Sprig, pitcher, footed, canary, 1 quart 65.00
Rose Sprig, relish, boat shape, vaseline 30.00
Royal Ivy, berry set, rainbow cracquelle 295.00
Royal Ivy, creamer, frosted . 55.00
Royal Ivy, master berry bowl, rainbow cracquelle satin . 125.00
Royal Ivy, water pitcher, frosted rubena 275.00
Royal Oak, butter with cover, frosted 175.00
Royal Oak, creamer, frosted rubena 150.00
Royal Oak, sugar shaker with original lid, frosted rubena 165.00
Royal Oak, table set, frosted rubena 625.00
Ruby Thumbprint, compote, high standard, 5" 55.00
Ruby Thumbprint, milk pitcher 90.00
Ruby Thumbprint, sauce, 4½" 18.00
Ruby Thumbprint, spooner, ruby & clear 35.00
Sawtooth, bowl, ruby stained, 5" 8.00

Sawtooth, goblet, knob stem, flint 40.00
Sawtooth, spooner, non-flint . 14.00
Sawtooth, water pitcher, ruby stained 120.00
Sawtooth, wine, non-flint .. 7.00
Scroll with Flowers, creamer . 40.00
Scroll with Flowers, goblet . 22.50
Scroll with Flowers, sugar with lid 35.00
Scroll with Flowers, wine, amber 35.00
Shell & Tassel, bowl, oval, footed, 12" 85.00
Shell & Tassel, oyster plate . 160.00
Shell & Tassel, spooner, square 37.00
Shrine, butter with cover .. 45.00
Shrine, celery 45.00
Shrine, goblet 45.00
Shrine, lemonade tumbler .. 35.00
Shrine, shaker 22.00
Spirea Band, creamer, amber . 35.00
Spirea Band, goblet, etched . 26.00
Spirea Band, wine, amber . 25.00
Sprig, bowl, footed, 8" 42.00
Sprig, compote, covered, 10½" 60.00
Sprig, creamer 29.50
Sprig, sauce, flat 8.00
Three Face, cake stand, 8" . 95.00
Three Face, champagne, saucer shape 125.00
Three Face, compote, clear & frosted, 6x7½" 60.00
Three Face, creamer, frosted stem & base 110.00
Three Face, goblet, etched, frosted stem & base 85.00
Three Face, spooner, etched . 95.00
Three Panel, berry set, scalloped rims, footed, amber, 7 piece 108.00
Three Panel, compote, open, low pedestal, vaseline ... 35.00
Three Panel, goblet, blue .. 40.00
Three Panel, spooner 15.00
Thumbprint, berry bowl, boat shape, ruby stained, small 30.00

Thumbprint, cheese dish, ruby
stained, round, 7″ 55.00
Thumbprint, cup 20.00
Thumbprint, match holder,
ruby stained 20.00
Thumbprint, water pitcher,
bulbous, ruby stained . . 145.00

Thumbprint, water pitcher, $145.00.

Thumbprint, wine, ruby stain-
ed 28.00
Torpedo, berry bowl, ruby
stained, small 25.00
Torpedo, celery vase 40.00
Torpedo, goblet 49.00
Torpedo, spooner 35.00
Torpedo, sugar with lid . . . 65.00
Triple Triangle, goblet, ruby
stained 37.00
Triple Triangle, tumbler . . . 24.50
Triple Triangle, tumbler, ruby
stained 30.00
Triple Triangle, wine, ruby
stained 45.00
Two Panel, creamer 16.00
Two Panel, sauce, footed,
vaseline 19.00
Two Panel, spooner, vaseline . 27.00
Two Panel, wine, vaseline . 25.00
US Coin, cake stand, 25¢ &
$1, frosted 450.00
US Coin, compote, 25¢ & 10¢,
5½″ 250.00
US Coin, spooner, 25¢ 200.00

Washington Centennial, egg
cup, clear 45.00
Washington Centennial,
goblet 40.00
Washington Centennial, plat-
ter, bear paw handle, In-
dependence Hall 95.00
Washington Centennial, wine 45.00
Westward Ho, butter dish . 180.00
Westward Ho, creamer 80.00
Westward Ho, milk pitcher . 175.00
Westward Ho, sugar with lid . 175.00
Wheat & Barley, compote,
covered 42.00
Wheat & Barley, goblet,
amber 32.00
Wheat & Barley, spooner . . 22.50
Wheat & Barley, tumbler,
amber 38.00
Wildflower, bread platter, ap-
ple green 25.00
Wildflower, butter with cover,
collared base 50.00
Wildflower, celery 23.00
Wildflower, goblet, apple
green 35.00
Wildflower, sauce, flat,
square, amber 15.00
Wildflower, sauce, flat,
vaseline 16.00
Wildflower, sugar with lid,
green 50.00
Wildflower, tray, oblong,
vaseline 43.50
Wildflower, tumbler, apple
green 29.00
Wildflower, tumbler, vaseline 20.00
Wildflower, water pitcher,
amber 42.00
Wildflower, water tray, apple
green 50.00
Willow Oak, butter with
cover, amber 50.00
Willow Oak, compote, open,
scalloped edge 20.00
Willow Oak, pitcher 50.00
Willow Oak, plate, closed
handles, blue, 9″ 28.00
Willow Oak, plate, 9″ 22.00

Willow Oak, sugar with lid,
amber 68.00
Wisconsin, bowl, 4½x6¼"
diameter 28.00
Wisconsin, celery tray,
10½x5½" 45.00
Wisconsin, pitcher 65.00
Wisconsin, tumbler 38.00
Wisconsin, wine 55.00
X-Ray, berry set, green with
gold trim, 7 piece 165.00
X-Ray, creamer, green with
gold trim 55.00
X-Ray, sugar, open, green
with gold trim, individual
size 20.00
X-Ray, sugar with lid,
amethyst 88.00

Peters and Reed

Peters and Reed founded a pottery
in Zanesville, Ohio, around the turn of
the century. By 1922, the firm became
known as Zane Pottery. Several lines
of artware were produced which are today attracting the interest of pottery
collectors: High Glaze Brown Ware,
decorated with in-mold relief; Moss
Aztec, relief designs molded from red
clay with a green washed exterior;
Chromal, with realistic or suggested
scenics done in soft matt colors; Landsun, Shadow Ware, and Wilse Blue.

Bowl, Landsun, blue, #24,
2½x8" 26.00
Bowl, Landsun, 3" diameter . 20.00
Bowl, Moss Aztec, green,
#602, 2½x5" 15.00
Bowl, Pereco, dark blue with
berries & leaves, 8½x3¼" . 60.00
Bowl, Pereco, lattice with
flower band at top, 4¾" . 25.00
Bowl, Wilse Blue, Zane stamp,
#656, 4x6½" 30.00
Bud vase, Moss Aztec,
tapered, 10x3½" 40.00
Bud vase, Wilse Blue, 8x4" . 25.00

High Glaze Brown Ware vase, relief
florals, 3" x 6", $35.00.

Ginger jar, Shadow Ware,
green & black, with lid, 6" . 90.00
Hanging basket, Moss Aztec,
small 15.00
Jug, High Glaze Brown Ware,
ear of corn decor, 7" 285.00
Pitcher, High Glaze Brown
Ware, cavalier portraits in
relief 95.00
Planter, Moss Aztec, square,
4x7¼" 20.00
Pot, Shadow Ware, high glaze
green with blue drip, 5x5" . 35.00
Tankard, High Glaze Brown
Ware, swirl, Weller shape,
grapes & leaves 165.00
Umbrella stand, Moss Aztec,
flowers, signed Ferrell, 17" 150.00
Vase, Chromal, scenic, field
with trees & fence, #6, 8x4" 220.00
Vase, Chromal, scenic, house
with trees, etc, 8x7" 200.00
Vase, Chromal, scenic, islands
& palm trees, #1, 5x4" .. 140.00
Vase, Chromal, scenic, slight-
ly concave sides, 5¾x4¾" 130.00
Vase, High Glaze Brown
Ware, florals in relief,
trumpet shape, 9" 55.00
Vase, High Glaze Brown
Ware, sprigged floral, 10" . 60.00
Vase, Landsun, green & blue,
flared, 5x5" 30.00
Vase, Landsun, Herringbone,
#40C, 10x3½" 45.00

Vase, Landsun, tan, blue &
green, marked Zaneware,
3¾" 20.00
Vase, Moss Aztec, flowers &
berries, 12" 65.00
Vase, Moss Aztec, iris decor,
waisted shape, 15" 170.00
Vase, Pereco, green, 11½" . 20.00
Wall pocket, Moss Aztec, dark
red with green branches,
8¼" 50.00

Pewter

A metal alloy combining tin, lead,
copper or brass, pewter was molded or
spun to form utensils, tableware,
lamps, inkwells, and miscellaneous
items of every sort. Artisans in
England marked their wares with
touch marks, signs or initials used to
identify themselves or their companies, and until the Revolution pro-
vided America with nearly all of the
pewter on the market. With the end of
the war and the abolition of the
English law restricting the import of
raw materials needed for its production, the Colonists themselves began
to make pewter on a much larger scale.
This practice continued until the Civil
War.

**Charger, Boardman & Co., New
York, 19th century, 13½", $165.00.**

Basin, American, cleaned &
polished, no mark, 2x8" . 90.00
Basin, Richard Rustin, 8" . 800.00
Bowl, Continental touch
mark, side handles,
3¾x11¾" 85.00
Bowl, French touch marks on
rim, hammered, 12¼" ... 45.00
Candlestick, Cincinnati, no
mark, 10" 175.00
Candlestick, slender pear-
shaped standard, unmark-
ed, 8½", pair 175.00
Chalice, Reed & Barton, 7",
pair 190.00
Chamber stick, H Hooper, 6",
with 5" saucer 160.00
Charger, crowned rose touch
mark, worn, 13¾" 125.00
Charger, Richard King, Jr,
Prescott 1757, 15" 200.00
Communion flagon, Waters &
Thorp, incomplete finial,
12½" 225.00
Flagon, acorn thumb piece,
5½" 25.00
Flagon, Hermand Fres & Cie,
'3' & 'Liter', 5" 90.00
Grape scissors, butterfly
hinge, shell above each han-
dle, 1880, 6½" 75.00
Lamp, saucer base & whale oil
burner, 6" 115.00
Lamp, weighted base, original
brass & pewter burner,
repaired, 8½" 105.00
Lamp, whale oil, Smith & Co,
8½", pair 450.00
Measure, English, bellied, gill
size 65.00
Measure, English, bellied, ¼
gill 35.00
Measure, tankard; marked
Pint, glass bottom, 4½" . 20.00
Mug, Samuel Danforth, S han-
dle with bud, quart 475.00
Pitcher, Austrian, Wien mark,
Fein Zinn, 12" 80.00
Plate, English, set of 6, 9" . 300.00

Plate, James Dixon & Sons, 9¼″ diameter	30.00
Plate, no mark, engraved initials on rim, heavy, 9″	55.00
Plate, Richard Lee, single reed, 8″	800.00
Plate, Thomas, Townsend & Company, 8″	50.00
Porringer, Rhode Island original, solid handle, 5″	125.00
Spoon, Hall & Bailey, shell on back of bowl, 7″	28.00
Spoon, J Ozenne, 12¼″	20.00
Stein, devil finial on lid, 16″	275.00
Tall pot, HB Ward in rectangle, black paint on handle, 11¼″	285.00
Tankard, CH mark, English, with lid, 5½″	275.00
Tankard, James Yates mark, quart, with spout, circa 1800-1840	140.00
Teapot, American, no mark, repaired, 8″	75.00
Teapot, eagle touch mark with JB Woodbury, 7¼″	350.00
Teapot, footed base, wood handle & finial, 10″	75.00
Teapot, Gleason, ovoid with panels & leaf-form foot, 9″	95.00
Teapot, unmarked American, steeple lid, 8¼″	70.00
Tobacco jar, acorn finial, 9″	105.00
Wine, 4½″	55.00

Phoenix Bird China

Since early in the 1900s, Japan potteries have been producing a line of blue and white china decorated with the Japanese bird of paradise and vines of Chinese grass. The design will vary slightly, and newer ware is whiter than the old, with a more vivid blue.

Bowl, 5½″	12.00
Bowl, 7¼″	20.00
Butter with lid & liner, gold trim	85.00
Chocolate pot	85.00

Cream soup	25.00
Creamer & sugar with lid, large	46.50
Cup & saucer	12.50
Egg cup, large	21.50
Ice bowl	55.00
Lamp, 11″	110.00
Marmalade, round, open	55.00
Mustard pot	25.00
Plate, 6″	9.00
Plate, 9½″	15.00
Platter, 12½″	22.00
Salt & pepper, ball shape, small, pair	12.00
Teapot, footed	36.00
Tumbler, 2¾″	16.50
Tureen, small	85.00

Mustard pot, $25.00.

Phonographs

The first phonograph was invented by Thomas Edison in 1877. Other companies soon hit the market with their own variations. Some played discs, others wax cylinders. Many types of amplifying devices were used, but today's collectors especially treasure the large morning-glory horns.

Aeolian Vocalion, ornate case, Graduola control	200.00
Busy Bee, front mount, all original, morning-glory horn	400.00

Columbia AT 350.00

Columbia BS, coin-operated
cylinder, all original 2,000.00

Columbia EE 325.00

Columbia Q, replacement
horn, metal base 275.00

Edison Amberola #75 ..... 300.00

Edison Amberola Model III,
oak cabinet, opera works . 1,200.00

Edison Diamond Disc, Chippendale lowboy, M 300.00

Edison Fireside, Combination
K 400.00

Edison Gem, black, 2 minute,
C reproducer, crank, small
horn 450.00

Edison Home, 2 minute, C
reproducer 300.00

Edison Home, 4 minute, 14"
horn 425.00

Edison Home C reproducer, 11
panel large Home morning-
glory horn 385.00

Edison Opera, oak case, con-
cert plate, all original, VG . 3,500.00

Edison Standard, C repro-
ducer 210.00

Edison Standard, complete,
no horn 240.00

Edison Triumph, A 575.00

Eldridge R Johnson, Model C,
M original 2,000.00

Maestrophone, German,
mahogany, large horn .. 750.00

Pathe, coin-operated, disc,
floor model 1,100.00

Perophone, disc, large black
outside horn 350.00

Regina Hexaphone, coin-
operated, 6 cylinder positions 6,200.00

Sonora, Chippendale, console,
wood arm 850.00

Standard Phonograph Com-
pany, Model X, black bell
horn, all original 450.00

Victor C, front mount, metal
top, concert reproducer,
brass bell 900.00

Victor D, fancy oak case, wood
horn, EX original 1,200.00

Victor E, front mount, complete, original 750.00

Victor II, humpback 640.00

Victor IV, small mahogany
horn, refinished 1,100.00

Victor Jr, small black bell
horn, all original 650.00

Victor MS, front mount all
brass horn, concert
reproducer 1,450.00

Victor R, front mount, EX . 600.00

Victor Schoolhouse, no horn,
early version, EX 950.00

Victor V, 24" 11 petal nickel
plated horn, 1908 ...... 1,200.00

Victor VV50, suitcase, wood . 150.00

Victrola, style 16, flared,
upright 185.00

Zonophone, glass sides 2,000.00

Photographica

Early cameras and the images
they produced are today becoming
popular collectors' items. The earliest
type of image was the daguerrotype,
made with the use of a copper plate
and silver salts; ambrotypes followed,
produced by the wet-plate process on
glass negatives. Tintypes were from
the same era as the ambrotype, but
were developed on japanned iron, and
were much more durable. Size, subject
matter, esthetics, and condition help
determine value. Stereo cards, viewing
devices, albums, photographs, and
advertising memorabilia featuring
camera equipment are included in this
area of collecting.

Albumen print, Niagara Falls,
close-up shot, in frame,
16x19" 350.00

Ambrotype, 6th plate, family
of nine, boy with sailboat,
cased 125.00

Bank, cast iron in shape of box
Brownie, 1903 .... 325.00

Camera, AGFA Clipper Special, $15.00.

Camera, AGFA Clipper
Special 15.00
Camera, AGFA Karat Model
12 .... 20.00
Camera, Air King, 120 film,
with built-in radio 115.00
Camera, Ansco Automatic,
motor driven, 2x2″ roll film 240.00
Camera, Argus C-3 Range-
finder 35, circa 1941 .... 20.00
Camera, Balda, 35mm, 1950s 30.00
Camera, Bell & Howell 127
Electric Eye, 1960s 15.00
Camera, Brownie #1 Improv-
ed, original carton with
Brownies 85.00
Camera, Brownie #2, 120 roll
film, in Brownie box, 1901 110.00
Camera, Burke & James #3
REXO, Jr 24.00
Camera, Ciroflex TLR, circa
1950 .... 35.00
Camera, Eastman Kodak #4,
circa 1907 .... 20.00
Camera, Ebner, German-made
in late 1920s, 120 folder,
rare 115.00
Camera, Flexaret TLR,
Czechoslovakia 50.00
Camera, Graflex, Home Por-
trait, revolving back 150.00
Camera, Guthe & Thorsche,
Germany, Praktina II .. 130.00

Camera, ICA, Dresden, Ger-
many, Delta, double exten-
sion 45.00
Camera, Kalart, press camera
with lens & shutter 160.00
Camera, Kalimar Aires V .. 50.00
Camera, Kodak Petite 175.00
Camera, Kodak Vallenda .. 40.00
Camera, Leader, Japanese
made, plastic body, stereo,
1950s 45.00
Camera, Mycro, Sanwa Co,
with filters, tripod, 25 rolls
of film, MIB 65.00
Camera, National Color
Camera, multiple filters,
Goerz lens, 1930s 245.00
Camera, Polaroid 110-A, with
range-finder, 1950s 75.00
Camera, Rolleicord 1A, twin-
lens reflex, Art Deco, 1929,
with case 100.00
Camera, Tom Thumb, radio-
camera, 1940 .... 130.00
Camera, Universal Radio
Cameradio, 127 film, top-
mount reflex viewer 100.00
Camera, Voigtlander Superb,
twin-lens, horizontal film
transport, 1930 .... 150.00
Camera, Zeiss Ikon Contessa
35 .... 160.00
Camera, Zeiss Miroflex, 9x12
cm, no lens 30.00
Carte de visite, Confederate
soldier, full-length view . 45.00
Carte de visite, fireman, in red
shirt with gold badge ... 45.00
Carte de visite, James Garfield, profile, VG 9.00
Chromotrope, counter-
rotating lantern slide set
with 12 discs, 1880s 245.00
Cigarette card, camera
shaped, lady's face in
center of camera 22.00
Daguerreotype, 6th plate,
pretty girl, hair in long
ringlets, tinted 60.00

Camera, Kodak Super Six, $750.00.

Daguerreotype, 9th plate, gent in large bow tie, Beard's Institution	95.00
Fan, Austin Bump advertising, Victorian design, circa 1909	35.00
Lantern slide, mechanical, 'Snow Storm'	85.00
Midget Movies, 'Reel Movie Show', cardboard box, crank for flip books	125.00
Stereo view, California, Dam on Caspar River, Soule #1102	22.50
Stereo view, lady photographer in long skirt, HC White #701	25.00
Stereo view, Oregon, 3 views, Buchtel & Stolte	15.00
Stereo view, Red River Trail, Indian portraits, Martin .	55.00
Stereo view, Shooting Wen-Ga-Rah (Ducks), Bennett #275	55.00

Stereo view, 4th of July parade, Ryder's Gallery .	35.00
Tintype, half plate, St Bernard, mat & preserver, EX	48.00
Tintype, 4th plate, boy with drum decorated with 13-star flag, tinted	50.00
Tintype, 6th plate, Union soldier, bayonetted rifle, tinted, half case	145.00
Viewer, Graphoscope, burled & inlaid wood, stereo lenses	285.00
Viewer, magnifies carte de visites, wood with ebonized accents	135.00
Viewer, NY Stereoscopic Co, leather covered Brewster style	145.00

Pickard

When first founded in Chicago in 1897, the Pickard China Company was merely a decorating studio. Because they imported blanks from European firms such as T&V Limoges, Noritake, and Haviland, you may find the manufacturer's backstamp alongside Pickard's. Much of their ware was decorated with hand painted fruits, florals, and scenics, often signed by the artist. By the late 1930s, Pickard had developed their own formula for a fine china body, and began producing their own blanks. Today they are located in Antioch, Illinois.

Bowl, berries decor, open handles, 8″	130.00
Bowl, gold with colorful flowers, 14″	550.00
Cake plate, gold rim & handles, 3-color roses, signed Seidel, 1898	152.00
Candlesticks, Aura Argenta Linear, signed OP, early circle mark, 5″	167.00
Charger, raspberries, scalloped gold border, 1894-04 mark, 12½″	186.00

Left to right: toothpick holder, match holder, gold with pine cones, either piece worth about $20.00.

Coffee set, Aura Argenta Linear, gold & silver, signed, 3 piece 327.00
Creamer & sugar, Art Deco, violets, signed FC, 1905, Limoges 226.00
Dish, square with bamboo corners, allover gold etched florals, small 42.00
Dresser set, tray, hair receiver, scent bottle, pin tray, florals 175.00
Nappy, currants decor, 8″ . 96.50
Perfume, cream with pink flowers outlined in gold, gold stopper 105.00
Pitcher, Aura Argenta Linear, signed Podlaha, 8″ 200.00
Pitcher, florals in blue & tan, black bands, gold, signed Hessler, 8″ 285.00
Plate, multi-florals, gold reserve, floral center, signed, 9″ 85.00
Relish, gold center with band of fruits, signed Schoner, 1900, 8¾″ 126.50

Salt & pepper, currants decor, pair 42.50
Sugar bowl, allover gold etched florals 35.00
Tankard, Dutch girl decor, artist signed, 8½″ 135.00
Tazza, allover gold etched florals 37.00
Teapot, allover gold etched florals 90.00
Vase, harbor scene, signed Sgiltori, 1898, 7″ 253.00
Vase, wide scenic shoulder band, artist signed, 1912, 9¾″ 180.00

Pickle Castors

A popular table accessory during the Victorian era, pickle castors consisted of a fancy silver plated frame with a glass insert, either pressed pattern glass or art glass, and tongs or a pickle fork.

Beatty Rib, blue opalescent, with silver plated holder . 225.00
Cane & Fan on clear insert, silver plated fancy frame with tongs 100.00
Cranberry, enamel florals .. 285.00
Cranberry, Inverted Thumbprint, Middletown frame with tongs 225.00
Daisy & Button, apple green with silver plated holder . 185.00
Diamond, clear, large, ornate silver 11″ frame & tongs . 85.00
Diamond Quilt, blue mother of pearl, with silver trim .. 275.00
Elk Medallion, with tongs, rare 177.00
Floral etched clear, in Reed & Barton frame, leaves & flowers, tongs 97.00
Frosted glass, silver plated frame with claw tongs .. 75.00
Panel & Groove insert, blue, trimmed frame with tongs & lid 157.00

Paneled Cane & Stars, with plated frame 92.00

Paneled Sprig, cranberry & clear, with silver plated holder 240.00

Peachblow, butterfly & flowers 350.00

Pigeon blood, Torquay, original footed frame & tongs, EX 277.50

Rubena, Inverted Thumbprint, with tongs, silver plated lid 165.00

Ruby insert, Meriden, ornate frame with cut-out birds, 14″ 125.00

Stork in Bushes, Webster tongs 75.00

Swirl, pink satin, in Pairpoint frame 213.00

Swirl, rose-mauve cased, NE glass insert, excellent silver plate 255.00

Pickle castor, aquamarine swirl insert, Rogers frame, 12½″, $220.00.

Pin-back Buttons

Most of the advertising buttons prior to the 1920s were made of celluloid; these are called 'cellos.' Many were issued in sets on related topics. Some buttons had paper inserts on the back that identified the company or the product they were advertising. After the 1920s, lithographed metal buttons were produced -- these are referred to as 'lithos.' Political buttons are listed in the section called Campaign Collectibles.

Aircraft Warning Service Volunteer Observer, red plane on white 4.00

Arcade Hook & Ladder Co, with torch, axe, hoist & ladder 20.00

Balloon route trolley trip, Pacific Electric, 1¼″ ... 20.00

Boy Sout, celluloid & metal, scout in campaign hat, 1925 .... 15.00

Buffalo Cocoa Creams, celluloid, patented 1894, 1½″ 8.00

Buster Brown 17.00

Clean Up Week, Dutch Cleanser girl, 1930s 5.00

Dairy Air Rifles 5.00

Downflake Donuts 5.00

Effanbee Dolls 5.00

Elvis, flasher type, dated 1956, 2½″ 4.50

Ford, 1949 .... 5.00

Gold Dust Twins, celluloid, ¾″ 10.00

Grapenuts, Roy's (Rogers) Boots 50.00

Greek War Relief, WWI, black insignia on white 4.00

Indian Motorcycle, with Indian head, ⅞″ 20.00

Merchants Biscuit Company, celluloid, ¾″ 10.00

Mickey Mantle, full color, 1950s, 3″ 7.50

Left to right: Blue Ribbon Doughnuts; Chevrolet, Watch the Leader; Drink More Milk; Palmer Method Writing; each worth from $1.00 to $5.00.

Pep, comic character, complete set of 86, 1942-45	385.00
Peters Ammunition, with cartridge, ⅞″	28.00
Rainbow Route through Colorado, 1¼″	15.00
Remember the Maine, with battleship, patented 1896	10.00
Santa bust, surrounded by holly, 1¼″	22.00
Shirley Temple, picture on green, 1¼″	25.00
Spirit of St Louis, Lindbergh with flags, multicolor, 1½″	20.00
Studebaker	5.00
Sweet Caperal Tobacco, name on back, multicolor illustrator art decor	15.00
Ted Williams, Boston Red Sox, 1940s, 1¼″	5.00
Toledo Springless Scales, 1¾″	12.00
US flag, 48 stars, flag on white, 1930s	3.00
USO, WWI	4.00
Welcome Home Slim Lindy, pictures Lindy with plane, 1½″	20.00
Winchester	25.00
Wool Soap, celluloid, ¾″	10.00
Yellow Kid, 1896, 1¼″	20.00

Pink Pigs

Made in Germany, these amusing pigs and piglets are portrayed driving a roadster, sitting in a suitcase, bowling, beside the feeding trough, or typing on a typewriter. While some figurines are easy to find, others are scarce and may bring prices in excess of $100.00.

Pink Pig barometer, 4½″, $125.00.

Beside pocketbook, souvenir, marked Germany	45.00
Beside rust Boston Bean pot, bisque	46.00
Facing typewriter, marked Germany	91.00
In green suitcase looking through binoculars	51.00

In polk, off to market	76.00	Alarm clock, Lux, Mr Peanut	45.00
Looking out of commode	41.00	Belt buckle	10.00
Public Telephone Call Office Engaged, top opens, 4″	39.00	Jar, Barrel, all original	200.00
		Jar, Clipper	65.00
Sitting by green hat match holder, 2x3″	75.00	Jar, Fish Bowl, with label & original lid, large	105.00
Standing on back legs bowling by green fence, 4½″	112.00	Jar, Football, peanut finial lid	185.00
Standing on green horseshoe ash tray with 2 gold rings, 2x3½″	85.00	Jar, Four Corner, large blown-out peanuts on each	245.00
		Jar, Leap Year, tin lid in excellent condition, 1940	50.00
Two in front of inverted hat	45.00	Jar, Octagon, Pennant 5¢ Salted Peanuts, 12″	85.00
Two sitting in open suitcase, gold trim	75.00	Jar, Octagon with T label	125.00
		Jar, round, frosted, original lid	45.00

Planters Peanuts

Since 1916 Mr. Peanut has represented the Planters Peanuts Company. Today he has his own fan club of collectors who specialize in this area of advertising memorabilia. More than fifteen styles of the glass display jars were made; the earliest was issued in 1926 and is referred to as the 'pennant' jar. The rarest of them all is the 'football' jar from the early '30s. Premiums such as glass and metal paperweights, pens, and pencils were distributed in the late 1930s; after the war, plastic items were offered.

Jar, six sides, yellow transfer 85.00
Jar, square, 1934 70.00
Jar, Streamline, original lid 45.00

Counter display bowl, $20.00.

Salt and pepper shakers, plastic figurals, large size, $8.00.

Plastic nut vending machine, $35.00.

Knife & fork, Mr Peanut,
Carlton silver plate, pair . 30.00
Letter opener, enameled ... 120.00
Mr Peanut, plastic windup
walker 125.00
Peanut butter grinder, Mr
Peanut 15.00
Pocket knife 20.00
Scoop, tin, 5¢ 95.00
Shakers, ceramic, pair 50.00
Tin, Jumbo Bar, 10 pound . 50.00
Wrist watch 75.00

Postcards

The first postcards were printed in Austria in 1869, but it was the Columbian Exposition in 1893 that started the postcard craze that swept the country for years to come. Today's collectors tend to specialize in cards of a particular theme or by a favorite illustrator. Among the famous artists whose work you may find are Rose O'Neill, Philip Bouileau, Alphonse Mucha, and John Winsch.

Adolph Hitler, signed
Schindler, printed in Germany, G 45.00
Advertising, Autocar Company, Ardmore, Pennsylvania 12.50
Advertising, Coffee Culture,
set of 16, unused, EX .. 32.00
Advertising, Swift's Butterine, national girls, airships, 1910 .... 14.00
Advertising, Walkover Shoes,
set of 9, in delft, unused,
EX 27.00
Alligator border, Ramble & Cove, Palm Beach, Florida,
#8520, Langsdorf....... 24.00
Bathing Beauties, On the
Beach, embossed, 1909,
Taggert Company, #25 .. 8.00
Bouileau, Philip; Blue Ribbon,
#294 .... 18.00
Bouileau, Philip; My Big Brother, older girl hugging younger boy 17.00

Halloween postcards, Jack-O'-Lantern with verse, $7.00; Jack-O'-Lantern with elves, $10.00; Witch, cat, owl, and duck, $10.00.

Bouileau, Philip; The Dreamy Hour, #824 . . . . 20.00

Boy Scouts, Guarding Sleeping Baby, signed Fred Spurgin, #445, color 12.00

Brooklyn Bridge, three panel fold-out souvenir, Underhill, 1906, G 5.00

Brundage, Art Series, Dutch girl, series #6374 . . . . . . 17.00

Campbell Kid, Dimples, signed Grace Dayton, VG . . 22.00

Chief Sitting Bull, #3420, nicely embossed, signed Peterson, Tammen 8.00

Clappsaddle, Christmas, 2 children in pajamas yawning, Wolfe Company 15.00

Clappsaddle, Valentine's Day, mechanical, kaleidoscope heart, G 23.00

Coins, gold & silver from Belgium, heavy embossing 15.00

Colby Cats & Dogs, set of 3, unused, VG 12.00

Fantasy, Street in Bern, bear vendors, bear tourists . . 12.00

Fisher, Harrison; Beauties, girl holds tiger cat 15.00

Gods & Goddesses, Apollo & the Muses, set of 10, black & white 25.00

Halloween, Schmucker lady . 35.00

Hold-to-light, child angel praying, DRGM 27.00

HSM Money Card, Russia, unused, NM 20.00

Klein, Catherine; Birthday, birds, fruit, flowers, EX . 5.00

Labor Day, Nash, G 55.00

Leap Year, Come Birdie Come to Me, S Gabriel, signed DWIG 7.00

Military, set of 6, signed Wall, illustrated PC Company, M 30.00

Ottmat Zieher Stamp Card, Brazil, #38, unused, NM . 18.00

Panama Canal Poster Card, embossed map, unused, EX 20.00

Parrish, Maxfield; The Broadmoor, poster painting of hotel, signed 28.00

Patriotic, Canadian, 1890, unused 36.00

PFB Company, To My Valentine, 3 cherubs playing, M . 13.00

Roosevelt Bears, #1, At Home, NM 25.00

Roosevelt Bears, #18, 4th of July 10.00

Santa, 2 girls at window, Santa in gondola, Winsch 1913 15.00

Ship, RMS Carmenia, woven in silk 20.00

Shirley Temple, glossy sepia photo, Hawaiian outfit, with Buddy Ebsen 14.00

Sunbonnet Babies, Last Day of Summer, 1905 . . . . 15.00

Sunbonnet Babies, Paying Toll, signed Dixon, Ullman, copyright 1905, G 10.00

Tuck, Among The Darkies, Oilette series #9297 . . . . 7.00

Tuck, Fantasy Egg Faces: man & lady in rain, used, G 8.00

Tuck, Rulers of England, Stephen, Series #614, unused, M 15.00

US Stamp Card, flat printing, eagle & shield, unused, EX 23.50

Valentine, mechanical, boy & girl with swiveling heads, G 2.00

Washington's Birthday, portrait in wreath, Nash #9, rich color 8.00

Women's Suffrage, Campbell Art #310, unused, M . . . 32.00

WWI, Rockwell, posted, VG . 100.00

Posters

The most collectible posters are those from the early days of the circus, war posters or those with a patriotic theme, early advertising posters, or those illustrated by noted artists such as Parrish, Fisher, Flagg, and Christy. Condition is important, also consider subject matter. Foxing and fading colors, as with any print, detract from their value.

War, Uphold Our Honor, Join Army-Navy-Marines, $30.00.

Advertising, El Principal Cigars, 2 fold-out stands, paper & cardboard 50.00
Advertising, Goodyear Pathfinder, truck, 1935, 25x 36″ 190.00
Advertising, Moore's Ice Cream, giant cone, 1940s, 15x21″ 85.00
Airline, United Over San Francisco, plane over bridge, 16x21″ 150.00
Army recruiting, Hazelton illustrated, soldiers charging, 1914 . . . . 145.00
Army recruiting, I Want You, James Montgomery Flagg, 30x40″, EX 650.00

Circus, Barnum & Bailey, Jupiter the Balloon Horse, 30x40″, 1940, M 240.00
Magic, Dante--A Mystery Review, photo insets, 1930s, 11x33″ 35.00
Magic, Frederik the Great, World's Greatest Magician, 1912, 6½x19″ 20.00
Magic, Prince Karmi & His Hindoo Troupe, devils & spirits, 60x44″ 200.00
Minstrel, Apollo Club, 1889, 13x38″ 100.00
Minstrel, Bryant's, stars & stripes letters, banjo & guitar, 1869 . . . . 85.00
Minstrel, Lew Dockstater's, Al Jolson in Black face . 95.00
Minstrel, Uncle Tom's Cabin, scenes from play, 1895, 20x28″, EX 72.00
Minstrel, Vogel's, man in Black face, 1903, 28x40″ . 325.00
Political, G McGovern, '72 Yes!, portrait, heavy stock, 23x23″, EX 7.00
Political, This Home is for Hoover, window poster, 1928, 8x12″ 17.50
Railroad, Night Freight, Condor Locomotive, British Railroad, 1946 . . . . 225.00

Red Cross, Christmas Roll Call, color lithograph, December 16/23, 28″ . . . 15.00
Theatrical, A Modern Cinderella, Ackermann, man & chorus line, 1900s . 75.00
Theatrical, Ben Hur, Klaw & Erlanger Production, 1904, 20x30″, M 75.00
Theatrical, Biggest Little Show on Earth, vaudeville act, 9x13″, 1932 . . . . 14.00
Theatrical, Fantasies of 1929, Vaudeville Burlesque, 28x40″ 125.00

Minstrel, Al Jolson, Lew Dockstater's, $100.00.

Theatrical, Jesse James, Missouri Outlaw, scene from play, 1890, 45″ ... 125.00

Travel, Denmark, Bendix illustrated, cyclists in country, 39x25″ 85.00

War, A Careless Word, A Needless Loss, sailor on the beach, AO Fisher 35.00

War, Attack, Attack, Attack- -Buy War Bonds, 28x40″, VG 47.50

War, Award for Careless Talk, hand with Iron Cross, 20x30″, EX 85.00

War, Be Patriotic, Columbia with out-stretched arms, 20x30″ 85.00

War, Become A Nurse, Your Country Needs You, Uncle Sam, 20x30″ 50.00

War, Columbia Calls, 1916, 30x40″ 195.00

War, E-E-E-Yah Yip, Go Over with the Marines, Falls, 20x30″, M 75.00

War, He's Home Over There, Herter, 41x28″, EX 30.00

War, I Want My Daddy Back, Daugherty 26.00

War, Let's Go Get 'Em, marines in jungle, 1942, 28x40″ 100.00

War, Look Who's Listening, rat-like Big 3, Seagram's Distilling 50.00

War, They Shall Not Perish, Douglas Volk, 40x28″, EX 75.00

War, 2nd Liberty Loan of 1917, American Lithograph Company, 34x46″ . 90.00

World's Fair, Penn Railroad, 24x40″ 200.00

Theatrical, Miss Billie Burke, The Runaway, $40.00.

Powder Horns and Flasks

Although of interest mainly to collectors of antique firearms, powder horns with scrimshawed decoration are admired by many and evaluated by

Powder horn, copper with brass cap and loops, B.A. Paris, 6½″, $75.00.

the workmanship of the artist. They were used to store the black powder and shot used to fire primitive weapons.

Flask, Batty, eagle, clasped hands, US in shield, 1854, 7½″	250.00
Flask, copper, with dispenser, G&JW Hawksley, Sheffield, 7″	65.00
Flask, copper, 13 stars, eagle & shield, garland, crossed swords, 4″	85.00
Flask, Dixon, measures to 4½ drams	65.00
Horn, brass cap, carved top, 8″	40.00
Horn, copper & brass, James Dixon Sons, 7x2½″	255.00
Horn, engraved eagle, shield, ship, primitive, 1870, 6½″	105.00
Horn, engraved Nov 1823, 5¾″	40.00
Horn, wood horn shape with silver spout, leather covered, 24″ long	50.00

Primitives

From the early days of our country until the industrial revolution of the latter 1800s, tools, utensils, furniture and even toys were made almost entirely by hand from readily available materials. Even factory-made items were finished by carvers, smithies, and other artisans who augmented the basic work of the machine with their handiwork. Primitives are evaluated by age, condition, workmanship, uniqueness of form, and desire to own.

Agitator, used to break up sugar in barrel, patented 1886, 14″	50.00
Bed warmer, copper, engraved birds flying, turned walnut handle	210.00
Bed warmer, copper with florals, 12″ diameter, 32″ wood handle	150.00
Bill holder, iron, wall hanging, fancy	13.00
Box, hanging; poplar, crest with side ears, painted, no lid, 16″ wide	135.00
Box, knife; pine, 2 section, turned handle, old paint, 9x14″	50.00
Box, knife; 2 section, scalloped sides, heart cut-out handle, 9x14″	135.00
Box, spice, hanging; 8 drawer, inset porcelain knobs, wire nails	105.00

Butter press, stand & level, signed Nesbit, patented 1879 .... 80.00

Candle box, hanging; pine, scalloped edges, worn repaint, 12½" 80.00

Candle mold, 1 tube, single handle, hanging type ... 80.00

Candle mold, 18 tube, repaired, 10½" 155.00

Candle mold, 2 tube, tin, 1 handle, hanging type ... 75.00

Candle mold, 36 tube, tin, double handles, 12" 200.00

Candle mold, 4 tube, tin, round base & top, 10¾" . 72.00

Cheese press, heavy mortised frame, adjustable lever, old red, 52" 95.00

Cheese strainer, punched tin, heart shape, 13½x5¾x6" . 125.00

Churn, Dazey, 3 quart 41.00

Clothes washing stick, wood with metal turned-up prongs on bottom 15.00

Bee smoker, tin with leather bellows, $35.00.

Corn grater, wood & hand punched curved tin on 17x5" board 62.00

Curd knife, pistol grip handle, 1 piece hand carved wood, 25" 75.00

Dough box, pine, turned legs, old green paint, 17x46x27" 350.00

Candle box, dovetailed construction, 9½" x 12", $100.00.

Dough scraper, iron, 3½"
wide 25.00

Feather bed fluffer, wood,
carved decor, 21" 145.00

Fly cover, screen wire, small . 36.00

Foot warmer, carpet covered,
The Clark Heater, 12" .. 20.00

Foot warmer, tin with pierced
sides, soapstone top,
4x5x10" 52.00

Hatchel, iron on wood base,
6x27½" 18.00

Ice tongs, chain handle 14.00

Kraut cutter, decorative cut-
out circle top, adjusts,
8x21" 36.00

Kraut cutter, poplar, good
detail with cut-out heart,
7x20" 165.00

Noise maker, wood, 16" long . 25.00

Pie rack, wire, holds 4 pies . 35.00

Pine sap bucket, lap banded,
14" 58.00

Quilt rack, walnut, accordion
folding, 8 bars, 45" 76.00

Quilting frame, folding base, 8
foot long 15.00

Roaster, tin, with handle, 2
rows hooks, drip pan ... 195.00

Salamander, iron with long
handle, spade end, 1830 . 65.00

Scouring box, walnut, pumice
kept in top, lower section
slants 40.00

Skimmer, sheet brass bowl,
wrought iron handle, 20"
long 55.00

Stone stomper, wood, wrought
iron, for road building, 1860 26.00

Taster, wrought iron & copper, hanging hook, 10" long 110.00

Tool carrier, pine, 4 sections,
center curved handle ... 33.00

Towel bar, green paint over
original blue, mortised, pin
joints, 24" 295.00

Washboard, all wood, Na-
tional Washboard Com-
pany 61.00

Washboard, National #801,
23½x12½" 15.00

Wick trimmer, iron scissors,
6" 25.00

Wick trimmer, scissors, iron
with tin tray 35.00

Prints

Prints, as with any article of collectible ephemera, are susceptible to certain types of damage. Staining and foxing (brown spots caused by microscopic mold) are usually present to some extent, and should be weighed against the desirability of the print. Margin tears may be acceptable if the print is a rare one, but avoid tears that affect the image itself. If margins have been trimmed to less than ¾", the value is considerably lowered.

Currier and Ives

Amelia, N Currier, small folio   60.00

American Fruit Piece, large
folio 1,500.00

American Homestead, Winter,
small folio 500.00

April Shower, medium folio . 150.00

Battle of Fair Oaks, Virginia,
large folio 500.00

Battle of Williamsburg,
Virginia, large folio 500.00

Bouquet of Roses, small folio . 80.00

Brush for the Lead, large folio,
G 1,000.00

Cottage Life, Summer,
medium folio 200.00

Dawn of Love, small folio . 45.00

Death of Stonewall Jackson,
small folio 75.00

Dotty Dimple, small folio .. 70.00

English Winter Scene, small
folio 275.00

Father's Pride, small folio . 55.00

First Ride, small folio 50.00

Frontier Lake, small folio .. 175.00

George Washington, black &
white, small folio 60.00

Grand Horse St Julien, King
of Trotters, small folio .. 250.00
Great West, small folio 700.00
Haunted Castle, small folio . 85.00
High Bridge at Harlem, New
York, small folio 400.00
Home in the Country, medium
folio 400.00
In the Mountains, small folio . 200.00
Julia, small folio 50.00
Life of a Fireman, Night
Alarm, N Currier, large
folio 1,850.00
Lincoln Family, black & white,
small folio 75.00
Little Brothers, small folio . 70.00
Little Playfellow, N Currier,
small folio 50.00
Maiden Rock, Mississippi
River, small folio 300.00
Mammoth Iron Steamship
Laviathan, small folio .. 225.00
Martha Washington, black &
white, small folio 50.00
My Three White Kitties, small
folio 75.00
Niagara Falls from the
Canada Side, small folio . 150.00
Old Ruins, small folio 100.00
Race on the Mississippi,
Steamboats Eagle &
Diana, small folio 350.00
Roadside Cottage, medium
folio 350.00
Rural Lake, medium folio .. 325.00
Saratoga Springs, small folio . 180.00
Scene on the Susquehanna,
small folio 250.00
Season of Joy, small folio . 80.00
Soldier's Memorial, small folio 95.00
Squirrel Shooting, small folio 375.00
Storming Stony Point, black
& white, medium folio .. 25.00
Sunny Side, Residence of Late
Washington Irving, large
folio 700.00
Surrender of Port Hudson,
Louisianna, July 8th, 1863,
small folio 175.00

A Crack Trotter, medium folio,
margins trimmed, $535.00.

Tick, Tick, Tickle!, small folio 50.00
Trotters on the Snow, small
folio 500.00
Washington, First in War,
First in Peace, N Currier,
small folio 65.00
Woodcock Shooting, N Cur-
rier, large folio 3,000.00
Year After Marriage,
Mother's Jewel, small folio 50.00
Young Cavalier, N Currier,
small folio 50.00

Plaza de Toros, #228 of 250, signed in
pencil, Salvador Dali, 29½" x 21",
$420.00.

Questionable Companionship, wood engraving published in Harper's Weekly after Frederick Remington, $50.00.

Fisher, Harrison; book, American Beauties 185.00

Fox, R Atkinson; Loves Paradise 38.00

Gutmann, Bessie Pease; Awakening 18.00

Icart, Louis; Blue Butterflies, oval, signed, circa 1922, 19½x14" 550.00

Icart, Louis; Green Screen, stamped, foxed, 1928, Paris, framed 220.00

Icart, Louis; Two Women & Monkey, signed, 1922 FH Bresler, framed 385.00

Kurz & Allison, Battle of Nashville, large folio . . .   150.00

Kurz & Allison, Landing of Columbus, large folio . . .   130.00

Nutting, Wallace; Bonny Dale, framed, 9½x7" . . .   35.00

Nutting, Wallace; Peep at the Hills, in frame, 9x4" 35.00

Nutting, Wallace; Westfield Water, in frame, 13x5" .   35.00

Parrish, Maxfield; Arizona, original frame 45.00

Parrish, Maxfield; Christmas card, Evening #2 . . . .   7.50

Parrish, Maxfield; Daybreak, original frame, 22x34" . .   210.00

Autumn Shadows, Whitetail Deer, by Neelon, 23" x 17", $50.00.

Parrish, Maxfield; Evening, original frame, 14x17" . .   100.00

Parrish, Maxfield; Jell-O ad, Polly Put the Kettle On, in frame, 6x8" 35.00

Parrish, Maxfield; Sing a Song of Sixpence, original frame, 6x11" 42.00

Prang, Louis; Bay of Annapolis, Nova Scotia, small folio 165.00

Prang, Louis; Dog's Head II, 11½x9" 20.00

Prang, Louis; Pansies, 7½x10½" 15.00

Purses

From the late 1800s until well into the 1930s, beaded and metal mesh purses were popular fashion accessories. Flat envelope styles were favored in the twenties, and bags featuring tassels or fringe were in vogue. Enameled mesh bags were popular in the late twenties and into the thirties, decorated in Art Deco designs with stripes, birds, or flowers. Whiting and Davis, and the Mandalian Manufacturing Company were two of the most important manufacturers.

Beaded, allover beading, drawstring closure, 8½x4½" 35.00

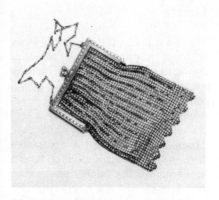

Mesh with alternating pink, black, and yellow vertical stripes, 6″, $35.00.

Beaded, checkerboard effect, blue, green, white, fringe, Czech, 7x9″ 70.00

Beaded, diamond shape, fringe, gold, 6¾x12″ 80.00

Beaded, hexagonal shape, 3 red roses, 3 tassels, 6¼x10″ 65.00

Beaded, iridescent navy clutch, 'diamonds' in ball closure 40.00

Beaded, mountain village scene, sterling frame, 7x12″ 225.00

Beaded, ribbon drawstring, openwork beading, 4½x13″ 35.00

Beaded, tapestry, castle, 6x8¼″ 85.00

Beaded, white with cream stripes, gold washed frame, 5x7″ 35.00

Chain mesh, with compact built into outside frame, sliding handle 35.00

Chiffon with white beading, embroidered flowers 25.00

Crochet flowers, allover metal beads, Metro Bag World, Paris 125.00

Enameled, turquoise border with white center & flowers, 2½x2½″ 50.00

Envelope, white sequin & pearls, 9x5″ 18.00

Faille, Art Nouveau metal cupids in panel, 4½x5½″ . 35.00

Mesh, Art Deco, yellow & black with spider, Whiting Davis 65.00

Mesh, flower center, V bottom, fringe, Mandalian, 3½x6½″ 45.00

Mesh, flowers in diamonds, green, Whiting & Davis, 4½x7″ 65.00

Mesh, rabbit foot shape, chain handle, Whiting & Davis, 1½x3½″ 25.00

Mesh, round with inside mirror & decorative handle, Armor 40.00

Mesh, sterling, ball drops, signed, 3½x2″ 42.00

Tapestry, with courting couple & sheep, jeweled frame, 7¼x8¼″ 200.00

Velvet, black with facing figural crayfish frame, Germany, 9½x9″ 150.00

Velvet, white with beaded front, peacock in design . 45.00

Victorian, jet beaded, twisted bead fringe 30.00

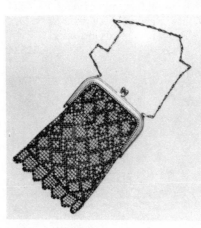

Mesh with black and white diamond patterns, 6″, $42.50.

Puzzles

Of most interest to collectors of vintage puzzles are those made of wood or plywood, especially the early hand cut examples, or those that are character related or have a special interest theme.

Battleship, Parker Brothers	145.00
Dissected Animals, sheep & goat, 1900s, original box	35.00
Down on the Farm, 300 combinations, in box, 11x 8½"	65.00
Fallowfield Hunt, wood, 141 pieces	45.00
Hood's Sarsaparilla, Rainy Day, advertising, 10x15"	95.00
Locomotive, 1900, with original box	65.00
Ocean liner, McLoughlin, professionally framed, cover on reverse, 1896	175.00
Railroad & County Map of New York, hand tinted, 1887, 13x17"	95.00
Victorian scenes with children, wooden, 5 in original wooden box	165.00
Wear Kenreign Raincoat, original box, advertising	45.00
White Sewing Machines & Bicycles, advertising, 12½x16"	125.00

Map of USA, heavy pressed cardboard, in original box, $15.00.

Quilts

The appreciation of quilting as an art form and the popularity of 'country' antiques have in recent months caused an increase in the sale of quilts; and prices, especially on the finer examples, have risen dramatically. There are several basic types of quilts: (1) appliqued: having the decorative devices applied onto a solid top fabric; (2) pieced: having smaller pieces that have been cut out in a specific pattern, then stitched together to form the quilt top; (3) crazy quilts: made by stitching pieces of various sizes and shapes together following no orderly design; (4) trapunto: devised by stitching the outline of the design through two layers of fabric, one very loosely woven, and inserting padding into the design through openings made by separating the loose fibers of the underneath fabric. Condition of a quilt is important; intricacy of pattern, good color composition, and craftsmanship contribute to its value. These factors are of prime concern whether evaluating vintage quilts or those of more contemporary artists.

Amish

Child's, blue on black, all wool, fine quilting	800.00
Crazy quilt, embroidered, multicolor flowers, 1930s	2,750.00
Crib, tree of life in center with tulip quilted border	170.00
Johnny in the Corner in Garden Maze, never washed	375.00
Nine Patch, cotton with vegetable dyes, some fading	440.00
Picture Frame, plain center, fine quilting, EX	250.00
Tumbling Blocks in green, navy & peach, unused, 80x92"	520.00

Amish quilt, shades of blue, lavender, black, gray, tan and brown, hand quilted ocean waves and tulips, machine stitched binding, initialed, 71″ x 82″, $550.00.

Appliqued

Butterflies applied with black
    embroidery, 1920s **75.00**
Floral design, pieced pink &
    green calico, 82x84″ **215.00**
Floral devices with diamond
    centers & flowers at points,
    74x90″ **185.00**
Flowers in solid colors, central
    bouquet, scalloped **350.00**
Hawaiian, red on white, swag
    with tassel border, early,
    84x65″ **475.00**
Oak Leaf, elaborate quilting,
    88″, EX **500.00**
Poppies with leaves in each
    corner & center, recent, M .   **375.00**
Tree of Life, dark yellow on
    white, 90½x88″ **750.00**

Pieced

Cake Stand, diagonal blocks,
    muslins, 57x82″ **225.00**
Crazy, mostly wool with fea-
    ther stitch, wool batting, G   **100.00**
Friendship Ring, 1932 . . . .   **100.00**
Grandmother's Flower Gar-
    den, scalloped border, ca
    1930s **235.00**
Pinwheels, red and white,
    74x90″ **450.00**
Rail Fence, old calicos, red &
    green with brown back,
    never washed **285.00**
Star design, all calico, 68x78″   **135.00**
Star of Bethlehem, EX **300.00**
Texas Stars, multicolored
    with red star centers within
    hexagons **165.00**

Trapunto

Block-type pattern, yellow on white with floral embroidery 150.00
Cherries with applied leaves, red, white & green, EX . 2,000.00
Leaves in border with pineapples in diamonds on pieced top 325.00
Mamie Rowe, red & white with florals, Texas, 1850s, 80x82" 400.00
Pinwheel within double wreaths, vintage, floral & pineapple, 86" 600.00
Tulip, cream, lavender & green, 70x85" 210.00

Radios

Collectors of vintage radios are especially interested in those made from the twenties through the fifties by companies such as RCA, Atwater Kent, Philco, and Crosley, though those produced by the smaller manufacturers are collectible as well. Cathedral and breadboard styles are popular, so are Art Deco styles and those with a unique type of speaker, power source, or cabinet.

AC Dayton XL20 .... 85.00
Atwater Kent, L Horn, radio speaker 50.00
Atwater Kent #10 Breadboard, with tubes 425.00
B Kennedy #5, exposed tubes on slant front panel 235.00
Chelsea Super Five, 3 dial TRF 175.00
Crosley #51, 3 tube portable . 125.00
Crosley VI, EX 145.00
Emerson #504, wood case .. 55.00
Federal Jr, crystal, with earphones 180.00
Freed Eisemann NR-7, EX . 75.00
Freshman Masterpiece, inside speaker 95.00

Jubilee, crystal, NM 100.00
Pearson, 3 dial, TRF 65.00
Philco #18, cathedral 195.00
Philco #45 .... 30.00
Radiola #1325-US, radio speaker 70.00
Radiola #17 .... 40.00
Radiola #20 .... 95.00
Radiola III 65.00
RCA Victor #224, 6-legged console 160.00
Sparton #79, console 75.00
Standardyne, 3 window dials . 65.00
Transamerica, 3 dial TRF . 87.50
Westinghouse, RA-DA, 3 tube 200.00
Zenith #75-633R 35.00

Railroadiana

Memorabilia relating to the more than 175 different railway companies that once transversed this great country of ours represents one of the largest and most popular areas of collecting today. Because the field is so varied, many collectors prefer to specialize. Lanterns, badges, advertising, dinnerware, silver, timetables, locks, and tools are only a sampling of the many types of relics they treasure.

Some enjoy toy trains, prints showing old locomotives -- in short, virtually anything that in any way represents the rapidly disappearing railway system is of value.

Dinnerware

Ash tray, George Washington, Buffalo, side mark, C&O, 7x3" 85.00
Bowl, cereal; Mimbreno, bottom stamp, ATSF, 7" .. 85.00
Bowl, Glory of the West, bottom stamp, GN, 6" 40.00
Celery dish, Centennial, oval, B&O RR 35.00
Creamer, Calumet, top mark, Pullman, 8 ounce 80.00
Cup & saucer, demitasse; Violets & Daisies, CB&O . 55.00

Cup & saucer, Lamberton Scammell, bottom stamp, B&O 85.00

Grapefruit dish, Desert Flower, bottom stamp, UPRR, M 17.00

Plate, Adobe, bottom stamp, ATSF, salad size, EX .. 40.00

Plate, Aristocrat, CB&Q, dinner size, average wear .. 160.00

Plate, Challenger, UPRR, salad size, EX 20.00

Plate, Galatea, no bottom stamp, Milwaukee Ry, 9″, EX 60.00

Plate, Peach Blossom, bottom stamp, Southern Ry, 10½″ 90.00

Platter, Prospector, D&RGW, 9″, M 40.00

Platter, Syracuse, top mark Eagle, bottom stamp, T&P, 12x8½″ 165.00

Platter, top logo, OSL Railway, 9″, VG 300.00

Saucer, coffee; Galatea, no bottom stamp, Milwaukee, NM 25.00

Soup, Prospector, wide flange, D&RGW, 7″, M 32.00

Teapot, Hall, cobalt with gold, buzz saw logo, MoPac .. 145.00

Underliner, Harriman Blue, bottom stamp, UPRR, 7″ . 15.00

Silver Flatware

Fork, condiment; stainless, bottom stamp, Rock Island, 6″ 15.00

Fork, dinner; Broadway, top mark, GM&O 17.50

Fork, dinner; Dartmouth, top mark, IC 18.00

Fork, oyster; Savoy, UPRR . 5.00

Fork, pickle; Dartmouth, top mark, IC 18.00

Knife, dinner; Broadway, top mark, CM St P&P 15.00

Knife, dinner; Elmwood, top mark, MK&T 15.00

Knife, dinner; International, #1 Century, SR 8.00

Knife, dinner; Savoy, UPRR . 4.00

Ladle, Century, top mark, NYC 25.00

Spoon, grapefruit; CM St P&P 20.00

Spoon, ice cream; Harrison & Howson Brothers, top mark, Fred Harvey 20.00

Spoon, serving; Savoy, UPRR 6.00

Spoon, soup; Dartmouth, top mark, IC 18.00

Spoon, table; Belmont, CB&Q 10.00

Spoon, table; Zephyr, Seaboard 8.00

Spoon, teaspoon; Cromwell, Fred Harvey 18.00

Spoon, teaspoon; Cromwell, 1912, Seaboard 15.00

Spoon, teaspoon; MCRR .. 20.00

Spoon, teaspoon; Westfield, 1903, UPRR 18.00

Silver Hollow Ware

Bouillon cup, Oriental, GN Ry, M 40.00

Coffee pot, International, bottom stamp, 1950, NYC . 75.00

Creamer, International, maple leaf logo, Canadian National, 4 ounce 60.00

Ice cream dish, International, 1951, UPRR 35.00

Menu holder, bottom stamp, half-moon shape, Deco stripes, footed, CZ 50.00

Platter, Gorham, bottom stamp, 1892 mark, C&EI . 100.00

Sugar bowl, Oriental, GN Ry, M 80.00

Sugar tongs, Empire by International, 1921, MoPac .. 65.00

Teapot, Reed & Barton, bottom stamp, dated 1947, UPRR, 1 pint 90.00

Toothpick holder, International, side mark, 1951, GN 45.00

Minnesota and International Moose-head cap badge, $75.00.

Miscellaneous

Ash tray, floor standing, Burlington	250.00
Berth lamp, brass, bulb in door lid, patented July 5, 1904, pair	150.00
Book, Rates & Rules, 1915, Virginian RW	15.00
Caboose lamp, wall, metal, Adams & Westlake, 10″ chimney	35.00
Calendar, perpetual, picture of steam train, MoPac	75.00
Cap badge, older, Roman lettering, Freight Conductor	9.00
Cap badge, ornate, silver with black, Vandalia/Baggage Master	95.00
Cap badge, standard, old, silver with black, C&O Ry	20.00
Catalog, Morton Company RR Parts, illustrated, 1927	50.00
Dater machine, Hill's Model A, UP System & Bancroft, IDA, restored	95.00
Engineer's oiler, tin, base mark, painted, N&W Ry	20.00
General lock, iron ET Fraim with numbered key, CCC & St L	30.00
Globe, clear cast, MP, 5⅜″	35.00
Journal gauge, Pratt & Whitney	5.00
Kerosene can, GN Ry	10.00
Lantern, A&W Adams, 5⅜″ clear globe, 1909, C&A RR, EX	75.00
Lantern, Adlake Kero, large lettering, red etched globe, N&W Ry	35.00
Lantern, Adlake 200 Kero, circle on dome, clear globe, B&O RR	35.00
Lantern, Dietz Vesta, red globe, 1954, GM&O RR, M	45.00
Lantern, Dresell, 3¼″ clear globe, PC, EX	27.00
Lantern, Handlan, 5⅜″ clear globe, painted, CM & St P Ry, VG	52.00
Lantern, inspector's; Dietz heavy iron body, Rock Island Lines	85.00
Letter opener, Route of the Great Big Baked Potato, bronze, NP	35.00
Magazine, Railway Age, 1920s	4.00
Mail bag lock, US Mail, for canvas mail bags, steel, no key	15.00
Match safe, Katy logo shape, cast iron, MKT	150.00
Newspaper, Rock Island 'Western Trail', 4 pages, 1887	15.00
Paperweight, Albert Lea Route, metal medallion, 1890s, BC R&N	50.00
Pass, eagles & flags, 1865, Chicago & Alton RR	45.00
Pencil, mechanical; Missouri-Ill	7.00
Pin, blue enamel on gold, Loyal Member 40 year service, B of LE	19.00
Pin, shield shape with blue stone in 10 karat gold, UP logo	22.50
Playing cards, double, used, Norfolk & Western	20.00
Playing cards, single deck, GM&O	12.00

Route checks, left to right: Baltimore and Ohio, with capitol dome, 1½" x 2¼", $30.00; Philadelphia and Reading, 1½" x 2¼", $30.00.

Scales, counter-top, ornate, 50 pound, Chatillion Express, VG 85.00

Sign, Package Received Here, double-sided porcelain, REA 150.00

Signal lock, brass padlock, marked Signal Dept, flat key, N&W Ry 15.00

Spittoon, standard style, re-painted, cast iron, N&W . 85.00

Steam whistle, brass, ornate finial, 14x3" diameter .. 75.00

Stepbox, Morton Company, top mark, painted, restor-ed, Pullman 125.00

Switch key, brass, circa 1900, DM&N RR, A&W, pocket wear 45.00

Switch key, Fraim, serial number, brass, 1950s, GN Ry 18.00

Switch key, long barrel, ser-vice number, FS/Keystone, B&O, worn 17.50

Switch lamp, Adlake, round top, glass lens, snow hoods, B&O RR 125.00

Switch lock, brass heart with key, CN RR, EX 35.00

Switch lock, iron heart, Bo-hannon, marked Slaymaker key, B&M RR 50.00

Switch lock, iron with chain, marked brass key, NC & St L Ry 35.00

Tallow pot, tin, B&O 15.00

Timetable, cut-out train, Harlem Extension, May 29, 1871 .... 65.00

Wheel coupler gauge, steel, Pratt & Whitney, 2½x5" . 9.00

Razors

Straight razors are prized for their beautifully decorated blades and handles, often portraying nudes, animals, scenes, or slogans popular at the time of their manufacture. Values are determined by assessing the blade style, pattern of the handle, and manu-facturer's mark. Corn razors, used to remove corns from the feet, are also collectible. An approximate manufac-ture date may be arrived at through study of the various types of blades. Those made before the 19th century were crude wedge shaped affairs that evolved through many improvements in shape as well as material to the fully hollow ground blades of the 1880s.

Blue Steel on stand, faux ivory with metal inlay ends	15.00
Boker & Company, Germany, black plastic tang	16.00
Challenge, fancy handle, straight	20.00
Collins Safety Razor, round head with ornate lined case, M	140.00
Curtin & Clark, imitation ivory with raised windmill, trees & boat	27.00
Electric Cutlery Company, celluloid with raised geometrics on 2 sides	25.00
ERN, checkered black handle with shield in relief	20.00
G Baker & Sons, celluloid with raised windmill and boat, etched blade	70.00
Genco DeRoma, faux ivory handle with metal inlay ends	16.00
Geraldus, faux ivory, Made in Sheffield	18.00
Henkel Corn Razor, slightly rounded with pearl handle, EX	54.00
Hub Corn Razor, Hub on blade, imitation ivory handle, EX	25.00

Claus Fremont, #11902, mother-of-pearl inlay in black handle, $15.00.

Imperial Razor Warranted, early auto & driver etched on blade	35.00
Jermania Cutlery Works, Germany, Oxford razor	10.00
Joseph Hollinger, faux ivory handle, Sheffield	16.00
Keen Kutter, #44	18.00
Krusius Brothers, black fancy carved handle	17.00
LE Champion, Switzerland, Qualite Garantie, Ad Abrenz	16.00
Nowill & Sons, Sheffield, glossy ivory handle, 1860s	21.00
Rector & Wilhelmy Company, XX Clean Clipper	12.00
Robeson Shuredge, black handle with relief decor, pair	36.00
Simmons Hardware Company, USA, Keen Kutter-Blue Steel	24.00
Southington, celluloid, red flowers, nude holds robe	36.00
Tonsorial, Sheffield Steel	10.00
Tony, yellow with 3 violin players inlaid in metal	15.00
Valentine & Yule, Chicago, #311	12.00
Wade & Butcher, Sheffield, By All the World Approved	20.00
Wade & Butcher, Sheffield, horse & wagon etched on blade	62.00
Wagner, Silver Steel, Germany, white celluloid	16.00

Corn razor, Centaur, etched blade, black celluloid handle, 5½″ open, with box, $10.00.

Waterville Cutlery, celluloid with fully-scrolled raised pattern 12.00

WM Gilchrist, Razor Steel . 11.00

Worchester Razor Company, Red Tobacco 12.00

Yankee Cutlery Company, Germany, Lion Brand .. 10.00

Yankee Magnetized, celluloid, relief nude with long hair on lily pad 52.00

Reamers

Though made for the simple task of extracting citrus juices, reamers may be found in fanciful figurals as well as the simple utilitarian styles. You may find even wood or metal examples, but the most popular with collectors are those made of glass and ceramics. Fry, Hazel Atlas, Hocking, Jeanette, and McKee are among the largest producers of the glass reamer, some of which (depending on color and rarity) may bring prices well into the hundreds of dollars.

Beswick, lemon figural 48.00

California Fruit Growers, Sunkist, crystal 18.00

Cambridge, crystal 15.00

Clown, ceramic, light yellow, 7" 35.00

Cottage, ceramic 45.00

Duck, ceramic yellow lustre . 35.00

Federal, amber, lemon reamer 18.00

Federal, pink ribbed with loop handle 20.00

Fleur-de-Lis, red slag with loop handle 250.00

Floral, 2 piece ceramic pitcher & reamer with tumblers, 7¾" 45.00

Fry, embossed, ruffled top, opalescent, loop handle . 33.00

Fry, embossed, straight sides, vaseline 125.00

Good Morning, 2 piece ceramic pitcher with reamer top 25.00

Hazel Atlas, cobalt, crisscross, orange reamer with loop handle 145.00

Hazel Atlas, cobalt, 2 cup measure with reamer ... 200.00

Hocking, blue, 1 piece orange reamer 375.00

Hocking, flashed-on black, ribbed with loop handle, orange reamer 10.00

Left to right: Cat face, made in Japan, 5½", $42.00; Happy face, made in Japan, 5", $35.00.

Hocking, green frosted 30.00
Japan, with matching ceramic
  pitcher, panels & florals . 18.00
Japan, 2 piece ceramic toby . 85.00
Jeannette, Jennyware, ultra-
  marine, loop handle 55.00
Jeannette, light jadite, tab
  handle, large 12.00
Jenkins Glass Company, short
  with tab handle 50.00
McKee, caramel opalescent . 375.00
McKee, custard, footed, em-
  bossed McK, small 30.00
McKee, green opaque, grape-
  fruit reamer 140.00
McKee, opaque yellow,
  Sunkist 42.50
Orange, ceramic figural with
  white top, 2 piece 45.00
Paden City, pink 110.00
Pear, ceramic, 3 piece 25.00
Servmor, US Glass, green . 50.00
Sunflower, jadite, 2 cup
  measure 30.00
Sunkist, pink 32.00
Valencia, green, EX 100.00
Vitrock white, orange reamer 12.00

Records

Records that made it to the 'Top
Ten' in their day are not the records
that are prized by today's collectors,
though they treasure those few which
best represent specific types of music:
jazz, rhythm and blues, country and
western, rock and roll, etc. Instead
they search for those cut very early in
the career of artists who later became
super stars, records cut on rare or interesting labels, or those aimed at
ethnic groups.

Alabama Jug Band, My Gal
  Sal, Decca, #7000 ...... 10.00
All-Star Orchestra, Add A Lit-
  tle Wiggle, Victor, #21423 . 8.50
Andrews, Ed; Barrel House
  Blues, Okeh, #8137 ..... 12.50

Arcadian Serenaders, The Co-
  Ed, Okeh, #40503 ...... 11.50
Arkansas Barefoot Boys,
  Eighth Of January, Okeh,
  #45217 .... 10.00
Arkansas Woodchopper, A
  Hard Luck Guy, Gennett,
  #7184 .... 20.00
Armstrong & Ashley, No
  More Dying, Paramount,
  #3291 .... 8.50
Atkins, Chet; In Three Dimen-
  sions, RCA Victor, #1197 . 17.50
Avalons, The; You Do
  Something To Me, Casion,
  #108 .... 17.50
Bare, Bobby; That's Where I
  Want To Be, Fraternity,
  #861 .... 5.00
Barefoot Bill, My Crime
  Blues, Columbia, #14510-D 42.50
Barnes, Walter & His Royal
  Creolians; Third Rail,
  Brunswick, #7072 ...... 30.00
Barr, Chuck & The Rockabil-
  lies; Susie Or Mary Lou,
  Elsan, #100 .... 10.00
Barry, Jeff; Lonely Lips, RCA
  Victor, #7797 .... 8.50
Beach Boys, Surfin', Candix,
  #301 .... 50.00
Beard, Dean; Party Party,
  Atlantic, #1162 .... 12.50
Beatles, All You Need Is
  Love, Capitol, DJ, #5964 . 17.50
Bee, Willie; Ramblin' Mind
  Blues, Vocalion, #03907 . 10.00
Bees, Toy Bell, Imperial,
  #5314 .... 30.00
Ben's Bad Boys, Wang Wang
  Blues, Victor, #21971 ... 10.00
Benny Benson's Orchestra,
  Honeysuckle Rose, #15932 9.50
Berry, Chuck; School Day,
  Chess, #1653, 78 rpm ... 8.50
Berry, Chuck; Sweet Little
  Sixteen, EP, Chess, #5121 . 10.00
Billy & Jesse, Put Your Mind
  On It, Brunswick, #7099 . 12.50

Black, Frankie; Wayback Blues, Champion, #50000 . 12.50

Black Boy Shine, Grey With Worry Blues, Vocalion, #03613 . . . . 12.50

Blind Blake, Skeedle Loo Doo Blues, Paramount, #12413 32.50

Blind Sammie, Razor Ball, Columbia, #14551-D 62.50

Breedlove, Jimmy; That's My Baby, Atco, #6094 . . . . . 8.50

Casanovas, That's All, Apollo, #471 . . . . 14.00

Cash, Johnny; Hey Porter, Sun, #221 . . . . 6.50

Cash, Johnny; I Walk The Line, Sun, #241 . . . . 4.00

Cats & The Fiddle, I Miss You So, RCA Victor, #50-0077 . 12.50

Chancellors, I'm Comin' Home, XYZ, #104 . . . . . . 6.50

Coon Hollow Boys, Coon Hollow Boys At The Still, Champion, #15748 . . . . . 12.50

Cox & Henson, National Blues, Champion, #16694 . 25.00

Cramer Brothers, Simpson County, Broadway, #8180 . 12.50

Crawford, Alvin; I Sit Broken Hearted, Superior, #2528 . 25.00

Crosby, Bing; Here Lies Love, Brunswick, #6406 . . . . . . 8.50

Crosby, Bing; Home On The Range, Brunswick, #6663 . 6.50

Crosby, Bing; Paradise, Brunswick, #6285 . . . . 8.50

Davis, Walter; Easy Goin' Mama, Bluebird, #7551 . 10.00

Davis, Walter; Moonlight Blues, Bluebird, #5192 . . 17.50

Delta Boys, Black Gal Swing, Bluebird, #8852 . . . . 14.00

Dickson, Tom; Worry Blues, Okeh, #8570 . . . . 50.00

Dixie Boys, I've Found A New Baby, Champion, #15227 . 62.50

Dixie Mountaineers, Hop Light Ladies, Edison, #52057 . . . . 12.50

Dixie Washboard Band, Gimme Blues, Columbia, #14188-D 12.50

Dorsey, Tom & His Novelty Orchestra; Tiger Rag, Okeh, #41178 . . . . 10.50

Dunham, Sonny & His Orchestra; Clementine, Vogue, #775 . . . . 8.50

East Texas Serenaders, Deacon Jones, Brunswick, #298 . . . . 8.50

Ed, Macon & Tampa Joe; Tickle Britches, Okeh, #8877 . . . . 32.50

Eddie's Hot Shots, That's A Serious Thing, Victor, #38046 . . . . 25.00

Effros, Bob; Tin Ear, Brunswick, #4620 . . . . . . 6.50

Fair, Jimmie; I'll Walk Alone, Kentucky, #532 . . . . 5.50

Fiddler Joe & His Boys, Turkey In The Straw, Okeh, #45042 . . . . 7.00

Fiddlin' Jim Pate, Texas Farewell, Victor, #40170 . 12.50

Flatt, Alan & His Band; I'm Movin' On, Jamboree, #511 6.50

Fort Worth Doughboys, Nancy Jane, Bluebird, #5257 . 30.00

Four Spades, Squabblin' Blues, Columbia, #14028-D 8.50

Friars Society Orchestra, Panama, Gennett, #4968 . 17.50

Fuller, Bob; I Ain't Got Nobody, Brunswick, #7006 12.50

Gross, Helen; Strange Man, Ajax, #17050 . . . . 32.50

Hardin, Lane; Hard Time Blues, Bluebird, #6242 . . 20.00

Hatcher, Willie; They're Mean To Me, Bluebird, #8003 . 10.00

Hickory Nuts, The Louisville Burglar, Okeh, #45169 . . 8.50

Hicks, Minnie; Sweet Rider Blues, Melotone, #12549 . 40.00

Holmes, Salty; I Want My Mama, Bluebird, #5303 . 10.50

Houchins, Kenneth & Slim Cox; Tennessee Blues, Champion, #16501 ..... 25.00

Jack Albin's Orchestra, The Two Of Us, Edison, #51831 12.50

Kelly, Willie; Kelly's Special, Victor, #23259 .... 50.00

Kentucky Jug Band, Walkin' Cane Stomp, Vocalion, #1564 .... 42.50

King, Francis; She's Got It, Okeh, #40854 .... 8.50

King Brady's Clarinet Band, Lazybones Blues, Gennett, #6393 .... 35.00

Lawrence, Sara; Don't Love Me, Oriole, #894 .... 8.50

Lee, Bessie; Sorrowful Blues, Silvertone, #3534 ...... 17.50

Lee, Johnny; I Came To See You Baby, Deluxe, #6009 . 6.50

Lee's Black Diamonds, Piggly Wiggly Blues, Broadway, #1294 .... 30.00

Little Richard, Good Golly, Miss Molly, 78 rpm, Specialty, #624 .... 10.50

Little Richard, Jenny, Jenny, Specialty, #606 .... 5.50

Little Richard, Tutti-Frutti, Specialty, #561 .... 6.50

Little Willie Littlefield, Boogie Woogie Playgirl, Eddie's, #1212 .... 8.50

Maple City Four, Roll Dem Bones, Supertone, #9193 . 6.50

Martin, Daisy; Sweet Daddy, Okeh, #8010 .... 6.50

McDonald Brothers, Poor Little Joe, Vocalion, #5406 . 10.00

McGhee, John; The Hatfield-McCoy Feud, Gennett, #6587 .... 20.00

McGinty's Oklahoma Cowboy Band, It Can't Be Done, Champion, #15446 ..... 10.00

Perkins, Dolly; My Doggone Lazy Man, Emerson, #10761 .... 10.00

Pickard Family, Down In Arkansas, Banner, #6283 . 6.50

Pickett, Dan; Chicago Blues, Gotham, #512 .... 15.00

Piedmont Melody Boys, Tell Him Now, Victor, #23660 . 17.50

Pigmeat Terry, Black Sheep Blues, Champion, #50043 . 12.50

Pleasant Family, Rabbit In The Pea Patch, Broadway, #8149 .... 6.50

Red Mike Bailey, Neck Bone Blues, Paramount, #13077 87.50

Rockin' Bradley, Look Out, Fire, #1007 .... 10.50

Tillis, Mel; Hearts of Stone, Columbia, #41026 ...... 6.50

Tillis, Mel; Teen Age Wedding, Columbia, #41115 . 6.50

Red Wing

Taking their name from the location in Minnesota where they located in the late 1870s, the Red Wing company produced a variety of wares, all of which are today considered noteworthy by pottery and dinnerware collectors. Their early stoneware lines, Cherry Band, Sponge Band (Gray Line), are especially valuable and often fetch prices of several hundred dollars on today's market. Production of dinnerware began in the thirties and lasted until the pottery closed in 1967. Some of their more popular lines -- all of which were hand painted -- were Bob White, Lexington, Tampico, Normandie, Capistrano, and Random Harvest. Commercial artware was also produced. Perhaps the ware most easily associated with Red Wing is their Brushware line, unique in its appearance and decoration. Cattails, rushes, florals, and similar nature subjects are 'carved' in relief on a stoneware type body, with a matt green wash its only finish.

Dinnerware

Black Rose Anniversary, dish, divided	12.00
Bob White, butter warmer with stand	15.00
Bob White, casserole, in copper frame, 4 quart	42.00
Bob White, cup & saucer	12.00
Bob White, pitcher, large	22.00
Bob White, plate, 10½"	8.00
Bob White, salt & pepper, tall, pair	25.00
Bob White, sugar with lid	9.00
Capistrano, platter, 13"	12.00
Damask, cup & saucer	7.00
Damask, sugar with lid	7.00
Driftwood, plate, 8"	4.00
Fondosa, batter pitcher, pink, with lid	25.00
Labrigo, French casserole	25.00
Lexington, cup & saucer	8.00
Lexington, dinner plate	8.00
Lexington, plate, 7"	5.00
Lexington Rose, cup & saucer	9.00
Lotus, bowl, 8½"	4.00
Lotus, cup	4.00
Lotus, gravy with attached plate	6.00
Lotus, plate, 6½"	3.00
Magnolia, cup & saucer	8.00
Magnolia, dinner plate	3.50
Morning Glory, plate, 10"	7.00
Normandie, cup & saucer	8.00
Orleans, bowl, 8¾"	5.00
Orleans, creamer	5.00
Orleans, teapot	12.00
Picardy, cup & saucer	6.50
Picardy, platter, well & tree, 12½"	9.00
Provincial Oomph, soup	7.00
Random Harvest, dinner plate	4.50
Random Harvest, shakers, pair	5.00
Random House, sauce	4.00
Random House, water pitcher	15.00
Tampico, creamer & sugar with lid	20.00
Tampico, dessert bowl	4.00

Normandie, dinner plate, $9.00.

Tampico, gravy	12.00
Tampico, pitcher, ice lip	24.00
Tampico, plate, 6½"	3.00

Stoneware

Batter jug, brown	65.00
Bean pot, with lid, brown glaze, Minnesota Stoneware, 8" diameter	45.00
Beater jar, no advertising, blue band	40.00
Butter jar, advertising, Moland Co-op, 5x7"	70.00
Canning jar, advertising, 2 gallons	320.00
Canning jar, 1 quart, dated 1899	95.00
Casserole, Gray Line, large	140.00
Churn, salt glaze, 4 gallons	120.00
Crock, large red wing, advertising, 1½ quart	185.00
Crock, salt glaze, 20 gallons	75.00
Ice tea cooler, 2 gallons	325.00
Jar, self drain, 5 gallons	45.00
Jar, Sponge Band with bail handle	110.00
Jug, Western, miniature	35.00
Jug, 5 gallons, large wing	35.00
Lid, for #15 crock	45.00
Pitcher, Cherry Band	40.00
Pitcher, Sponge Band, advertising, small, M	150.00

Elephant-ear churn, signed on base and stamped on front in oval 'Minnesota Stoneware Co., Red Wing, Minnesota,' $400.00.

Bowl vase, acorns & leaves, with handles, signed, Brushware 26.00
Candle holder, ivory matt, #529, pair 12.00
Christmas tree holder 295.00
Cookie jar, Chef, yellow ... 36.00
Cookie jar, Dutch girl, yellow 28.00
Cookie jar, King of Tarts .. 32.00
Cookie jar, Monk, blue 38.00
Figurine, Spanish dancers, 10″, pair 65.00
Jug, Commemorative, #5 .. 35.00
Mug, Hamm's Krug Klub . 65.00
Pitcher, black, #2315, 9″ .. 25.00
Planter, #11687 .... 7.00
Shoe, black, miniature 65.00
Umbrella stand, Brushware . 80.00
Urn, large, Brushware 90.00
Vase, fan flared, green, #416-12 .... 25.00
Vase, floral sprays, signed Union Stoneware, Brushware, 11″ 55.00

Reamer, Sponge Band 240.00
Rolling pin, flowers, original handles, with Minnesota advertising, M 225.00
Rolling pin, orange band, advertising 140.00
Salt crock, Sponge Band, advertising, dated 1934, hairline 300.00
Salt shaker, Sponge Band, rare, M 250.00
Water cooler, with lid, wing mark, 5 gallon 200.00
Water cooler, 6 gallon 165.00

Miscellaneous

Advertising card, Union Stoneware 135.00
Ash tray, Red Wing, wing shape, 7″ 40.00
Bookends, polar bears, gray, pair 60.00

Vase, brown glaze with cactus decoration and handles, 8½″, $22.00.

Redware

Simple utilitarian ware made from easily accessible deposits of red clay was a staple of the early American settlers. Though available throughout the country, it was utilized to the fullest extent in Pennsylvania, Ohio, and southern Appalachia. Occasionally yellow slip was used to add decorations of straight or wavy lines, or simple outlines of birds or tulips. Value is determined by size and form, age, decoration, and condition.

Bank, unglazed bell form, 4¾" 30.00
Bowl, dough mixing; original slate top, 11x22" 175.00
Bowl, 4 line yellow slip, 13½" 350.00
Charger, Breininger, sgraffito lady on horse, 1976, 12½" 85.00
Churn, allover cream slip with green spotting, 17" 45.00
Cookie mold, bunch of grapes, unglazed, 4" long 55.00
Crock, black glaze, 7" 35.00
Cuspidor, Morganville, New Jersey, speckled tan glaze, 3½x8½" 65.00
Dish, clear glaze with bittersweet color, 7¾" diameter 65.00
Dish, green-amber mottled, 3½" 45.00

Flask, tooled base with blackish-brown glaze, 6½" 45.00
Jar, apple butter; glazed within, 6½" 35.00
Jar, green-brown mottled, 2" . 210.00
Jar, ovoid with blackish-brown glaze, 12½" 40.00
Lighting stand, incised straight & wavy line, green with drips, 4" 340.00
Loaf pan, 3 line slip decor with coggled edge, 17" 425.00
Pie plate, clear glaze with dots of yellow, coggled rim, 9" . 95.00
Pie plate, swirled yellow slip, coggled edge, 9¼" 300.00
Pitcher, applied rosettes & incised design, 9" 250.00
Plate, coggled edge, 3 line yellow slip decor, 9" 200.00
Plate, slip decorated, 9" ... 125.00
Plate, 2 color tulip, yellow, green, brown, 8" 850.00
Porringer, green with brown sponge, 3¾x4x5" 115.00
Pot, impressed Henshaw Motor Company, interior glaze, 3" 18.00
Puzzle jug, sgraffito flowers & foliage, 'R+C pusle pot, 1884' 45.00
Tray, crosshatching on yellow slip, 11x14" 495.00
Urn, double handle, small . 45.00

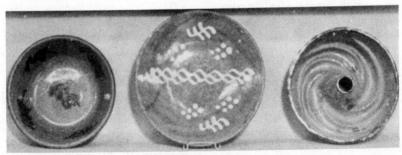

Left to right: bowl, clear glazed interior with brown splotches, 3" x 8¼", $50.00; pie plate, crows feet and dots in yellow slip, coggled edge, 9¾", $275.00; Turk's head food mold, swirled design, clear glaze with daubs of black on rim, 4½" x 8", $85.00.

Left to right: Dish, 11½″, $125.00; dish, 9½″, $70.00; dish, beaded rim, 12½″, $150.00.

Rockingham

A type of utilitarian ware favored in America from the early 1800s until after the 1920s, Rockingham is easily identified by its mottled brown sponged-on glaze. While some items are simple and unadorned, many are molded with high relief designs of animals, vines, leaves, cherubs, and human forms. Figural hound handles are often found on pitchers. Some of the finest examples of Rockingham was made at the Vermont potteries of Norton and Fenton, and you may find ill-informed dealers and collectors that mistakenly refer to this ware as 'Bennington.' However, hundreds of potteries produced goods of a very similar appearance; and proper identification of the manufacturer is often difficult, if not impossible.

Bank, book figural, 1840 .. 60.00
Bank, pig, embossed initials
  'JA', 5½″ 30.00
Cake mold, 9½″ 65.00
Creamer, beaded rim band,
  4½″ 45.00
Crock, with cover, 8x5″ ... 65.00
Cup, 2¾″ 85.00
Cuspidor, embossed shell top,
  8″ diameter 30.00
Cuspidor, marked Pruden, 9″ 95.00

Dish, oval, plain, 5½x8″ ... 35.00
Inkwell, seated dog on oval
  base, 5½″ 275.00
Jar, embossed leaves & vines,
  small handle flake, 1½″ . 45.00
Mixing bowl, rib pattern, base
  wear, 4½″ 85.00
Mold, Turk's head, 10½″
  diameter 85.00
Mug, vertical ribs, 3″ 55.00
Mug, 2 handles, woman &
  smoking man in relief, frog
  inside, 6½″ 225.00
Pie plate, small surface flakes,
  10½″ diameter 75.00
Pitcher, blackberry, American
  Pottery Company, 1860s,
  6″ 65.00
Pitcher, embossed neck band,
  7½″ 60.00
Platter, octagonal, small glaze
  imperfection, 15″ 225.00
Platter, oval, 13½″ 150.00
Stove support, bust of lady, 5″ 235.00
Teapot, Rebecca at the Well,
  6½″ 75.00
Wash bowl, 12 sides, flakes on
  rim & foot, 4x12¾″ 85.00

Rockwell, Norman

His first *Saturday Evening Post* cover was published in 1916; launching him on a lifetime career. He became famous for his ability to portray through his illustrations keen insight and understanding of the American way of life. In addition to his magazine covers, he illustrated advertisements and sheet music. All are highly collectible. Modern applications of his original art -- collector plates, figurines, Christmas ornaments, etc. -- are also valued.

Saturday Evening Post cover, January 13, 1962, $14.00.

Ad, Post Bran Flakes, 1920s .	6.00
Bell, Leapfrog, 6½", 1980 .	50.00
Blotter, American Oil, 1939 .	15.00
Calendar, Scout's Memories, 1931	50.00
Calendar top, Boy Scouts of America, 11x17", 1938 ..	12.50
Figurine, At the Doctors, 5½", 1978	112.00
Figurine, Dreams of Long Ago, 6", 1979	100.00
Figurine, Drum for Tommy, 6¾", 1976	62.00
Figurine, God Rest Ye Merry Gentlemen, Gorham	1,200.00
Figurine, Huckleberry Finn Secret, 5¼"	110.00
Figurine, Lazybones, Grossman	225.00
Figurine, Lighthouse Keeper's Daughter	50.00
Figurine, Love Letter, Grossman	45.00
Figurine, Schoolmaster, Grossman	225.00
Figurine, Schoolmaster, miniature, 4", 1979	34.00
Figurine, The Cobbler, Rockwell Museum	65.00
Figurine, Young Artist, Rockwell Club, Grossman, 1981	95.00
Magazine, American Boy, December, 1916	21.00
Magazine, Country Gentleman, July 31, 1920	18.00
Magazine, Jack & Jill, December, 1974	3.00
Magazine, Saturday Evening Post, October 8, 1938, EX	10.00
Movie poster, Stagecoach, 27x41", 1966	40.00
Ornament, Drum for Tommy, Saturday Evening Post, 1921 cover date	30.00
Print, Four Seasons, Autumn, 20x21"	1,500.00
Print, Marriage License, signed, 19x25"	500.00
Print, School Days, Baseball, 20x26"	1,850.00
Print, See America First, 17x24"	4,200.00
Sheet music, Over There ..	17.50
Spoon, Back to School, pewter, 6¾"	35.00
Stein, Four Seasons, Pride of Parenthood, 8", 1976 ...	70.00
Stein, Looking Out to Sea, Rockwell Museum, First Edition	150.00
Thimble, Going Steady, china, 1980	7.50
Tray, Ben Franklin, 12x14", 1975	13.00
Tray, Coca-Cola Company, 10½x13"	175.00

Rookwood

Fine art pottery was produced by the Rookwood Pottery Company, established in Cincinnati, Ohio, in 1879 by Maria Longworth Nichols Storer. Though it is not at all impossible to find examples of the early art lines at flea markets, the type most often encountered is their mass-production vases, bookends, paperweights, etc., made after the turn of the century, machine molded and relying upon in-mold details for their decorations. The company was faithful in marking their wares -- the most familiar mark is the reverse R and P device with the flame points above it. First used in 1886, each flame represents the succeeding years up to 1900. Roman numerals were used in addition to the flames from that time on. Early artware lines are judged and evaluated by scarcity of line and finesse of the artwork involved.

Figurine, blue and gray bird, 6337 XLVI, 5″, $120.00.

Advertising sign, 1915, Rookwood Soft Porcelain in floral square 330.00

Bookends, 1944, rooks, white matt, McDonald 100.00

Bowl, Jewell Porcelain, 1916, lavender, 2¾x6½″ 90.00

Bowl, Standard, 1889, floral, signed HEW, 2x5″ 210.00

Bowl, Standard, 1893, yellow floral, S Markland, 2x4″ . 160.00

Bud vase, Standard, 1889, crocus, Ed Diers, 7″ 285.00

Bud vase, Wax Matt, pink with yellow & green florals, #2307, 7¼″ 195.00

Bust of Madonna, Iris, 1959, #6949, 10″ 295.00

Candlestick, 1934, elephant figurals, black, green gloss, 4″, pair 80.00

Cigarette box, 1944, green gloss, florals, designed by KS, #6856 .... 55.00

Creamer, Iris, clover, Sara Sax, 'X' 135.00

Ewer, Sea Green, 1882, panels of fish, Harriet Wenderoth, 11¾″ 1,150.00

Ewer, Standard, lilac decor, signed ARB/L, #387, 14½″ 900.00

Ewer, Standard, 1899, orange floral, L Lincoln, 11″ ... 375.00

Figurine, cock pheasant, K Shirayamadani, #2832, 9x16″ 880.00

Flower frog, turtle, 1930, turquoise matt, signed KS, #2994 .... 150.00

Honey jug, 1883, reeds, birds, gold, red clay, M Rettig, 5″ 400.00

Jar, 1949, 'Nuts' in relief, blue gloss, hexagonal, 5x5″ .. 50.00

Jug, Limoges, 1883, black bird on brown glaze, impressed 360/R, 4¾″ 150.00

Jug, 1884, bisque, top handle, 2 spouts, reeds, butterflies, ARV, 9″ 1,300.00

Paperweight, 1933, squirrel,
yellow, white matt, S
Toohey, 4¼" 110.00

Paperweight, 1941, duck,
green gloss 60.00

Pitcher, Standard, 1896,
floral, C Steinle, 4½" ... 200.00

Pitcher, 1887, blue gloss with
white florals, ARV,
hairline, 7" 275.00

Plaque, Vellum, 1915, An
April Day, M Denzler, 9x5" 850.00

Plaque, Vellum, 1915, landscape with tall trees, signed,
8¾x11" 440.00

Platter, Iris, 1926, blue sailing
ship, 12" 195.00

Ash tray/paperweight, Devil's head,
3½" x 6", $75.00.

Ramekin, Limoges, 1883,
birds fly over marsh, AR
Valentien 325.00

Rose bowl, 1922, geometric
florals band on black, SS,
#1927, 4" 350.00

Teapot, Standard, yellow rose,
signed CS, #77 .... 420.00

Teapot, 1923, lobed, gray clay,
blue with white floral, Epply, 6" 675.00

Tray, Matt, 1922, brown,
leaves, acorns, rook,
2½x10½" 100.00

Tray, 1935, flower on rim,
orange glaze, 3½" 50.00

Trivet, 1922, grape clusters,
twining vines, 3 colors,
5¾" square 80.00

Vase, Incised Matt, 1920,
rust, green, red flowers,
Lincoln, 5½" 140.00

Vase, Iris, 1902, florals, excellent art, Ed Diers, 7" . 900.00

Vase, Iris, 1903, light green to
olive, crocus, CCl, #925,
6½" 500.00

Vase, Sea Green, 1894, school
of fish, ARV, #568C, 7" . 2,000.00

Vase, Sea Green, 1899, florals
by Sallie Toohey, #762/C,
5½" 700.00

Vase, Standard, 1896, pansy
decor, L Lincoln, 5" 280.00

Vase, Standard, 1899, autumn
leaves, Ed Hurley, #657C,
8x4" 595.00

Vase, Standard, 1900, florals,
K Hickman, 7" 375.00

Vase, Vellum, 1915, trees,
Lorinda Epply, #808, 8" . 595.00

Vase, Vellum, 1919, dark blue
scenic, Ed Diers, 7" 550.00

Vase, Vellum, 1919, scenic, excellent art, signed E, 14x8" 1,550.00

Vase, Vellum, 1922, scenic
with trees, Sally Coyne,
9¾" 1,100.00

Vase, Wax Matt, 1922, floral
decor, MH McDonald, 6" . 270.00

Vase, Wax Matt, 1926, blue,
ovoid, L Abel, 4¾" 220.00

Wall pocket, 1930, green high
glaze, cone shape, 8" ... 60.00

Rose Medallion

A lovely pattern of dinnerware
first exported from China in the early
1800s, Rose Medallion is decorated in
a rose pallate with figures, butterflies,
and florals within paneled reserves. It
sold well into the 20th century, and is

evaluated by age, condition, form, and color. Early examples were sometimes decorated with gold or heavily reticulated. Such items bring premium prices.

Basket, with tray, each piece reticulated, 4x10½"; 9½ x11" 625.00
Bowl, deep, Made in China, 7½" 75.00
Bowl, fruit; footed oval, genre center, 1840, 3½x14½" . 525.00
Candlestick, 8½" 245.00
Charger, 12" 150.00
Creamer, bulbous, circa 1800 . 195.00
Creamer, late, 4¼" 65.00
Cup & saucer, hexagonal, China 40.00
Dish, triangular, orange peel glaze, small flakes, 7½ x10¾" 100.00
Jar, no mark, with lid, 2¼" . 115.00
Plate, Made in China, 7½" . 45.00
Plate, 9½" 55.00
Platter, circa 1800, 11x8½" . 650.00
Punch bowl, four reserves of ladies & attendants in garden, late, 16" 650.00
Sugar, with lid, bulbous, no mark, 4½" 135.00
Teapot, bulbous, no mark, 7" . 300.00
Tureen with tray, early 1800s, tray 14½" long 2,600.00
Umbrella jar, family vignettes, insects, flowers, 1800s, 24" 1,000.00
Vase, applied gilded dragons & lions, 12" 200.00

Rosemeade

Novelty items made by the Whapeton Pottery Company of North Dakota from 1941 to 1960 are finding an interested following among collectors of American pottery. Though smaller items (salt and pepper shakers, figurines, trays, etc.) are readily found, the larger examples represent a challenge to collectors who prize them highly. The name of the novelty ware, 'Rosemeade,' is indicated on the paper labels, (many of which are still intact), or by the ink stamp.

Figurine, buffalo, 3" 35.00
Planter, double parakeets .. 15.00
Planter, swan figural, 5" .. 8.00
Tray, relief mouse in center, maroon glaze, small 15.00
Vase, lovebirds, blue & pink glaze, 6" 20.00
Wall pocket, figural deer, light pink glaze, 5x3¼" 20.00

Black bear salt and pepper shakers, Rosemeade label, $12.00, pair.

Roseville

Founded by George Young in 1892, the Roseville Pottery Company produced quality artware, utility ware, and commercial artware of the finest quality until they closed in the 1950s. Of the major American potteries, Roseville's production pieces are among the finest, and it is a rare flea market that will not yield several excellent examples from the 'middle period.' Some of the early artware lines require perseverance to acquire, while others such as their standard brown-glazed 'Rozane' is easy to locate. During the twenties and thirties they produced several lines of children's serving dishes decorated with Santa Claus, chicks, rabbits in jackets, Sunbonnet Babies, and various other characters, which are today treasured by their own band of devotees. While many pieces of Roseville are marked with some form of the company name, others that originally had paper labels are otherwise unmarked. Careful study of Roseville lines may result in your finding one of the few bargains left at the flea market today.

Apple Blossom, bookends, blue, pair	85.00
Apple Blossom, jardiniere, #302-8″	115.00
Apple Blossom, teapot	75.00
Artwood, planter, #1055-9″	30.00
Aztec, vase, tan, waisted with flared rim, 11″	300.00
Azurean, tankard, Dutch scene, 14″	1,350.00
Baneda, jardiniere, green, 4x5½″	65.00
Baneda, vase, small handle each side of neck, green, 9¼″	95.00

Dutch mug, 4″, $60.00.

Bittersweet, basket, #808-6″, green	45.00
Bittersweet, wall pocket, gray	52.00
Blackberry, bowl, oval, 13″	185.00
Blackberry, vase, straight top half, round bottom, side handles, 5″	125.00
Bleeding Heart, basket, 12″	110.00
Burmese, bookends, figural, green, pair	150.00
Bushberry, ash tray	65.00
Bushberry, bowl, #657-3″	30.00
Bushberry, vase, 10″	75.00
Carnelian I, urn, 7″	45.00
Carnelian II, urn, low angled bulge, large fancy handles, 8″	60.00
Cherry Blossom, bowl, 4x5½″	135.00
Cherry Blossom, jardiniere, brown, 4″	95.00
Cherry Blossom, jug vase, 6″	110.00
Cherry Blossom, vase, 12″	250.00
Chloron, vase, Art Nouveau style, relief berries, scroll handles, 9″	325.00
Clemana, bowl, #281-5, 4½″	65.00
Clematis, candlestick, #1159-4½″, pair	38.00
Clematis, ewer, #18	125.00
Clematis, vase, #110-10″, brown	52.00
Clematis, wall pocket, 8″	55.00
Columbine, basket, 12″	95.00
Columbine, bowl, #402-8″, tan	35.00
Columbine, vase, #22-9″, tan	52.00
Corinthian, vase, 8″	45.00
Cosmos, wall pocket, double	75.00
Creamware, ash tray, seascape scene, Fatima shape	120.00
Creamware, candlestick, Good Night, shield back	285.00
Creamware, Mug, Cornell Jr Law Smoker, with orange decoration, 1906	75.00
Creamware, tumbler, Conventional	40.00
Cremona, candle holders, 4″, pair	40.00
Dahlrose, bowl, 10″	40.00

Iris ewer, 10½", $80.00.

Dahlrose, hanging basket .. 100.00
Dahlrose, vase, with handles,
   8" 40.00
Dawn, vase, yellow, 7" 35.00
Della Robbia, mug, band with
   Dutch children, 4" 500.00
Dogwood I, hanging basket . 95.00
Dogwood II, basket, 8x8½" . 65.00
Donatello, candlestick, 8" .. 65.00
Donatello, compote, 5" 45.00
Donatello, jardiniere &
   pedestal, 28½" 375.00
Donatello, wall pocket, 9" . 95.00
Dutch, mug, 4" 45.00
Dutch, toothbrush holder .. 45.00
Earlam, bowl, 3x11½" 42.00
Early Pitcher, boy with horn . 175.00
Early Pitcher, poppy, full
   body, cream with orange,
   9" 130.00
Egypto, inkwell, 'In Hoc
   Signo Vinces' 210.00
Elsie the Cow, mug, #B1 . 70.00
Falline, vase, egg shape with
   large ear handles, 6¼" .. 150.00

Ferella, vase, brown, 10½" . 225.00
Florane, bowl, #63-10" 29.00
Florane, wall pocket, 9" ... 68.00
Florentine, basket, cream
   background, 9" 120.00
Florentine, vase, catalog
   #232-10" 75.00
Foxglove, basket, #373-8" . 50.00
Foxglove, cornucopia, 6" .. 20.00
Foxglove, ewer, 15" 125.00
Foxglove, hanging basket . 75.00
Foxglove, vase, #659-3", pink 22.00
Freesia, basket, #390-7" ... 55.00
Freesia, bud vase, blue, bulb-
   ous base, akimbo handles,
   7¼" 20.00
Freesia, tea set 145.00
Freesia, vase, #126-10" 60.00
Fuschia, bowl, #364-4" 37.00
Fuschia, vase, #904-15" ... 135.00
Futura, candlestick, akimbo
   handles, pointed panels, 4",
   pair 155.00
Futura, hanging basket ... 140.00
Futura, vase, flat sided fan
   with rectangular rim, blue
   & green, 6" 72.50
Futura, wall pocket, overlap-
   ping angle panels, akimbo
   handles, 8½" 180.00
Gardenia, basket, #608-8",
   brown 60.00
Gardenia, jardiniere, #601-6" . 45.00
Gardenia, vase, #684-8", green 45.00
Imperial I, dish, with handle,
   2¾x6½" 24.00
Imperial II, vase, bulbous
   body, flaring with incised
   rings, 7" 150.00
Iris, vase, #929-15", blue .. 115.00
Iris, vase, rose bowl shape,
   tan, 4" 25.00
Iris, wall shelf 135.00
Ivory II, candlestick, Topeo
   shape, double, paper label,
   pair 35.00
Ixia, jardiniere, #387-6", pink 45.00
Jonquil, bowl, with attached
   frog, #89, label, 10" 120.00

Jonquil, candlesticks, catalog
#1802-4″, with label, pair . 125.00
Jonquil, vase, U-form with low
handles, 7″ 80.00
Juvenile, bowl, chicks, 5½″ . 40.00
Juvenile, cup & saucer, chicks 60.00
Juvenile, plate, Sunbonnet
Baby, flat 35.00
La Rose, bowl, low, 6″ dia. 50.00
Landscape, casserole 175.00
Laurel, vase, red, 6″ 45.00
Lombardy, wall pocket,
straight top, 8″ 185.00
Lotus, wall pocket, 7½″ ... 175.00
Luffa, console bowl with
flower frog 75.00
Luffa, jardiniere, brown, 7″ . 95.00
Luffa, vase, full body, small
akimbo rim handles, 7″ . 60.00
Magnolia, basket, #384-8″ . 50.00
Magnolia, cider pitcher 110.00
Magnolia, cornucopia, #185-
8″, tan 35.00
Magnolia, tea set, tan 145.00
Mayfair, cornucopia, #127-6″,
brown, pair 60.00
Ming Tree, basket, #508-8″,
blue 75.00
Ming Tree, ewer, #516, blue . 85.00
Ming Tree, vase, #572-6½″,
white 60.00
Mock Orange, bowl, #941-5″,
with handles 26.00
Moderne, compote, #295-5″ . 55.00
Monticello, vase, with
handles, 8½x5″ 70.00
Morning Glory, candlestick,
white, 5″, pair 110.00
Moss, bowl, #292-8″, pink . 38.00
Moss, console bowl, #293-10″ 45.00
Moss, urn vase, with handles,
#779-8″ 45.00
Mostique, planter, arrowhead,
8½x10″ 85.00
Orian, vase, tan, 7″ 60.00
Pauleo, vase, ovoid, short
neck, no decor, 9½x6½″ . 600.00
Pine Cone, candle holder, tri-
ple, brown, pair 135.00

Vintage vase, 5½″, $45.00.

Pine Cone, cornucopia,
#422-8″, brown 65.00
Poppy, jardiniere & pedestal,
large 550.00
Raymor, coffee pot, paper
label, no stand .... : 125.00
Raymor, dinner plate 12.00
Raymor, mustard, white, 3½″ 26.00
Rosecraft Black, ginger jar
with lid 180.00
Royal Capri, basket, #509-8″,
green 60.00
Rozane, jug, blackberries,
signed, wafer mark, 6″ .. 220.00
Russco, candle holder, 4½″,
pair 35.00
Silhouette, ash tray, red ... 25.00
Silhouette, basket, #710-10″,
white with green trim .. 55.00
Silhouette, candlestick, #751-
3″, white, pair 22.00
Snowberry, bookends, pair . 65.00
Snowberry, bud vase, 7″ .. 28.00
Snowberry, hanging basket,
blue, 8½″ 55.00
Sunflower, bowl, with handles,
4″ 60.00

Sunflower, vase, U-form, rim to base handles, 5″ 50.00
Sunflower, vase, with handles, black sticker, 10½″ 140.00
Teasel, vase, 2 handles, #889-15″ 125.00
Tuscany, console bowl, 15″ . 50.00
Velmoss, urn, catalog #265-6″ 60.00
Victorian Art Pottery, bowl vase, floral & beetle band, 4″ 85.00
Water Lily, basket, #381-10″ . 68.00
Water Lily, cookie jar 110.00
Water Lily, vase, #77-8″, aqua 48.00
White Rose, candle holder, pair 42.00
White Rose, teapot with lid, blue 85.00
White Rose, wall pocket, #1288-6″ 58.00
Wincraft, console bowl, #229-14″ 35.00
Wincraft, hanging basket .. 95.00
Wincraft, vase, #274-7″ ... 40.00
Wisteria, jardiniere, 5x6½″ . 75.00
Wisteria, vase, wide top, sides flare slightly, small rim handles, 8″ 90.00
Zephyr Lily, bowl, #474-8″, blue 40.00
Zephyr Lily, compote, #8-10″, blue 45.00
Zephyr Lily, jardiniere, #571-8″ 85.00

Royal Copley

Produced by the Spaulding China Company of Sebring, Ohio, Royal Copley is a line of novelty planters, vases, ash trays, and wall pockets modeled after appealing puppy dogs, lovely birds, innocent eyed children, etc. The decoration is airbrushed and underglazed; the line is of good quality and is well-received by today's pottery collectors.

Ash tray, pink bird on green flower, 5″ 4.00

Bank, rooster, 'Chicken Feed', coin slot at top of tail, 7½″ 16.00
Bud vase, yellow with parrot on branch, 5″ 5.00
Figurine, bird on apple, yellow, green & teal, 7″ . 10.00
Pitcher, daffodil 13.00
Planter, bluebird, open center 10.00
Planter, deer head, open center, 8″ 12.00
Planter, hen & rooster, original label, 8¼″ 25.00
Planter, leaf sprays in relief, chartreuse & brown, 7½″ . 8.00
Planter, mailbox with baby duck sitting underneath, 6¾″ 20.00
Planter, mallard duck, 8½″ . 15.00
Planter, ram head, 6½″ ... 9.00
Vase, cornucopia, floral decal, gold trim, 8¼″, pair 14.00
Vase, dogwood, rose on gray with brown & cocoa, 9″ . 22.50
Vase, raised ivy, 7″ 5.00
Wall pocket, brown spaniel head, signed 14.00
Wall pocket, Chinese girl .. 12.00
Wall pocket, fruit decor ... 8.00

Tanager-bird planter, 6¾″, $7.50.

Roycroft

Elbert Hubbard, whose name is familiarly associated with the Arts and Crafts movement, established a community called Roycroft in New York at the turn of the century. There, in addition to the original print shop, furniture, metal items, leather goods, and a variety of other items were made, bearing the 'R' in circle mark of the Roycrofters.

Ash tray, hammered, silver finish, 3½″	22.00
Book, Notebook of Elbert Hubbard, 1927, Roycrofters	45.00
Book, Selected Writings, Elbert Hubbard, leather, set of 14	50.00
Book rack, oak, 2 shelves with exposed tenons, shoe foot base, 27″	225.00
Bookends, hammered copper, Roycrofter's Hallmark, large, pair	50.00
Bowl, copper, 2½x4″	40.00
Bowl, hammered copper, Deco flowers in center, signed, 8″	75.00
Cake plate, Buffalo Pottery, 11″	95.00
Candlestick, single, brass finish, 7¾″, pair	95.00
Desk set, with tray, knife, frame, rolling blotter, hammered copper	135.00
Incense burner, hammered copper	45.00
Inkwell, brass cylinder with dome cover, glass insert	65.00
Letter holder, 3 part, hammered copper	40.00
Letter opener, hammered copper	30.00
Postcard	3.00
Stamp box, copper	55.00
Tray, copper, round, small	35.00
Vase, hammered copper, American Beauty, 21″	350.00
Vase, hammered copper, 8½″	150.00

Rugs, Hooked

Today recognized and admired as folk art, vintage hooked rugs as well as contemporary examples are prized for their primitive appeal, workmanship, and originality of design.

Autumn leaves, 23x36″	75.00
Clipper ship with American flag, 29x42″	125.00
Dog in barrel with playful kitten, 27x50″	200.00
Floral in oval reserve, simple, stylized, 18x36″	40.00
Geometric design, multicolor, 27x39″, EX	100.00
Horse, primitive styling, stylized background design, 1916, 18x36″	175.00
Pair of prancing horses in oval reserve, good detail, 18x22″	400.00

Stylized design with flying bird in olive with red and magenta wings, elaborate background, 32″ x 38″, $625.00.

Russel Wright Dinnerware

Dinnerware designed by one of America's top industrial engineers is today attracting the interest of many. Some of his more popular lines are American Modern, manufactured by the Steubenville Pottery Company (1939-'59), and Iroquois, introduced in 1944.

Clover Leaf pattern, Harker Ware, sugar and creamer, $24.00, pair; cup and saucer, $5.00.

American Modern, celery dish, Bean Brown 22.00

American Modern, coaster . 10.00

American Modern, coffee pot, demitasse, Black Chutney 43.00

American Modern, covered vegetable, Chartreuse Curray 18.00

American Modern, cup, Black Chutney 10.00

American Modern, lug soup . 5.00

American Modern, mug, Black Chutney 30.00

American Modern, plate, 10″ . 5.00

American Modern, salad bowl, Chartreuse Curray 16.00

American Modern, salt & pepper shakers, pair 8.50

American Modern, sherbet, stemmed 17.00

American Modern, teapot .. 38.50

American Modern, water pitcher, Black Chutney 52.00

Highlight, dinner plate 8.00

Highlight, vegetable bowl . 16.00

Iroquois, bowl, 10″ 15.00

Iroquois, covered vegetable, divided, avocado 32.00

Iroquois, creamer, stack ... 9.00

Iroquois, gumbo, nutmeg, blue, or yellow 10.00

Iroquois, plate, 9″ 6.50

Iroquois, saucer 2.00

Iroquois, shaker, stacking . 5.50

Iroquois, sugar, stacking, brown 6.00

Sterling, bouillon 7.00

Sterling, plate, 10¼″ 5.00

Sterling, plate, 9″ 4.00

Sterling, soup 8.00

Sterling, teapot 22.00

Sterling, water pitcher 25.00

Salesman's Samples

Commonplace during the late 1800s and early 20th century, salesman's samples were small scale copies of a particular product, often exact working models that enabled the salesman to demonstrate his wares to potential customers.

Axe, double-bitted, 2¾x6″, 13″ handle 45.00

Battery, lead, 'Diller, Made in Iowa' 20.00

Boiler, with wood handles, 7x5″ 50.00

Candy case, with 12 vials of
sealed candy 65.00
Chamber pot, yellowware with
white stripes, 3½" 20.00
Chest, walnut, 4 drawers, late
wire nail construction,
15x14x8" 100.00
Chest of drawers, inlaid
mahogany, bow front,
Federal, 18x19" 900.00
Chest of drawers, William &
Mary, walnut bow front,
1840, 3½", pair 935.00
Churn, with dasher & turned
top, wood burned decor,
Norwegian, 8" 105.00
Cooking set, pewter, 11 pieces
with 4 lids, largest 1¼" . 50.00
Corn cultivator, with written
documentation 150.00
Cup, pewter, footed, 1", set of
4 . . . . 10.00
Dinner pail, with coffee cup,
tin, 3x2" 60.00
Farmer's grain cradle, wood
curved tines 150.00
Flatware, knife, fork, spoon,
pewter, 4½" long 10.00
Folding table, Paris Manufac-
turing Company 75.00
Globe, mahogany, George III,
L Smith, London, 1818,
6½" 2,500.00

**Butcher block made of maple, mark-
ed 'Michigan Maple Block Co.', 6" x 7",
$85.00.**

Hat box, Stetson, with 12 hats 40.00
Meat grinder, JP Company,
New York, cast iron 25.00
Organ stool, heavy oak 110.00
Plate, pewter, 2" diameter, set
of 5 . . . . 40.00
Portage Shoes for men,
original see-through box . 20.00
Stove, Eagle, cast iron, ornate 175.00
Stove, potbelly, Spark, 13" . 110.00
Tea set, Queen Style, 2 pots,
cream & sugar, sterling,
¾" 175.00
Vice, Hollands Manufacturing
Company, cast iron 50.00
Wicker fernery 125.00

Salt Shakers

Though salt has always been a
valuable commodity, shakers as we
know them today were not used until
1863 when a patent was issued for a
mechanism capable of breaking up the
lumps of salt in a bottle. In 1901, a
method was developed that rendered
the salt less apt to absorb moisture,
and salt shakers began to be produced literally by the thousands, in
any available material -- art glass,
ceramics, wood, silver, brass, pot
metal, and plastic.

Acorn, Hobbs, Brockunier &
Company, mold blown,
black opaque 55.00
Acorn, pink to white, pair . 65.00
Barrel, vaseline, pair 20.00
Beaded Dahlia, pink, pair . . 65.00
Beehives, honey colored,
ceramic, pair 7.00
Briefcase & hat, ceramic, pair 7.00
Buckets, wooden, pair 7.00
Bulging Loop, cased in yellow,
pair 70.00
Butterfly, Eagle Glass, opales-
cent with butterflies in
relief 35.00
Christmas, electric blue, pair . 175.00

Organ grinder and lift-off monkey, ceramic, $20.00, pair.

Christmas Panel, agitator, dated lid, amber	75.00
Circle, Jefferson Glass Co, double, blue with opalescent sheen	63.00
Colonial English, McKee, pressed brilliant crystal, 3¼″	18.00
Corn, custard, pair	95.00
Cotton Bale, green opaque	19.00
Cranberry frost, in castor, pair	75.00
Curved Body, 'S'	25.00
Diamond & Star, TG Hawkes, cut crystal, 3″	38.00
Diamond Point & Leaf, white	50.00
Dice figurals, opaque glass with hand painted florals	120.00
Domino, mold blown, white opaque with black intaglio dots, 3″	78.00
Egg, Mt Washington, blue flowers	30.00
Eyewinker, blue, pair	35.00
Fan Band Double, white	15.00
Feet with faces, ceramic, pair	4.00
Fishscale	25.00
Forget-Me-Not, regular, white	27.00
Hand & Fishscale	18.00
Heart, Dithridge, mold blown, opaque, any color	56.00

Horseshoe, amber	12.00
Huggers, Dutch couple, white with blue & yellow, ceramic, pair	10.00
Jewel & Flower, clear opalescent	65.00
Leaf Mold, blue opaque, pair	85.00
Leaf Umbrella, cased in pink	45.00
Liberty Bell, original pewter top	55.00
Log cabins, pot metal, bronze colored, pair	7.00
Milk glass, fluted tubular body with spelter tops, 4″, pair	30.00
Outhouses, wooden, pair	7.00
Pineapples, wooden, pair	7.00
Quilted Phlox	19.00
Royal Oak, frosted rubena, pair	150.00
Sawtooth Bulbous, amber	22.00
Scroll, green opaque, footed	16.50
Spanish Lace, clear opalescent	45.00
Sunrise, pink opaque	22.00
Swirl Windows, cranberry opalescent	32.00

Loop and Daisy, satin glass, 2 ⅝″, $80.00, each.

Tea & coffee pot, brown ceramic, pair	5.00
Telephone & directory, ceramic, pair	7.00
Toltec	10.00
Wild Flower, amber	30.00
Wild Rose with Bow Knot	15.00
X-Ray, pair	87.00

Samplers

Samplers were designed and embroidered by very young ladies from colonial times until the late 1800s. Many signed their efforts with their names, their ages, and the date the sampler was completed. Through the application of various stitches, the less complicated examples display the alphabet, numbers, or a simple verse; but depending upon the skill and dedication of the seamstress, others depicted buildings of brick, American eagles, all sorts of animals and other birds, and complete family registers.

Vining floral border with sawtooth edging, pots of flowers, birds, panel with tree, deer and oversized bird in tree; poem 'The Day of Life', and signature and '1892' in floral wreath, 24″ x 27″, $1,325.00

Alphabet, homespun linen, dated 1819, 10x12″	135.00
Alphabets, stars, homespun, faded, in cherry frame, 10½″ square	225.00
Alphanumerics, deer, vining border, homespun, 1820, 14x17″	260.00
Alphanumerics, house, trees, vines, homespun, 1826, 19x20″	395.00
Alphanumerics, signed & dated, homespun, 1848, 9x12″	145.00
Alphanumerics, verse, schoolhouse & trees, dated 1881, 8x12½″	255.00
Building, trees, birds, animals, people, poem, in frame, 21″ square	350.00
Buildings, moralistic verse, 2 large cats, vines, 1847, 12x22″	700.00

Family record, vining border, alphabets, pine trees, 1830s	750.00
Farm scene with house, sheep, fence, birds, 1840s, 17x21″	2,090.00
Flowers, practice stitches, homespun, 8x10″	275.00
House, shepherdess, sheep, dog, squirrel, excellent detail, 1794, 20″	3,100.00
Miniature, alphanumerics & name, no frame, 7½x9½″	175.00
Needlepoint, birds, building, animals, 1855, 19x20″	550.00
Poem, floral garlands, cherubs, excellent work, homespun, 20x33″	315.00
Verse, house, animals, angels, flowers, 1845, framed, 13x17″	350.00
Verses, florals above house, vine border, 1800s, 16x13″	275.00
Windmill, cottage, trees, excellent workmanship, 1828, 14″ square	450.00

Scouting Collectibles

Founded in England in 1907 by Major General Lord Baden-Powell, scouting remains an important institution in the life of young boys and girls everywhere. Recently, scouting-related memorabilia has attracted a following, and values of many items have escalated dramatically in the last few years. Early 1st edition handbooks often bring prices of $100 and more; vintage uniforms are scarce and highly valued; and one of the rarer medals, the Life Saving Honor Medal is worth several hundred dollars to collectors.

Award, Silver World, globe with silver on blue enamel, old type 450.00

Axe & knife, combination .. 38.00

Bugle, Boy Scout, brass mouthpiece attached with chain 47.00

Calendar, 1925, Boy Scouts of America, 1st Rockwell, complete 59.00

Canteen, Girl Scout, multicolor plaid cloth over metal, MIB 15.00

Compass, pin-back, brass .. 20.00

Flag, 1950 Boy Scout Jamboree, New Jersey Troop, red & white 115.00

Handbook, For Scoutmaster, 2nd edition, 15th print, 1930, red cover 17.50

Handbook, Girl Scout, January 1932 .... 10.00

Lithographs, advertising Bordens Evaporated Milk, 1912, 10 in series 195.00

Manual, BSA Official, 1910, original edition, hard bound, VG 185.00

Medal, WWI War Savings Service, Boy Scouts, pinback button 8.00

Paperweight, pewter with 3¢ Boy Scout stamp on marble base, 1948 .... 7.50

Patch, Segment-Naturalist, blue twill, brown mesa, green tree, 1950s 9.00

Pocket knife, Boy Scout, Remington, 1930s 35.00

Poster, 1957 BSA National Jamboree, promotional, large 20.00

T-shirt, 1950 BSA National Jamboree, official, with package, M 20.00

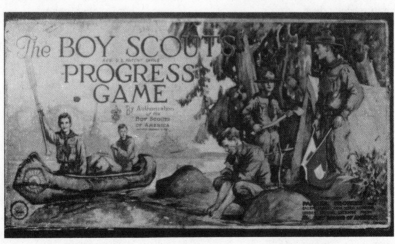

Boy Scout Progress Game by Parker Bros., 1924, $45.00.

Uniform, Boy Scout, 1910-20,
with badges 50.00
Uniform, Girl Scout, 1927,
coat-style dress, official
buttons 35.00
Yearbook, 4 Rockwell color
plates 45.00

Sewing Items

Sewing notions from the 1800s
and early 20th century, such as whimsical figural tape measures, beaded satin pincushions, blown glass darning eggs, and silver and gold thimbles are pleasant reminders of a bygone era -- ladies' sewing circles, quilting bees, and beautifully hand-stitched finery.

Booklet, Singer Sewing
Library, 1930, 4 in case . 10.00
Box, dresser shaped with 3
drawers, 1850s, 9½x9½x6″ 250.00
Box, tiny oak table with
drawer & cushion top,
1910, 4½″ 30.00
Button, Cupid, sterling,
English 10.00
Button, high wheel bicycle,
½″ 5.00
Button, ocean pearl, Occupied
Japan, set of 4 on original
card, 1948 .... 10.00
Cabinet, pine with spool pegs
& drawer, pincushion,
1900s 50.00
Clamp, with mirror & thimble
holder 85.00
Crochet hook, bone handled
with tiny hook, Milwerd .12 3.50
Darning egg, dated November
8, 1907 .... 15.00
Hem gauge, The Parisian, cast
iron, early 10.00
Kit, celluloid fish, 6″ 15.00
Machine, cast iron, hand
crank, B Eldridge, Wanamaker, 1880s 65.00
Machine, Kayanee, Berlin, US
Zone Germany 30.00

Thimble case, mother of pearl, 2″ wide, $45.00.

Needle box, ivory, 1½″ 22.00
Needle case, ivory parasol
figural, 4½″ long 125.00
Needle case & thread holder,
3 grooved chanels & tape
measure 55.00
Pincushion, Black doll, worn,
6″ 35.00
Pincushion, decorated bucket
with lift-off top, mirror
within, 2″ 65.00
Scissors, baby faces, brass, 4″ 16.50
Scissors, Cut Your Costs, Buy
CWS Goods 14.00
Scissors, Winchester 27.50
Sewing bird, brass embossed,
clamp-on with pincushion . 95.00
Spool stand, sterling, plain
with fancy monogram .. 65.00
Tape measure, banjo, celluloid 45.00
Tape measure, basket of
flowers, celluloid 65.00
Tape measure, champagne
bottle in cooler, 1800s .. 165.00
Tape measure, clown head
with hat, celluloid 95.00
Tape measure, dog in captain's hat with binoculars,
white celluloid 80.00
Tape measure, doghouse with
dog tape pull, 1½″ 55.00
Tape measure, fishing reel,
wooden 60.00
Tape measure, John Deere . 32.00

Figural clock tape measure, pull tape to rotate hands, marked Germany, 2″, $50.00.

Tape measure, mechanical windmill, brass	45.00
Tape measure, pig, brass	55.00
Tape measure, pirate ship, red celluloid, Japan	28.00
Tape measure, tea kettle, copper, 2¼″	75.00
Tape measure, terrier, celluloid	90.00
Tape measure, walnut, celluloid	40.00
Tatting shuttle, Lydia Pinkham	38.00
Thimble, aluminum with advertising	12.00
Thimble, child's size	25.00
Thimble, sterling with etched scene	50.00
Thimble, sterling with overall relief scroll & floral, marked	25.00
Thimble, sterling with tiny rubies & colored glass top, engraved	125.00
Thimble, 14k, beading with engraved band	90.00
Thimble, 14k, Simmons	135.00
Thimble, 14k, with original leatherette case	60.00
Thimble, 14k, 12-sided, plain ½″ band, marked, size 12	95.00

Thread holder, brass with enamel decor	20.00
Thread waxer, cylinder shaped with inlaid wood top & base, Victorian	75.00
Travel kit, enamel & sterling, opalescent glass top thimble/scissors	125.00

Shaker Items

Made by an all-but-vanished religious sect that was founded in America in 1776, Shaker items are exquisitely simple and are prized for their flawless construction and originality of design. The Shakers established self-contained communities, each of which produced all the necessities required for day-to-day living. They were weavers, brick makers, printers, farmers, and cabinetmakers. Besides their furniture, which collectors value highly, Shaker finger-constructed boxes, finely woven baskets, original handmade clothing, and advertising items relating to the sale of their seeds are the most sought-after memorabilia.

Three step stool, pine with traces of old orange paint, 26″ x 19″ x 16½″, $175.00.

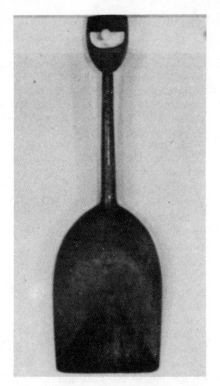

Wooden shovel, maple, carved from one piece of wood, Sabbathday Lake, circa 1840, 36″ long, $400.00.

Basket, fine weave splint, flared sides, bentwood handles, 4x12″ 150.00

Basket, woven cane, double-hinged lids, minor wear, 7½x10x14″ 70.00

Basket, woven grass, melon ribbed, slight wear, 3½x7½″ 33.00

Berry bucket, staved, yellow exterior, white interior, bail handle 120.00

Bonnet, woven poplar, hood shape, 1880s 100.00

Book, Life & Gospel Experience of Mother Ann Lee, HC Blinn 125.00

Bottle, embossed Fluid Extract Valerian, aqua, pontiled, 3½″ 40.00

Box, oval, copper nails, 4 fingers, light green paint, late 1800s 320.00

Box, red stained, 3 fingers, 9¼″ 275.00

Box, worn flame graining, oval, 1 finger, 3x4″ 275.00

Calf weaner, wood, 4x6″ ... 50.00

Churn, tin, with wooden dasher, 1860s, small dents 200.00

Clothes hanger, maple, marked 'Sister's side' 58.00

Curd drainer, tin, circa 1870 . 165.00

Dipper, tin, 6½″ long 50.00

Pincushion, treen, table clamp, plush pad, 5″ ... 75.00

Rolling pin, turned wood, 14″ long 30.00

Rug beater, wire loop with maple handle, 'Mt Lebanon NY', 1880s 120.00

Shampoo comb 68.00

Whisk broom, from broom corn, turned maple handle, 1850s 75.00

Pair of side chairs, early Alfred, Maine, original red paint and splint seats, 38½″, $350.00.

Shaving Mugs

Often as elegant as the handlebar mustache sported by its owner, the shaving mug was usually made of china or earthenware, well decorated with floral sprays, gold trim, depictions of the owner's trade, or his name. Today, the 'occupationals' are most highly valued, especially those representing an unusual trade or fraternal affiliation.

Advertising, Golden Knight Shaving Soap, St Louis, glass	30.00
Advertising, hand painted elk	60.00
Eagle, two 25-star flags, name	180.00
Four Aces, scuttle	35.00
Milk glass, Robin & Wheat pattern, pedestal, soap divider, 1870s	100.00
Moss Rose, ironstone	25.00
Occupational, artist, pallette & brushes with name, NM	110.00
Occupational, farmer with horses & plow, gold name, EX	165.00
Occupational, horse & buggy	100.00
Occupational, railroad, wood-burning locomotive, Limoges	175.00
Occupational, tailor, working	175.00
Occupational, trolley, BL RR	200.00
Roses, marked 3 Crown China, Germany	22.00

German china with hand painted florals, 3½", $35.00.

Shawnee

The novelty planters, vases, cookie jars, salt and pepper shakers, and 'Corn' dinnerware made by the Shawnee Pottery of Ohio are attractive, fun to collect, and are still available at reasonable prices. The company operated from 1937 until 1961, marking their wares with 'Shawnee, U.S.A.' and a number series, or 'Kenwood.'

Ash tray, orange with silver & gold spots, #219	7.00
Basket, #640	15.00
Bookend planter, Buddha, #524, pair	28.00
Bud vase, #1402, green & black	10.00
Console bowl, Kenwood, pink, oval with scalloped top, #1510, 14"	10.00
Cookie jar, Cinderella	75.00
Cookie jar, Dutch Boy	45.00
Cookie jar, Dutch Girl, gold trim	60.00
Cookie jar, Mugsey, gold trim	65.00
Cookie jar, Puss 'n Boots, plain	35.00
Cookie jar, Winking Owl	50.00
Corn, bowl, #5	12.00
Corn, bowl, #6	14.00
Corn, butter with cover, #72	28.50
Corn, casserole, individual, #73	35.00
Corn, cookie jar, #66	50.00
Corn, cup, #90	12.50
Corn, salt & pepper, 3½", pair	12.00
Creamer, pig, yellow	27.00
Creamer & sugar, pig with flower decor	47.00
Figurine, Oriental girl, #601	6.00
Figurine, teddy bear	16.00
Flowerpot holder, figural clown, marked USA #619	10.00
French casserole, lobster, Kenwood, #900	10.00
Pitcher, Chanticleer	22.00
Pitcher, fruit, tilt style	35.00

**Corn line covered casserole, 11½",
$35.00.**

Planter, black & white, Kenwood, #2112	10.00
Planter, bow tie, gold traced, #434	4.00
Planter, Cameo, #2506	9.00
Planter, clown, gold trim, #607	12.00
Planter, doe, gold trim, #624	12.00
Planter, duck, #752	6.50
Planter, elf, gold trim, #536	6.50
Planter, girl with book, #574	6.50
Planter, Oriental lady, #896	6.00
Planter, pump	10.00
Planter, white with scalloped edge, oval, 14"	5.00
Planter, 2 Orientals carrying basket, #537	6.00

Bo-Peep pitcher, 8", $35.00.

Shakers, cats, 2½", pair	8.00
Shakers, Farmer Pig with shovel, 2½", pair	8.00
Shakers, Mugsy, large, pair	29.00
Shakers, Puss 'n Boots, small, pair	10.00
Shakers, sailor & girl, pair	15.00
Teapot, Granny Anne, with basket, gold detail & decals	70.00
Teapot, rose	25.00
Vase, Cameo, blue with cream, fluted top, #2505, 5½"	12.50
Vase, swan figural, wine with much gold trim	12.00
Vase, wood grain, #868	8.00
Watering can, red flowers, blue bands, 3½"	6.50

Sheet Music

The most valuable examples of sheet music are those related to early transportation, ethnic themes, Disney characters, a particularly popular artist or composer, or with a cover illustration done by a well known artist. Production of sheet music peaked during the 'Tin Pan Alley Days', from the 1880s until the 1930s. Covers were made as attractive as possible to lure potential buyers, and today's collectors sometimes frame and hang them as they would a print. Flea markets are a good source for sheet music, and prices are usually very reasonable.

All Mixed Up, Dionne Quintuplets in Alpine costumes, 1938	20.00
Because He Did His Duty, photo Sophie Tucker, 1913, large size	8.00
Blue Shadows On The Trail, from Melody Time	5.00
Casablanca, Bogart & Bergman	15.00
Celebratin' Day In Tennessee, photo Emma Carcus, 1914, large	8.00
Coo-Coo, Al Jolson	10.00

Fifty Chubby Tiny Toes, Dionne Quintuplets as babies, tinted, 1935 .... 10.00

Fire Drill March, fire engine cover 12.00

Freckles, Hess & Ager, pictures Nora Bayes, 1919, VG 5.00

Go Way Back & Sit Down, Black man at rear of restaurant, 1901 ...... 10.00

God Is Love, 1844, calligraphic cover, publisher George Reed, 8 pages .. 9.00

Hurrah For Henry, HL Brown, 1923 .... 12.00

Hush-A-Bye Island, from Smash Up, Susan Hayward, 1946 .... 6.00

In My Merry Oldsmobile, couple in red convertible, 1905, EX 6.00

In The City Of Broken Hearts, large photo Theda Bara, 1916, large 10.00

Lady In Red, full-figure Dolores Del Rio in red gown, 1935 .... 8.00

Little Ford Rambled Right Along, 1914 .... 8.00

Lovin' Sam The Shiek Of Alabam, photo Al Harman, 1922, VG 4.00

Midnight Fire Alarm, EJ Paull 17.50

Minstrels March Two Step, Al J White, humorous minstrel cover 15.00

Muchacha, yellow cover with Dolores Del Rio, 1935 .. 12.50

Next President, The; Al Smith 26.00

Peerless Polka, stove ad cover, 1857 .... 28.00

Perfect Song, The; Amos 'n Andy, 1919 .... 10.00

President Johnson's Grand March & Quick Step, 1865 32.50

Ragging The Chopsticks, 2 kids at piano, 1919, VG . 5.00

Rio Grande Quick March, John Andrews, 1846 .... 55.00

Shift In High & Let Her Go, 1923 .... 15.00

Sit Down You're Rocking The Boat, 1913 .... 10.00

Six Women, from George Whites Scandels, Alice Faye 15.00

Solace, A Mexican Serenade; by S Joplin, couple by wall, 1909 .... 20.00

Tammy, Debbie Reynolds in pigtails, Universal, 1957 . 3.00

Thank God We've Found The Man 14.00

Warmin' Up In Dixie, Black folk dancing around fire, 1899, VG 25.00

When I'm Alone I'm Lonesome, I Berlin, 1911, large size, VG 15.00

Whistle My Love, from Robin Hood 7.00

Who's Afraid, graphic faces of E Taylor & R Burton, 1966 6.00

Your's For A Song, 1939, World's Fair cover 12.00

Slot Machines

Now legal in many states, old 'one-arm bandits' are being restored, used for home entertainment, or simply amassed in collections. Especially valuable are those from the turn of the century, rare or unique models, and those with unusually fancy trim.

Bally 25¢ Reliance 3,000.00
Buckley Pointmakers, electric 495.00
Caille Sphinx, EX original . 1,800.00
Caille 5¢ Doughboy, restored 800.00
Caille 5¢ Superior, 3 reel with jackpot, restored, 24" ..1,400.00
Dewey 5¢ floor model, original 6,900.00
Dutchess 1¢, restored 1,450.00
Jennings Airplane Chief, EX . 1,150.00
Jennings Little Duck 1,750.00

Mill's Roman Head, Silent-Golden Bell, $2,600.00.

Jennings 1¢ Silver Club, restored 1,300.00
Jennings 10¢ 4-Star Chief with jackpot, restored .. 1,500.00
Jennings 5¢ Dutch Boy, restored 1,650.00
Jennings 5¢ Peacock 1,300.00
Jennings 5¢ Standard Chief . 950.00
Jennings 5¢ Vest Pocket, restored 550.00
Keeney 5¢ Bonus Super Bell 795.00
Mills $1 Golden Falls, with jackpot, restored 2,700.00
Mills Jumbo Parade, floor model, free game feature, 1930s 975.00
Mills 1¢ Firebird QT, orig... 1,600.00
Mills 10¢ Black Cherry 985.00
Mills 10¢ Golden Nugget with jackpot, restored .. 2,100.00
Mills 10¢ Midas Touch, cast iron, chrome with formica trim 500.00
Mills 10¢ 7-7-7 Hi-Top 1,200.00
Mills 5¢ Bursting Cherry, restored 1,850.00

Mills 5¢ Club Extraordinary, EX 1,400.00
Mills 5¢ Hi-Top 21, guaranteed jackpot, EX 1,200.00
Mills 5¢ Illusion, curved glass with cast iron front & top, restored 2,100.00
Mills 5¢ Lion Head, chrome plated, hand painted, restored 1,650.00
Mills 5¢ Mask Cowboy, restored 4,200.00
Mills 5¢ Vest Pocket 225.00
Pace $1 Cowboy, restored . 4,750.00
Pace 1¢ Bantam, EX 1,350.00
Pace 5¢ All Star Comet Bell................. 1,200.00
Starlite 5¢ Aristocrat 675.00
Watling 1¢ Blue Seal Gumball, restored 2,000.00
Watling 10¢ Torch Front .. 1,450.00
Watling 25¢ Rol-A-Top Coin Front with jackpot, restored 4,500.00
Watling 5¢ Bird of Paradise, G original 3,500.00
Watling 5¢ Operator's Bell, cast iron, 3 reel, payout, restored, 24″ 1,210.00

Soda Fountain Collectibles

The days of the neighborhood ice cream parlor are gone; the soda jerk, the mouth-watering confections he concocted, the high counter and bar stools a thing of the past -- but memories live on through the soda glasses, ice cream scoops, milk shake machines and soda fountain signs that those reluctant to forget treasure today.

Back bar, white opalite top, 8 foot 850.00
Bucket, wood, 'Lemon Ice' . 50.00
Canister, aluminum, Van Houten's, boy with soda in relief 50.00

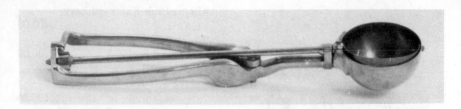

Scoop, Gilchrist, brass, 10″, $35.00.

Chair, nickel over iron, set of 4 .... 360.00
Cup holder, pewter, Vortex, Patented 1915, 4½″ 8.00
Dispenser, Brazilla, milk glass with claw & ball feet, dated 10/26/15 .... 175.00
Milk shake machine, Horlick's 100.00
Mixer, Hamilton Beach, green porcelain, single, 1919 .. 135.00
Scoop, Fry dispenser 175.00
Scoop, Gilchrist, brass, 10″ . 35.00
Scoop, Toledo, Ohio, EZ Roll, aluminum 125.00
Stool, bases swivel, cast iron, pair 20.00
Straw holder, with domed lid, green, ornate, EX 295.00
Tray, Imperial Ice Cream, shows strawberry sundae, VG 38.00

Spongeware

Utility earthenware from the last quarter of the 1800s decorated with sponged-on colors is popular with today's collectors, especially those interested in primitives, country antiques, and American pottery. Usually the color was applied at random, although occasionally simple patterns were attempted. Blue on white are the most treasured colors; but red, green, rust, black, and tan were also used, sometimes in combination. You may find some items trimmed with gold.

Batter pitcher, blue & white, original lid, 7″, EX 175.00

Batter pitcher, bulbous, ribbed sides, flow sponging, 5x7x5½″ 70.00
Bean pot, blue & white 275.00
Bowl, blue, putty on gray, molded, late 1800s, 4x10½″ 60.00
Bowl, blue & white, 3x4″ .. 35.00
Bowl, green & brown on cream, 9″ 36.00
Bowl, mixing; plain & blue bands, 6½x14″ 150.00
Casserole, individual, brown & yellow, 2x5″ diameter, set of 6 .... 140.00
Chamber pot, blue & white . 95.00
Chamber pot, embossed rose trellis, blue & white, 5½x9″ 25.00
Creamer, green & brown on yellowware, no advertising, 4½″ 75.00
Crock, blue & white, ears for wires, no lid, 3¾x5½″ .. 70.00
Crock, blue & white, 12 gallons 385.00
Cup, handleless, blue & white, small 30.00
Cup & saucer, blue with red rose & green leaves, EX . 175.00
Dish, rectangular, blue & white, 8x9¾″ 220.00
Gypsy kettle, with lid, blue & white, no handle, 4¾″ .. 65.00
Jar, 6″ diameter 65.00
Jardiniere, brown on cream, 7½″ 55.00
Kettle, blue & white, original bail & clips, 1870s, 4½x8½″ 215.00

Mixing bowl, clear and blue bands, 5″ x 14″, $150.00.

Mug, blue & white, marked
Imperial 95.00

Pitcher, blue & brown on
cream, embossed corn,
5½″ 95.00

Pitcher, blue & white, bulbous,
embossed diamonds, large 150.00

Pitcher, blue & white, bulbous,
1½ quart 140.00

Pitcher, blue & white, straight
sides, white base band,
6½″ 115.00

Pitcher, blue on yellow with
embossed floral, 7½″ ... 115.00

Pitcher, brown, green &
yellow, 7″ 67.50

Pitcher, green & tan, straight
sided, 6″, EX 40.00

Planter, hanging, blue & white 225.00

Plate, scalloped rim, blue &
white, 9½″ 120.00

Platter, scalloped rim, blue &
white, 6½x9¼″ 190.00

Salt & pepper, blue & white, 4″ 65.00

Salt box, hanging, blue &
brown on cream, hinged
walnut top, 6″ 195.00

Sauce dish, Virginia, cut-
sponge decor, 5½″ 90.00

Soap dish, rectangular, edge
flakes, 3½x4¾″ 65.00

Spittoon, green on cream with
gold traces 225.00

Teapot, brown & green on
yellow, minor flakes, 5½″ . 65.00

Spoons

Since the 1890s, spoons have been issued as souvenirs, to commemorate an event, in honor of a famous person, or on the occasion of a holiday. Today's collectors prefer those with high relief designs on handle as well as bowl, Indian or other full-figure handles, enameled or gold-washed trim, and spoons that are dated or from a limited edition. While the design is more important than the material, silver is much preferred over silver plate.

Alligator handle, Jackson
Statue, New Orleans em-
bossed in bowl, P&B Co. 18.00

Black boy eating watermelon,
Memphis, TN, engraved
bowl 100.00

California on handle, embossed ostrich in bowl, MB Mfg, 4″ 15.00

Canada, enameled leaf handle, Niagara Falls engraved in bowl, BM Co 9.00

Cheyenne, WY, 'Let 'Er Buck' in bowl, cut-out cowboy & horse 35.00

Faneuil Hall embossed in bowl, Boston, MA, on stem, 4″ 15.00

Fish handle, Venice, CA, engraved in bowl, pennant on handle, 4″ 18.00

Glacier Nat'l Park & lake in bowl, Indian, swastika & skull handle 57.50

Goldenrod on handle, bowl engraved Jacksonville, FL, 4″ 10.00

Helena, MT, state seal, miners panning gold in bowl, engraved on back 26.00

Indian, full-figure handle, Spokane engraved in bowl, 4″ 35.00

Indian, full-figure handle, Toronto & Parliment in bowl, view on back 60.00

Indian, kneeling full figure on handle, NY subway embossed in bowl 35.00

Indian head, corn, bow & arrows handle, teepee & canoe on back, Watson .. 35.00

Indian head on handle, embossed Landing of the Spanish in bowl 25.00

Indian head on handle, Ft Dearborn, 1830, embossed in bowl, Chicago 45.00

Indian with shield, full-figure handle, Yosemite Valley, view on back 115.00

Lake Shore & Michigan Southern Railway embossed in bowl, Pan Am handle.............. 10.00

Landing of Columbus on handle, Administration Building relief in bowl 18.00

Las Vegas, cut-out handle with cowboy on horse, demitasse 12.00

Mary Poppins, figural 22.00

Miner & donkey on handle, St Louis Union Station engraved in bowl 25.00

Minnesota State on handle, plain bowl, Crown Mfg, 4⅞″ 18.00

Morman Temple embossed in bowl, P&B Mfg, 4″ 8.00

New York skyline, Statue of Liberty embossed in bowl . 75.00

Niagara, full-figure Indian with oar on handle, view of falls on back 45.00

Niagara, Maid of the Mist, Red Man's Fact 30.00

Portland scenes on handle, Mt Hood embossed in bowl, MB Mfg 15.00

Possums climbing tree, San Xavier, MS, P&B Mfg .. 15.00

Pyramids & sphinx in bowl, scarab enameled on handle, gold washed 65.00

Salem witch, broom & cat . 60.00

Santa Claus head & stocking on handle, engraved bowl . 125.00

Santa coming down chimney, Gorham Mfg, 4¼″ 35.00

Springfield, MO, rifle shape, Nat'l Cemetery engraved in bowl 100.00

St Louis Cathedral embossed in bowl, flower handle, demitasse 12.00

Starved Rock, IL, on handle, plain bowl, sterling 15.00

Stork with baby in beak, St Louis engraved in bowl . 50.00

Tri-State Telephone Co, girl & phone embossed on handle 75.00

Walker's Grape Juice, bottle on handle, embossed bowl . 40.00

Sports Collectibles

Memorabilia related to sports of any kind -- hunting, fishing, golfing, baseball, bicycling, etc. -- is attracting a following of collectors, many of which specialize in the particular sport that best holds their interests. See also Fishing Collectibles.

Baseball bat, Hutchinson Brothers, Jackie Robinson, 30½″	24.00
Bat rack, wooden, Stan Musial, 1964	20.00
Bicycle lamp, carbide, Solar, brass with jeweled sides, 1896	95.00
Book, Who's Who in American Sports, 964 pages, 1928	35.00
Boxing ring gong, brass with lever action, 9¾″ diameter	70.00
Calendar print, well dressed tennis player, M Stewart, 1901	25.00
Pennant, Hank Aaron, Home Run King	20.00
Photo, 1950s Philadelphia Whiz Kids team with names, 30″	20.00
Pin-back, Baseball Stars, 1950	10.00
Putter, wood shaft	40.00
Record, Mickey Mantel's Farewell to Baseball, in original sleeve	1.50
Skis, handmade, 1904	85.00
Sled, oak with metal tipped runners, primitive, 13x49″	35.00
Turkey caller, wood, patent 1807	35.00
Watch fob, Babe Ruth	100.00

Staffordshire

The Staffordshire district of England is perhaps the best known pottery-producing area in the world. Since the early 1700s, hundreds of potteries have operated there, producing wares as varied as their names. While many examples are extremely rare and expensive, it is still possible to find small but interesting Staffordshire items at nearly any good market. See also Historical Blueware.

Bowl, Sicilian, brown transfer, 1850s, 11½″	70.00
Bowl, vegetable; Surrey, F Winkle	18.00
Bust, George Washington, multicolored enamel, 8″	265.00
Chamber pot with lid, green scenic transfer, circa 1830s	75.00
Chimney piece, fortune teller, base & top flakes, 12½″	95.00
Cottage, bank, children in windows with parents on each side, 4½″	300.00
Cottage, pastille burner, 6″	325.00
Cup & saucer, handleless, Lombardy, light blue transfer	28.00

Pastille burner cottage, creamware with applied multicolored flowers, circa 1820, 5″, $275.00.

Cup & saucer, handleless, rose lustre, blue & green flowers, 4 for 70.00

Cup & saucer, handleless, Venetian Temple, red transfer 30.00

Cup plate, Canova, green, Mayer 30.00

Cup plate, Corinth, light blue, Edwards 30.00

Figurine, cat on orange pillow with gold ribbon, sponge decor, 7″ 85.00

Figurine, dog with green lustre trim, 12″ 175.00

Figurine, girl riding goat, coleslaw decor, 5″ 125.00

Figurine, girl with pink tunic, 1850s, 7″ 45.00

Figurine, poodle on cushion, white, coleslaw decor, 2½x3″ 150.00

Figurine, Queen Victoria & Prince Albert, late 1800s, 7½″ 130.00

Figurine, rooster on domed base, polychrome, 4″ ... 45.00

Figurine, Spaniel, sitting, russet & white coat, 1875, 9½″ 125.00

Incense hutch, polychrome cottage figural, 4″ 190.00

Money box, bell-shaped Derbyshire souvenir, 1870, 7″ . 65.00

Mug, Cut Finger, green transfer, 2¾″ 35.00

Pitcher, Cupid in wreath, white with multicolor, 7″ . 75.00

Pitcher, purple transfer birds & flowers, green & yellow enamel, 10″ 55.00

Plate, Trentham Castle, wall hanging, 1880 .... 75.00

Platter, blue & green landscape, Wedgwood, Eturia, 8½x10½″ 30.00

Satyr jug, pearlware with multicolored enamels & pink lustre decor 295.00

Sauce tureen, with lid, underplate & ladle, Sicilian, brown transfer 175.00

Spill, boy milking cow, flat back, slight repairs, 6½″ . 135.00

Spill, Burns & His Mary, 1850, 12″ 150.00

Toddy, embossed florals, black transfer of children by stream, 5″ 25.00

Vase, deer & hound figural, 12″, pair 125.00

Vase, Victorian lady & man, black & white, 4″, pair .. 45.00

Stained Glass

Stained glass is an art medium popularly used in the early 1900s for lamp shades, windows, architectural panels, etc., and it is currently enjoying a revival. The more valuable examples are those signed by the artist or studio. Number of pieces, intricacy of design, and presence of seliniumbased colors (red, orange, yellow) should be considered when evaluating stained glass items.

Tiffany Favrile glass shade, together with a Moe Bridges Egyptian-style lamp base, $7,150.00.

Door, tulip design with wood beading effect & clear glass area, 60x23″ 600.00

Panel, yellow borders with frosted center, ovals & arcs, 48x16″ 150.00

Shade, hanging; flowers with jewel center border, brickwork, 18″ 750.00

Window, art glass with 80 bevels, 25x25″ 150.00

Window, central peacock rondel, 26x26″ 375.00

Window, pennant with anchor, 27x29″ 340.00

Stangl Birds

Birds modeled after the prints of Audubon were introduced by the Stangl Pottery Company in the early 1940s. More than one hundred different birds were produced, most of which are marked with 'Stangl' and a four-digit number to identify the species. Though a limited few continue to be produced, since 1976 they have been marked with the date of their production.

Bird of Paradise, #3813, 5″, $70.00.

Allen Hummingbird, #3634, oval mark, 3½″	60.00
Bird of Paradise, #3408, 5½″	65.00
Blue-Headed Vireo, #3448 .	48.00
Bluebird, #3276	50.00
Bob-O-Link, #3595, 4″	50.00
Brewer's Blackbird, #3591 .	40.00
Broadtail Hummingbird, #3626, blue flower, signed RTF, M	80.00
Cardinal, #3444, sample ...	80.00
Carolina Wren, #3590	55.00
Chestnut-Backed Chickadee, #3811	45.00
Chestnut-Sided Warbler, #3812	55.00
Cockatoo, #3580, VR, 9″ ..	75.00
Duck, flying, #3443, blue glaze	250.00
Gray Cardinal, #3596	65.00
Hen, #3446	65.00
Kentucky Warbler, #3598, signed, 3″	30.00
Key West Quail Dove, #3454, 9″, M	160.00
Kingfisher, #3406	55.00

Nuthatch, #3593	22.00
Parrot with worm, #3449 ..	125.00
Parula Warbler, #3583	40.00
Penguin, #3274	275.00
Pheasant, old mark, pair ..	255.00
Prothonatary Warbler, #3447	55.00
Redstarts, #3490D	125.00
Rooster, #3445, yellow, 9″ .	100.00
Rufous Hummingbird, #3585, MMF, 3″	50.00
Titmouse, #3592	40.00
Wilson Warbler, #3597	45.00
Yellow Warbler, #3850	60.00

Stocks and Bonds

Interest has recently developed in collecting old stocks and bonds from defunct industries. There are several factors that determine their worth: (1) autograph value (2) the industry represented -- railways, mining, and energy being the most popular fields (3) attractiveness -- those with vignettes of old trains, classical figures, or eagles, for example. While most may be purchased for well under $25.00, some of the very rare bring several hundred dollars at the market.

Adventure Consolidated Copper, vignette with Michigan seal, 1899 .... 12.00

Alaska-United Mining Company, issued, 1895 ..... 25.00

American Drug Company, South Dakota, eagle with train, 1902 .... 10.00

Baltimore Consolidated Railroad, unissued certificate, circa 1890 ..... 15.00

Bank of Kentucky, issued, 1865 .... 75.00

Boston & Hartford Railroad, bond, issued, 1874 ..... 75.00

Cambrian Oil Company, issued certificate with gushers & eagle, 1920 .. 23.00

Charleston City Railroad, issued certificate with trolley, 1890s 45.00

Colony Railroad, bond, 1930 . 50.00

Comstock Tunnel Company, issued bond, 1889 ...... 40.00

Durant Motors Incorporated, issued certificate, 2 allegoricals, 1925 ...... 85.00

Ford Motor Company, stock, early auto, 1977 .... 5.00

Germantown Passenger Railway, Philadelphia; 3 vignettes, 1929 .... 28.00

Gold Exploration Company, issued, 1905 .... 20.00

Irving Trust Company, New York, 1930s 4.00

Little Rock Oil & Gas, oil field vignette, 1917 .... 12.00

Montana Territorial Drafts, lot of 2, 1867, 4x8" 50.00

New Century Oil Company, issued, 1910 .... 15.00

Realty Syndicate, bond, California, 1898 .... 9.00

Ross Oil Company, stock certificate with revenue stamp, 1865 .... 50.00

Tonopah Divide Mining Company, issued, 1918 ..... 15.00

Union Traction, stock certificate, 1899 issue 4.00

William Whitman Company, orange vignette with 2 ladies, 1922 .... 5.00

Stoneware

From about 1840 and throughout the next hundred years, stoneware clay was used to pot utility wares such as jugs, jars, churns, and pitchers. Though a brown Albany slip was applied to some, by far the vast majority was glazed by common salt that was thrown into the kiln and vaporized. Decorations of cobalt were either slip trailed, brushed on, or stenciled; sgraffito (incising) was used on rare occasions. The complexity of the decoration has a great deal of bearing on value, and examples bearing the mark of a short-lived company are often at a premium.

Bottle, unsigned, impressed initials on gray salt glaze, ½ qt, EX 15.00

Churn, CW Braun, Buffalo, NY, oak leaves & 4 in cobalt, 16" 400.00

Churn, Seymour Bosworth, scroll with 3 Xs in cobalt, 3 gal, EX 300.00

Churn, Whites Utica, 4 cobalt rickrack stripes, restored, 3 gal 135.00

Crock, A Conrad, stenciled decoration in cobalt, 4 gal . 90.00

Crock, AP Donaghho, stenciled geometric band & name in cobalt, 2 gal ... 225.00

Crock, butter, unsigned, leaves & vines in cobalt, ½ gal 300.00

German harvest jug, from Whithall, New York, dated 1891, 11″, $110.00.

Flask, gray salt glaze, 8″ .. 30.00
Funnel, White Hall Pottery . 25.00
Jar, Bennington Factory, 2 & handle trim in cobalt, 2 gal, lid, VG 800.00
Jar, canning; flowers in cobalt, 9¼″ 65.00
Jar, canning; Palatine Pottery & dog in cobalt, wax sealer, ½ gal 200.00
Jar, canning; unsigned, 6 cobalt bands, 1 gal, EX . 95.00
Jar, T Mabbett & Co, number 3 in cobalt, wide mouth, 3 gal, EX 275.00
Jar, unsigned, simple cobalt flower, cobalt smeared handles, 10½″ 225.00
Jar, Whites Utica, parrot on stump in cobalt, 1 gal, EX 325.00
Jug, Binghampton, NY, slip-trailed bird on branch with leaves, 11″ 345.00
Jug, Boyers & Harden, cobalt stenciled name, 2 gal ... 145.00
Jug, Dillon, Henry & Porter, 6-petal tulip, ovoid, 2 gal, EX 345.00
Jug, Drink Everett Crystal Spring Water, freehand in cobalt, 5 gal 290.00
Jug, E Wantell Olean, NY, leaf in cobalt 100.00
Jug, Ft Edward Stoneware Co, freehand name in cobalt, 11″ 115.00
Jug, FW Merril, cobalt brush stroke over impressed name, ovoid, 3 gal 120.00
Jug, N Clark, Athens, cobalt accent around impressed name, ovoid, 13″ 175.00
Jug, NA White & Son Utica, pine tree in cobalt, 1 gal . 115.00
Jug, Nichols & Boynton, flowers in cobalt, 12″ ... 115.00
Jug, OS Gifford, turtle, three flowers & branches in cobalt, 2 gal 900.00

Crock, EA Montell, leaves in wreath in cobalt, 4 gal .. 125.00
Crock, Hamilton & Jones, stenciled name & bands in cobalt, 3 gal 95.00
Crock, J Burger, flowers with leaves in cobalt, lug handles 105.00
Crock, John Burger, well done 4 petaled flower, 4 gal .. 375.00
Crock, L Willard & Sons, stenciled cow in cobalt, 12″, VG 900.00
Crock, Lyons, NY, flowers, leaves & number 2 in cobalt 175.00
Crock, S Hart, Fulton, pair of doves in cobalt, 3 gal, restored 500.00
Crock, SB Bosworth, bird on stalks, brushed on in cobalt, 2 gal, EX 400.00
Crock, unsigned, large cobalt leaf, 1½ gal, EX 125.00
Crock, unsigned, large hen pecking corn in cobalt, 4 gal, EX 550.00
Crock, Whites Utica, fantailed bird on fern in cobalt, 2 gal, EX 400.00

Jug, PS Proctor, foliage
wreath in cobalt, 2 gal .. 85.00
Jug, S Risley, Norwich, flower
in cobalt, ovoid, 1840s .. 220.00
Jug, TS Taft & Co, leaves in
cobalt, 1 gal 120.00
Jug, unsigned, Albany slip, 1
gal 55.00
Jug, unsigned, handwritten
name in cobalt, circa 1875,
16½" 115.00
Jug, unsigned, indistinct floral
on brown-gray, 2 gal ... 120.00
Jug, Whites Utica, bird in
cobalt, 2 gal 200.00
Jug, Woolever & Skinner, leaf
in cobalt, 1 gal 65.00
Milk pan, flowers in cobalt, 1
gal, 5x11" 215.00
Pitcher, FB Norton Co, floral,
1½ gal, NM 485.00
Pitcher, unsigned, 3-leaf
clover, 8", EX 350.00
Spittoon, Cowden & Wilcox,
large flower buds in cobalt,
4½x7½" 350.00

Two-gallon jug with cobalt flower, die-stamped 'Lyon', 11", $225.00.

String Holders

Until the middle of this century, spools of string contained in devices designed for that purpose were a common sight in country stores, as well as many other businesses. Early examples of cast iron or wire and those with advertising are the most desirable and valuable, but later figurals of chalkware or ceramics are also quite collectible.

Apple, red turned wood with
yellow highlights & metal
tube stem 30.00
Ball shape, iron, 2 part with
open design 35.00
Beehive, cast iron, original
paint only fair, large ... 30.00
Chef, chalkware 15.00
Little girl, chalkware 15.00
Lovebird, porcelain 15.00
Mammy, Black woman's
head, wall type, plaster,
7½" 20.00
Sewer tile, man's head, string
pulls through mouth, 5x6" 225.00
Thousand Eye, pattern glass . 29.50

Sugar Shakers

Once a commonplace table accessory, the sugar shaker was used to sprinkle cinnamon and sugar onto toast or muffins.

Acorn, excellent decor 95.00
Alba, custard glass with O-top 75.00
Baby Thumbprint, amber,
enamel decor 70.00
Banded Portland 45.00
Block & Fan 32.50
Bohemian, ruby with clear et-
ching 150.00
Bulbous base, white with
lavender 110.00
Challinor's Blue Forget-Me-
Not 140.00
Chandelier 75.00

China, hand painted with peach colored flowers ... 45.00
Cone, blue satin 75.00
Daisy & Fern, Northwood, blue opalescent 125.00
Floral & bird, hand painted & cased in yellow 65.00
Leaf Mold, cranberry spatter 175.00
Leaf Umbrella, cased in yellow 100.00
Melligo, blue opaque 70.00
Mt Washington, egg shape with delicate blue florals . 135.00
Opal Lattice, ribbed cranberry 80.00
Paneled Daisy 35.00
Paneled Sprig, amethyst .. 110.00
Question Mark 35.00
Quilted Phlox, with pink flowers 30.00
Ring Neck, cranberry optic . 65.00
Royal Ivy, cased spatter .. 150.00
Royal Oak, frosted rubena . 170.00
Swirled Windows, cranberry opalescent 165.00
Twelve Panels, cranberry with plated domed top 72.00
Windermere's Fan, pink & yellow opaque 40.00

Floral decorated milk glass, $65.00.

Syrups

Syrup dispensers have been made in all types of art glass, china, stoneware, and in many patterns. Together they make a lovely collection.

Marked WCP, Stone China, hand painted over transfer, 1883, 8½", $80.00.

Alabama 65.00
Alba 45.00
Apollo, etched, metal handle . 32.50
Beaded Band, dated top ... 39.50
Block & Fan 57.50
Box in Box, floral etched .. 22.00
Chrysanthemum Base Speckled, blue 210.00
Clear Circle 42.00
Coin Dot, blue with blue handle, metal cover 85.00
Coin Spot, 9-panel mold, green opalescent 85.00
Cord Drapery, chocolate ... 210.00
Florette, pink frosted 100.00

Henrietta	45.00	Bowl, fluted, 9½"	40.00

Henrietta 45.00
Hercules Pillar, blue 145.00
Interlocking Hearts 42.50
Leaf Flower, clear with amber
  stain 165.00
Maize, Libbey, custard with
  gold leaves 280.00
Pennsylvania 35.00
Polka Dot, cranberry opales-
  cent 220.00
Rope & Thumbprint, amber . 90.00
Sawtooth & Star 35.00
Spanish Lace, cranberry ... 97.50
Sunflower, opaque chartreuse 190.00
Torpedo 80.00
US Coin, frosted 1892 coins . 475.00

Tea Leaf Ironstone

Ironstone decorated with a copper lustre design of bands and leaves became popular in the 1880s. It was produced by potters in both England and America until the early 1900s.

Bacon rasher 45.00
Bone dish, gold lustre, some
  wear, no mark 20.00
Bowl, covered vegetable;
  Wedgwood 95.00

Bowl, fluted, 9½" 40.00
Bowl, fruit; scalloped rim,
  Wilkinson, 10x10" 60.00
Bread plate, Meakin, Fish
  Hook 50.00
Butter pat, Meakin 12.00
Cake plate, 6-sided 95.00
Casserole with lid, Meakin,
  6x10½" 100.00
Cracker jar, Meakin 60.00
Creamer, Meakin, Bamboo . 115.00
Creamer, Shaw, 5" 150.00
Cup & saucer, Meakin, square
  handle 40.00
Cup & saucer, Mellor Taylor . 60.00
Gravy boat, Anthony Shaw,
  with underplate 95.00
Pancake dish, with cover,
  Malkin, 'buttery yellow',
  rare 265.00
Pitcher, Cable, 8" 150.00
Pitcher, Meakin, Bamboo, 9" . 265.00
Pitcher & bowl, AJ Wilkinson 375.00
Plate, Furnival, 7" 10.00
Plate, Grindley, 10" 22.50
Plate, Meakin, 8" 12.00
Platter, Meakin, 9" 15.00
Platter, Shaw, oval, 12" ... 24.00
Platter, Shaw, oval, 16" ... 45.00
Platter, 17½" 75.00

Vegetable bowl with cover, marked Mellor, Taylor and Co., 3½" x 11" x 7 $90.00.

Salt & pepper	50.00
Sauce tureen, Meakin, Bamboo, with ladle, lid & underplate	425.00
Shaving mug, Meakin	125.00
Spittoon, gargoyle heads at sides, EX	750.00
Spooner, flat	50.00
Sugar with lid, Anthony Shaw	95.00
Sugar with lid, Meakin	175.00
Teapot, Shaw	135.00
Toothbrush holder	55.00
Wash bowl; Meakin, very simple, 14½″	90.00

Teddy Bears

Only teddies made before the 1940s can be considered bona fide antiques, though character bears from more recent years are also quite collectible. The 'classic' bear is one made of mohair, straw stuffed, fully jointed, with long curving arms tapering at the paw and extending to the knees. He has very long skinny feet, felt pads on all paws, embroidered claws, a triangular, proportionately small head, a long pointed snout, embroidered nose and mouth, and a hump on the back torso at the neck. But above all, he is adorable, endearing, cuddly, and he loves you.

Baby bottle, embossed Teddy, 1920s	45.00
Bear, balloon blowing, lighted eyes & voice, MIB	45.00
Bear, clockworks, automation, 1800s	450.00
Bear, Cowboy Teddy, circa 1940, 14″	600.00
Bear, fully jointed, bicycle rider, marked PW, 5″ ...	120.00
Bear, fully jointed, blue mohair, 19″	300.00
Bear, fully jointed, glass eyes, 1920s, 11½″	160.00
Bear, fully jointed, growler, 42″	230.00

Early Steiff teddy, mohair, fully jointed, shoe button eyes, embroidered nose and mouth, felt paws, 12½″, $250.00.

Bear, fully jointed, long arms & paws, circa 1920, 12″ .	185.00
Bear, fully jointed, outside button joints & eyes, large hump, 21″	110.00
Bear, fully jointed, straw stuffed, early, 16″	250.00
Bear, Hermann Prince growler, white mohair, jointed ...	85.00
Bear, mohair, yellow gold, long arms, 22″	275.00
Bear, Shaggy Cinnamon Bear, 10″	225.00
Bear, yellow, long hair, jointed arms & legs, 9½″	95.00
Book, Moving Picture Teddies, 1907	65.00
Book, Teddy Bears Come to Life, 1907	20.00
Cup & saucer, china, Roosevelt Bear decor	45.00
Doll, Bewley's Milk, flour sack	45.00

Figurine, large white bear
pouring water on baby bear 95.00
Fork & spoon, ABCs on back,
Teddies on handle, pair . 65.00
Hatpin, sterling Teddy head,
1909 .... 75.00
Mush set, bowl & creamer,
dolls, Teddies & horses on
wheels 60.00
Paper dolls, Cook's Teddy
Bear, uncut sheet 175.00
Plate, tin, Teddies & kids on
border, girl in center, 1907 50.00
Rattle, sterling silver Teddy
with mother of pearl han-
dle, 4″ 225.00
Sheet music, March of Teddy
Bears, Dedicated to 3rd
Term 15.00
Valise, round with tin handle,
mamma, papa & baby bear,
1920s 35.00
Wood carving, bear on sled . 45.00

Tinware

From 1800 until the early 20th
century, American tinsmiths imported
sheets of tin plate from Europe, from
which they hand fashioned kitchenware items, footwarmers, lamps, etc.
Some pieces, such as lamps and
lanterns, were sometimes decorated
with simple pierced designs. Often
they were painted, either freehand or
stenciled; this type of decoration is
referred to as tole. Cookie cutters, very
popular with today's collectors, were
made in every shape imaginable. The
very early, more unusual detailed
forms sometimes sell for well in excess
of $100.00.

Bathtub, round with high
back 82.00
Bird cage, architectural form
with tubular bars, 29x13″ . 75.00
Bucket, square handle with
wood grip, factory made . 30.00

Bucket, wire handle, 4x5″ . 12.50
Candle holder, with saucer &
snuffer, 4x8½″ 125.00
Coffee pot, cone shape with lift
lid, copper bottom, 1860, 9″ 20.00
Coffee pot, side spout, 12″ . 45.00
Cookie cutter, bird with
crimped wings & tail, 5″ . 70.00
Cookie cutter, deer, good
stylized form, 5x5½″ ... 245.00
Cookie cutter, eagle with
spread wings, 4½″ 32.50
Cookie cutter, lion, 4″ 12.50
Cookie cutter, pipe, 4¾″ ... 20.00
Cookie cutter, rooster, 4″, late
1800s 33.00
Cookie cutter, Victorian lady
in feathered hat, man in
coat, 7½″ 80.00
Dispenser, soldered, handmade, 1890, 5x3″ diameter 14.00
Dust pan, 12½″ 20.00
Fly sprayer, quick loader .. 7.50
Hearing horn, telescoping
length 45.00
Hot water bottle, oval with
oval top lid & screw cap,
7x10″ 15.00
Lamp filler, tapered shape
with angled spout & lid,
3¾″ 65.00
Lantern, semi-cylinder, sliding
glass front & hinged back
door 90.00
Loaf pan, 4 sections, with lid,
22x13″ 25.00
Lunch pail, 3 part, with in-
tegral cup 45.00
Measure, mug shape with handle, 5¾″ 37.50
Mug, 4½x4½″ 37.50
Noodle cutter, S curve with
grooves, 12½″ 70.00
Nutmeg grater, wood handle,
5¼″ 35.00
Sconce, round reflector back,
7¾″, pair 170.00
Shaker, with handle & hand
pierced top, 4″ 40.00

Lamp filler, 6¼″, $45.00.

Tinderbox, with candle socket
  & damper, 4½″ **65.00**
Wash tub, japanned, handles
  on each side, 6½x17″ . . . **65.00**
Water can, AT&S Fry, 1 gal. **25.00**

Tobacciana

    Now gone the way of the barber
shop and the ice cream parlor, the
cigar store with its carved wooden Indian at the door and the aroma of fine
tobacco in the air is no more. But the
clever figural cigar cutters, the hand
carved Meerschaum pipes, the cigar
molds, and the humidors are still en-
joyed as reminders of our country's
younger days and for the workmanship of long-ago craftsmen.

Ash pot, Black man with red
  wagging tongue, 2¼″ . . . **125.00**
Ash tray, bronze Cocker Span-
  iel with duck in mouth . . **45.00**
Card photo, cigar store Indian
  outside shop, signed, 1890s **75.00**
Cigar box, Stratton & Briggs,
  wood, 1883 . . . . **22.00**
Cigar box opener, Dolly
  Madison **25.00**
Cigar box opener, San Felice . **25.00**
Cigar cutter, counter; Betsy
  Ross, 5¢, cast iron,
  original picture **385.00**
Cigar cutter, desk; ivory with
  engraved monkeys, 4½″ . **220.00**

Cigar cutter, King Alfred,
  complete **450.00**
Cigar cutter, Old Hindu, dated
  1861 . . . . **200.00**
Cigar cutter, pocket; brass &
  sterling bullet **50.00**
Cigar cutter, pocket; inscribed
  sterling loving cup with
  black case **275.00**
Cigar cutter, pocket; silver &
  enamel arrowhead **135.00**
Cigar cutter, pocket; silver
  scissors with etching . . . **29.00**
Cigar cutter, table; Dachshund
  rocking blade, cast iron . **58.00**
Cigar holder, amber & burl-
  wood, 14k gold bands, 3″ . **28.00**
Cigar holder, carved rose-
  wood, figural thistle **20.00**
Cigar mold, cast iron, makes
  20 cigars, 20″ **20.00**
Cigar mold, wood with metal
  clamp, makes 1 cigar,
  primitive **16.00**
Cigarette card, camera shape
  with pretty lady, 2″ **22.00**

**Humidor, painted tin with mother of
pearl inlay, bird and flower decor,
marked Japan, 4¾″ x 3½″, $50.00.**

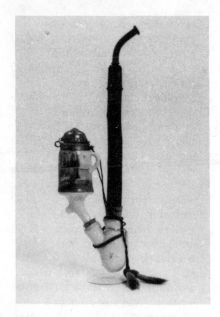

Pipe, hunt scene with dog and deer, marked Czech., 10¼″ x 3″, $42.50.

Cigarette case, 18k gold, dragons in neillo, Chinese, signed	1,000.00
Cigarette dispenser, crank mule's ear to release	17.50
Cigarette holder, amber stem with carved horse, 3″	58.00
Cigarette holder, ivory with carved rose band	20.00
Cigarette silk, Flags of the World	2.00
Cigarette silk, Indian Chief	20.00
Humidor, Germany, skull on book with muliticolored cap, 4½″	60.00
Humidor, hippopotamus figural	150.00
Humidor, LaPalina Senators, brass	48.00
Humidor, owl, porcelain, marked Austria	95.00
Lighter, Art Deco, globe on stand, copper & chrome, 5″	35.00
Lighter, baby grand piano, chrome, Occupied Japan	45.00
Lighter, hand grenade	20.00
Lighter, Happy Joe, lights from top of hat, 1931	60.00
Lighter, Midland Jump Spark, oak base	175.00
Lighter, Nestles, in box, musical	40.00
Lighter, Sir Walter Raleigh tobacco can	75.00
Pipe, Austrian porcelain, hinged, 15″	25.00
Pipe, Meerschaum, Arabian Chief with headdress	60.00
Pipe, Meerschaum, eagle claw holds bowl	35.00
Pipe, Meerschaum, large semi-nude figural	225.00
Pipe, Meerschaum, lion & lioness with sterling band	65.00
Pipe, Meerschaum, standing elk, in original case, 3x2⅛″	60.00
Pipe, Art Nouveau, majolica, lady's head	125.00
Pipe, pottery, decorated, rough briar stem	145.00
Pipe bowl, burl, primitive	40.00
Pipe holder, F Jones Ales advertising	50.00
Sampler case, Van Bibber Cigars	35.00
Store card, Buecher's Corn Cob Pipes, 25¢, with 6 original pipes	45.00
Tobacco card, Helmar Turkish, seal of the United States	50.00
Tobacco card, Players miniatures, set of 25	7.00
Tobacco cutter, battle axe	210.00

Tobacco cutter, figural horse blade, 6½″, $175.00.

Tobacco cutter, figural horse
blade, 6½" 175.00
Tobacco cutter, little boy
thumbing nose 85.00
Tobacco cutter, Star, Save the
Tags 75.00
Tobacco cutter, Superior .. 50.00
Tobacco holder, leather lion
head with ring in nose .. 30.00
Tobacco press, brown metal
mule 8.00

Tools

Considering the construction of
early tools, one must admire the hand
shaped wood, the blacksmith-wrought
iron, and the hand tooled leather. Even
factory made tools from the late 1800s
required a good deal of hand finishing.
Most desirable to tool collectors are
those with the touch mark of the crafts-
man, or early examples marked by the
manufacturer. Value is determined by
scarcity, condition, usefullness, and
workmanship.

Adze, wrought, dated 1776 . 75.00
Anvil, clip horn type, signed &
dated 183? 60.00
Auger bits, single twist with
thimble handle, Sanford
1847, 6 for 45.00

Axe, goose-wing; marked MP
within heart, incised decor,
10" 55.00
Axe, wood splitting; German,
1831 .... 50.00
Bill poster's hammer, 1 joint,
both brass clips intact,
signed 85.00
Blacksmith's cone, solid,
1700s, 36" 190.00
Blacksmith's tray, original
red, labeled A Smith ... 40.00
Brace, gentleman's, polished
steel, ornate head, Peugeot
Freres 65.00
Brace, Sheffield style, wood . 40.00
Calipers, double, hand forged,
18" 85.00
Clamp, violin maker's; wood,
curved jaws, 4 for 55.00
Clap board splinter, wrought
iron 22.50
Cobbler's bench, wood, 4
drawers, nail bins, 17x46" . 90.00
Divider, oak, brass tips, fer-
rules, wing nut, 1¾x24" . 125.00
Ice spade, wrought iron ... 55.00
Line level, Stanley, ornate cast
iron, 3¼" 20.00
Mortise gauge, dark rose-
wood, polished brass ... 55.00
Parallel rule, ebony with
brass, 6" long 20.00

Slitting gauge, cherrywood, circa 1850, $39.00.

Plane, coach maker's radius plow; walnut, slide arm fence, 13" 385.00

Plane, jack; floor model with guides, wood 60.00

Plane, Stanley #100½ 85.00

Plumb bob, brass, suspended from wood frame level, 43" 70.00

Pump auger bit, marked Gilpin 35.00

Router, bronze, right & left bead, 11" 33.00

Screwdriver, Wards Spiral Ratchet 18.00

Shingle splitter, 2 piece, blade & beetle, 13½" 20.00

Splint squeeze, mechanical, wood 20.00

Square, brass & steel, A McKenzie patented 1857 Boston, 12" blade 79.00

Tinsmith's mandrel, wood . 25.00

Trammel, brass with bird's head, late 1800s, 16¾" .. 125.00

Wood sampling tool, wrought iron 40.00

Wrench, hand ratchet, ¾" square drive, 9" long ... 22.00

Toothpick Holders

Toothpick holders have been made in hundreds of patterns, in art glass, pattern glass, opalescent and translucent glass of many colors, in novelty designs and figural forms. Today they are all popular collectibles, relatively easy to find and usually affordable.

American Belleek, orange trees & orange decor, palette mark 35.00

Banded Portland, clear with maiden blush 40.00

Beatty Honeycomb, blue opalescent 55.00

Bird on Stump, amber 30.00

Black amethyst with enamel decor 40.00

Bundle of Sticks, blue 20.00

Button & Star Panel, clear . 18.00

Cactus, chocolate 65.00

Chrysanthemum Base Swirl, cranberry 95.00

Colorado, green with gold, footed 34.00

Continental, Heisey 75.00

Cupid & hat, figural, silver plate, MSP Company, 3½" 65.00

Custard, St Marys, Ohio .. 45.00

Daisy & Button, blue 25.00

Daisy & Button, Coal Hod, blue 20.00

Daisy & Button with Red Dots 55.00

Diamond Peg, custard with rose decor 45.00

Diamond Quilted, amberina, 2½" 175.00

Dog with top hat, blue, rectangular base, 2¼" 58.00

Double Eye Hobnail, amber . 28.00

Duncan & Miller, #42 ..... 32.00

Fan, amber 19.00

Fleur-de-lis, figural 16.00

Flower & Pleat, clear & frosted 55.00

Frazier, cranberry with enamel decoration 45.00

Gatling Gun 15.00

Girl on hoop, Germany 22.00

Hat shape, clear blown with polished pontil, 2½x3¼" . 25.00

Holly Amber, flat 225.00

Iowa 20.00

Klondike 145.00

Lean Queen 15.00

Liberty Torch, blue 62.00

Manhattan, with gold 30.00

New Jersey, no gold 38.00

Pillar Ribbed, crystal with cranberry & white spatter . 50.00

Plain Band, Heisey 75.00

Ribbed Lattice, blue opalescent 68.00

Rising Sun, gold flashed ... 25.00

Scalloped Panel, plain, green . 35.00

Scroll with Cane Band, dark ruby stain 50.00

Ribbed Opal Lattice, blue, $90.00.

Sunk Daisy	12.00
Thousand Eye, blue	32.00
Tramp's Shoe, milk glass	38.00
Vermont, amber	25.00
Zipper Swirl	14.00

Toys

Toy collecting is a very popular hobby, and if purchases are wisely made, there is good potential for investment. Toys from the 1800s are rarely if ever found in mint condition, but should at least have all their original parts and be working. More recently manufactured toys are evaluated more critically. Compared to one in excellent condition, original box intact, even a slightly damaged toy may be worth only about half price. Character-related toys, space toys, toy soldiers and toy trains are among the more desirable from the 20th century.

Guns

Daisy, BB gun, 1901	125.00
Dewey, large cap bomb, nickeled cast iron	65.00
Humpty Dumpty, japanned cast iron, recast	20.00
Lion, patent June 21, 1887, 5½"	145.00
Mattel, Shootin' Shell Fanner, 1956, MIB	20.00
Red Ryder, Daisy, BB gun, wood stock	32.50

Penny Toys

Auto	110.00
Coach, France, original paint, 3"	80.00
Fire truck, pumper with fireman	125.00
Man in cart pulled by 3-D horse, good original color, 4"	110.00
Man shoots pool, mechanical	85.00
Truck with driver, German, lithographed tin, EX	100.00

Pipsqueaks

Birds, facing each other, animated, tin, box torn but working, 3"	75.00
Cardinal, bellows repaired, 5"	160.00
Dog, good original, 3½"	150.00
Elephant, tip of trunk repaired, 4½"	180.00
Parrot, composition, original paint, some flaking but working, 7"	175.00
Rooster, composition, multicolored paint, leather bellows, 9½"	150.00
Two face, 1 side with man's & other side with lady's, 3"	340.00

Toy Soldiers

Barclay, cameraman	25.00
Barclay, mechanic, with engine	25.00
Barclay, parachutist	15.00
Barclay, rangefinder	15.00
Berdou, Marshall Davout on horseback, signed, 1960	450.00
Britains, Circus Set figures, 17 piece	275.00

Tootsie Toy from the 1930s, 1½″ x 4½″, $85.00.

Britains, Egyptian Cavalry lancers & officers, #115, original box 135.00
Britains, Guard Room, #1734 950.00
Britains, Imperial Yeomanry, mounted at trot, #105 . . 300.00
Britains, Infanteria Espanola, #92, in original box 145.00
Britains, Royal Air Force Monoplane, #433, with 4 extra 1,100.00
Britains, Royal Army Medical Corps, #137, VG 250.00
Britains, Royal Navy, #35, in original box 135.00
Britains, Serbian Infantry, charging, #173, 1935 . . . 500.00
Britains, Sudanese Infantry, marching at trail, #116 . 325.00
Elastolin, brown bear, standing, #6230 . . . . 20.00
Elastolin, Indian, walking, with tomahawk, D/6825 . 19.00
Elastolin, lion, sitting, #6216 . 14.00
Elastolin, trapper, standing, firing rifle, #6866 . . . . . . 19.00
Manoil, Navy deck gunner, M76 . . . . 16.50
Manoil, observer with periscope 15.00
Manoil, soldier in poncho, M189 . . . . 36.50
Manoil, trench digger 25.00
Wood cut-out with chromolithographic paper cover, 14″, pair 25.00

Trains

American Flyer, engine & tender, marked Penn #312 50.00
Bing, #1425, locomotive, tender, 3 coaches 320.00
Buddy L, locomotive, tender, original labels, painted steel, G 450.00
Lionel, engine #390-E, standard gauge, 11″, G 200.00
Lionel, Mickey Mouse Handcar, #1100, original box . 750.00
Lionel, Santa Handcar, Santa with Mickey Mouse on pack 1,250.00
Marx, Stream Line, steamtype electric, 6 parts in original box 65.00

Miscellaneous

Allis Chalmers, tractor, D17 . 110.00
American Stove, cast iron, with pots & pans, 8½″ . . 100.00
American Yellow Cab, German, Lenox 530, doors open 275.00
Arcade, Andy Gump 348 Car, painted cast iron, restored, 7″ 400.00
Asahi, tin violin in original box, 12″ long 25.00
B&R Company, windup boy riding tricycle, 1920s . . . 250.00
Bavaria, sedan with driver, windup, black tin 240.00
Bing, touring car, lithographed tin windup, 6″, VG . . 400.00
Book, Humpty Dumpty Circus, G 45.00
Carter Toy Company, windup Chinaman pulls cart, 1910 150.00
Case, tractor, Spirit of '76 . 75.00
Champion, gasoline truck, cast iron, 8″ 200.00
Charlie Chaplin, carrying luggage, celluloid windup, 7″ . 75.00
Chein, Clown in Barrel, 7½″, EX 110.00

Chein, Happy Hooligan, tin windup, 6¼″, VG 170.00
Chein, Popeye, windup walker, 1930s 250.00
Chein, Walking Teddy Bear, tin, 5″, G 35.00
Chein, Yellow Taxi, Main 7570, 6″, VG 140.00
Chicken, pecking, lithographed tin windup 28.00
Coal wagon, cast iron, repainted, 16″ 90.00
Comical Kat, German, windup walker, 1920s 150.00
Courtland Manufacturing, Ice Cream Scooter, original box, EX 140.00
CR Company, French bus with driver, windup, 1929 . 375.00
Cymbal player, composition head, key wind, early, 9½″ 200.00
English, auto with long front end, windup, 1920s 195.00
Fire truck, pumper with driver, 1920s, 9½″ 175.00
Fisher, Toonerville Trolley, Cracker Jack size, EX .. 325.00
Franmonia, lady bug, metal windup, 5¾x4½″ 35.00
Fun-E-Flex, large Mickey Mouse figure 150.00
German, black cat squeeze toy, lithographed wood & tin, 4½″, EX 120.00
German, Distler roadster, painted tin clockwork, 1940s, 9½″ 250.00
German, rolly polly, good original paint, 12″ 105.00
GFN Germany, tanker, painted & lithographed tin windup, 20″ 90.00
Gilbert, Erector set, #7½ .. 45.00
Hose reel, cast iron, painted, 13″, VG 100.00
Hubley, airplane, P-38 .... 45.00
Hull & Stafford, tin lamb pull toy on wheels, 1800s, 5x3½″ 190.00

Emenee organ, plastic case, 15″ wide, $35.00.

International Harvester, tractor, #560 .... 50.00
Japan, duck & 3 ducklings on wheels, tin windup, worn, 12″ 10.00
Japan, Louis Armstrong, tin, plastic, cloth, windup in original box 210.00
Japan, Monkey Sheriff, windup, marked TN 40.00
Japan, skunk, windup, G .. 30.00

Stuffed dog, rotating head, glass eyes, circa 1900, 8″, $85.00.

Japan, Video Robot, battery operated, in original box . 50.00

John Deere, combine, #12A, very good repaint 75.00

John Deere, spreader, model R 107.50

John Deere, tractor, high post A 95.00

Kallus, Pete the Pup, wood jointed, 11″ 135.00

Kenton, elephant pulling clown in chariot, painted cast iron, G 260.00

Keystone, truck loader, painted pressed steel, 17″ . 190.00

Lehmann, Climbing Miller, original box 400.00

Lehmann, Going to the Fair, painted lithographed tin . 650.00

Lehmann, seal, windup 150.00

Lindstrom, Sweeping Lady, 8″, EX 140.00

Linemar, Minnie Mouse knits in rocker, windup 225.00

Linemar, Popeye balances Olive Oyl in chair 850.00

Lionel, electric range, #455, 1932, 33″ 220.00

M Drolet & Company, Joy Wash Machine 325.00

Martin Company, man plays piano, musical, 1900 .... 650.00

Marx, Beat It, The Komikal Kop, VG 150.00

Marx, Bunny Express, lithographed tin, original box, NM 400.00

Marx, Charleston Trio, 1921, 9″, EX 560.00

Marx, College Crazy Car, EX 90.00

Marx, Dick Tracy Police Station, in box, VG 100.00

Marx, Drummer Boy, 9″, VG 120.00

Marx, Merry Makers Mouse Band, EX 650.00

Marx, Moon Mullins & Kayo handcar, lithographed tin clockwork, 6″ 450.00

Marx, Mysterious Pluto, wind-up, metal, in original box 150.00

Marx, Popeye Express, lithographed tin windup, EX . 260.00

Marx, Tidy Tim the Clean-Up Man, lithographed tin, 8x8½″ 175.00

Marx, Whoopee Car, EX .. 175.00

Matchbox, 1919 Open Coupe . 15.00

Mickey Mouse, celluloid wind-up walker, 7½″ 1,350.00

Atomic Tank, battery operated, tin litho with siren, marked KKK, Made in Japan, 5¾″, $35.00.

Occupied Japan, Lucky
Sledge, MIB 65.00
Ohio Art, Mickey Mouse
mechanical tin washer .. 150.00
Pull toy, cow on wheels, hide
covered, 6½x9" 150.00
Pull toy, horse, wood & papier
mache, 9" 105.00
Pull toy, man on horse, tin
with worn original paint,
3¼" 125.00
Reed, Floating Palace,
lithographed paper on
wood, G 900.00
Schoenhut, airplane, with box 35.00
Schoenhut, alligator with
painted eyes, 12½", EX . 225.00
Schoenhut, clown, painted
eyes, replaced clothing, 8" 125.00
Schoenhut, duck with jointed
head, with tag & button, 8" 65.00
Schoenhut, giraffe, painted
eyes, original paint, 11" . 150.00
Schoenhut, hippopotamus
with glass eyes, 9½", EX . 260.00
Schoenhut, kangaroo with
painted eyes, original paint,
9" 300.00
Schoenhut, mule, replaced tail 100.00
Schoenhut, piano, 6 keys &
original red finish, some
repairs, 6x8" 58.00
Schoenhut, ringmaster, bisque
head, 7" 150.00
Schoenhut, U-Build House in
box, small 75.00
Schuco, boy playing violin,
with key, 4½", EX 100.00
Schuco, Hor-Zu, dressed,
1950, 11", MIB 125.00
Schuco, mouse, windup, 4",
VG 145.00
Schuco, Packard Hawk, tin &
plastic, battery operated,
10½" 250.00
SG Company, pumper-type
fire truck with 3 firemen,
windup, 1920s 375.00
Steiff, bat, Eric, 8" 250.00

American handmade tin train steam
engine, circa 1930s, New York Central,
#3267, with coal car and individual
track, 12" high, $650.00.

Steiff, bear, Cosy Orsi, 7x8" . 85.00
Steiff, bear, Cosy Teddy, with
tag & button, 8" 85.00
Steiff, bear, Zotty, fully
jointed, with squeaker, 11" 85.00
Steiff, bison, mohair, with tag,
6x9" 125.00
Steiff, crocodile, with button,
21½" long 110.00
Steiff, dog, Floppy Cocki, with
tag & button, 7" 47.50
Steiff, dog, Peky, Pekinese,
jointed head with tag &
button, 5x6" 75.00
Steiff, doll, Cappy, with tag &
button, 12", M 95.00
Steiff, dwarf, Gucki, with tag
& button, 7", M 75.00
Steiff, elephant with bells, tag
& button, 10" 135.00
Steiff, gazelle, 55x58" 750.00
Steiff, hedgehog, with button,
2½" 15.00
Steiff, horse, with button,
6x6½" 85.00
Steiff, monkey on handcar,
tag & button 195.00
Steiff, pelican, mohair, 6½" . 85.00
Steiff, ram, Snucki, with tag &
button, 8" 85.00

Fisher-Price paddle toy, fully-jointed dog, 10½″ long, $23.00.

Steiff, snake, 6 foot long	595.00
Steiff, tiger, standing, with tag & button, 10″	55.00
Steiff, zebra, mohair, with button, 8″	65.00
Strauss, Flying Air Ship, #1017 Gray Zeppelin, EX	350.00
Strauss, Interstate double-decker bus, 1920s	350.00
Strauss, Leaping Lena, wind-up, 8½″, EX	200.00
Strauss, Tombo, Alabama Coon Jigger, 1910	295.00
Tonka, fire truck, sheet metal, all original, 6x17″	25.00
Tootsie Toy, Corvette, 1954	25.00
Tootsie Toy, Ford convertible, 1949	20.00
Tootsie Toy, Herbie & Smitty on Motorcycle	195.00
Tootsie Toy, Wrecker	35.00
Unique Art, Howdy Doody & Bob Smith Piano, EX	435.00
Unique Art, Unique Artie, original box, EX	125.00
Wells of London, Opera Car with driver, lithographed tin windup	300.00
Wilkins, goat cart, painted cast iron, 6½″, VG	210.00
Wolverine, Sandy Andy Merry Go Round, #108, MIB	150.00

Traps

Recently attracting the interest of collectors, old traps are evaluated by their condition and by the condition of the manufacturer's trademark. Traps listed here are in fine condition, that is with the trademark legible in its entirety, with strong lettering.

Allsteel #2 Long Spring	30.00
Blake & Lamb #40 Double Under Spring	25.00
Diamond #15 Coil	80.00
Eclipse #3 Folding Trap	45.00
Fut-Set, rattrap	15.00
Gibbs Gladiator, rattrap	35.00
Good Luck #0	45.00
Hector #1 Long Spring	8.00
Jack Frost Nev-R-Lose #1	12.00
Kompakt #3 Jump	30.00
Master Grip #34X Triumph Coil	125.00
Montgomery #2 Digger	20.00
Newhouse #0, Oneida Community, riveted pan	32.00
Oneida Marsh Special #1	18.00

Rival, mousetrap 12.00
Sargent #22 Long Spring .. 130.00
Tree Trap #3 .... 35.00
Triumph #0 Long Spring .. 15.00
Union Hardware #2 .... 65.00
Victoria, PSW & Co 70.00
Wiggington Mousetrap, glass 18.00

Van Briggle

Van Briggle pottery has been made in Colorado Springs since 1901. Fine art pottery was made until about 1920, when commercial wares and novelties became more profitable products. The early artware was usually marked with the date of production and a number indicating the shape. After 1920 'Colorado Springs' in script letters was used; after 1922 'U.S.A.' was added. Van Briggle is most famous for his Art Nouveau styling and flat matt glazes.

Ash tray, spiral interior, mark-
ed Colorado Springs, 5½" 22.00
Bookends, owls, blue to dark
blue, 5", pair 115.00
Boudoir lamp, Colonial girl &
boy, with shades, 16½",
pair 150.00
Bowl, dragonflies, with 3 frogs
flower holder 90.00
Bowl, leaf decor, Persian rose,
dark clay, pre-1930 ..... 125.00
Bowl, leaf relief, cobalt & rose,
USA, 7" 55.00
Bowl, leaves at top, golden
brown matt, 1917, 2x4½" 80.00
Bowl, with frog, tulips, tur-
quoise, marked Colorado
Springs, 8x5¾" 32.00
Bud vase, lime matt drip on
yellow-green, bun base,
#88, 1902, 6" 475.00
Bunny, turquoise, 3" 35.00
Candlestick, muted brown
tones, signed Anna Van
Briggle, 4" 20.00

Candlestick, seven sides,
marked Colorado Springs,
10¼x5½" 35.00
Creamer, turquoise, hex-
agonal, marked Colorado
Springs, 2⅛" 10.00
Donkey, turquoise, 3¾x4" . 40.00
Jar, with lid, blue & rose, knob
finial, 1917, 5½" 75.00
Pitcher, light blue matt,
squat, 1908-11, 3½" 150.00
Pitcher, Ming, original VI
mark, 3¾" 90.00
Vase, blue & green, 1920s, Colorado Springs, 4½" 30.00
Vase, butterflies, rose, Colorado Springs, #688, 4x4" . 30.00
Vase, floral decor, purple,
1906, 8" 350.00
Vase, leaf & stem, dark red,
1919, 2" 45.00
Vase, leaf decor, dark blue,
dark maroon, USA
(1923-29 period), 5" 50.00

Nude with shell, blue matt, $135.00.

Tile, blue-green matt, signed Colorado Springs, 7″, $125.00.

Vase, leaf design, red & blue, collar with teardrop base, 1920, 8¼″ 50.00
Vase, leaves & violets, brown, #645, 4¼″ 20.00
Vase, Lorelei, blue 130.00
Vase, poppies, mustard, dated 1904, crazed, 10″ 650.00
Vase, turquoise, dark clay, marked AA & VB, #684 . 35.00
Vase, 4 shoulder handles, matt green peacock feather, #229/1915, 13″ 200.00

Vernon Kilns

From 1931 until 1958, Vernon Kilns produced hundreds of lines of fine dinnerware, which today's collectors enjoy reassembling. They also made novelty items designed by famous artists such as Rockwell Kent and Walt Disney, examples of which are at a premium.

Anytime, serving bowl, round, 7½″ 5.00
Ash tray, Petrified Forest . 15.00
Brown Eyed Susan, cup & saucer 5.00
Calico, plate with transparent cake cover 25.00

Coral Reef, bowl, Don Blanding, maroon, 11½″ 25.00
Coral Reef, salt & pepper, pair 25.00
Early California, creamer .. 7.50
Early California, demitasse cup & saucer 15.00
Early California, oval vegetable, 9″ 10.00
Early California, salt 5.00
Gingham, torte plate, 2 tiered 20.00
Gingham, tumbler 9.50
Gingham, water pitcher, 3 quart 17.00
Heyday, creamer 3.50
Heyday, gravy boat 6.00
Heyday, plate, 7½″ 3.00
Heyday, salt & pepper, pair . 6.00
Homespun, coffee server .. 20.00
Homespun, egg cup 10.00
Homespun, pitcher, ½ pint . 12.00
Homespun, salt & pepper, pair 6.50
Lei Lani, coupe soup 25.00
Lei Lani, demitasse cup ... 24.00
Lei Lani, serving bowl, Ultra shape, 9″ 27.50
Mayflower, butter with lid . 28.00
Mayflower, cup & saucer .. 10.00
Mayflower, oval platter, 14″ . 20.00
Mayflower, vegetable, 10″ diameter 12.00
Melinda, egg cup 12.00
Melinda, platter, 12″ 16.00
Melinda, soup bowl, rimmed, 8″ 9.50
Monterey, cup 5.00
Monterey, sugar with lid .. 8.00
Organdie, bowl, 9″ 9.50
Organdie, creamer & sugar with lid, individual 12.00
Organdie, platter, 14″ diameter 15.00
Organdie, torte plate, 2 tiered 20.00
Our America, plate, brown, 14″ 82.00
Plate, California, with map, brown 8.00
Plate, Franklin D Roosevelt, signed Goode, 1st edition . 35.00
Plate, Mission San Juan, 8½″ 10.00

Brown-Eyed Susan pitcher, 11½ ″, $24.00; tumblers, 5½ ″, $15.00 each.

Plate, Texas Centennial, 1846-1946	40.00
San Fernando, olive dish, 10″	15.00
San Fernando, oval serving bowl, 10″	14.00
San Fernando, teapot with lid, 6 cup	35.00
San Marino, ash tray, round, 5½″	7.50
San Marino, covered casserole, 8″	24.00
San Marino, mug, 9 oz	12.00
Shadow Leaf, cereal bowl	4.00
Shadow Leaf, cup & saucer	6.00
Tam-O'-Shanter, chop plate, 12″	8.00
Tam-O'-Shanter, pitcher, 2 quart	18.00
Tam-O'-Shanter, tumbler, 5½″	10.00
Tickled Pink, cereal bowl	6.00
Tickled Pink, creamer	6.00
Tickled Pink, cup & saucer	7.50
Tickled Pink, plate, 10″	7.50
Tweed, coffee server with lid	20.00
Tweed, creamer	8.00

Ultra California, butter tray & cover, oblong	28.00
Ultra California, chop plate, pink, 12½″	6.50
Ultra California, cup & saucer, blue	12.00
Ultra California, mixing bowl, 8″	14.00
Ultra California, vegetable bowl, red, 9¼″	10.00
Vernon Rose, sauce boat with attached underplate	25.00
Winchester 73, plate, Davidson, 6″	8.00
Year 'Round, trio buffet server	10.00

Watch Fob

Watch fobs were popular during the last quarter of the 19th century, and remained in vogue well into the 20th. Retail companies issued advertising fobs, and these are especially popular with collectors. Political, commemorative and souvenir fobs may also be found. They were made from brass, cast iron, bronze, copper or celluloid.

Advance Rumely, silver metal, factory, man with flag	60.00
American Bottlers	25.00
Armour's Simon Pure Lard	40.00
Art Nouveau style lyre in relief, dark metal	7.00
Battle Axe Shoes, silver metal, with axe & shoe	25.00
Bloodstone, carved charm & chain	50.00
Buffalo Bill, Pawnee Bill	75.00
Bull Durham	5.00
Case Eagle	45.00
Chapman Drug Company, White Lion Drugs, silver metal, lions	21.00
Dan Patch	200.00
DuBois Budweiser, Lucky 1949, Lincoln penny drilled charm	7.50
Eagle, with flag shield, bronze	15.00
Fireman's hat, leather strap, gold plate	15.00
Firestone, with picture of tire	60.00
Gesanguerein Concordia, Altoona, Pennsylvania, gold washed, 1916	18.00
Gipps Amberlin Beer, porcelain	85.00
Hamilton Brown Shoes	50.00
Harold Lloyd, dated 1950	15.00
Hughes Tool, tri-con rock bit	98.00
Indian, seated, smoking peace pipe, enamel on brass	20.00
International Harvester Spreaders, brass, with horse-drawn spreader	22.00
John Deere, silver deer figural	50.00
Keen Kutter, strap type	75.00
Lion's head, brass	20.00
Masonic, round 2 tone yellow gold, blue enamel, gold plated chain	45.00
Massey-Ferguson, keychain type	30.00

Memorial to Friendly Cooperation Between States, 1931	8.00
Mohawk Trail, brass, embossed elk on boulder	24.00
Northwest Shovel, Denver, Colorado	22.00
Oklahoma Indian Territory Bankers Association, 1907, brass	48.50
Olive Crawler	45.00
Panama, with RR steam shovel, silver plate	50.00
Paul Revere Life Insurance Company	10.00
Phoenix Fire Company, Hollidaysburg, Pennsylvania, ornate, 1971	12.50
Pointer Stoves & Ranges, embossed dog, brass	45.00
Racine, Wisconsin, 1909	25.00
Rock Island American Legion, airplane shape, 1929	30.00
Roosevelt Dam	15.00
Saxon, pop-out	85.00
Sechler Carriages, Indian	75.00
Shapleigh Diamond Edge	55.00
St Louis Expo, Village of Liberal Arts, 1904, 3 sections	60.00
St Louis Livestock Remedy Company, celluloid on brass, animals & box	48.50
Sugar Glen, canned in Memphis, embossed dog & can	35.00
Taft & Sherman	28.00
Uncle Sam, Chicago	35.00
US Steel, 5 years service	18.00
Watab Pulp Paper Company, Sartell, Minnesota, Indian Chief	45.00
White Motor Company	110.00
XEA fraternity, Ames, Iowa, suede strap	25.00

Weathervanes

As early as 1000 B.C the weathervane was used as a religious symbol, but by 17th and 18th century

America, they were used as much for decoration as an indicator of wind velocity and direction. The most valuable examples are those cast in well detailed dimensional molds with an especially unusual or dynamic theme. Patina, the natural corrosion of the metal, is desirable, and should under no circumstances be removed or painted over. Two-dimensional sheet metal weathervanes are gaining in popularity due to the rarity and extremely high cost of the full-bodied type.

Handmade sheet metal rooster, $1,400.00.

Circus horse jumps through hoop, with directionals, 30" long 4,500.00
Cow, copper, cast iron head, worn paint, battered, bullet holes, 28" 200.00
Deer, leaping, copper, full rack of cast iron antlers, 30" . 3,250.00
Duck, hand carved, wood eyes, New England, 16x17½" . 135.00
Eagle with spread wings on ball & arrow, copper with gold, 37x34" 1,800.00
Fish, figure only, wood with metal fins & tail, paint, 37" 425.00
Horse, flying, sheet copper head & body, cut-out mane & tail, 31" 2,750.00
Horse, galvanized sheet metal with sphere & cone finial, 26" wide 400.00
Horse & rider, stylized, gilt on sheet copper, 1800s, 26x25" 5,000.00
Hunter with gun on arrow, directionals, small components, pine 525.00
Pig, zinc & cast iron, 25" directional arrow, early 1900s, 9x5" 115.00
Rooster, copper & zinc, J Howard, bullet holes, 31x26" 3,080.00
Rooster, on arrow, primitive sheet metal part galvanized, 29" 100.00
Rooster, sheet tin, painted, early 1900s, 15x13" 235.00

Weller

Sam Weller's company made pottery in the Zanesville, Ohio, area from before the turn of the century until 1948. They made lovely hand decorated artware, commercial lines, garden pottery, dinnerware, and kitchenware. Most examples are marked with the company name, either in block letters or script.

Ardsley vase with cattails, 10½", $85.00.

Alvin, bud vase, yellow with fruit on branches, paper label 75.00
Ardsley, candle holders, 3", pair 50.00
Ardsley, vase, 10½" 85.00
Aurelian, mug, hunting dog, silver lid, signed K, 7" ..1,400.00
Aurelian, pillow vase, 4 feet, floral, Karl Kappes, 5x6½" 335.00
Baldin, umbrella stand 360.00
Barcelona, vase, ruffled & pinched, with handles, 8" .. 120.00
Blo' Red, vase, 7" 70.00
Blossom, double cornucopia, 6" 25.00
Blue & Decorated, vase, white band, florals allover front, 8¾" 150.00
Blue Drapery, bowl, 3x5½" . 35.00
Blue Drapery, lamp, 12" .. 100.00
Blue Ware, jardiniere, classic figure, 10" 100.00
Bonito, bowl, high gloss finish, 7" 35.00

Bouquet, console bowl, B-12, 5x12½" 37.50
Brighton, figurine, woodpecker, 5" 75.00
Burntwood, bowl, swimming ducks, 3x3" 45.00
Cactus, cat 75.00
Cameo, ewer, footed, green with white roses, 10" ... 35.00
Cameo, vase, square, blue, 8½" 25.00
Chase, vase, blue, footed, 10½x5¾" 250.00
Chengtu, jar, flat cover, 3½" 60.00
Classic, wall pocket, very wide, 6" 80.00
Claywood, mug, 5-petal flower, 5" 75.00
Claywood, spittoon, spider webs, 3½x4½" 40.00
Coppertone, candle holder, turtle with water lily on back, 3¼" 110.00
Copra, basket, rust, orange, green flowers, 11" 190.00
Cornish, candle holder, 3½", pair 30.00
Darsie, vase, blue, 7½" 22.00
Delsa, pitcher, #10, 7" 32.00
Dickens, 1st Line, vase, Indian portrait, A Daugherty, 10" 350.00
Dickens, 2nd Line, humidor, skull, 5½" 1,175.00
Dickens, 2nd Line, vase, golfer, 7½" 375.00
Dickens, 3rd Line, mug, 2 handles, cavalier with pipe, 4¼" 475.00
Dickens, 3rd Line, vase, King, 11" 450.00
Dupont, planter, square, 3½" 50.00
Eocean, Late Line, bud vase, cherries, 7" 80.00
Eocean, mug, charcoal, green with pink carnations, 4¼" 90.00
Eocean, vase, florals, artist signed, marked Eocean Rose, 6¼" 175.00

Hudson vase with hand painted white daisies, signed S. Timberlake, 8″, $185.00.

Etna, vase, gray & pink with dark pink flowers, 4½″	55.00
Fairfield, wall pocket, 11″	120.00
Flask, All's Well, 4″	140.00
Flask, Never Dry, 6″	135.00
Flemish, planter, tub shape, with handles, 4″	50.00
Flemish, wall pocket, 9½″	55.00
Fleron, bowl, 3x7½″	35.00
Floral, vase, blue with pink flowers, 9¼″	30.00
Florenzo, basket, 5½″	55.00
Florenzo, vase, 7″	55.00
Floretta, tankard, matt, blue & tan, 10½″	135.00
Forest, bowl, 3x7″	60.00
Forest, fan vase, 8″	65.00
Fruitone, bowl, green & brown, 3x5¾″	30.00
Gloria, vase, double, 4½″	25.00
Greenbriar, vase, full body, 6½″	85.00
Greora, vase, triangular, 3 feet, 4½″	50.00
Hobart, bowl, 3x9½″	45.00

Hudson, candlestick, blue to gray, blue flowers at base, AP, 9″	120.00
Hudson, vase, lavender to white with white florals, detailed, 10″	200.00
Hudson, vase, raspberries on pastel, 10¾″	160.00
Hudson Perfecto, vase, spider mums, bulbous, signed Leffler, 9½″	360.00
Hunter, vase, flying gulls on brown glaze, 7½″	600.00
Ivoris, console set, 14″ footed bowl & pair 7″ 2-branch sticks	50.00
Ivory, jardiniere & pedestal, 10x13″ jardiniere, 18½″ pedestal	335.00
Jap Birdimal, vase, gray with white goose, 3 feet, signed VMH, 5″	215.00
Jewel, mug, 6½″	250.00
Knifewood, jar with lid, blue bird, matt glaze, 8″	350.00
Lavonia, vase, slender bottom with 3 vertical handles, 9″	65.00

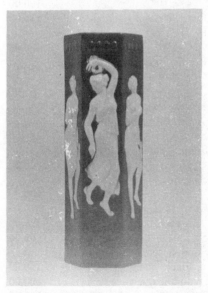

Narona vase, hexagonal, brown with white classical figures, 17½″, $250.00.

325

Lido, cornucopia, turquoise, footed, 7¼x4¾" 20.00
Lorbeek, candlesticks, pair . 30.00
Louella, bowl, 8½" 55.00
Louwelsa, mug, mulberries, Levi Burgess, 5" 100.00
Louwelsa, punch bowl, signed Lybarger, 7x13½" 495.00
Louwelsa-Blue, vase, florals in dark blue, 11" 900.00
Luxor, bud vase, 7½" 30.00
Malvern, console bowl with frog, 10" 70.00
Mammy Line, cookie jar, 11" . 200.00
Mammy Line, teapot, 8" .. 190.00
Marbleized, vase, brown & cream, 4½" 35.00
Marvo, vase, 9" 68.00
Melrose, basket, grapes, 10" . 180.00
Modeled Etched Matt, planter, footed 60.00
Muskota, fence, 5" 140.00
Orris, umbrella stand, lotus & miscellaneous flowers, 19x10" 200.00
Patricia, bowl, 4 geese with necks entwined, white, 4¾x10" 100.00
Pearl, vase, 4 handles, 9½" . 115.00
Pierre, creamer, lavender, 2½x4" 20.00
Roma, planter, medallions with lady's head, 4x4½" square 55.00
Rosemont, vase, bluebird, flowering branch, 10" ... 300.00
Sabrinian, pitcher, 10½" ... 165.00
Senic, vase, pillow shape, #S-11, 7½" 40.00
Sicardo, vase, cylinder, light green & blue, 5½" 195.00
Silvertone, console bowl with flower holder 125.00
Softone, hanging basket, 10" . 55.00
Souevo, tobacco jar, tan, buff, black designs, 6x5" 150.00
Sydonia, fan vase, 9½" 90.00
Turada, bowl, 3½x8" 165.00
Turkis, vase, 3½" 35.00

Tutone, wall pocket, 10½" . 55.00
Warwick, planter, 1 handle, 3 feet, 3½" 60.00
White & Decorated, vase, large red & white roses, 13" 365.00
Wild Rose, ewer, 7" 25.00
Woodcraft, bud vase, 9" ... 35.00
Woodrose, jardiniere, 7" ... 115.00
Zona, bowl, rabbit & bird decor, 5½" 30.00
Zona, child's plate, duck decal, rolled lip, 7½" 42.00

Western Collectibles

The romance of the Old West lives on with collectors of relics related to those bygoné days of the cowboys, Wild West shows, frontier sheriffs, and boom-town saloons.

Autograph, WF Cody, Buffalo Bill, ink on show program, 1908 .... 160.00
Branding iron, Bar S 26.50
Branding iron, 2 brass letters, 5½x4", 11" handle 16.00
Chaps, dyed red for rodeo, with conchos 280.00
Chaps, leather, shotgun style, pair 150.00
Cuffs, full-beaded buckskin, from Wild West show, 8¾" long 450.00
Freight receipt, Adams Express Company, from Virginia, 1865 .... 15.00
Holster, fold-over Mexican type, basketweave & tooling 75.00
Holster, marked King's Ranch, single, 7½" 55.00
Mittens, sheepskin, from frontier days 30.00
Postcard, cowboys playing cards, going for guns, color, circa 1900 .... 19.00
Print, Range Ponies, Olaf Wieghorst, signed 195.00

Program, Ranch & Real Wild
  West Show, 1916, 36 pages,
  7x9" 30.00
Saddle, McClellan 375.00
Saddle bags, leather, 1860,
  small, pair 30.00
Spade bit, silver mounted with
  copper roller in mouthpiece 325.00
Spurs, Mexican, silver
  overlays, no straps 50.00
Spurs, Spanish SW, white
  metal with brass mounts,
  16 point rowels 72.50
Statue, Buffalo Bill on horse,
  cast iron, copper wire lasso,
  9x8x3" 85.00
Wagon jack, Conestoga, wood
  & wrought iron, dated 1822 65.00
Whip, leather, braided & link-
  ed with wood handle, 53" . 20.00
Wrist cuffs, leather, pair .. 75.00

Wicker

Wicker became a popular medium
for furniture construction as early as
the mid-1800s. Early styles were closely woven and very ornate; frames were
of heavy wood. By the turn of the century the weaving was looser and styles
were simple. Today's collectors prefer
tables with wicker tops as opposed to
wooden tops, matching ensembles, and
pieces that have not been painted.

Armchair, Nouveau styling,
  Heywood Brothers, Wake-
  field, 1920s 450.00
Baby buggy, red interior with
  black parasol 400.00
Baby stroller, adjustable
  hood, side diamond design 110.00
Basket, wall hanging, rattan,
  simple weave, 8x8½" ... 45.00
Bassinet, loose weave, braid
  trim, no hood, bottom rack 80.00
Chair, round back, fancy
  panel, fretwork, fancy
  scroll legs, 32" 245.00

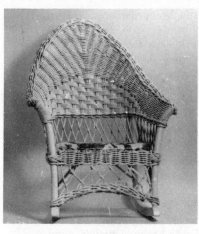

Child's rocker, circa 1930s, $100.00.

Child's rocker, arms & half of
  back loose weave, 1915,
  20½" 135.00
Desk with chair, tight weave,
  drawers, curved top, high
  back 380.00
Doll's cradle, very open weave,
  1920s, 16x15" 90.00
Fern stand, loose weave, rec-
  tangle, with arch & bird-
  cage 280.00
Footstool, cane legs, floral
  cushion, rectangular 55.00
Highchair, loose weave, braid
  trim, high back 165.00
Kneeling bench, with ram's
  horn at top edge, late 1800s 450.00
Lounge, back & arm rest,
  cushioned, tight weave . 390.00
Plant stand, simple design,
  straight legs, 25x32" long . 125.00
Rocker, loose weave, square
  back with high arm rest . 110.00
Settee, tight weave, curved
  back with partial loose
  weave 200.00
Settee, with arms, heart-
  shaped scrollwork back,
  sides & legs, 58" 365.00
Sewing basket, white 175.00
Sofa, braided look, rounded
  back & arms, cushioned . 400.00

Sofa, floral cushioned, curved
back & seats, loose woven . 240.00
Sofa, open arms, upholstered
back & cushions, simple
weave, 75″ 190.00
Table, round, tight weave diamond design in square
woven base, large 325.00
Table, 2 tier, wood top, wide
lower apron, 30″ diameter . 180.00
Table lamp, round wicker
base, wood standard, open
weave shade, 15″ 90.00
Tea cart, tight weave, bottom
shelf, front wheels, top tray 260.00
Waste basket, circular, tight
weave 15.00
Youth stroller, EX 450.00

Willow Ware

Inspired by the lovely blue and
white Chinese exports, the Willow pattern has been made by many English,
American, and Japanese firms from
1750 until the present. Many variations of the pattern have been noted;
mauve, black, green, and multicolor
Willow ware can be found in limited
amounts. The design has been applied
to tinware, linens, glassware, and
paper goods, all of which are treasured
by today's collectors.

Ash tray, fish novelty, Japan,
1950s, MIB 8.00
Baking dish, Hall, 4 pattern
repeats, 3x9″ 15.00
Baking dish, Oven Proof,
Japan, 2½x5″ 15.00
Bone dish, Minton, pattern in
oval reserve, 8¼″ 25.00
Bowl, Adams, Staffordshire,
9″ 22.00
Bowl, cereal; Homer Laughlin
.... 5.00
Bowl, Japan, no mark, 10″ . 20.00
Bowl, vegetable with lid;
Wood & Son, with handle,
11″ 100.00

Coffee pot, marked Willow Etruria
Wedgwood, Made in England,
Detergent Proof, 8″, $70.00.

Butter dish, Moyott & Sons,
round with willow band . 75.00
Butter pat, England, 3″ ... 15.00
Cake plate, flow blue, marked
Balmoral with lion, 10″
square 35.00
Carafe & warmer, marked
Japan, 10″ overall 150.00
Charger, Allerton, 13″ 45.00
Child's cup, 2¾″ 9.00
Child's grill plate, Made in
Japan, 4½″ 8.50
Child's plate, Made in Japan,
4⅜″ 10.00
Child's plate, tin, no mark,
1½″ 5.00
Child's saucer, 3½″ 2.50
Coaster, advertising, York-
shire Relish, English, 4″ . 150.00
Compote, Cambridge Glass
Company, no mark, 3x5½″ 50.00
Creamer, Homer Laughlin . 5.00
Cup, demitasse; Arabia, Made
in Finland, 2½″ 12.00
Cup & saucer, Allertons,
1930s-40s, large 23.00
Cup & saucer, Homer
Laughlin 8.00

Egg cup, Japan, double ... 15.00
Gravy boat with 9" underplate, Allerton, 1930s-40s, 4x8" 60.00
Honey dish, WR Midwinter, 4" 16.00
Meat drainer, marked Iron Stone China, English, 10x7¼" 50.00
Mug, Royal, stacking 4.00
Piggy bank, 3 tier, Japan, 1950s, MIB 20.00
Plate, Alfred Meakin, Old Willow, 9½" 10.00
Plate, grill; Maastricht, 11" . 15.00
Plate, grill; SM Willow, made in England, 10¾" 15.00
Plate, Japan, 6" 3.00
Plate, made in Japan, good color, 6" 4.00
Plate, rolled edge, no mark, 7¼" 3.00
Plate, Samuel Radford Ltd, fishtail birds, circa 1928, 4" 10.00
Platter, Wedgwood, Eturia, 7x10¼" 80.00
Punch bowl, no mark, inside rim border, pattern front & back, 6x9" 130.00
Sauce dish, Johnson Brothers, 5" ..../ 4.00
Saucer, Homer Laughlin ... 2.00
Shakers, pedestal base, scroll handle, circa 1950s, 4", pair 15.00
Soap pad holder with lid, Japan, 1950s, MIB 20.00
Sugar, Royal, open 4.00
Tea tile, Wiltshaw & Robinson, 4¾" 60.00
Toothpick holder, English, 2½" 30.00
Wash set, Doulton & Company, 1890-1902 .... 600.00

Winchester

Originally manufacturing only guns and ammunition, after 1920, the Winchester Company produced a vast array (over 7,500 items) of sporting goods and hardware items which they marked 'Winchester Trademark, USA.' The name of the firm changed in 1931, and the use of the trademark was discontinued. Examples with this mark have become collectors' items.

Axe, original handle, VG .. 45.00
Bait reel, #2245 .... 45.00
Box opener 35.00
Bullet mold, #2520 .... 30.00
Calendar, 1930, framed, with all pads, M 355.00
Can opener 25.00
Casting rod, bamboo 70.00
Catalog, 1909, 182 pages, EX 135.00
Drill bit 15.00
Envelope, man pointing out game to hunter 20.00
Flashlight 10.00
Grapefruit knife, EX 19.50
Hatchet 38.00
Padlock, 6 lever, no keys .. 60.00
Plane, #4 .... 70.00
Pliers, lineman's 40.00
Safety razor 16.00
Sewing shears, 6" 30.00
Wood brace, #10 .... 85.00
Wrench, open end, 10" 17.50

Woodenware

Most of the primitive hand crafted wooden bowls and utensils on today's market can be attributed to a period from late in the 1700s until about 1870. They were designed on a strictly utilitarian basis, and only rarely was any attempt made toward decoration. The most desirable are those items made from burl wood -- the knuckle or knot of the tree having a grain that appears mottled when it is carved, or utensils with an effigy head handle. Very old examples are light in weight due to the deterioration of the wood; expect age cracks that develop as the wood dries.

Bowl, burl, ash, hairline, 2x6½" 200.00

Bowl, burl, with cover, 3½x5" 800.00

Bowl, long oval, worn old finish, 5½x13x25" 75.00

Bowl, poplar, worn blue paint outside, chip, 12½x18½" . 135.00

Box, turned poplar, good original red & yellow grain-paint, 8¼" 525.00

Bucket, mounted with mop ringer, all wood, hoop construction 125.00

Butter paddle, maple, peacock-head handle, edge wear, 9½" 275.00

Butter paddle, maple, spade end, bent handle with knob 65.00

Butter scoop, maple, square shaped hooked handle .. 90.00

Canteen, oak, 2 wrought iron hoops, original red, wire & wood handle 75.00

Case, bird's eye maple burl, 4 parts fold, wood hinges, 3x3½" 200.00

Cookie board, 4 part, with fruit & 2 horses, 3½x4¾" . 70.00

Cream skimmer, shell shaped, tab, brass pierced filter center 160.00

Cup, burl, 3x4½" 160.00

Dipper, curved handle, thin bowl, 11½" 70.00

Firkin, stave constructed, old repaint, 9¼" 45.00

Container, barrel shape, twist-off lid, carved, 5" 65.00

Cookie board, each side with lady in long dress with fan, 15x7" 295.00

Cookie board, pine with carved inset, relief florals, 7x10½" 60.00

Knife tray, bird's eye maple, cut-out handle, 9x12" ... 70.00

Ladle, burl, effigy bird head . 175.00

Ladle, maple, effigy head, hanging hole, large 85.00

Noggin, maple, with handle, 1 piece, 6" 185.00

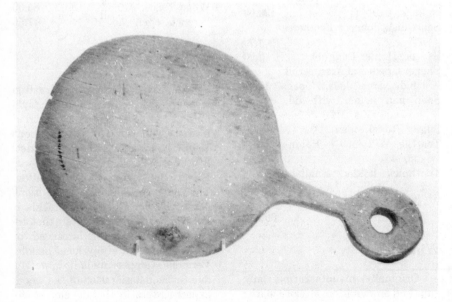

Pie paddle, light weight wood, late 1700s, 17½" x 10", $85.00.

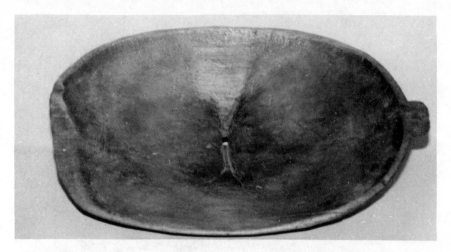

Cheese mixing bowl, maple, with drain hole, 1700s, $250.00.

Paddle, geometric carving on
blade, 16½″ 45.00
Pie crimper, wood with wood
handle, primitive 55.00
Plate, turned treen, early,
6½″ 90.00
Rolling pin, tiger maple, one
end handle, 16″ 40.00
Salt, turned, worn brown
patina, 1¾x3¼″ 50.00
Spoon, tiger maple, long han-
dle, 14″ 140.00
Spoon, well shaped, 7½″ . . 10.00
Trencher, pine, tab handles,
hand hewn, 4x14x24″ . . . 260.00
Tub, 2 iron hoops & lid,
original green, 8½″ 230.00

World's Fairs and Expositions

Souvenir items have been
distributed from every fair and exposition since the mid-1850s. Examples
from before the turn of the century are
challenging to collect, but those made
as late as for the 1939 New York and
San Francisco fairs are also desirable.

1876 Centennial, Philadelphia
Pin, Liberty Bell figural,
enameled red, white & blue 20.00
Print, Machinery Hall,
Thomas Hunter Litho-
graphers, color, 7x11″ . . 15.00

1893 Columbian, Chicago
Beer foam scraper, wood,
Machinery Hall scene,
10½″, EX 35.00
Book, Story of Columbus &
World's Columbian Expo . 35.00
Paperweight, clear glass with
Utah State Building, Lib-
bey Co 45.00
Token, aluminum, embossed
with Columbus & men land-
ing in America 15.00

1895 Atlantic City Expo
Change purse, abalone 25.00
Decanter with stopper, clear
with etching, plus 6 cups . 125.00

1898 Omaha
Demitasse spoon, Administration Building, canal, boats,
detailed 15.00
Sheet music, Sod Shanty . . 25.00

Hot plate, 1939 New York World's Fair, aluminum over cardboard, 7" x 10", $15.00.

1901 Pan American
Poster, diamond shaped, by
Rafael Beck, official,
13x13" 145.00
Tumbler, etched, Temple of
Music 45.00

1904 St. Louis
Book, Samantha at the St
Louis Expo 5.00
Jewelry box, with lid, metal
filigree 20.00
Spoon, ornate 20.00
Vase, Palace of Liberal Arts,
white metal, 3½" 45.00

1909 Alaska Yukon Pacific
Plate, views of fair 40.00
Tray, metal, highly embossed
scenes with gilt outlining,
7" diameter 27.50

1915 Panama Pacific
Album of Views, 25 separate
cards, full color, EX 25.00

Match safe, cannon design,
Are You Ready, 1915,
Panama, VG 20.00
Plate, polished metal, with
many views, 12" 30.00

1933 Chicago
Marbles, colorful agate, 28 in
Century of Progress bag, M 45.00
Plate, pierced border with
Chicago scenes, set of 4 . 16.50

1939 New York
Belt buckle, goldtone, enamel-
ed Trylon & Perisphere,
dated 1939 .... 20.00
Globe, silver lustre, on black
glass base, dated 1940 .. 15.00
Program, American Jubilee . 5.00
Viewer, with original box .. 45.00

1939 San Francisco
Hot plate, aluminum with
many scenes 8.00
Plate, multicolored, 10" ... 15.00

Yellow Ware

Utility ware made from buff-burning clays took on a yellow hue when covered with a clear glaze, hence the name 'yellow ware'. It is a type of 'country' pottery that is becoming quite popular due to today's emphasis on the 'country' look in home decorating. It was made to a large extent by the Ohio potters, though some was made in the eastern states as well. Very seldom do you find a marked piece. Bowls, pitchers, and pie plates are common; mugs, rolling pins and lidded jars are more unusual and demand higher prices -- so do items with in-mold decoration.

Mug, brown and white bands, 3", $55.00.

Bank, spotted hen on nest with brown base, 3½" ..	95.00
Bowl, brown sponging, 2x4½"	20.00
Bowl, mixing; tan & white stripes, 6½x14"	45.00
Bowl, rolled rim, 2 white & 2 narrow brown bands, 7¼"	20.00
Bowl, tan with white stripes, 5¼" diameter	10.00
Chamber pot, miniature with white stripes, 2¾"	25.00
Creamer, embossed dark brown checkerboard decor, 3½", M	40.00
Mold, 6-petal flower, 3" diameter	35.00
Mug, sand finish with blue bands	75.00
Pie plate, small rim hairline, 11" diameter	25.00
Pudding mold, corn pattern, 8x5½"	35.00
Rolling pin, turned wood handles, 15" long	130.00
Teapot, Rebecca at the Well, blue mottled, spout flake, 9"	125.00
Watering can, girl in garden, repeat design, 9"	28.00

Index

Two Important Tools For The
Astute Antique Dealer, Collector and Investor

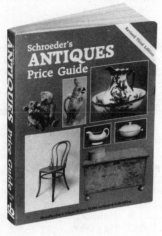

Schroeder's Antiques Price Guide

The very best low cost investment that you can make if you are really serious about antiques and collectibles is a good identification and price guide. We publish and highly recommend **Schroeder's Antiques Price Guide.** Our editors and writers are very careful to seek out and report accurate values each year. We do not simply change the values of the items each year but start anew to bring you an entirely new edition. If there are repeats, they are by chance and not by choice. Each huge edition (it weighs 3 pounds!) has over 56,000 descriptions and current values on 608 - 8½x11 pages. There are hundreds and hundreds of categories and even more illustrations. Each topic is introduced by an interesting discussion that is an education in itself. Again, no dealer, collector or investor can afford not to own this book. It is available from your favorite bookseller or antiques dealer at the low price of $9.95. If you are unable to find this price guide in your area, it's available from Collector Books, P. O. Box 3009, Paducah, KY 42001 at $9.95 plus $1.00 for postage and handling.

Schroeder's INSIDER and Price Update

A monthly newsletter published for the antiques and collectibles marketplace.

The **"INSIDER"**, as our subscribers have fondly dubbed it, is a monthly newsletter published for the antiques and collectibles marketplace. It gives the readers timely information as to trends, price changes, new finds, and market moves both upward and downward. Our writers are made up of a panel of well-known experts in the fields of Glass, Pottery, Dolls, Furniture, Jewelry, Country, Primitives, Oriental and a host of other fields in our huge industry. Our subscribers have that "inside edge" that makes them more profitable. Each month we explore 8-10 subjects that are "in", and close each discussion with a random sampling of current values that are recorded at press

time. Thousands of subscribers eagerly await each monthly issue of this timely 16-page newsletter. A sample copy is available for $3.00 postpaid. Subscriptions are postpaid at $24.00 for 12-months; 24 months for $45.00; 36 months for $65.00. A sturdy 3-ring binder to store your **Insider** is available for $5.00 postpaid. This newsletter contains NO paid advertising and is not available on your newsstand. It may be ordered by sending your check or money order to Collector Books, P. O. Box 3009, Paducah, KY 42001.

26. For further study, check out the Mars Hill blog by Pastor Mark Driscoll: http://blog.marshillchurch.org/2008/03/31/the-trinity/.

27. L. B. Cowman, *Streams in the Desert*, August 27 entry, 328.

28. Dawson Trotman, *Born to Reproduce* (Colorado Springs, CO: NavPress, 2008), 13.

29. L. B. Cowman, *Streams in the Desert*, February 10 entry, 69.

30. *Merriam-Webster's Collegiate Dictionary*, 11th ed., s.v. "meek."

31. Kathleen Curtin, "The First Thanksgiving," History.com, http://www.history.com/content/thanksgiving/the-first-thanksgiving (accessed September 25, 2009).

32. http://en.wikipedia.org/wiki/TANSTAAFL.

33. John C. Maxwell, "Breakthroughs That Build Your Dream," *Maximum Impact*, 13: 6.

34. Idea taken from *Leadership Moments: 365 Inspirational Thoughts for the Leader's Year* (Johns Creek, GA: EQUIP, 2008). *Leadership Moments* is the daily radio ministry of EQUIP, www.equip.org. Used by permission.

35. Idea taken from *Leadership Moments*. Used by permission.

36. John C. Maxwell, "Let God Work in Your Life" and "Pursue the Heart of God," *Leadership Moments: 365 Inspirational Thoughts for the Leader's Year*, March 26 and March 25 entries, 92, 91.

37. *Leadership Moments*. Used by permission.

38. John C. Maxwell, "You Can Do It," *Leadership Moments*, April 26 entry, 124.

39. John C. Maxwell, "Empowerment," *Leadership Moments*, May 26 entry, 154.

40. "Is America's Faith Really Shifting?" Barna Group, http://www.barna.org/barna-update/article/5-barna-update/116-is-americas-faith-really-shifting.

41. John C. Maxwell, *The 21 Most Powerful Minutes in a Leader's Day* (Nashville: Thomas Nelson, 2007), 355.

42. http://www.youtube.com/watch?v=CuYD2cwMbpw.

43. Dr. Henry Cloud, *Integrity* (New York: Harper Paperbacks, 2009).

44. "Proud People vs. Broken People," www.ReviveOurHearts.com. *Revive Our Hearts* is an outreach of Life Action Ministries.

ABOUT THE AUTHOR

Renee Johnson is a spirited speaker and writer to twentysomethings. She graduated from Biola University and has had the pleasure of working with the top nationally known Christian speakers and writers at Outreach Events. Her devotional blog reaches hundreds of readers. Renee's mission in life is to "spur others forward" (Hebrews 10:24) using the lessons learned from her own trials to encourage others in their walk with God. Sign up for weekly devotionals at www.devodiva.com. Learn more about Renee and her ministry at www.devotionaldiva.com.

DATE DUE